*i*BT TOEFL VOCABULARY

토플 보카

iBT TOEFL VOCABULARY 토플 보카

지은이 Keith Kyung
펴낸이 임상진
펴낸곳 (주)넥서스

초판 1쇄 발행 2011년 3월 25일
초판 4쇄 발행 2011년 4월 10일

2판 1쇄 발행 2014년 5월 25일
2판 12쇄 발행 2024년 5월 1일

출판신고 1992년 4월 3일 제311-2002-2호
10880 경기도 파주시 지목로 5
Tel (02)330-5500 Fax (02)330-5555

ISBN 978-89-6790-877-5 13740

저자와 출판사의 허락 없이 내용의 일부를
인용하거나 발췌하는 것을 금합니다.

가격은 뒤표지에 있습니다.
잘못 만들어진 책은 구입처에서 바꾸어 드립니다.

본책은 〈넥서스 보카〉의 개정판입니다.

www.nexusbook.com

iBT TOEFL VOCABULARY

토플 보카

Keith Kyung 지음

넥서스

Preface

📁   나는 지난 10년간 영어 사교육 시장에서 다양한 학습 목적을 가진 학생들을 가르치며 시중의 어휘 책은 모두 보았다고 자신 있게 말할 수 있다. 어휘는 영어 실력의 기초이며, TOEFL · TEPS · SAT 등의 공인 인증시험에서 좋은 점수를 따려면 어휘 실력이 절대적이라는 것은 누구나 아는 사실이다.

📁   어휘 책 집필을 위하여 오랜 기간 조사를 하면서 보니 책마다 특징이 있지만 대부분 단어 설명이 복잡하고 지나치게 많은 정보를 주려는 경향이 있었다. 가르치는 입장에선 어휘별 부연 설명의 필요성은 이해하나 학생들은 단어의 핵심적인 의미를 빨리 파악하여 쉽게 암기하고자 한다. 그러다 보니 실제로 학생들은 책에서 제공하는 추가 정보를 무시하는 경향이 많다. 즉, 수많은 동의어, 반의어, 어원, 다의어로 가득 찬 책은 정작 학생들에게 큰 도움이 되지 못하였고, 가르치는 나의 입장에서도 예외는 아니었다. 따라서 시중에 있는 어휘 책이 가지고 있는 단점을 극복하여 간결하고 일목요연하게 정리된 VOCA책을 만들겠다는 결심을 하게 되었다.

📁   수많은 영단어 중에서 시험에 자주 출제되는 단어를 고르고, 또 그중에서도 가장 중요한 단어만 뽑아낸다는 것은 결코 쉬운 작업이 아니었다. 각종 영어 시험 문제를 분석하여 자주 출제되는 단어를 모아 보니 어마어마한 양이었다. 다시 꼼꼼하게 선별한 어휘들을 영어 교육에 종사하는 여러 지인들에게 보내어 의견을 구했지만 각자 의견이 분분하여 최종적으로 난이도에 따라 단어를 선정하기보다는 시험에 자주 출제되는 빈도수가 높은 단어를 우선으로 삼았다.

📁   책에 실린 몇몇 어휘는 너무 쉽거나 어렵게 느껴질 수 있지만 그만큼 매우 중요하기 때문에 꼭 넣어야 했다. 또 정확한 의미 전달을 위해 동의어와 반의어를 고르는 일도 쉽지 않았다. 가끔씩 동의어와 반의어가 표제어와 관련 없는 것으로 보일 때가 있는데 영어 문화권에서는 충분히 대체할 수 있는 의미이므로 안심해도 좋다.

📁   이 책의 저자로서 책의 대부분을 집필하였지만 나 혼자만의 주관적 관점을 피하고 좀 더 객관적인 설명을 싣고자 여러 전문가의 도움을 받았다. 나의 현재와 과거의 동료들, 영어 관련 책을 출판한 경험이 있는 저자들도 이 책을 완성하는 데 큰 도움을 주었다. 작업을 수월하게 마무리 할 수 있도록 도와주신 Kevin, Michelle, Jay, Paul, Tongpa, 의진, 새별에게 고마움을 표한다. 특히 이 책의 틀과 방향을 같이 고민해준 오랜 동료 넥서스의 김신영 과장님에게 감사를 드린다.

Contents

- Preface — 5
- 구성과 특징 — 8
- 약어 및 기호 — 11
- 학습 스케줄 — 12

- **Day 1** — 16
- **Day 2** — 21
- COMPREHENSIVE QUIZ — 26

- **Day 3** — 27
- **Day 4** — 32
- COMPREHENSIVE QUIZ — 37

- **Day 5** — 38
- **Day 6** — 43
- COMPREHENSIVE QUIZ — 48

- **Day 7** — 49
- **Day 8** — 54
- COMPREHENSIVE QUIZ — 59

- **Day 9** — 60
- **Day 10** — 65
- COMPREHENSIVE QUIZ — 70

- **Day 11** — 71
- **Day 12** — 76
- COMPREHENSIVE QUIZ — 81

- **Day 13** — 82
- **Day 14** — 87
- COMPREHENSIVE QUIZ — 92

- **Day 15** — 93
- **Day 16** — 98
- COMPREHENSIVE QUIZ — 103

- **Day 17** — 104
- **Day 18** — 109
- COMPREHENSIVE QUIZ — 114

- **Day 19** — 115
- **Day 20** — 120
- COMPREHENSIVE QUIZ — 125

- **Day 21** — 126
- **Day 22** — 131
- COMPREHENSIVE QUIZ — 136

- **Day 23** — 137
- **Day 24** — 142
- COMPREHENSIVE QUIZ — 147

- **Day 25** — 148
- **Day 26** — 153
- COMPREHENSIVE QUIZ — 158

- **Day 27** — 159
- **Day 28** — 164
- COMPREHENSIVE QUIZ — 169

- **Day 29** — 170
- **Day 30** — 175
- COMPREHENSIVE QUIZ — 180

- **Day 31** — 181
- **Day 32** — 186
- COMPREHENSIVE QUIZ — 191

- **Day 33** — 192
- **Day 34** — 197
- COMPREHENSIVE QUIZ — 202

Day 35	203
Day 36	208
COMPREHENSIVE QUIZ	213

Day 37	214
Day 38	219
COMPREHENSIVE QUIZ	224

Day 39	225
Day 40	230
COMPREHENSIVE QUIZ	235

Day 41	236
Day 42	241
COMPREHENSIVE QUIZ	246

Day 43	247
Day 44	252
COMPREHENSIVE QUIZ	257

Day 45	258
Day 46	263
COMPREHENSIVE QUIZ	268

Day 47	269
Day 48	274
COMPREHENSIVE QUIZ	279

Day 49	280
Day 50	285
COMPREHENSIVE QUIZ	290

Day 51	291
Day 52	296
COMPREHENSIVE QUIZ	301

Day 53	302
Day 54	307
COMPREHENSIVE QUIZ	312

Day 55	313
Day 56	318
COMPREHENSIVE QUIZ	323

Day 57	324
Day 58	329
COMPREHENSIVE QUIZ	334

| 정답 및 해설 | 336 |

| Voca Plus | 346 |

| Index | 358 |

구성과 특징

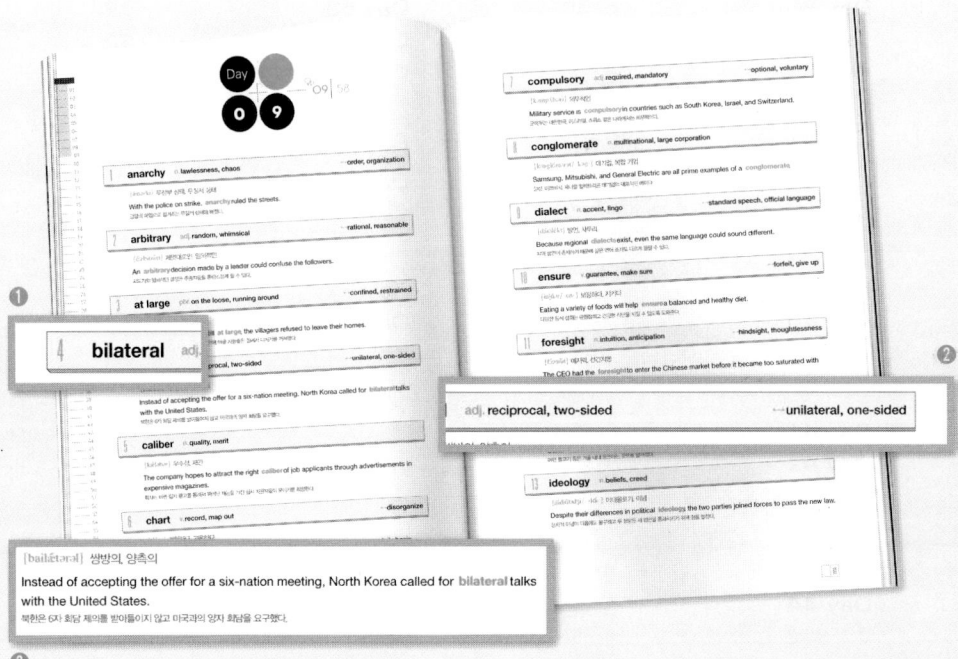

1 표제어
가장 큰 글씨로 되어 있는 표제어는 각종 공인 영어 시험의 100% 기출 어휘입니다.

2 동의어 및 반의어
표제어의 의미를 가장 잘 나타내는 동의어와 반대 의미를 설명합니다. 표제어와 동의어는 예문과 퀴즈에 계속 등장하므로 무한 반복 학습을 통해 자연스러운 암기가 가능합니다.

3 예문과 해석
표제어의 이해를 돕기 위해 명쾌한 예문과 정확한 번역을 실었습니다. 예문의 번역 문장은 흐리게 처리하여 학습자가 스스로 문장을 해석해 보도록 했습니다.

4 Daily Quiz

매일 학습한 어휘는 간단한 용례를 통해 연습할 수 있습니다.

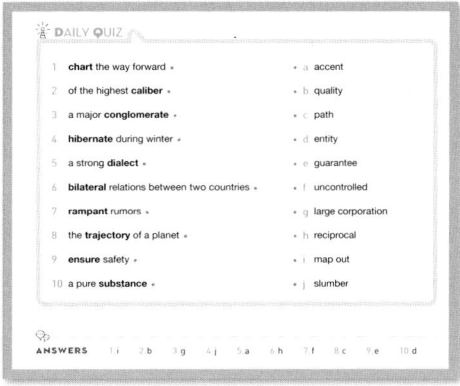

5 Comprehensive Quiz

Day 2개씩 묶은 난이도 높은 어휘 문제를 풀면서 확장 학습이 가능합니다.

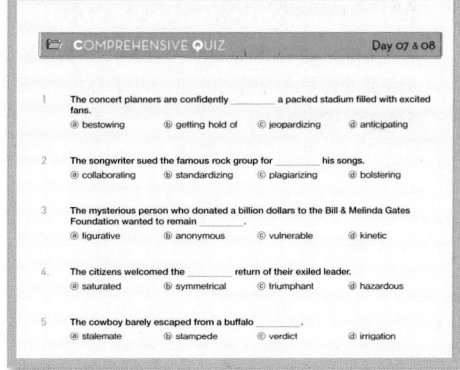

6 Voca Plus

중요한 빈출 단어이나 표제어로 싣지 않은 추가 단어와 숙어를 공부할 수 있는 보너스 페이지입니다.

7 Index
이 책에 수록된 모든 단어를 언제든지 찾아볼 수 있어 사전처럼 활용 가능합니다.

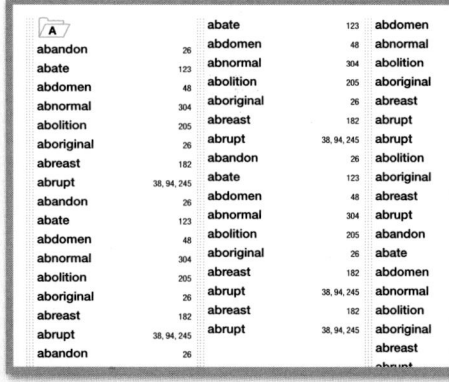

8 MP3 (www.nexusbook.com)
www.nexusbook.com에서 원어민의 발음을 통해 표제어와 예문을 학습할 수 있습니다. 표제어의 의미는 한국어 성우가 아닌 원어민이 들려줍니다.

9 무료 추가 어휘 테스트지 제공
교재에 실린 Quiz를 모두 끝낸 학습자는 www.nexusbook.com에서 추가 어휘 문제지를 무료로 다운받아 풀어볼 수 있습니다.

약어 및 기호

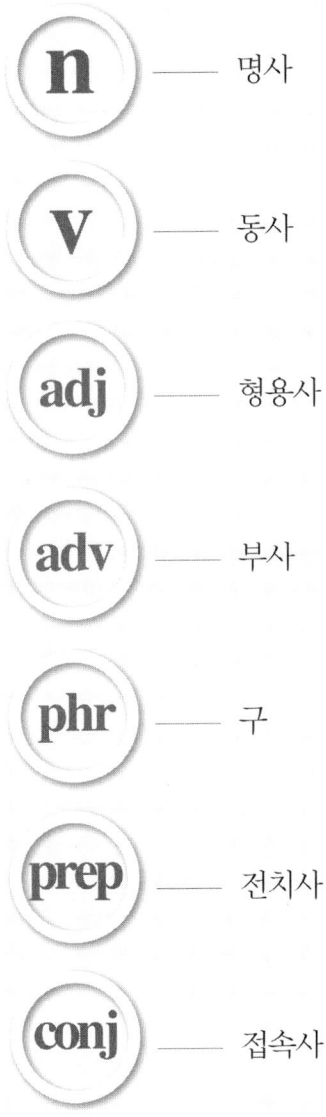

- **n** — 명사
- **v** — 동사
- **adj** — 형용사
- **adv** — 부사
- **phr** — 구
- **prep** — 전치사
- **conj** — 접속사

🔍 — 네이티브는 잘 쓰는데 나만 몰랐던, 숨겨진 의미를 지닌 어휘와 TOEFL, SAT, TEPS 등의 고득점을 위한 필수 어휘

VOCA 학습 스케줄

📁 **TYPE 1** 60일 장기 완성

: 1일 Day 1 VOCA Plus (a)	: 2일 Day 2 VOCA Plus (a)	: 3일 Day 3 VOCA Plus (a)	: 4일 Day 4 VOCA Plus (a)	: 5일 Day 5 VOCA Plus (a)	: 6일 Day 6 VOCA Plus (a)	: 7일 Day 7 VOCA Plus (a)
: 8일 Day 8 VOCA Plus (b)	: 9일 Day 9 VOCA Plus (b)	: 10일 Day 10 VOCA Plus (b)	: 11일 Day 11 VOCA Plus (b)	: 12일 Day 12 VOCA Plus (c)	: 13일 Day 13 VOCA Plus (c)	: 14일 Day 14 VOCA Plus (c)
: 15일 Day 15 VOCA Plus (d)	: 16일 Day 16 VOCA Plus (d)	: 17일 Day 17 VOCA Plus (d)	: 18일 Day 18 VOCA Plus (e)	: 19일 Day 19 VOCA Plus (e)	: 20일 Day 20 VOCA Plus (e)	: 21일 Day 21 VOCA Plus (e)
: 22일 Day 22 VOCA Plus (f)	: 23일 Day 23 VOCA Plus (f)	: 24일 Day 24 VOCA Plus (f)	: 25일 Day 25 VOCA Plus (g)	: 26일 Day 26 VOCA Plus (g)	: 27일 Day 27 VOCA Plus (g)	: 28일 Day 28 VOCA Plus (h)
: 29일 Day 29 VOCA Plus (h)	: 30일 Day 30 VOCA Plus (i)	: 31일 Day 31 VOCA Plus (i)	: 32일 Day 32 VOCA Plus (i)	: 33일 Day 33 VOCA Plus (i)	: 34일 Day 34 VOCA Plus (i)	: 35일 Day 35 VOCA Plus (j)
: 36일 Day 36 VOCA Plus (j)	: 37일 Day 37 VOCA Plus (k)	: 38일 Day 38 VOCA Plus (k)	: 39일 Day 39 VOCA Plus (l)	: 40일 Day 40 VOCA Plus (l)	: 41일 Day 41 VOCA Plus (l)	: 42일 Day 42 VOCA Plus (m)
: 43일 Day 43 VOCA Plus (n)	: 44일 Day 44 VOCA Plus (o)	: 45일 Day 45 VOCA Plus (o)	: 46일 Day 46 VOCA Plus (o)	: 47일 Day 47 VOCA Plus (p)	: 48일 Day 48 VOCA Plus (p)	: 49일 Day 49 VOCA Plus (p)
: 50일 Day 50 VOCA Plus (r)	: 51일 Day 51 VOCA Plus (r)	: 52일 Day 52 VOCA Plus (s)	: 53일 Day 53 VOCA Plus (s)	: 54일 Day 54 VOCA Plus (s)	: 55일 Day 55 VOCA Plus (s)	: 56일 Day 56 VOCA Plus (t)
: 57일 Day 57 VOCA Plus (t)	: 58일 Day 58 VOCA Plus (u), (v), (w)	: 59일 VOCA Plus Review	: 60일 VOCA Plus Review			

📂 TYPE 2 30일 완성

1일 Day 1~2	2일 Day 3~4	3일 Day 5~6	4일 Day 7~8	5일 Day 9~10	6일 Day 11~12	7일 Day 13~14
8일 Day 15~16	9일 Day 17~18	10일 Day 19~20	11일 Day 21~22	12일 Day 23~24	13일 Day 25~26	14일 Day 27~28
15일 Day 29~30	16일 Day 31~32	17일 Day 33~34	18일 Day 35~36	19일 Day 37~38	20일 Day 39~40	21일 Day 41~42
22일 Day 43~44	23일 Day 45~46	24일 Day 47~48	25일 Day 49~50	26일 Day 51~52	27일 Day 53~54	28일 Day 55~56
29일 Day 57~58	30일 VOCA Plus					

📂 TYPE 3 15일 초단기 완성

1일 Day 1~4	2일 Day 5~8	3일 Day 9~12	4일 Day 13~16	5일 Day 17~20	6일 Day 21~24	7일 Day 25~28
8일 Day 29~32	9일 Day 33~36	10일 Day 37~40	11일 Day 41~44	12일 Day 45~48	13일 Day 49~52	14일 Day 53~56
15일 Day 57~58 VOCA Plus						

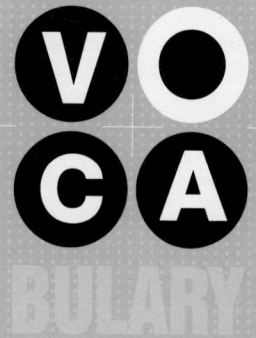

Day 1 ~ 58

표제어 암기
동의어 및 반의어 학습
예문 학습
DAILY QUIZ
COMPREHENSIVE QUIZ

Day 01

01 | 58

1 ambiguous   adj. vague, confusing   ↔ clear, understandable

[æmbígjuəs] 애매모호한

The question on the test was so **ambiguous** that many students had to ask the professor to explain it to them clearly.
시험 문제가 너무 애매모호해서 많은 학생들이 교수에게 명확하게 설명해 줄 것을 요청해야 했다.

2 analysis   n. study, finding

[ənǽləsis] 분석, 해석

The CSI agents sent the blood samples to the lab for DNA **analysis**.
CSI 요원들은 DNA 분석을 위해 혈액 샘플을 실험실로 보냈다.

3 bring about   phr. produce, induce   ↔ hinder, prevent

야기하다, 초래하다

The new law is expected to **bring about** major changes in the way companies run their businesses.
새로운 법은 회사가 사업을 운영하는 방식에 주요 변화를 가져올 것으로 예상된다.

4 buzzword   n. in-word, catchword

[bʌ́zwə̀ːrd] 유행어, 통용어

"Globalization" has been a very popular media **buzzword** for quite a long time.
'세계화'는 꽤 오랫동안 언론에 아주 인기 있는 유행어이다.

5 cause   n. belief, principles

[kɔ́ːz] 신념, 대의, 원칙

Not many people are willing to die for a **cause** they believe in.
많은 사람들이 자신이 믿는 대의를 위해 죽을 각오가 되어 있는 것은 아니다.

6 consistency   n. harmony, uniformity   ↔ variation, change

[kənsístənsi] 일관성

The lawyer lost the trial because his arguments lacked **consistency**.
변호사는 일관성이 부족한 주장 때문에 재판에서 졌다.

7 contradict — v. deny, challenge ↔ support, accept

[kὰntrədíkt] 부정하다, 반박하다

The professor's latest theory **contradicts** everything we know about the universe.
교수의 최신 이론은 우리가 우주에 대해 알고 있는 모든 것을 부정한다.

8 disposable — adj. dispensable, consumable ↔ irreplaceable, reusable

[dispóuzəbl] 일회용의

Using paper cups, plastic utensils, and other **disposable** items are bad for the environment.
종이컵, 플라스틱 용품 및 기타 일회용품을 사용하는 것은 환경에 안 좋다.

9 elaborate¹ — adj. fancy, extravagant ↔ humble, unpretentious

[ilǽbərət] 화려한

The actor was famous for inviting many celebrities to his **elaborate** parties.
배우는 많은 유명 인사들을 자신의 화려한 파티에 초대하는 것으로 유명했다.

10 elaborate² — v. clarify, specify ↔ simplify, abridge

[ilǽbərèit] 상세히 설명하다

Mr. Smith had to **elaborate** because the students did not know what he was talking about.
그가 하고 있는 말을 학생들이 이해하지 못했기 때문에 스미스 씨는 상세히 설명해야 했다.

11 expectancy — n. chance, probability ↔ certainty, reality

[ikspéktənsi] 기대

Over the last hundred years, human life **expectancy** has increased significantly.
지난 100년 동안 인간의 기대 수명은 상당히 늘어났다.

12 facilitate — v. promote, expedite ↔ block, delay

[fəsílətèit] 가능하게 하다, 촉진하다

There are many who doubt that milk can actually **facilitate** physical growth.
우유가 실제로 신체의 성장을 촉진시킬 수 있다는 것을 의심하는 사람이 많다.

13 genuine — adj. real, authentic ↔ fake, deceptive

[dʒénjuin] 진짜의, 진실한

Parents raise their children not out of duty, but out of **genuine** love.
부모들은 의무감이 아니라 진실한 사랑으로 자녀를 키운다.

14 guarantee v. promise, assure

[gæ̀rəntíː] 보장하다, 확보하다

The king sent seventy extra knights in order to **guarantee** the safety of the princess.
왕은 공주의 안전을 보장하기 위해 70명의 기사를 추가로 보냈다.

15 incorporate v. include, integrate ↔ drop, exclude

[inkɔ́ːrpərèit] 포함시키다

The bank decided to **incorporate** new ideas to improve its customer service.
은행은 고객 서비스를 향상시키기 위한 새로운 아이디어를 포함시키기로 했다.

16 industrious adj. hardworking, diligent ↔ lazy, lethargic

[indʌ́striəs] 부지런한

Ants are perhaps the most **industrious** insects on Earth.
개미는 아마도 지구상에서 가장 부지런한 곤충일 것이다.

17 layman n. amateur, unprofessional ↔ specialist, expert

[léimən] 비전문가

For a **layman**, Joseph surprisingly knows so many difficult medical terms.
조셉은 비전문가치고 놀랍게도 어려운 의학 용어를 많이 안다.

18 lucrative adj. profitable, rewarding ↔ useless, unproductive

[lúːkrətiv] 이득이 있는, 수익성이 좋은

China is considered to be a **lucrative** market because the country's economy is growing rapidly.
중국은 국가 경제가 빠르게 성장하고 있기 때문에 수익성이 좋은 시장으로 여겨진다.

19 naked eye phr. unaided vision

맨눈, 육안

Venus is so bright that it is visible to the **naked eye**.
금성은 너무 밝아서 육안으로 볼 수 있다.

20 obligation n. duty, responsibility ↔ freedom, exemption

[àbləgéiʃən] 의무

Rich people have a moral **obligation** to help the poor.
부자들은 가난한 사람들을 도울 도덕적 의무가 있다.

21 phenomenon   n. happening, development

[finάmənàn] 현상

The snowfall in May is quite an unusual **phenomenon**.
5월에 내리는 눈은 매우 보기 드문 현상이다.

22 primitive   adj. old, ancient   ↔ modern, latest

[prímətiv] 원시 사회의, 초기의

The **primitive** tools found by the scientists prove that cavemen were able to make sharp weapons.
과학자들이 발견한 원시 도구는 원시인들이 뾰족한 무기를 만들 수 있었음을 증명한다.

23 productive   adj. effective, practical   ↔ fruitless, unhelpful

[prədʌ́ktiv] 생산적인, 효율적인

Studying right before the vocabulary test is not very **productive**.
어휘 시험 직전에 공부하는 것은 별로 효율적이지 않다.

24 pseudonym   n. alias, pen name   ↔ name, autonym

[súːdənim] 필명

Samuel Clemens, who used the **pseudonym** Mark Twain, became famous after creating characters like Huckleberry Finn and Tom Sawyer.
마크 트웨인이라는 필명을 사용했던 사무엘 클레멘스는 허클베리 핀과 톰 소여와 같은 캐릭터를 만든 후 유명해졌다.

25 relatively   adv. comparatively, nearly   ↔ definitely, precisely

[rélətivli] 비교적

Although Jake is **relatively** smarter than the rest of his family, he is one of the dumbest students in his class.
제이크는 그의 가족보다 비교적 똑똑하지만 반에서는 제일 멍청한 학생들 중 하나이다.

26 salvage   v. save, retrieve

[sǽlvidʒ] 구조하다, 인양하다

He went back into his burned home to **salvage** anything that could be still useful.
그는 아직 쓸 만한 어떤 것이든 가져오기 위해 불에 타버린 집으로 돌아갔다.

27 stringent   adj. severe, demanding   ↔ flexible, tolerant

[stríndʒənt] 엄중한

The government passed a **stringent** law regarding smoking in public.
정부는 공공장소에서의 흡연에 관한 엄중한 법률을 통과시켰다.

28 trivial   adj. unimportant, ordinary   ↔ valuable, significant

[tríviəl] 사소한

Unlike the President, the Vice-President can make decisions only on **trivial** issues.
대통령과 달리 부통령은 사소한 문제에 대해서만 결정할 수 있다.

29 understatement   n. oversimplification, underestimation   ↔ exaggeration, hyperbole

[ʌ̀ndərstéitmənt] 절제된 표현

To say simply that Einstein was a smart man is a severe **understatement**.
아인슈타인을 단순히 똑똑한 사람이었다고 말하는 것은 절제된 표현이다.

30 wreak havoc   phr. destroy, devastate   ↔ construct, build

[ríːk hǽvək] 피해를 입히다

Hurricane Katrina **wreaked havoc** in Louisiana and other nearby states.
허리케인 카트리나는 루이지애나와 주변 주에 엄청난 피해를 입혔다.

DAILY QUIZ

1	a **lucrative** business	a	assure
2	**bring about** positive results	b	real
3	a scientific **analysis**	c	diligent
4	**guarantee** freedom	d	profitable
5	a **genuine** effort	e	ancient
6	a **trivial** matter	f	study
7	an **industrious** worker	g	unimportant
8	a **primitive** weapon	h	destroy
9	a unique **pseudonym**	i	produce
10	a strong storm **wreak havoc**	j	alias

ANSWERS   1. d   2. i   3. f   4. a   5. b   6. g   7. c   8. e   9. j   10. h

Day 02

02 | 58

1 aptitude *n.* capability, proficiency ↔ inability, disinclination

[ǽptətjùːd] 소질, 적성

He was placed in an advanced English class by his school counselor because of his **aptitude** for the subject.
영어에 대한 소질 때문에 상담 교사는 그를 고급반에 배치하였다.

2 arduous *adj.* difficult, rigorous ↔ easy, facile

[áːrdʒuəs] 고된

Volunteering may be an **arduous** task, but most people find it worthwhile.
자원봉사는 고된 일일 수 있으나 대부분의 사람들은 가치 있는 일이라고 생각한다.

3 baffle *v.* perplex, confound ↔ clear up, enlighten

[bǽfl] 어리둥절하게 만들다

The formation of crop circles in remote farmlands has continued to **baffle** scientists.
외딴 농지에 크롭 서클의 형성은 과학자들을 계속 당황스럽게 한다.

4 catchphrase *n.* motto, slogan

[kǽtʃfreiz] 유명 문구

The politician running for Mayor worked with his campaign staff to come up with a **catchphrase** that could make him famous.
시장 선거에 출마하는 정치인은 선거 운동원들과 함께 자신을 유명하게 해 줄 선전 문구를 만들고자 했다.

5 competent *adj.* capable, dexterous ↔ inept, inefficient

[kάmpətənt] 능숙한

The President's new interpreter is **competent** in five languages.
대통령의 새로운 통역사는 5개 국어에 능통하다.

6 comprehensive *adj.* broad, extensive ↔ specific, exclusive

[kὰmprihénsiv] 포괄적인

Researchers are able to understand the behavior of chimpanzees because of Jane Goodall's **comprehensive** study.
연구원들은 제인 구달의 포괄적인 연구 덕분에 침팬지의 행동을 이해할 수 있다.

21

7 conventional adj. customary, predominant ↔ unusual, irregular

[kənvénʃənl] 관습적인

Parents are expected to teach children proper manners and **conventional** behaviors.
부모는 자녀에게 적절한 매너와 관습적 행동을 가르쳐야 한다.

8 eavesdrop v. overhear, snoop ↔ ignore, pass over

[íːvzdrɑ̀p] 엿듣다

The federal agent was able to **eavesdrop** successfully on his suspect's conversation.
연방 수사관은 용의자의 대화를 용케도 엿들을 수 있었다.

9 expenditure n. payment, expense ↔ savings, accumulation

[ikspénditʃər] 지출, 비용

Much of the government **expenditure** is spent on national defense.
국비의 대부분은 국방에 쓰인다.

10 frugal adj. economical, thrifty ↔ lavish, wasteful

[frúːgəl] 절약하는, 검소한

She realizes that she has to live a **frugal** life if she wants to save enough money to buy a house in the city.
그녀는 도시에 집을 살 만큼의 돈을 저축하고 싶다면 검소한 생활을 해야 한다는 것을 깨달았다.

11 hamper v. inhibit, impede ↔ encourage, promote

[hǽmpər] 방해하다

Economists warn that low birth rate can **hamper** economic growth by reducing the number of laborers.
경제학자들은 낮은 출생률이 노동자의 수를 감소시켜 경제 성장을 방해할 수 있다고 경고한다.

12 illusion n. deception, delusion ↔ reality, certainty

[ilúːʒən] 환상, 착각

The magician used mirrors to create optical **illusions**.
마술사는 착시를 일으키기 위해 거울을 사용했다.

13 inept adj. clumsy, incompetent ↔ skilled, adroit

[inépt] 서투른

The shy teenage boy was unpopular at school because he was socially **inept**.
수줍은 10대 소년은 사교적으로 서툴렀기 때문에 학교에서 인기가 없었다.

14 insulate v. protect, envelop ↔ harm, impair

[ínsəlèit] 보호하다

The city hired additional police officers to **insulate** citizens from rising crime.
시는 증가하는 범죄로부터 시민을 보호하기 위해 경찰을 더 채용했다.

15 keep abreast of phr. follow, keep up with

~에 뒤떨어지지 않다

In order to **keep abreast of** the latest fashion trends, Linda spends all her money on clothes.
린다는 최신 패션 트렌드에 뒤처지지 않기 위해 옷 사는 데 모든 돈을 쓴다.

16 luminous adj. bright, radiant ↔ dark, gloomy

[lú:mənəs] 빛나는, 밝은

Her room is always **luminous** because she is afraid of the dark.
어둠을 무서워하기 때문에 그녀의 방은 항상 밝다.

17 minute adj. tiny, diminutive ↔ huge, gigantic

[mainjú:t] 극히 작은

Bacteria are too **minute** for us to see with the naked eye.
박테리아는 육안으로 보기에는 너무 작다.

18 molecular adj.

[məlékjulər] 분자의, 분자로 된

The **molecular** structure of our DNA is quite complex.
인간의 DNA 분자 구조는 상당히 복잡하다.

19 momentum n. thrust, impetus ↔ hindrance, impediment

[mouméntəm] 탄력, 추진력

After winning eight straight games, the team hoped to carry the **momentum** into the finals.
8연승 후에 팀은 기세를 몰아 결승까지 가기를 원했다.

20 penal adj. punitive, disciplinary

[pí:nl] 형벌의, 형법상의

A strong **penal** system is necessary to ensure a safe society.
엄격한 형벌 제도는 안전한 사회를 보장하기 위해 필요하다.

21 perseverance n. diligence, persistence ↔ laziness, lethargy

[pə̀ːrsəvíərəns] 인내, 끈기

Without **perseverance**, one cannot achieve success.
끈기 없이는 성공할 수 없다.

22 pessimistic adj. cynical, discouraged ↔ confident, optimistic

[pèsəmístik] 비관적인

The soccer team became **pessimistic** about winning the game when its star player left the field with an injury.
축구팀은 스타 선수가 부상으로 경기를 뛰지 못하게 되자 승리에 대해 비관적이 되었다.

23 profusely adv. abundantly, substantially ↔ inadequately, insufficiently

[prəfjúːsli] 넘치게

Allen sweated **profusely** throughout his debut concert.
앨런은 데뷔 콘서트 내내 땀을 뻘뻘 흘렸다.

24 revered adj. respected, esteemed ↔ disliked, unappreciated

[rivíərd] 존경받는

Gandhi still remains as one of the most **revered** figures in history.
간디는 지금까지도 역사상 가장 존경받는 인물 중 한 명이다.

25 rite n. ritual, ceremony

[ráit] 의식, 의례

Drawing tattoos is an important religious **rite** in certain cultures.
어떤 문화에서는 문신하는 것이 중요한 종교 의식이다.

26 span v. extend, stretch over ↔ compress, condense

[spǽn] (넓은 범위에) 걸치다

The actor's career **spans** nearly half a century.
배우의 이력은 거의 반세기에 걸쳐 있다.

27 spatial adj.

[spéiʃəl] 공간의

Most 3D animators have an excellent sense of **spatial** relationship.
대부분의 3D 애니메이터는 공간적 관계에 대한 뛰어난 감각을 가졌다.

28 succumb v. surrender, give in ↔ survive, come through

[səkʌ́m] 굴복하다, 무릎을 꿇다

Helen Keller did not **succumb** to her physical disabilities.
헬렌 켈러는 자신의 신체적 장애에 굴복하지 않았다.

29 tariff n. tax, duty

[tǽrif] 관세

The two countries decided to lower all **tariffs** imposed on each other.
두 국가는 서로 부과했던 모든 관세를 낮추기로 결정했다.

30 versatile adj. flexible, all-purpose ↔ limited, confined

[və́ːrsətl] 다재다능한, 다용도의

Cell phones are rapidly becoming more **versatile** and less expensive.
휴대 전화는 급속도로 용도가 더 다양하고 저렴해지고 있다.

DAILY QUIZ

1	**baffle** everyone	a protect
2	a **frugal** housewife	b keep up with
3	a **revered** leader	c confound
4	**insulate** children from harm	d overhear
5	**keep abreast of** the latest news	e expense
6	hire a **competent** worker	f slogan
7	cut military **expenditure**	g thrifty
8	**minute** shoes of a baby	h tiny
9	**eavesdrop** on secret conversation	i capable
10	come up with a **catchphrase**	j respected

ANSWERS   1. c   2. g   3. j   4. a   5. b   6. i   7. e   8. h   9. d   10. f

COMPREHENSIVE QUIZ — Day 01 & 02

1. Defending one's country is a(n) _____ worth fighting for.
   ⓐ rite   ⓑ cause   ⓒ momentum   ⓓ pseudonym

2. It is difficult for a(n) _____ person to achieve happiness in life.
   ⓐ revered   ⓑ productive   ⓒ pessimistic   ⓓ industrious

3. Reporters try to _____ the current events that are happening around the world.
   ⓐ insulate   ⓑ keep abreast of   ⓒ hamper   ⓓ wreak havoc

4. Many developing nations impose _____ to protect their economies.
   ⓐ tariffs   ⓑ illusions   ⓒ obligations   ⓓ aptitudes

5. Top universities try to recruit _____ students.
   ⓐ conventional   ⓑ disposable   ⓒ competent   ⓓ inept

6. During financially difficult times, it is important to be _____.
   ⓐ elaborate   ⓑ luminous   ⓒ penal   ⓓ frugal

7. Mr. Johnson was so busy that he did not want to hear the _____ details.
   ⓐ minute   ⓑ genuine   ⓒ versatile   ⓓ stringent

8. The professor had to _____ on the ambiguous terms that filled the textbook.
   ⓐ incorporate   ⓑ guarantee   ⓒ elaborate   ⓓ contradict

9. The day was so clear that people were able to see the canyon with _____.
   ⓐ analysis   ⓑ the naked eye   ⓒ perseverance   ⓓ phenomenon

10. The small village did not _____ to the huge invading army.
    ⓐ succumb   ⓑ facilitate   ⓒ span   ⓓ salvage

Answers: p.338

Day 03

1. abbreviate   v. shorten, abridge   ↔ expand, lengthen

[əbríːvièit] 줄여 쓰다, 간략화하다

Many words in the dictionaries are **abbreviated** in order to keep their contents short and simple.
사전에 있는 많은 단어는 내용을 짧고 간결하게 하기 위해 축약되어 있다.

2. address   v. approach, deal with

[ədrés] 논의하다

None of the presidential candidates **addressed** the most important social issues.
대통령 선거 후보자 어느 누구도 가장 중요한 사회 문제를 논의하지 않았다.

3. authorize   v. allow, empower   ↔ reject, disapprove

[ɔ́ːθəràiz] 재가하다, 권한을 부여하다

The police chief was fired because he had **authorized** the use of firearms to stop the union strike.
경찰청장은 노조 파업을 막기 위해 총기 사용을 허가했기 때문에 파면되었다.

4. buffer   n. shield, fortification

[bʌ́fər] 방패, 완충제

The Great Wall of China acted as a **buffer** against the invading Mongols.
중국의 만리장성은 몽골 족의 침입을 막아 주는 방패 역할을 했다.

5. circumvent   v. avoid, shun   ↔ face, confront

[sə̀ːrkəmvént] 피하다

The suspect tried to **circumvent** the questions asked by the police.
용의자는 경찰관의 질문을 피하려 했다.

6. coerce   v. compel, intimidate   ↔ discourage, talk out of

[kouə́ːrs] 강요하다, 강압하다

His parents tried to **coerce** him not to quit his job.
그의 부모님은 그가 직장을 그만두지 않도록 강요하려고 했다.

7 delve into   phr. examine, follow up

[délv-] 캐다, 철저히 조사하다

Nosy reporters tend to **delve into** the personal lives of celebrities.
캐기 좋아하는 기자들은 유명 인사의 사생활을 파내는 경향이 있다.

8 enactment   n. legislation, authorization

[inǽktmənt] (법의) 제정

The professor criticized the **enactment** of the new law, arguing that it could harm various minority groups.
교수는 여러 소수 집단에 해가 될 수 있다고 주장하며 새로운 법안의 제정을 비판하였다.

9 eradicate   v. remove, root out   ↔ establish, bring into being

[irǽdəkèit] 근절하다, 뿌리 뽑다

The new mayor promised to **eradicate** corruption during his term of office.
신임 시장은 임기 동안 부정부패를 뿌리 뽑겠다고 약속하였다.

10 foster   v. support, stimulate   ↔ dampen, suppress

[fɔ́:stər] 발전시키다, 성장시키다

Group projects can **foster** friendship among students.
그룹 프로젝트는 학생들 사이에 우정을 발전시킬 수 있다.

11 futile   adj. hopeless, vain   ↔ fruitful, productive

[fjú:tl] 헛된, 쓸데없는

The rescue team knew that it was **futile** to continue the search for the lost child in the dark.
구조대는 어둠 속에서 실종된 아이를 계속 찾는 것이 소용없다는 것을 알았다.

12 hinge on[upon]   phr. depend on, be subject to

~에 달려 있다

The possibility of John's getting accepted to the university **hinges upon** the quality of his application essays.
존이 대학교 입학 허가를 받을 가능성은 지원서 에세이의 질에 달려 있다.

13 inspiration   n. a divine influence

[ìnspəréiʃən] 귀감, 감화

Mother Teresa's unselfish service remains a source of **inspiration** for millions of people around the world.
테레사 수녀의 헌신적인 봉사는 여전히 전 세계의 많은 사람들에게 귀감의 원천으로 남아있다.

14 integration n. unification, assimilation ↔ disassociation, exclusion

[ìntəgréiʃən] 통합

A nation cannot maintain peace and prosperity without a successful social **integration** of its minority groups.
사회에서 소수 집단이 성공적으로 통합되지 못하면 국가는 평화와 번영을 유지할 수 없다.

15 loathe v. detest, abhor ↔ adore, relish

[lóuð] 혐오하다

Most people **loathe** cockroaches.
대부분의 사람들은 바퀴벌레를 혐오한다.

16 mar v. tarnish, spoil ↔ heal, alleviate

[má:r] 손상시키다, 해를 끼치다

The recent scandal **marred** the Prime Minister's clean image.
최근 스캔들은 총리의 깨끗한 이미지를 손상시켰다.

17 medium n. means, mechanism

[mí:diəm] (대중 전달용) 매체

The Internet is an important **medium** that connects people around the world.
인터넷은 전 세계 사람들을 연결해 주는 중요한 매체이다.

18 periodical n. journal, publication

[pìəriádikəl] 정기 간행물

Students need to read various **periodicals** to keep abreast of the rapidly changing world.
학생들은 급변하는 세계에 뒤처지지 않기 위해 다양한 정기 간행물을 읽어야 한다.

19 periodically adv. regularly, every now and then ↔ rarely, seldom

[pìəriádikəli] 주기적으로

Floods during the rainy season **periodically** wreak havoc in Korea.
장마 때 생기는 홍수는 주기적으로 한국에 피해를 준다.

20 plausible adj. reasonable, credible ↔ improbable, unbelievable

[plɔ́:zəbl] 타당한 것 같은, 그럴듯한

Mr. Higgins made Serena stay after school because she could not provide a **plausible** excuse for coming late to class.
히긴스 씨는 세레나가 수업에 늦은 타당한 이유를 대지 못했기 때문에 방과 후에 남게 했다.

21 propel v. steer, stimulate ↔ hold, impede

[prəpél] 나아가게 하다, 몰고 가다

The newly recruited player **propelled** the worst team in the league to win the title.
새로 영입된 선수는 리그에서 최악인 팀을 우승하도록 몰고 갔다.

22 quota n. allotment, allowance

[kwóutə] 한도(량), 할당량

In order to protect the farmers, the authorities decided not to lift the import **quota** on beef.
당국은 농가를 보호하기 위해 쇠고기 수입 한도를 폐지하지 않기로 결정했다.

23 recipient n. receiver, beneficiary ↔ giver, presenter

[risípiənt] 수령인, 수상자

The **recipient** of the Nobel Peace Prize donated over a million dollars of the prize money to charity.
노벨 평화상 수상자는 자선 단체에 백만 달러가 넘는 상금을 기부하였다.

24 resort to phr. employ, make use of ↔ refuse, renounce

(좋지 못한 것을) 쓰다, 기대다

The union members had to **resort to** violence when their demands were ignored.
노조원들은 요구 사항들이 무시되자 폭력을 쓸 수밖에 없었다.

25 sarcastic adj. mocking, cynical ↔ kind, respectful

[sɑːrkǽstik] 빈정대는, 비꼬는

Newspaper editorials are usually filled with **sarcastic** remarks that target incompetent politicians.
신문 논설은 대개 무능한 정치인을 겨냥해 비꼬는 발언으로 가득 차 있다.

26 sibling n. brothers and sisters

[síbliŋ] 형제자매

Although Tim and Tom are **siblings**, they do not have anything in common.
팀과 톰은 형제지만 닮은 구석이 없다.

27 somber adj. gloomy, depressing ↔ cheerful, buoyant

[sámbər] 침울한, 우울한

He was in a **somber** mood for weeks after the death of his pet fish.
그는 애완물고기가 죽은 뒤 몇 주 동안 우울했다.

28 spearhead   v. lead, direct   ↔ follow, bring up the rear

[spíərhèd] 주도하다, 선봉에 서다

Spearheaded by Dr. Johnson, a top scientist in the field of biology, the research team successfully cloned a chimpanzee.
생물학 분야의 최고 과학자인 존슨 박사의 주도 하에 연구팀은 성공적으로 침팬지를 복제했다.

29 tuition   n. fee, payment for instruction

[tjuːíʃən] 등록금, 수업료

The students protested the university's decision to raise **tuition**.
학생들은 대학 등록금 인상 결정에 항의했다.

30 wary   adj. careful, on guard   ↔ reckless, indiscreet

[wέəri] 경계하는, 조심하는

It is important for parents to teach their children to be **wary** of strangers.
부모가 자녀에게 낯선 사람을 조심하라고 가르치는 것이 중요하다.

DAILY QUIZ

1	**address** an important problem •	• a regularly
2	**eradicate** crime •	• b allowance
3	water plants **periodically** •	• c employ
4	a **plausible** reason •	• d journal
5	set **quota** on car imports •	• e deal with
6	**propel** economic development •	• f allow
7	**resort to** cheating in a test •	• g credible
8	read a **periodical** •	• h hopeless
9	**authorize** the use of physical force •	• i root out
10	a **futile** effort to save a dying person •	• j stimulate

ANSWERS   1. e   2. i   3. a   4. g   5. b   6. j   7. c   8. d   9. f   10. h

Day 04

1. abrupt   adj. sudden, unanticipated   ↔ gradual, expected

[əbrʌ́pt] 갑작스러운

The students were surprised by the **abrupt** change in school policy.
학생들은 학교 방침의 갑작스러운 변화에 놀랐다.

2. abide by   phr. follow, comply with   ↔ disobey, ignore

준수하다

When people travel to a foreign country, they must **abide by** the local laws.
외국을 여행할 때에는 현지 법을 반드시 따라야 한다.

3. ancestral   adj. genealogical

[ænséstrəl] 조상의

Native Americans were driven from their **ancestral** lands when the European settlers arrived in America.
유럽 이주자들이 미국에 도착했을 때 북미 인디언들은 조상의 땅에서 쫓겨났다.

4. availability   n. accessibility, opportunity

[əvèiləbíləti] 이용 가능도, 유용성

Beth was told that she may be able to get on board an airplane tonight depending on seat **availability**.
베스는 좌석이 있는지 여부에 따라 오늘 밤 비행기에 탑승할 수도 있다고 들었다.

5. breakthrough   n. advancement, progress   ↔ impediment, a step backward

[bréikθrù:] 큰 발전

Recently, there have been many **breakthroughs** in cancer research.
최근 암 연구에 큰 발전이 있었다.

6. byproduct   n. side effect, derivative   ↔ root, source

[báiprɑ̀dʌkt] 부산물

Radioactive waste is perhaps the most dangerous **byproduct** of nuclear power plants.
방사성 폐기물이 아마 원자력 발전소의 가장 위험한 부산물일 것이다.

7 celestial adj. heavenly, cosmic ↔ earthly, terrestrial

[səléstʃəl] 천체의, 하늘의

Stars are the main **celestial** bodies in the night sky.
별은 밤하늘의 주된 천체이다.

8 compensate v. make up for, settle ↔ deprive, penalize

[kámpənsèit] 보상하다, 배상하다

Employees are **compensated** for overtime if they work on the weekends.
직원들은 주말에 근무할 경우 초과 근무에 대해 보상을 받는다.

9 diversify v. expand, branch out ↔ specialize, narrow down

[daivə́:rsəfài] 다각화하다

Many companies choose to **diversify** into different products in order to continue growing.
많은 회사는 지속적인 성장을 위해 다양한 상품으로 다각화를 꾀하고자 한다.

10 erratic adj. unpredictable, irregular ↔ steady, consistent

[irǽtik] 불규칙한, 변덕스러운

The current **erratic** weather patterns are caused by global warming.
최근의 변덕스러운 날씨 패턴은 지구 온난화 때문이다.

11 forecast v. predict, estimate

[fɔ́:rkæst] 예측하다

Economists are **forecasting** a positive turnaround in the economy in the coming year.
경제학자들은 내년에 경기가 호전되리라는 낙관적인 전망을 하고 있다.

12 harness v. exploit, tap

[há:rnis] 활용하다, 동력화하다

Energy can be **harnessed** from alternative sources such as steam, wind, and water.
에너지는 증기, 바람, 물과 같은 대체 가능한 원천으로부터 끌어낼 수 있다.

13 incentive n. inducement, stimulus ↔ prevention, deterrent

[inséntiv] 장려책

A cash bonus from the carmaker is a major **incentive** for salespeople to sell more cars.
자동차 회사가 주는 현금 보너스는 영업 사원들이 더 많은 차를 팔도록 하는 주된 장려 정책이다.

14 inevitable adj. unavoidable, certain ↔ unlikely, preventable

[inévətəbl] 불가피한, 필연적인

When people become careless, accidents are **inevitable**.
사람들이 부주의해지면 사고는 피할 수 없다.

15 innovative adj. creative, inventive ↔ unimaginative, unoriginal

[ínəvèitiv] 획기적인

It takes **innovative** thinking to solve difficult problems.
어려운 문제를 해결하기 위해서는 획기적인 생각이 필요하다.

16 intrinsic adj. inborn, inherent ↔ acquired, extrinsic

[intrínsik] 본질적인, 고유한

One cannot put a price on the **intrinsic** value of education.
교육의 본질적인 가치는 돈으로 매길 수 없다.

17 mandatory adj. required, compulsory ↔ voluntary, optional

[mǽndətɔ̀:ri] 의무의

Serving in the military is **mandatory** for all men in Korea.
군 복무는 모든 한국 남자의 의무이다.

18 mutate v. modify, alter ↔ persist, remain

[mjú:teit] 돌연변이하다, 변화하다

If a virus **mutates**, the existing vaccine may no longer be effective.
바이러스가 변형되면, 현재 백신은 더 이상 효과가 없을지도 모른다.

19 notorious adj. infamous, disreputable ↔ esteemed, renowned

[noutɔ́:riəs] 악명 높은

Al Capone is an example of a **notorious** crime lord during the 1920s.
알 카포네는 1920년대 악명 높은 범죄 두목의 예이다.

20 penetrate v. go through, enter ↔ exit, withdraw

[pénətrèit] 침투[진출]하다

In order to **penetrate** a new market, companies need to consider the local tastes in products.
새로운 시장에 진출하기 위해 업체들은 지역의 상품 취향을 고려해야 한다.

21. per capita phr. per person, for one

[pər-kǽpitə] 1인당

Per capita income in large cities tends to be higher than that in rural areas.
대도시의 1인당 수입은 지방 도시보다 높은 경향이 있다.

22. predator n. hunter, pursuer ↔ prey, game

[prédətər] 포식자, 포식 동물

The polar bear is the world's largest land **predator**.
북극곰은 세계에서 가장 큰 포식 동물이다.

23. proficient adj. skilled, accomplished ↔ incompetent, inept

[prəfíʃənt] 능숙한

He is so **proficient** in PowerPoint that he can create a presentation in an hour.
그는 파워포인트에 아주 능숙해서 한 시간 안에 프레젠테이션을 만들 수 있다.

24. renounce v. abandon, give up ↔ adopt, uphold

[rináuns] 포기하다, 버리다

If a priest **renounces** his faith in God, he must leave the Catholic Church.
신부가 신에 대한 믿음을 버린다면 그는 카톨릭 교회를 떠나야 한다.

25. speculate v. guess, hypothesize ↔ realize, understand

[spékjulèit] 추측하다

Many experts continue to **speculate** that heart disease will become the number one cause of death in the next few decades.
많은 전문가들은 몇십 년 후에 심장병이 사망 원인 1위가 될 것이라고 여전히 추측한다.

26. subsequent adj. following, ensuing ↔ preceding, antecedent

[sʌ́bsikwənt] 차후의, 그 다음의

Although the judge allowed the interruption once, he insisted that there be no **subsequent** ones.
판사는 한 차례의 중단은 허용하였지만, 더 이상은 허락하지 않는다고 주장했다.

27. transition n. changeover, progression

[trænzíʃən] 이행, 인수인계

In order to ensure a smooth **transition** of power, the outgoing President met constantly with the newly-elected leader.
순조로운 권력 인계를 보장하기 위해 퇴임하는 대통령은 차기 대통령과 계속 만났다.

28 underestimate v. underrate, make light of ↔ overrate, expect too much of

[ʌ̀ndəréstəmèit] 과소평가하다

Because the general **underestimated** the enemy's military strength, he suffered a surprising defeat.
장군이 적의 군사력을 과소평가한 탓에 예상치 못한 패배를 겪었다.

29 uniformity n. consistency, homogeneity ↔ unevenness, variation

[jùːnəfɔ́ːrməti] 균등성, 획일

For the sake of **uniformity**, all students were given the test on the same day.
균등을 위하여 모든 학생들에게 같은 날 시험을 보게 했다.

30 venue n. site, location

[vénjuː] 장소

The sudden downpour caused the change of game **venue** from the outdoor volleyball pit to the indoor gym.
갑작스런 폭우로 경기 장소는 야외 배구장에서 실내 체육관으로 변경되었다.

DAILY QUIZ

1. come to an **abrupt** stop
2. **harness** energy from nature
3. energy consumption **per capita**
4. **underestimate** the stock value
5. the championship **venue**
6. a hungry **predator**
7. **compensate** for the damages
8. **abide by** the guidelines
9. a scientific **breakthrough**
10. one's **intrinsic** nature

a. per person
b. site
c. follow
d. make up for
e. advancement
f. tap
g. inherent
h. hunter
i. underrate
j. sudden

ANSWERS 1. j 2. f 3. a 4. i 5. b 6. h 7. d 8. c 9. e 10. g

COMPREHENSIVE QUIZ   Day 03 & 04

1. The _____ stock market confused the investors.
   ⓐ proficient   ⓑ erratic   ⓒ sarcastic   ⓓ intrinsic

2. The Best Director _____ thanked the people who came to the awards ceremony.
   ⓐ transition   ⓑ enactment   ⓒ recipient   ⓓ incentive

3. The college student took a job during school vacation to help pay for _____.
   ⓐ quota   ⓑ medium   ⓒ buffer   ⓓ tuition

4. The Mayor _____ the union leader to stop the strikes.
   ⓐ coerced   ⓑ fostered   ⓒ speculated   ⓓ renounced

5. A bonus system was used as a(n) _____ to push the employees to work harder.
   ⓐ venue   ⓑ incentive   ⓒ integration   ⓓ availability

6. All players must _____ the game rules.
   ⓐ forecast   ⓑ abide by   ⓒ penetrate   ⓓ harness

7. There was finally a(n) _____ in the dispute between the two rival parties.
   ⓐ byproduct   ⓑ predator   ⓒ breakthrough   ⓓ periodical

8. Missing the bus is not a(n) _____ reason for coming late to work.
   ⓐ futile   ⓑ plausible   ⓒ mandatory   ⓓ subsequent

9. Because she was an only child, Candice has always wanted a(n) _____.
   ⓐ inspiration   ⓑ uniformity   ⓒ sibling   ⓓ forecast

10. After failing the doping test, the boxer was forced to _____ his championship belt.
    ⓐ renounce   ⓑ propel   ⓒ underestimate   ⓓ authorize

Answers: p.338

Day 05

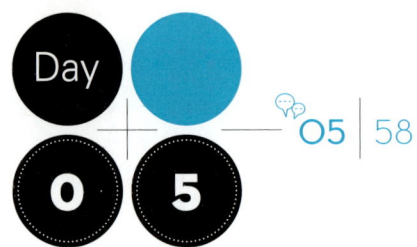

1 abstain   v. refrain, hold back   ↔ indulge

[əbstéin] 자제하다

Recovering alcoholics should **abstain** from drinking even a single glass of beer.
알코올 중독에서 회복되려면 단 한 잔의 맥주라도 마시는 것을 자제해야 한다.

2 accelerate   v. quicken, speed up   ↔ decelerate, slow down

[əksélərèit] 가속하다

Visual aids can **accelerate** the learning process.
시청각 자료는 학습 과정을 가속할 수 있다.

3 awe   n. amazement, reverence   ↔ contempt, indifference

[ɔ́ː] 경외감

All the boys from the countryside stared at the skyscrapers in **awe** as their bus passed the bridge.
시골에서 온 소년들은 모두 버스가 다리를 건널 때 고층 건물을 경외롭게 바라보았다.

4 biodegradable   adj. decomposable, eco-friendly

[bàioudigréidəbl] 생분해성의

Many supermarkets have switched to paper bags because they are **biodegradable** while plastic ones are not.
많은 슈퍼마켓은 비닐봉지와 달리 종이봉투는 자연 분해되기 때문에 종이봉투로 바꾸었다.

5 budget   n. spending plan, estimated expenses

[bʌ́dʒit] 예산, (지출 예상) 비용

Because of the tight travel **budget**, Paul stayed in cheap motels.
빠듯한 여행 비용 때문에 폴은 저렴한 모텔에 머물렀다.

6 bustling   adj. busy, active   ↔ tranquil, quiet

[bʌ́sliŋ] 바쁜 듯한, 번잡한

The family moved to a quiet resort town in order to get away from the **bustling** city life.
그 가족은 번잡한 도시 생활에서 벗어나기 위해 조용한 휴양 도시로 이사했다.

7 camouflage   n. disguise, concealment   ↔ exposure, uncovering

[kǽməflà:ʒ] 위장, 위장 수단

The white fur coat of a polar bear acts as a **camouflage** in the whiteness of the Arctic.
북극곰의 흰 털가죽은 순백의 북극에서 위장 수단의 역할을 한다.

8 come to the fore   phr. emerge, come out   ↔ disappear, go away

표면화되다, 주목을 받다

The same major issues **come to the fore** during every election.
매 선거 때마다 동일한 주요 쟁점들이 부각된다.

9 controversial   adj. contentious, disputable   ↔ agreeable, unquestionable

[kàntrəvə́:rʃəl] 논쟁의

Politicians tend to avoid making **controversial** remarks that may anger their supporters.
정치인들은 지지자를 화나게 할 수 있는 논쟁적 발언을 피하는 경향이 있다.

10 debris   n. remains, waste

[dəbríː] 잔해

The Red Cross workers had to remove the **debris** from the earthquake before they could save the victims under the fallen building.
적십자 직원들은 무너진 건물 아래의 희생자들을 구할 수 있기에 앞서 지진의 잔해를 치워야 했다.

11 denounce   v. condemn, criticize   ↔ approve, commend

[dináuns] 비난하다

The United States once again **denounced** North Korea for its nuclear weapons program.
미국은 북한의 핵무기 계획을 다시 한번 비난했다.

12 detect   v. discover, make out   ↔ miss, overlook

[ditékt] 발견하다, 감지하다

Some animals can **detect** an earthquake before it actually occurs.
어떤 동물들은 실제로 지진이 일어나기 전에 감지할 수 있다.

13 deteriorate   v. worsen, degenerate   ↔ improve, get better

[ditíəriərèit] 악화하다

When his relationship with his wife **deteriorated** beyond repair, he had to seek divorce.
아내와의 관계가 회복될 수 없을 만큼 악화되었을 때 그는 이혼을 요구해야 했다.

14 emulate   v. imitate, follow

[émjulèit] 모방하다

Children often try to **emulate** the behaviors of the adults they respect.
아이들은 종종 존경하는 어른들의 행동을 모방하려고 한다.

15 humidity   n. wetness, dampness   ↔ dryness, aridity

[hju:mídəti] 습도

Laundry does not dry very easily in summers due to high **humidity**.
여름에는 높은 습도 때문에 세탁물이 쉽게 마르지 않는다.

16 hypothesis   n. theory, assumption   ↔ fact, proof

[haipáθəsis] 가설, 추측

After years of gathering evidence, the scientists were finally able to prove their **hypothesis**.
수년간의 증거 수집 후에야 과학자들은 마침내 그들의 가설을 증명할 수 있었다.

17 impoverished   adj. poor, poverty-stricken   ↔ wealthy, plentiful

[impávərist] 빈곤한, 결핍된

There are too many **impoverished** children dying of hunger in Ethiopia.
에티오피아에는 굶주림으로 죽는 빈곤한 아이들이 너무 많다.

18 inhale   v. breathe in, draw in   ↔ exhale, breathe out

[inhéil] (숨을) 들이마시다

The rescued victims from the burning building were taken to the hospital for **inhaling** smoke.
불타는 건물에서 구조된 희생자들은 연기를 들이마셔서 병원으로 실려 갔다.

19 installation[1]   n. setup

[ìnstəléiʃən] 설치

Internet access has become easier with the numerous wireless internet **installations** around the city.
도시 주변에 수많은 무선 인터넷 설치로 인터넷 접속이 더 수월해졌다.

20 installation[2]   n. base, facility

[ìnstəléiʃən] (특수) 시설

Military **installations** are usually not indicated in maps.
군사 시설은 보통 지도에 표시되어 있지 않다.

21 investigate v. probe, inspect

[invéstəgèit] 수사하다, 조사하다

The police **investigated** the crime scene for evidence.
경찰은 증거를 찾기 위해 범죄 현장을 조사하였다.

22 irrational adj. illogical, unreasonable ↔ rational, sensible

[irǽʃənl] 무분별한, 불합리적인

People who are under stress often make **irrational** decisions.
스트레스를 받는 사람들은 종종 무분별한 결정을 한다.

23 loom v. approach, impend ↔ disappear, fade

[lúːm] 불안하게 다가오다

As the deadline for submitting her paper **loomed**, she became worried that she might not finish it on time.
과제 제출 마감이 다가오자 그녀는 제시간에 끝내지 못할 것 같아 걱정이 되었다.

24 mediocre adj. average, run-of-the-mill ↔ outstanding, extraordinary

[mìːdióukər] 평범한, 썩 좋지는 않은

Despite receiving **mediocre** reviews, the movie was a big hit at the box office.
평범한 평을 받았지만 영화는 박스 오피스에서 크게 흥행하였다.

25 misconception n. error, mistaken belief ↔ perception, understanding

[mìskənsépʃən] 오해, 잘못된 인식

The idea that men are better drivers than women is a common **misconception**.
남자가 여자보다 운전을 잘한다는 생각은 흔한 오해이다.

26 onset n. beginning, commencement ↔ completion, conclusion

[ánsèt] (안 좋은 일의) 시작, 발단

It is often a good idea to seek professional help right from the **onset** of depression.
흔히 우울증이 발병할 때부터 바로 전문가의 도움을 구하는 것이 좋다.

27 phobia n. fear, anxiety

[fóubiə] 공포증

Because of his **phobia** of snakes, he was afraid to enter the jungle.
뱀 공포증 때문에 그는 정글에 들어가는 것을 무서워했다.

28 portrayal n. depiction, representation

[pɔːrtréiəl] 묘사

The actor's realistic **portrayal** of a dying cancer patient won him a nomination for Best Actor at the Academy Awards.
배우는 죽어 가는 암 환자를 실감나게 연기해서 아카데미 남우 주연상 후보에 올랐다.

29 species n. kind, type

[spíːʃiːz] 종 (생물 분류의 기초 단위)

Human beings are not the only **species** of mammals on the planet.
인간은 지구상 포유류의 유일한 종이 아니다.

30 validate v. approve, authenticate ↔ reject, invalidate

[vælədèit] 입증하다, 인증하다

In order for a new theory to be accepted by the general public, it must be **validated** by many scientists.
새로운 이론이 일반 대중들에게 수용되려면 여러 과학자들이 입증해야 한다.

DAILY QUIZ

1. **accelerate** physical growth •   • a   inspect
2. **investigate** corruption •   • b   kind
3. **debris** from volcanic eruption •   • c   breathe in
4. protect endangered **species** •   • d   spending plan
5. a **mediocre** result •   • e   amazement
6. **inhale** hazardous gas •   • f   speed up
7. **humidity** during rainy season •   • g   waste
8. a low **budget** to save money •   • h   poor
9. stand in **awe** of the famous movie star •   • i   average
10. **impoverished** people in Africa •   • j   wetness

ANSWERS 1. f 2. a 3. g 4. b 5. i 6. c 7. j 8. d 9. e 10. h

Day 06

1 abode   n. home, dwelling

[əbóud] 거주지, 거처

An igloo is the traditional **abode** used by Eskimos, or the Inuit.
이글루는 에스키모 혹은 이누잇 족의 전통 가옥이다.

2 advent   n. emergence, appearance

[ǽdvent] 출현, 도래

The **advent** of the Internet has allowed users to search information directly from a variety of sources.
인터넷의 출현으로 이용자들은 다양한 출처에서 직접 정보를 찾을 수 있게 되었다.

3 alienate   v. exclude, turn away   ↔ accept, embrace

[éiliənèit] 소원하게 하다

A restaurant playing loud rock music can **alienate** older diners.
큰 소리의 록음악을 연주하는 식당은 나이 든 손님들을 멀어지게 할 수 있다.

4 beacon   n. guide, beam

[bíːkən] 신호등, 불빛

Gandhi acted as a **beacon** of hope for the people of India in their desire for independence from the British rule.
간디는 영국의 지배로부터 독립을 갈망하는 인도 국민에게 희망의 불빛의 역할을 했다.

5 bliss   n. (extreme) happiness, ecstasy   ↔ misery, grief

[blís] 더없는 기쁨, 행복

People say ignorance is **bliss**, but having knowledge is the true pleasure in life.
모르는 것이 약이라고 하지만, 앎은 삶의 진정한 기쁨이다.

6 configuration   n. arrangement, structure

[kənfìgjuréiʃən] 배치, 배열

The desks were arranged in a circular **configuration** with the teacher in the middle.
책상은 선생님을 가운데 두고 원형으로 배치되었다.

43

7 contemporary   adj. modern, concurrent   ↔ old, separate

[kəntémpərèri] 동시대의, 현대의

To reach a wider audience, an orchestra must be able to play both classical and **contemporary** music.
더 다양한 관객에게 다가가려면 오케스트라는 고전 음악과 현대 음악 둘 다 연주할 수 있어야 한다.

8 contest   v. challenge, question   ↔ agree, concede

[kəntést] 이의를 제기하다

The opposing party **contested** the decision by the President to increase the police force.
야당은 경찰력을 강화하겠다는 대통령의 결정에 이의를 제기했다.

9 dissident   n. separatist, nonconformist

[dísədənt] 반체제자

China was displeased with the awarding of the Nobel Peace Prize to a political **dissident**.
중국은 정치적 반체제자의 노벨 평화상 수상에 못마땅했다.

10 engender   v. arouse, give rise to   ↔ desist, back out

[indʒéndər] 불러일으키다

Her short but timely speech **engendered** pride and passion in the audience.
그녀의 짧지만 시기적절한 연설이 청중의 긍지와 열정을 불러일으켰다.

11 entity   n.

[éntəti] 실체, 독립체

A corporation is an **entity** separate from the people who own it.
법인은 소유주와 분리된 독립체이다.

12 homogeneous   adj. similar, consistent   ↔ dissimilar, heterogeneous

[hòumədʒíːniəs] 동질의, 같은 종류의 것으로 된

Despite a shared national identity, the states in the U.S. are not culturally **homogeneous**.
미국 주들은 하나의 국가 정체성을 공유하고 있음에도 문화적으로 동질적이지 않다.

13 inception   n. beginning, onset   ↔ conclusion, completion

[insépʃən] 시작, 발단

The club has been active in the community since its **inception** in 1991.
클럽은 1991년 결성된 이후 지역 사회에서 활발하게 활동하고 있다.

14 **inherent** adj. hereditary, built-in ↔ acquired, extrinsic

[inhérənt] 타고난, 내재하는

Everyone is born with an **inherent** ability to master language.
모든 사람은 언어 습득 능력을 가지고 태어난다.

15 **interval** n. break, intermission ↔ continuation, progression

[íntərvəl] 간격, (중간의) 휴식 시간

There was a long **interval** between the two acts in the play.
연극의 두 막 사이에 긴 휴식 시간이 있었다.

16 **legislation** n. measure, enactment

[lèdʒisléiʃən] 제정법, 입법

Most companies were unhappy with the new **legislation** that limited overtime.
대부분의 회사들은 초과 근무를 제한하는 새로운 법안을 못마땅해 했다.

17 **offspring** n. child, baby ↔ parent, begetter

[ɔ́fsprìŋ] 자손, 새끼

A liger is the **offspring** of a male lion and a female tiger.
라이거는 수사자와 암호랑이 사이에서 난 새끼이다.

18 **on behalf of** phr. for someone, as an agent of

~을 대신하여, ~을 대표하여

A spokesperson is the one who generally makes announcements **on behalf of** his or her political party.
대변인은 일반적으로 정당을 대표해서 발표하는 사람이다.

19 **perception** n. understanding, apprehension ↔ misinterpretation, misunderstanding

[pərsépʃən] 인식, 지각

Psychologists agree that a **perception** of reality can be as powerful as the reality itself.
심리학자들은 현실 자각이 현실 그 자체만큼이나 강력할 수 있다는 데 동의한다.

20 **policy** n. rule, procedure

[páləsi] 정책, 방침

Tens of thousands of teachers marched in the streets to protest the government's new school **policy**.
수만 명의 교사들이 정부의 새로운 학교 정책에 항의하기 위해 거리 행진을 했다.

21 resolve¹   v. solve, clear up   ↔ question, mull

[rizálv] 해결하다

They had to **resolve** the first problem before they could discuss the next one.
그들은 다음 문제를 논의하기 전에 첫 번째 문제를 해결해야 했다.

22 resolve²   v. pledge, promise   ↔ waver, shift back and forth

[rizálv] 다짐하다, 결심하다

The student **resolved** to never cheat again after he was caught looking at his classmate's test.
학생은 반 친구의 시험지를 보다가 발각된 후 다시는 부정행위를 하지 않기로 했다.

23 rigorous   adj. severe, brutal   ↔ lax, easy-going

[rígərəs] 엄격한, 혹독한

Training for the Special Forces is **rigorous**.
특수 부대 훈련은 혹독하다.

24 shrine   n. sanctuary, holy ground

[ʃráin] 성지

Primitive societies were known to build **shrines** in honor of various gods.
원시 사회는 여러 신을 기리기 위해 신전을 세운 것으로 알려졌다.

25 subtle   adj. faint, insinuated

[sʌ́tl] 미묘한, 포착하기 힘든

The smell was so **subtle** that he barely noticed it at first.
냄새가 너무 미묘해 그는 처음에 거의 알아차리지 못했다.

26 superstitious   adj.

[sù:pərstíʃəs] 미신을 믿는, 미신적인

Although he was not usually **superstitious**, he believed that there was a ghost in the house.
그는 보통 미신을 믿지 않았지만 집안에 유령이 있다고 생각했다.

27 suppress   v. restrain, put down

[səprés] 진압하다, 참다

Armed with water cannons, the police easily **suppressed** the demonstrations in the streets.
물대포로 무장한 경찰은 거리 시위를 쉽게 진압했다.

28 symptom   n. sign, indication

[símptəm] 증상, 징후

Coughing and sneezing are some of the **symptoms** of the flu.
기침과 재채기는 독감의 몇몇 증상이다.

29 transaction   n. deal, trading

[trænzǽkʃən] 거래, 매매

Credit card **transactions** allow consumers to keep a record of their purchases.
신용 카드 거래를 통해 소비자는 구입 내역을 기록해 둘 수 있다.

30 transient   adj. temporary, fleeting   ↔ enduring, permanent

[trǽnziənt] 일시적인

Like the weather, most emotions are **transient**.
날씨와 마찬가지로 대부분의 감정은 일시적인 것이다.

DAILY QUIZ

1	**contest** the wrong answer	a	modern
2	a warm and comfortable **abode**	b	exclude
3	**suppress** the enemy	c	beginning
4	**alienate** minority groups	d	as an agent of
5	**on behalf of** the people	e	severe
6	**contemporary** environmental issues	f	home
7	**resolve** an important issue	g	restrain
8	**inception** of a new idea	h	challenge
9	go through **rigorous** training	i	sign
10	a **symptom** of a cold	j	clear up

ANSWERS   1. h   2. f   3. g   4. b   5. d   6. a   7. j   8. c   9. e   10. i

COMPREHENSIVE QUIZ — Day 05 & 06

1. _____ products can help reduce pollution level.
   ⓐ Mediocre   ⓑ Biodegradable   ⓒ Bustling   ⓓ Homogeneous

2. The speaker discussed the _____ flaws in the theory of communism.
   ⓐ superstitious   ⓑ impoverished   ⓒ inherent   ⓓ rigorous

3. _____ home decorations are usually very simple and modern.
   ⓐ Contemporary   ⓑ Controversial   ⓒ Irrational   ⓓ Transient

4. No one dared to _____ the general's orders.
   ⓐ loom   ⓑ contest   ⓒ resolve   ⓓ engender

5. Real estate _____ practically froze during the recent economic recession.
   ⓐ symptoms   ⓑ transactions   ⓒ portrayals   ⓓ debris

6. Cable _____ is necessary in order to watch a wide range of television programs.
   ⓐ beacon   ⓑ perception   ⓒ interval   ⓓ installation

7. The department store owner took the escalator because he had a(n) _____ of elevators.
   ⓐ turbine   ⓑ budget   ⓒ phobia   ⓓ camouflage

8. _____ is especially high on tropical islands.
   ⓐ Misconception   ⓑ Humidity   ⓒ Awe   ⓓ Onset

9. The IAEA investigators were sent to inspect North Korea's nuclear _____.
   ⓐ hypotheses   ⓑ abodes   ⓒ installations   ⓓ species

10. No one will ever be able to _____ the original dance moves of the legendary Michael Jackson.
    ⓐ emulate   ⓑ accelerate   ⓒ abstain   ⓓ deteriorate

Answers: p.338

1 ambiance   n. atmosphere, milieu

[ǽmbiəns] 분위기, 주변의 상황

The designers have created a peaceful **ambiance** by painting the ceiling and the walls blue.
디자이너는 천장과 벽을 푸른색으로 칠해 평화로운 분위기를 자아냈다.

2 anonymous   adj. nameless, unnamed   ↔ named, identified

[ənánəməs] 익명의

The police are attempting to locate the **anonymous** caller who claimed there was a bomb in the airport.
경찰은 공항에 폭탄이 있었다고 주장한 익명의 전화 제보자를 찾고자 애쓰고 있다.

3 anticipate   v. predict, foresee   ↔ doubt, be surprised

[æntísəpèit] 예상하다, 기대하다

The Electronic Entertainment Expo planners **anticipate** a larger crowd this year.
E3 Expo 기획자들은 금년에 더 많은 사람들이 올 것으로 예상하고 있다.

4 bestow   v. award, bequeath

[bistóu] 수여하다

The Queen of England **bestows** knighthood only to her subjects.
영국 여왕은 자국민에게만 기사 작위를 수여한다.

5 calculate   v. compute, estimate

[kǽlkjulèit] 계산하다, 추정하다

Sara **calculated** that it would take her two hours to complete her homework.
사라는 숙제를 끝내는 데 두 시간이 걸릴 것으로 추정했다.

6 concede   v. give in, accept   ↔ dispute, repudiate

[kənsíːd] 인정하다

He **conceded** that his friend's answer was better.
그는 친구의 답이 낫다고 인정하였다.

49

7 contour   n. outline, silhouette

[kántuər] 윤곽, 외형

The round **contour** of the tire looked like that of a donut.
타이어의 둥근 윤곽이 도넛처럼 보였다.

8 decree   n. legal order, mandate

[dekríː] 법령, 포고

By presidential **decree**, gasoline prices were frozen for a week.
대통령령에 의해 휘발유 가격이 1주일 동안 동결되었다.

9 distinction   n. difference, discrepancy   ↔ similarity, congruence

[distíŋkʃən] 구별, 차이

Sometimes it is difficult to make a **distinction** between right and wrong.
때로는 옳고 그름을 구분하기 어려울 때가 있다.

10 eligible   adj. worthy, acceptable   ↔ ineligible, undeserving

[élidʒəbl] ~을 가질 수 있는, 적임의

Only those with GPAs of 3.5 or better were **eligible** for scholarship.
평점이 3.5 이상인 학생만 장학금을 받을 자격이 있었다.

11 eliminate   v. remove, get rid of   ↔ accept, keep

[ilímənèit] 탈락시키다, 제거하다

If the national team loses this match, it will be **eliminated** from the Round of 16.
국가 대표팀이 이번 시합에서 지면 16강전에서 탈락할 것이다.

12 figurative   adj. symbolic, metaphorical   ↔ literal, straightforward

[fígjurətiv] 비유적인

Calling someone a pig would be using a **figurative** speech.
누군가를 돼지라고 부르는 것은 비유적인 말을 쓰는 것이다.

13 groundbreaking   adj. innovative, cutting-edge   ↔ traditional, conventional

[gráundbrèikiŋ] 획기적인

The television was a **groundbreaking** discovery at a time when the radio was the main source of entertainment.
TV는 라디오가 주요 오락 제공 수단이었던 시절에 획기적인 발명품이었다.

14 in lieu of phr. instead of, as an alternative to

[-lú:-] ~의 대신에

Milk can be used **in lieu of** cream when drinking coffee.
커피를 마실 때 크림 대신 우유를 넣을 수 있다.

15 insight n. understanding, acumen ↔ ignorance, stupidity

[ínsàit] 통찰력

To gain **insight** into human behavior, people should look into themselves first.
인간의 행동에 대한 통찰력을 가지려면, 먼저 자기 자신부터 들여다보아야 한다.

16 irrigation n.

[irəgéiʃən] 관개

The farmers used **irrigation** to bring water to their dry rice paddies.
농부들은 마른 논에 물을 대기 위해 관개 시설을 이용했다.

17 jeopardize v. put at risk, endanger ↔ protect, guard

[dʒépərdàiz] 위태롭게 하다, 위험에 빠뜨리다

Cindy's poor school grades **jeopardized** her chances of getting accepted into an Ivy League university.
신디의 학교 성적이 좋지 않아서 아이비리그 대학 진학의 기회가 위태로워졌다.

18 kinetic adj. active, energetic ↔ inactive, idle

[kinétik] 동적인

Simply put, **kinetic** energy is the energy of motion.
간단히 말해서, 운동 에너지는 움직임의 에너지이다.

19 metabolism n. absorption, digestion

[mətǽbəlìzm] 신진대사, 대사

Her high **metabolism** helped her stay slim even though she ate as much as anyone her age.
그녀는 또래들만큼 먹었지만 활발한 신진대사 덕분에 날씬함을 유지했다.

20 monsoon n. rainstorm, deluge ↔ aridity, dryness

[mɑnsúːn] 폭풍우, (동남아 지역의) 계절풍

The town was soon flooded with the rains from the **monsoon**.
계절풍에 의한 비로 인해 시내는 곧 범람했다.

21 rationale   n. reason, justification

[rǽʃənæl] 근거, 이론적 설명

There seemed to be no **rationale** behind the abrupt change in policy.
갑작스런 정책 변화의 이면에 근거가 없는 것처럼 보였다.

22 recession   n. decline, depression ↔ expansion, boom

[riséʃən] 침체, 불경기

Due to the economic **recession**, companies stopped hiring new employees.
경기 침체로 인해 회사들은 신입 사원 채용을 중단했다.

23 soot   n.

[sút] 그을음, 검댕

The rescued miners were covered in **soot** from having spent too much time in the caves.
구조된 광부들은 갱도에 너무 오래 갇혀 있었기 때문에 몸이 검댕 투성이었다.

24 subjective   adj. personal, individual ↔ objective, unbiased

[səbdʒéktiv] 주관적인

Without supporting evidence, his statements were seen as highly **subjective**.
입증 자료가 없는 그의 진술은 매우 주관적으로 보였다.

25 subsidy   n. support, assistance

[sʌ́bsədi] 보조금

Many kindergartens around the country are operated with government **subsidies**.
전국의 많은 유치원들이 정부 보조금으로 운영된다.

26 symmetrical   adj. balanced, proportional ↔ asymmetrical

[simétrikəl] 대칭적인

The Twin Towers are **symmetrical** to each other.
쌍둥이 빌딩은 서로 대칭이다.

27 terminate   v. end, do away with ↔ begin, initiate

[tə́ːrmənèit] 끝나다, 종료하다

The discount store chain **terminated** selling its famous fried chicken.
할인점 체인은 유명한 프라이드 치킨 판매를 종료했다.

28 tread v. walk, ambulate

[tréd] 디디다, 밟다

At home, many people like to **tread** on the carpet with their bare feet.
많은 사람들이 집에서 맨발로 카펫 밟는 것을 좋아한다.

29 verdict n. decision, ruling

[vɔ́:rdikt] 평결, 판결

When the jurors returned with the **verdict** in one hour, everyone in the courtroom was surprised.
한 시간 후 배심원들이 돌아와 평결을 내렸을 때 법정에 있던 모든 사람들이 놀랐다.

30 vibrant adj. colorful, animated ↔ colorless, pale

[váibrənt] 활기에 넘치는

In the autumn, the leaves of the trees in the mountains are **vibrant** with colors.
가을에 산의 나뭇잎은 색색으로 활기 넘친다.

DAILY QUIZ

1	**calculate** the distance	a nameless
2	floods caused by the **monsoon**	b end
3	a questionable **verdict**	c symbolic
4	**concede** defeat	d mandate
5	an **anonymous** donator	e innovative
6	**terminate** a contract	f personal
7	a **subjective** view	g accept
8	speak in a **figurative** way	h ruling
9	a royal **decree**	i rainstorm
10	a **groundbreaking** idea	j compute

ANSWERS   1. j   2. i   3. h   4. g   5. a   6. b   7. f   8. c   9. d   10. e

Day 08

1 abstract   adj. complex, conceptual   ↔ actual, concrete

[ǽbstrækt] 추상적인

The artist's paintings were too **abstract** to be understood by ordinary people.
화가의 그림은 일반인들이 이해하기에 너무 추상적이었다.

2 blunder   v. err, mess up   ↔ correct, remedy

[blʌ́ndər] 큰 실수를 하다

The soldier **blundered** by forgetting to salute the captain.
병사는 대위에게 경례를 하지 않은 큰 실수를 저질렀다.

3 bolster   v. support, buttress   ↔ hinder, undermine

[bóulstər] 북돋우다, 지지하다

The audience's positive reaction **bolstered** his confidence during his speech.
청중의 긍정적인 반응이 연설을 하는 동안 그의 자신감을 북돋았다.

4 cater to   phr. satisfy, serve   ↔ turn away, ignore

[kéitər-] ~의 구미에 맞추다, …에 영합하다

Locals should avoid expensive restaurants that **cater to** tourists.
현지인들은 관광객의 구미에 맞추는 비싼 식당을 피해야 한다.

5 chamber   n. room, compartment

[tʃéimbər] 방, 실

The old castle has many secret **chambers** of different sizes.
오래된 성에는 다양한 크기의 많은 비밀의 방이 있다.

6 collaborate   v. work together, cooperate

[kəlǽbərèit] 협력하다

George Lucas and Steven Spielberg **collaborated** on some of the most successful movies of all time.
조지 루카스와 스티븐 스필버그는 전무후무한 가장 성공적인 영화 몇 편을 합작했다.

7 deterrent   n. obstacle, impediment   ↔ encouragement, incentive

[ditə́:rənt] 제제 수단, 방해물

Many people believe that surveillance cameras can be a **deterrent** to crime.
많은 이들은 감시 카메라가 범죄를 억제할 수 있다고 본다.

8 exploitation   n. taking advantage, profiteering

[èksplɔitéiʃən] 착취

Too many factories in developing countries engage in child **exploitation** by using young children to produce goods.
개발 도상국의 아주 많은 공장들이 제품 생산에 아동을 이용함으로써, 아동 착취에 연루되어 있다.

9 fathom   v. understand, comprehend   ↔ misunderstand, misconstrue

[fǽðəm] 추측하다, 이해하다

The famous cook could not **fathom** why the guests avoided his new sauce.
유명 요리사는 손님들이 자신의 새로운 소스를 기피한 이유를 알 수 없었다.

10 geographic   adj.

[dʒì:əgrǽfik] 지리적인, 지리학(상)의

San Francisco has a mild climate due to its unique **geographic** location.
샌프란시스코는 독특한 지리적 위치 때문에 기후가 온난하다.

11 geological   adj.

[dʒì:əládʒikəl] 지질학의, 지질의

A volcano eruption or an earthquake is a **geological** event.
화산 폭발이나 지진은 지질학적 사건이다.

12 get hold of   phr. contact, communicate with

~와 연락이 되다

After repeated phone calls, the boss finally **got hold of** his slacking employee.
상사는 계속 전화를 한 후에야 마침내 태만한 직원과 연락이 닿았다.

13 grueling   adj. difficult, strenuous   ↔ easy, facile

[grú:əliŋ] 엄한, 대단히 힘든

He was tired after finishing the **grueling** task of shoveling snow.
그는 삽으로 눈을 치우는 힘든 작업을 끝내고 지쳤다.

14 hallucination   n. figment of the imagination, mirage   ↔ experience, reality

[həlùːsənéiʃən] 환각, 환영

It was discovered that the monsters and aliens he saw were only **hallucinations** caused by the drugs.
그가 보았던 괴물과 외계인은 단지 약으로 인한 환영이었던 것으로 밝혀졌다.

15 hazardous   adj. dangerous, precarious   ↔ safe, guarded

[hǽzərdəs] 위험한

Many smokers have quit when they realized that smoking was **hazardous** to their health.
많은 흡연자가 흡연이 건강에 유해하다는 것을 깨닫고 금연했다.

16 photosynthesis   n.

[fòutousínθəsis] 광합성

Plants use **photosynthesis** to convert sunlight into food.
식물은 햇빛을 양분으로 변환시키기 위해 광합성을 한다.

17 plagiarize   v. imitate, copy

[pléidʒəràiz] 표절하다

They believed that the second report was **plagiarized** because it was so similar to the first.
두 번째 보고서가 첫 번째 보고서와 매우 유사했기 때문에 그들은 표절이라고 여겼다.

18 procure   v. obtain, get ahold of   ↔ lose, give away

[prəkjúər] 구하다, 입수하다

They were surprised that she was able to **procure** the tickets to the Far East Movement concert.
그들은 그녀가 파 이스트 무브먼트 콘서트 티켓을 구할 수 있었다는 것에 놀랐다.

19 prominent   adj. celebrated, pronounced   ↔ unimportant, obscured

[prάmənənt] 유명한, 눈에 잘 띄는

As a **prominent** member of society, Mr. Bate was involved in many important clubs, including the Jaycees and the Lions Club.
사회에서 유명 인물인 베이트 씨는 청년 상공 회의소 및 라이온스 클럽을 포함한 많은 중요한 클럽에 몸담고 있었다.

20 quarantine   v. isolate, confine   ↔ release, liberate

[kwɔ́ːrəntìːn] 격리하다

The government **quarantined** those infected with the virus in one area of the hospital.
정부는 바이러스에 감염된 사람들을 병원의 한 구역에 격리했다.

21 reciprocal adj. mutual, complementary ↔ independent, unilateral

[risíprəkəl] 상호간의

She discovered that true love was **reciprocal**, not one sided.
그녀는 진정한 사랑은 일방적인 것이 아니라 주고받는 것이라는 것을 깨달았다.

22 revenue n. income, earnings ↔ debt, payment

[révənjù:] 수익, 수입

The store **revenue** was higher this year due to increased foot traffic.
행인 수의 증가로 인해 금년에 상점 수입이 늘었다.

23 saturated adj. full, crowded ↔ void, empty

[sǽtʃərèitid] 배어든, 가득한

The children found the cereal too sweet because it was **saturated** with sugar.
아이들은 시리얼이 설탕 범벅이라 너무 달다는 것을 알았다.

24 sovereignty n. domination, autonomy ↔ submission, capitulation

[sávərənti] 주권, 통치권

Both China and Japan claimed **sovereignty** over the island.
중국과 일본 모두 그 섬에 대한 주권을 주장했다.

25 stalemate n. deadlock, standstill ↔ progress, headway

[stéilmèit] 교착 상태

The match ended in a **stalemate** with no point scored by either side.
경기는 어느 편도 득점하지 못하고 무승부로 끝났다.

26 stampede n. rush, charge

[stæmpí:d] 쇄도, 한꺼번에 몰림

There was a **stampede** of eager shoppers to the doors when the discount store opened for its first day of business.
할인점 개장 첫날 열성 쇼핑객들이 우르르 몰려들었다.

27 standardize v. make regular, unify ↔ differentiate, waver

[stǽndərdàiz] 표준화하다, 통일하다

All the questions are similar because the school has **standardized** the tests.
학교가 시험을 표준화했기 때문에 모든 문제가 비슷하다.

28 supposedly   adv.   ↔ unlikely, dubiously

[səpóuzidli] 추정상, 겉보기에는

He was **supposedly** at work, but his wife knew he was playing golf.
그가 직장에 있는 것 같았지만 아내는 그가 골프를 치고 있었다는 것을 알았다.

29 triumphant   adj. successful, victorious   ↔ unproductive, defeated

[traiʌ́mfənt] 의기양양한, 성공한

The new video game was a **triumphant** success after years in development.
수년간의 개발을 마친 새로운 비디오 게임은 대단한 성공을 거두었다.

30 vulnerable   adj. open to attack, susceptible   ↔ guarded, protected

[vʌ́lnərəbl] ~에 취약한

Smokers are extremely **vulnerable** to lung cancer.
흡연자는 폐암에 매우 걸리기 쉽다.

DAILY QUIZ

1 **cater to** different tastes   • a isolate
2 **prominent** figures in history   • b autonomy
3 reduce **hazardous** waste   • c work together
4 a **saturated** market   • d strenuous
5 loss in **revenue**   • e dangerous
6 **quarantine** the affected areas   • f obstacle
7 **grueling** exercises   • g income
8 national **sovereignty**   • h satisfy
9 **collaborate** on a project   • i crowded
10 **deterrent** against missile attacks • j celebrated

ANSWERS   1. h   2. j   3. e   4. i   5. g   6. a   7. d   8. b   9. c   10. f

COMPREHENSIVE QUIZ — Day 07 & 08

1. The concert planners are confidently _____ a packed stadium filled with excited fans.
   ⓐ bestowing   ⓑ getting hold of   ⓒ jeopardizing   ⓓ anticipating

2. The songwriter sued the famous rock group for _____ his songs.
   ⓐ collaborating   ⓑ standardizing   ⓒ plagiarizing   ⓓ bolstering

3. The mysterious person who donated a billion dollars to the Bill & Melinda Gates Foundation wanted to remain _____.
   ⓐ eligible   ⓑ anonymous   ⓒ vulnerable   ⓓ kinetic

4. The citizens welcomed the _____ return of their exiled leader.
   ⓐ saturated   ⓑ symmetrical   ⓒ triumphant   ⓓ hazardous

5. The cowboy barely escaped from a buffalo _____.
   ⓐ decree   ⓑ stampede   ⓒ verdict   ⓓ irrigation

6. The general election resulted in a political _____ because each of the two parties won exactly fifty percent of the vote.
   ⓐ ambiance   ⓑ hallucination   ⓒ monsoon   ⓓ stalemate

7. Environmentalists are worried about the ongoing _____ of natural resources.
   ⓐ revenue   ⓑ exploitation   ⓒ soot   ⓓ contour

8. For people of average intelligence, it is nearly impossible to _____ the minds of geniuses.
   ⓐ fathom   ⓑ procure   ⓒ blunder   ⓓ quarantine

9. After allowing nine goals in the first half, the team had to _____ defeat early.
   ⓐ concede   ⓑ calculate   ⓒ eliminate   ⓓ terminate

10. The defendant used a lot of _____ language in order to avoid a direct answer.
    ⓐ groundbreaking   ⓑ subjective   ⓒ figurative   ⓓ geographic

Answers: p.338

Day 09

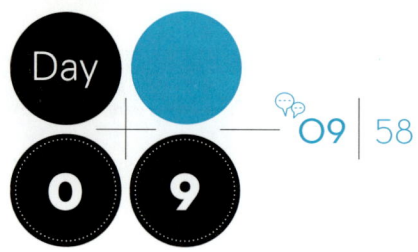

1 anarchy n. lawlessness, chaos ↔ order, organization

[ǽnərki] 무정부 상태, 무질서 상태

With the police on strike, **anarchy** ruled the streets.
경찰의 파업으로 길거리는 무질서 상태에 빠졌다.

2 arbitrary adj. random, whimsical ↔ rational, reasonable

[áːrbətrèri] 제멋대로인, 임의적인

An **arbitrary** decision made by a leader could confuse the followers.
지도자의 임의적인 결정은 추종자들을 혼란스럽게 할 수 있다.

3 at large phr. on the loose, running around ↔ confined, restrained

잡히지 않고

With the escaped bear still **at large**, the villagers refused to leave their homes.
탈출한 곰이 아직도 잡히지 않기 때문에 마을 사람들은 집에서 나서기를 꺼려했다.

4 bilateral adj. reciprocal, two-sided ↔ unilateral, one-sided

[bailǽtərəl] 쌍방의, 양측의

Instead of accepting the offer for a six-nation meeting, North Korea called for **bilateral** talks with the United States.
북한은 6자 회담 제의를 받아들이지 않고 미국과의 양자 회담을 요구했다.

5 caliber n. quality, merit

[kǽləbər] 우수성, 재간

The company hopes to attract the right **caliber** of job applicants through advertisements in expensive magazines.
회사는 고급 잡지 광고를 통해 뛰어난 재능을 가진 입사 지원자들을 유인하기를 희망한다.

6 chart v. record, map out ↔ disorganize

[tʃɑːrt] 계획하다, 기록하다

The new computer schedule software can **chart** the progress of a project on a daily basis.
새로운 컴퓨터 스케줄 소프트웨어는 매일 일의 진행을 기록할 수 있다.

7 compulsory adj. required, mandatory ↔ optional, voluntary

[kəmpʌ́lsəri] 의무적인

Military service is **compulsory** in countries such as South Korea, Israel, and Switzerland.
군복무는 대한민국, 이스라엘, 스위스 같은 나라에서는 의무적이다.

8 conglomerate n. multinational, large corporation

[kəngláməret] 대기업, 복합 기업

Samsung, Mitsubishi, and General Electric are all prime examples of a **conglomerate**.
삼성, 미쯔비시, 제너럴 일렉트릭은 모두 대기업의 대표적인 예이다.

9 dialect n. accent, lingo ↔ standard speech, official language

[dáiəlèkt] 방언, 사투리

Because regional **dialects** exist, even the same language could sound different.
지역 방언이 존재하기 때문에 같은 언어조차 다르게 들릴 수 있다.

10 ensure v. guarantee, make sure ↔ forfeit, give up

[inʃúər] 보장하다, 지키다

Eating a variety of foods will help **ensure** a balanced and healthy diet.
다양한 음식 섭취는 균형 잡히고 건강한 식단을 지킬 수 있도록 도와준다.

11 foresight n. intuition, anticipation ↔ hindsight, thoughtlessness

[fɔ́:rsàit] 예지력, 선견지명

The CEO had the **foresight** to enter the Chinese market before it became too saturated with foreign investments.
최고 경영자는 외국인 투자가 너무 포화되기 전에 중국 시장에 진출하는 선견지명이 있었다.

12 hibernate v. sleep, hole up

[háibərnèit] 동면하다

Certain species of fish are known to **hibernate** during winter.
어떤 물고기 종은 겨울 내내 동면하는 것으로 알려졌다.

13 ideology n. beliefs, creed

[àidiálədʒi] 이데올로기, 이념

Despite their differences in political **ideology**, the two parties joined forces to pass the new law.
정치적 이념이 달랐지만 두 정당은 새 법안을 통과시키기 위해 힘을 합쳤다.

14 immune adj. unaffected, insusceptible ↔ vulnerable, susceptible

[imjúːn] 면역의, ~에 영향을 받지 않는

Not even the President is **immune** to public criticism.
심지어 대통령조차도 대중의 비판을 면할 수는 없다.

15 parody n. imitation, satire

[pǽrədi] 패러디, 풍자

For a **parody** to work, it has to contain familiar elements that are exaggerated enough to be funny.
패러디가 효과 있으려면 재미있을 정도로 과장되어 친숙한 요소를 담고 있어야 한다.

16 perpendicular adj. vertical, at right angle to ↔ horizontal, on level

[pə̀ːrpəndíkjulər] 수직적인, 직각의

A building's columns should be **perpendicular** to the ground.
건물의 기둥은 땅 위에 수직으로 놓여야 한다.

17 physiological adj. bodily, biological ↔ mental, psychological

[fìziəládʒikəl] 생리적인

Physiological changes are natural as we age.
나이를 들면서 생리적인 변화는 자연스러운 것이다.

18 plunder v. steal, pillage

[plʌ́ndər] 약탈하다, 노략질하다

Hungry soldiers **plundered** the nearby village for food and water.
배고픈 군인들은 음식과 물을 찾아 인근 마을을 노략질하였다.

19 rampant adj. uncontrolled, out of hand ↔ controlled, restrained

[rǽmpənt] 걷잡을 수 없는, 만연한

Violence is **rampant** in most major cities around the world.
전 세계 대부분의 주요 도시에 폭력이 만연하고 있다.

20 in reserve phr. on the side, in store

예비의

It is wise to keep some money **in reserve** for any unexpected emergency.
어떤 예상치 못한 위급 상황을 위해 예비금을 가지고 있는 것이 현명하다.

21 reserved adj. soft-spoken, taciturn ↔ outgoing, extroverted

[rizə́:rvd] 말수가 적은, 수줍은
Unlike her **reserved** husband, she was talkative and outgoing.
말수가 적은 남편과 달리 그녀는 수다스럽고 사교적이었다.

22 spawn v. produce, generate ↔ destroy, ruin

[spɔ́:n] 낳다, 양산하다
The senator's careless remarks **spawned** public outrage and calls for resignation.
상원 의원의 부주의한 발언이 대중의 격노와 사퇴 요구를 낳았다.

23 sporadically adv. infrequently, now and then ↔ frequently, regularly

[spərǽdikəli] 산발적으로
Crimes involving guns occur only **sporadically** in countries like Korea.
한국과 같은 나라에서는 총기 관련 범죄가 이따금 발생한다.

24 stagnation n. inactivity, sluggishness ↔ boom, rise

[stægnéiʃən] 침체, 정체
Recovery usually follows a period of economic **stagnation**.
경제 회복은 주로 경기 침체기에 뒤따른다.

25 substance n. material, entity

[sʌ́bstəns] 물질, 본질
Plastic is not a natural **substance**.
플라스틱은 천연 물질이 아니다.

26 substantial adj. considerable, serious ↔ minor, insignificant

[səbstǽnʃəl] 상당한
The damage caused by the big earthquake was **substantial**.
대지진 때문에 생긴 피해가 상당했다.

27 suffrage n. right to vote

[sʌ́fridʒ] 선거권, 투표권
Universal **suffrage** does not exist in communist countries, where the power to govern is given only to a small number of people.
공산주의 국가에서는 보통 선거권은 존재하지 않고, 소수의 사람들에게만 통치권이 주어진다.

28 susceptible   adj. affected, be taken in   ↔ resistant, invulnerable

[səséptəbl] ~하기 쉬운, 민감한

Teenagers are especially **susceptible** to drug use because they are more open to new experiences.
10대는 새로운 경험에 더 개방적이기 때문에 약물 사용에 특히 빠지기 쉽다.

29 trajectory   n. course, path

[trədʒéktəri] 궤도, 탄도

The missile fell into the sea because someone had not calculated the **trajectory** correctly.
누군가 궤도를 정확하게 계산하지 않아 미사일은 바다로 떨어졌다.

30 unprecedented   adj. groundbreaking, exceptional   ↔ ordinary, unremarkable

[ʌ̀nprésədèntid] 전례 없는

This year the early monsoon has brought **unprecedented** rainfall to the country.
올해는 이른 장마로 전국에 유례없는 폭우가 내렸다.

DAILY QUIZ

1. **chart** the way forward   •
2. of the highest **caliber**   •
3. a major **conglomerate**   •
4. **hibernate** during winter   •
5. a strong **dialect**   •
6. **bilateral** relations between two countries   •
7. **rampant** rumors   •
8. the **trajectory** of a planet   •
9. **ensure** safety   •
10. a pure **substance**   •

- a   accent
- b   quality
- c   path
- d   material
- e   guarantee
- f   uncontrolled
- g   large corporation
- h   reciprocal
- i   map out
- j   slumber

ANSWERS   1. i   2. b   3. g   4. j   5. a   6. h   7. f   8. c   9. e   10. d

Day 10

1 analogy   n. comparison, similarity   ↔ disagreement, unlikeness

[ənǽlədʒi] 유사, 비유

She made an **analogy** between a light bulb and an idea.
그녀는 백열전구를 아이디어에 비유했다.

2 archaic   adj. out of date, obsolete   ↔ modern, state-of-the-art

[ɑːrkéiik] 형태가 오래된

Certain words in the English language are so **archaic** that only scholars are aware of their meanings.
영어의 어떤 단어들은 너무 고어라서 학자들만이 그 의미를 안다.

3 arithmetic   n. mathematics, computation

[əríθmətik] 산수, 셈

Because of his strong dislike for anything that dealt with numbers, he failed **arithmetic** in school.
그는 숫자에 관련된 것이라면 뭐든지 매우 싫어하기 때문에 학교에서 산수에 낙제했다.

4 beneficiary   n. inheritor, recipient   ↔ giver, benefactor

[bènəfíʃièri] 수혜자

Low-income families were the main **beneficiaries** of the new tax policy.
저소득 가정은 새로운 세금 정책의 주요 수혜자였다.

5 catalyst   n. stimulus, reactant   ↔ prevention, blockage

[kǽtəlist] 촉진제, 기폭제

The tragic accident proved to be a **catalyst** for changes in traffic laws.
비극적인 사고가 교통법 개정에 촉진제가 된 것으로 드러났다.

6 commute   v.

[kəmjúːt] 통근하다

He **commuted** two hours to work every morning.
그는 매일 아침 2시간을 통근했다.

7 condone v. excuse, look the other way ↔ forbid, censure

[kəndóun] 용납하다, 용서하다

Schools generally do not **condone** fighting among students.
학교는 일반적으로 학생들 간 싸움을 용납하지 않는다.

8 dubious adj. doubtful, skeptical ↔ definite, trustworthy

[djúːbiəs] 의심하는, 미심쩍어 하는

Although he was at first **dubious** about the trip, he was soon enjoying it.
그는 처음에는 여행에 대해 미심쩍어 했지만 얼마 안 있어 즐기게 되었다.

9 establish v. set up, organize ↔ destroy, invalidate

[istǽbliʃ] 설립하다, 창설하다

FIFA was **established** in 1904.
FIFA는 1904년에 설립되었다.

10 exposure n. uncovering, laying open ↔ concealment, hiding

[ikspóuʒər] 노출

Exposure to radiation can cause sickness and even death.
방사선 노출은 질병을 일으키거나 심지어 죽을 수도 있다.

11 fissure n. crack, crevice

[fíʃər] 갈라진 틈, 균열

There was a coin stuck in a **fissure** in the ground.
동전이 땅의 갈라진 틈에 박혀 있었다.

12 forage v. seek, rummage

[fɔ́ːridʒ] 마구 뒤지며 찾다

The wild boar came into the village to **forage** for food.
멧돼지는 먹이를 찾기 위해 마을로 왔다.

13 heritage n. tradition, custom

[héritidʒ] 유산, 전통

Every country has its own unique cultural **heritage**.
모든 국가는 각기 독특한 문화유산이 있다.

14 hierarchy n. chain of command, ranking

[háiərɑ̀ːrki] 계급, 계층제

Among a group of monkeys, there is also a social **hierarchy** with the leader at the top.
원숭이 무리에서도 최고 우두머리가 있는 사회 계급이 있다.

15 inscription n. message, epitaph

[inskrípʃən] 적힌 글, 비문

The **inscription** they found on the stone tablet was in Chinese characters.
그들이 석판에서 발견한 비문은 한자로 쓰여 있었다.

16 instill v. implant, disseminate

[instíl] 서서히 주입시키다, 서서히 심어주다

It is the role of the parents to **instill** values and beliefs into their children.
자녀에게 가치와 신념을 서서히 심어주는 것은 부모의 역할이다.

17 juvenile adj. childish, naive   ↔ grown-up, mature

[dʒúːvənàil] 청소년의, 유치한

Playing violent games can lead to **juvenile** crime.
폭력적인 게임을 하는 것은 청소년 범죄를 유발할 수 있다.

18 kinship n. connection, affinity   ↔ dissimilarity, antagonism

[kínʃip] 연대감, 혈족 관계

When he discovered that she was from his hometown, he felt a strong sense of **kinship** with her.
그는 그녀가 자기 고향 출신이라는 것을 알고 강한 연대감을 느꼈다.

19 legitimate adj. well-founded, valid   ↔ unwarranted, illegal

[lidʒítəmət] 타당한, 정당한

Unless Nate has a **legitimate** excuse for his absences, he will be suspended.
결석에 대해 타당한 이유가 없다면 네이트는 정학 당할 것이다.

20 membrane n. covering, film

[mémbrein] (동·식물 조직의) 막

Cells have thin **membranes** that act as barriers.
세포에는 방벽 역할을 하는 얇은 막이 있다.

21 monotonous   adj. unchanging, boring   ↔ ever-changing, lively

[mənátənəs] 단조로운, 지루한

The lecture was so **monotonous** that several students fell asleep.
강의가 너무 지루해서 여러 학생들이 잠들었다.

22 patent   n. copyright, protection

[pǽtnt] 특허권

Patents allow their holders to protect their inventions.
특허는 특허 소유자가 발명품을 보호할 수 있도록 한다.

23 persistent   adj. determined, unrelenting   ↔ lazy, yielding

[pərsístənt] 끈질긴, 끊임없이 지속되는

The **persistent** headache lasted for hours.
끊임없는 두통은 몇 시간 동안 지속되었다.

24 pragmatic   adj. practical, realistic   ↔ idealistic, unreasonable

[prægmǽtik] 실용적인, 실용주의적인

Although they were twins, Kevin was idealistic while Keith was **pragmatic**.
쌍둥이임에도 불구하고 케빈은 이상주의적인 반면에 키스는 실용주의적이었다.

25 proclaim   v. make known, declare   ↔ conceal, obscure

[prəkléim] 선포하다

Each side **proclaimed** victory over the other.
각 편은 상대편에 대한 승리를 선포했다.

26 replica   n. duplicate, imitation   ↔ original, prototype

[réplikə] 복제품

The art dealer was furious when he discovered the sculpture he had bought was a **replica**.
미술상은 그가 구입한 조각품이 복제품인 것을 알고 몹시 화가 났다.

27 respiratory   adj. breathing, inhaling

[réspərətɔ́:ri] 호흡 기관의, 호흡의

Smog and pollution can cause many types of **respiratory** problems.
스모그와 오염 물질은 여러 가지 호흡기 질병을 야기할 수 있다.

28 streak n. uninterrupted series, roll

[strí:k] 연속

The player's winning **streak** was broken when he suffered an injury during a game.
그 선수의 연승은 경기 도중에 입은 부상으로 인해 물거품이 되었다.

29 substitute n. alternate, equivalent ↔ original, standard

[sʌ́bstətʃù:t] 대리인, 대체물

Margarine is a good **substitute** for butter.
마가린은 버터의 좋은 대체물이다.

30 torrential adj. abundant, abounding ↔ lacking, sparse

[tɔːrénʃəl] 억수 같은, 들이붓듯이 내리는

Flooding is a major concern during a **torrential** rain.
비가 억수같이 내릴 때에는 홍수가 가장 큰 걱정이다.

DAILY QUIZ

1. **archaic** words no longer in use •   • a   tradition
2. make **pragmatic** decisions •   • b   declare
3. **proclaim** independence •   • c   message
4. **heritage** of the African tribe •   • d   boring
5. **exposure** to sunlight •   • e   copyright
6. a **monotonous** song •   • f   valid
7. receive a **patent** •   • g   obsolete
8. **legitimate** leaders voted by the people •   • h   practical
9. **beneficiary** of a will •   • i   inheritor
10. **inscription** on the ancient statue •   • j   laying open

ANSWERS 1. g 2. h 3. b 4. a 5. j 6. d 7. e 8. f 9. i 10. c

COMPREHENSIVE QUIZ Day 09 & 10

1. The real estate bubble burst acted as a(n) _____ for the nation's financial crisis.
   ⓐ dialect   ⓑ catalyst   ⓒ beneficiary   ⓓ conglomerate

2. Many men who were eligible voters also fought for women's _____.
   ⓐ fissure   ⓑ anarchy   ⓒ substance   ⓓ suffrage

3. The police chief advised the citizens to lock their doors because the escaped convicts were still _____.
   ⓐ reserved   ⓑ archaic   ⓒ at large   ⓓ in reserve

4. There is a huge _____ of the Statue of Liberty near the City Museum.
   ⓐ trajectory   ⓑ analogy   ⓒ replica   ⓓ catalyst

5. People who are _____ to caffeine can sleep well at night even if they drink several cups of coffee.
   ⓐ bilateral   ⓑ immune   ⓒ saturated   ⓓ grueling

6. The lungs are perhaps the most important part of the _____ system.
   ⓐ compulsory   ⓑ unprecedented   ⓒ rampant   ⓓ respiratory

7. The record snow fall caused great difficulties for the citizens who had to _____ to work.
   ⓐ commute   ⓑ plunder   ⓒ condone   ⓓ forage

8. Health officials warned that babies and senior citizens may be more _____ to the new flu virus.
   ⓐ pragmatic   ⓑ physiological   ⓒ perpendicular   ⓓ susceptible

9. Many of the calls made by the referee were largely _____.
   ⓐ substantial   ⓑ arbitrary   ⓒ juvenile   ⓓ monotonous

10. Last night's victory finally ended the rugby team's ten-game losing _____.
    ⓐ parody   ⓑ caliber   ⓒ streak   ⓓ patent

Answers: p.339

1 advocate — v. argue for, bolster ↔ oppose, criticize

[ǽdvəkèit] 지지하다, 주장하다

NGOs generally **advocate** positive changes in society and government.
일반적으로 비정부 기구는 사회와 정부의 긍정적인 변화를 지지한다.

2 articulate — v. say clearly, verbalize ↔ bumble, misrepresent

[ɑːrtíkjulèit] 명료하게 표현하다, 분명하게 발음하다

He had an ability to **articulate** his ideas clearly and simply.
그는 자신의 생각을 명확하고 간결하게 표현하는 능력이 있었다.

3 aura — n. feeling, atmosphere

[ɔ́ːrə] 기운, 기

The professor had an **aura** of authority and confidence.
교수는 권위와 자신감의 기운이 있었다.

4 cognitive — adj. rational, observant

[kágnətiv] 인식의, 인지의

Chimpanzees have surprisingly high **cognitive** skills.
침팬지는 놀라울 정도로 높은 인지력을 가지고 있다.

5 confidential — adj. secret, off the record ↔ public, well-known

[kànfədénʃəl] 비밀의, 은밀한

The government employee was arrested for leaking **confidential** information.
그 공무원은 기밀 유출 혐의로 체포되었다.

6 confiscate — v. seize, take away ↔ offer, bestow

[kənfískeit] 몰수하다, 압수하다

His driver's license was **confiscated** after he drove 50 kilometers over the speed limit.
제한 속도를 초과해 50킬로미터로 달린 후에 그의 운전면허증이 취소되었다.

7. deviate   v. digress, bear off   ↔ continue, abide by

[díːvièit] 벗어나다, 이탈하다

His parents were disappointed when he **deviated** from his plan to attend college.
그가 대학교 입학 계획에서 벗어나자 부모님은 실망하셨다.

8. entrepreneur   n. businessperson, industrialist

[à:ŋtrəprənə́ːr] 사업가, 기업가

Bill Gates and Steve Jobs are two examples of **entrepreneurs** who started their companies in their garages.
빌 게이츠와 스티브 잡스는 차고에서 사업을 시작한 사업가의 대표적인 두 예이다.

9. exorbitant   adj. excessive, overboard   ↔ moderate, reasonable

[igzɔ́ːrbətənt] 과도한, 엄청난

The hotels in tourist areas were charging **exorbitant** prices for rooms.
관광지에 있는 호텔들은 과도한 객실 요금을 부과하였다.

10. fortification   n. defense, bulwark   ↔ opening, breach

[fɔ̀ːrtəfikéiʃən] 방어 시설, 요새

By king's orders, stronger **fortifications** were built around the castle.
왕의 명령에 의해 더 강력한 요새가 성 주위에 지어졌다.

11. imminent   adj. on the verge, approaching   ↔ distant, beyond range

[ímənənt] 임박한, 급박한

During the Cold War, many Americans believed that nuclear war was **imminent**.
냉전 시대에 많은 미국인들은 핵전쟁이 임박했다고 생각했다.

12. instigate   v. provoke, bring about   ↔ prevent, halt

[ínstəgèit] 부추기다, 선동하다

It was believed that a handful of people **instigated** the riots.
소수의 인원이 폭동을 선동한 것으로 여겨졌다.

13. jurisdiction   n. authority, hegemony

[dʒùərisdíkʃən] 관할권, 사법권

The island falls under the **jurisdiction** of South Korea.
그 섬은 대한민국의 관할에 속한다.

14 lethal   adj. fatal, malignant   ↔ harmless, beneficial

[líːθəl] 치명적인

Eating blowfish can be **lethal** if it is not prepared by a certified cook.
자격 있는 요리사가 조리하지 않으면 복어를 먹는 것은 치명적일 수 있다.

15 metaphor   n. analogy, symbol   ↔ plain speech, dissimilarity

[métəfɔːr] 은유, 비유

The story of Cinderella was the **metaphor** the media used to describe the actress's success.
신데렐라 이야기는 언론이 그 여배우의 성공을 묘사하기 위해 쓴 비유였다.

16 omnipotent   adj. all-powerful, supreme   ↔ powerless, impotent

[ɑmnípətənt] 전능한

The **omnipotent** power of the conqueror instilled fear throughout the empire.
정복자의 전능한 힘이 제국 전체에 두려움을 심어 주었다.

17 omnipresent   adj. universal, ubiquitous   ↔ rare, scarce

[ɑ̀mniprézənt] 어디에나 존재하는

Many complain that the **omnipresent** surveillance cameras invade their privacy.
많은 사람들은 어디에나 존재하는 감시 카메라가 사생활을 침해한다고 불평한다.

18 omniscient   adj. all-knowing, preeminent   ↔ unknowing, oblivious

[ɑmníʃənt] 전지한, 모든 것을 다 아는

Specialists in different fields exist because no one can be **omniscient**.
어느 누구도 모든 것을 다 알 수 없기 때문에 다양한 분야의 전문가가 존재한다.

19 phase out   phr. weed out, eliminate   ↔ increase, spread

단계적으로 폐지하다

The car model will be **phased out** by next year because of its low sales.
판매 저조로 그 자동차 모델은 내년까지 단종될 것이다.

20 pilgrimage   n. crusade, excursion

[pílgrəmidʒ] 순례, 성지 순례

Muslims try to make the **pilgrimage** to Mecca at least once in their lifetime.
이슬람교도들은 평생 적어도 한 번은 메카로 성지 순례를 하려고 한다.

21 reign n. rule, dominion ↔ subservience, subordination

[réin] 통치, 지배

Ivan the Terrible's **reign** of terror made life miserable for many Russian nobles.
폭군 이반의 공포 정치 이래 러시아의 많은 귀족들의 삶이 비참했다.

22 relic n. antique, vestige ↔ invention, novelty

[rélik] 유물, 유적

Cassette players are now considered **relics** from the past.
카세트 플레이어는 이제 과거의 유물로 여겨진다.

23 reminiscence n. remembrance, nostalgia

[rèmənísns] 추억담, 회상

Everyone listened with awe at his **reminiscence** of the hunting trip in Africa.
모두들 아프리카에서 있었던 그의 사냥 얘기를 두려운 마음으로 들었다.

24 stationary adj. fixed, motionless ↔ mobile, ambulatory

[stéiʃənèri] 정지된

The truck remained **stationary** while the men loaded it with boxes.
남자들이 상자를 싣는 동안 트럭은 정지 상태로 있었다.

25 stationery n. writing materials, office supplies

[stéiʃənèri] 문구류, 필기 용지

She often used a fountain pen to write personal notes on expensive **stationery**.
그녀는 비싼 용지에 사적인 메모를 적기 위해 종종 만년필을 사용했다.

26 subordinate adj. secondary, lesser ↔ chief, paramount

[səbɔ́ːrdənət] 하위의, 하급의

A **subordinate** officer must obey every command given by his commander.
하사관은 사령관이 지시하는 모든 명령에 복종해야 한다.

27 unsolicited adj. unwelcome, uninvited ↔ asked, requested

[ʌ̀nsəlísitid] 요청받지 않은

If you receive an **unsolicited** commercial e-mail, it is recommended that you erase it immediately.
원치않는 광고성 이메일을 받는다면 바로 삭제할 것을 권장한다.

28 variable   adj. changing, fickle   ↔ unchanging, perpetual

[vέəriəbl] 변덕스러운, 가변적인

The weather is highly **variable** in tropical islands, so it is a good idea to keep an umbrella at all times.
열대섬에서는 날씨가 매우 변덕스럽기 때문에 항상 우산을 가지고 다니는 것이 좋다.

29 vivid   adj. clear, lively   ↔ dull, lackluster

[vívid] 생생한, 선명한

The nightmare remained so **vivid** in his mind that he could not sleep all night.
악몽이 그의 머리에 너무 생생하게 남아 있어서 밤새 잠을 잘 수 없었다.

30 zeal   n. passion, enthusiasm   ↔ indifference, apathy

[zí:l] 열의, 열성

It was her **zeal** for life that gave her the will to survive ten days in the desert.
그녀가 사막에서 10일 동안 살아남을 수 있는 의지를 준 것은 바로 삶에 대한 그녀의 열의였다.

DAILY QUIZ

1 a successful **entrepreneur**   a approaching
2 **vivid** description   b businessperson
3 breaking through the **fortification**   c motionless
4 an **imminent** death   d provoke
5 **instigate** a fight   e remembrance
6 a **stationary** train   f authority
7 **confiscate** a driver's license   g all-powerful
8 a **reminiscence** of the glory days   h lively
9 state versus federal **jurisdiction**   i take away
10 the **omnipotent** emperor   j defense

ANSWERS   1. b   2. h   3. j   4. a   5. d   6. c   7. i   8. e   9. f   10. g

Day 12

1 adjacent   adj. next to, contiguous   ↔ separate, detached

[ədʒéisnt] 가까이 있는

The jogging lane is **adjacent** to the bike lane.
조깅 도로는 자전거 도로 가까이에 있다.

2 admonish   v. scold, reprimand   ↔ praise, laud

[ædmániʃ] 질책하다

His doctor **admonished** him for continuing to smoke.
그의 주치의는 계속해서 담배를 피우는 그를 나무랐다.

3 benefactor   n. donor, contributor   ↔ opponent, antagonist

[bénəfæktər] 후원자, 은인

What keeps the orphanages open are the generous donations from wealthy **benefactors**.
고아원이 운영을 지속할 수 있는 건 부유한 후원자들의 후한 기부금 때문이다.

4 complement   v. supplement, accompany   ↔ take away, neglect

[kámpləmént] 보완하다, 보충하다

Wine lovers know red wine **complements** any dish.
와인 애호가들은 레드와인이 어떤 음식과도 잘 어울린다는 것을 안다.

5 compliment   v. praise, speak highly of   ↔ criticize, find fault

[kámpləmént] 칭찬하다, 찬사를 보내다

His girlfriend **complimented** him on his new haircut.
그의 여자 친구는 그의 새로운 헤어스타일을 칭찬했다.

6 concession   n. compromise, give and take   ↔ quarrel, disagreement

[kənséʃən] 양보, 타협

The new **concessions** from both the company and the union signaled the end of the long strike.
회사와 노조간의 새로운 타협은 긴 파업이 끝났다는 것을 시사했다.

7 counterpart   n. opposite number, alter ego

[káuntərpà:rt] 상대방, 대응하는 사람
The Mayor of New York called his counterpart in San Francisco.
뉴욕 시장은 샌프란시스코 시장에게 전화를 했다.

8 designate   v. select, nominate

[dézignèit] 지정하다, 지명하다
She was designated as the school spokesperson because she was the most articulate of all the teachers.
그녀는 모든 교사 중에서 가장 말소리가 분명했기 때문에 학교 대변인으로 지명되었다.

9 erudite   adj. knowledgeable, well-educated   ↔ uneducated, empty headed

[érjudàit] 박식한, 학식 있는
The adults were surprised when the boy joined the erudite discussions on the current economic stagnation.
소년이 현 경제 침체에 대한 학술 논의에 참여하자 어른들이 놀랐다.

10 forte   n. strong point, faculty   ↔ weakness, Achilles heel

[fɔ:rt] 강점, 장기
Although he occasionally made sculptures, painting was his real forte.
그는 가끔 조각을 만들었지만, 진짜 강점은 그림 그리는 것이었다.

11 hygienic   adj. clean, germ-free   ↔ contaminated, unsanitary

[haidʒénik] 위생적인
Malaria can spread in poor hygienic conditions.
위생 상태가 안 좋으면 말라리아가 퍼질 수 있다.

12 inclination   n. soft spot, tendency

[ìnklənéiʃən] 성향, 경향
Since childhood, the singer had a strong inclination for music.
가수는 어린 시절부터 강한 음악적 성향을 가졌다.

13 invoice   n. itemized bill, bill of sale

[ínvɔis] 송장, 청구서
The amount on the invoice the consultant sent him was higher than expected.
컨설턴트가 그에게 보낸 청구서의 금액은 예상보다 높았다.

14 magnitude n. amount, extent

[mǽgnətʃùːd] 규모

The **magnitude** of the damage caused by the earthquake surprised even the most experienced rescuers.
지진으로 인한 피해 규모는 가장 경험이 많은 구조대원들조차도 놀라게 했다.

15 mimic v. imitate, impersonate ↔ be original, differ

[mímik] 흉내를 내다

The comedian **mimicked** people so well that he sounded almost exactly like them.
코미디언은 사람 흉내를 매우 잘 냈기 때문에, 그들과 거의 똑같은 목소리를 냈다.

16 preservative n. chemical preserving agent

[prizə́ːrvətiv] 방부제

For health reasons, the family avoided food containing artificial **preservatives**.
건강상의 이유로 가족은 인공 방부제가 함유된 음식을 피했다.

17 pressing adj. life-and-death, urgent ↔ trivial, insignificant

[présiŋ] 긴급한

A more **pressing** issue than the threat of disease was the water shortage.
질병의 위협보다 더 긴급한 문제는 물 부족이었다.

18 register v. sign up, enlist ↔ cancel, call off

[rédʒistər] 등록하다

Students are required to **register** for classes no later than a week after the start of the semester.
학생들은 학기 시작 후 1주일 이내에 수강 신청을 해야 한다.

19 rehabilitation n. recovery, rejuvenation

[rìːhəbílətéiʃən] 재활, 갱생

Rehabilitation of criminals leaving prison is a major social concern.
출감하는 범죄자의 갱생은 중요한 사회적 관심사이다.

20 relevant adj. appropriate, pertaining to ↔ unrelated, beside the point

[réləvənt] 관련 있는, 타당한

Only the **relevant** points should be included in an essay or a presentation.
논문이나 발표에는 관련된 요점만 포함되어야 한다.

21. satellite¹   adj. subordinate, subsidiary   ↔ main, primary

[sǽtəlàit] 위성(도시 근교)의, 지사의

A great number of residents in nearby **satellite** cities commute to the capital every day.
인근 위성 도시의 많은 주민들이 매일 수도로 통근한다.

22. satellite²   n. moon, orbiting spacecraft

[sǽtəlàit] 위성

The world's first artificial **satellite** was launched into earth's orbit in 1957.
세계 최초의 인공위성이 1957년에 지구 궤도로 발사되었다.

23. staple   n. food, diet

[stéipl] 기본 식료품

Potatoes were the main **staple** of the Irish before the famine.
감자는 기근이 발생하기 전 아일랜드 사람들의 주식이었다.

24. strategically   adv. tactically, critically

[strətíːdʒikəli] 전략적으로

The U.S. has always considered South Korea to be a **strategically** important ally in Asia.
미국은 항상 한국을 아시아에서 전략적으로 중요한 동맹국으로 여겨 왔다.

25. subconsciously   adv. without full awareness   ↔ knowingly, deliberately

[sʌbkɑ́nʃəsli] 무의식적으로

We all **subconsciously** avoid things that scare us.
우리는 모두 자신을 놀라게 하는 것들을 무의식적으로 피한다.

26. subject to   phr. conditional, contingent on   ↔ unlimited, unrestricted

~을 조건으로 하는, ~될 수 있는

The company explained that the warranty conditions on its products are **subject to** change without notice.
회사는 자사 제품에 대한 보증 조건이 예고 없이 변경될 수 있다고 설명했다.

27. terrestrial   adj. earthly, earthbound   ↔ cosmic, heavenly

[təréstriəl] 육생의, 지구의

Although there are hardly any **terrestrial** animals in the Antarctic, its waters are full of seals and penguins.
남극에는 육상동물이 거의 없지만 바다에는 물개와 펭귄이 가득하다.

28 tyrannical adj. oppressive, ironhanded ↔ compassionate, sympathetic

[tirǽnikəl] 폭군의, 위압적인

Hitler's **tyrannical** rule ended in 1945.
히틀러의 폭군 통치는 1945년에 끝났다.

29 universal adj. common, widespread ↔ local, confined

[jùːnəvə́ːrsəl] 보편적인, 일반적인

Love and hate are **universal** emotions shared by all people on earth.
애증은 지구상의 모든 사람들이 공유하는 보편적인 감정이다.

30 volatile adj. up-and-down, inconsistent ↔ stable, set in stone

[vάlətl] 불안정한

The stock markets in developing countries are especially **volatile**.
개발도상국의 주식 시장은 특히 불안정하다.

DAILY QUIZ

1. using fancy candles to **complement** dinner settings • • a common
2. **register** to vote • • b clean
3. **mimic** animal sounds • • c strong point
4. love as the **universal** language • • d sign up
5. an individual's **forte** • • e appropriate
6. **relevant** answers • • f compromise
7. **terrestrial** birds • • g supplement
8. maintaining a **hygienic** environment • • h earthbound
9. **strategically** located • • i imitate
10. a political **concession** • • j tactically

ANSWERS 1. g 2. d 3. i 4. a 5. c 6. e 7. h 8. b 9. j 10. f

COMPREHENSIVE QUIZ — Day 11 & 12

1. Being able to _____ your ideas is a great asset for working with other people.
   ⓐ articulate   ⓑ phase out   ⓒ confiscate   ⓓ deviate

2. The gift shop sells souvenirs, _____ and other accessories.
   ⓐ fortification   ⓑ stationery   ⓒ stationary   ⓓ forte

3. His boss _____ him on a job well done.
   ⓐ registered   ⓑ differed   ⓒ admonished   ⓓ complimented

4. Many high school students plan to protest the _____ price of college tuition.
   ⓐ subordinate   ⓑ exorbitant   ⓒ adjacent   ⓓ erudite

5. Citizens believe that the new law will make teenagers _____ unwarranted suspicion.
   ⓐ complement   ⓑ mimic   ⓒ advocate   ⓓ subject to

6. The speech was delivered with such _____ that everyone stood up to clap at the end.
   ⓐ zeal   ⓑ benefactor   ⓒ invoice   ⓓ pilgrimage

7. Repeated brain injury can lead to decreased _____ function.
   ⓐ cognitive   ⓑ hygienic   ⓒ variable   ⓓ omniscient

8. In order to have an organized discussion, _____ a person to speak for your team.
   ⓐ confiscate   ⓑ designate   ⓒ deviate   ⓓ admonish

9. Rice is a main _____ in many Asian diets.
   ⓐ jurisdiction   ⓑ counterpart   ⓒ entrepreneur   ⓓ staple

10. Due to poor profits, the food division will be _____ by next year.
    ⓐ phased out   ⓑ instigated   ⓒ nominated   ⓓ praised

Answers: p.339

1 aesthetic adj. beautiful, artful ↔ distasteful, not much to look at

[esθétik] 미학적, 심미적

Many smart phones are chosen for their multiple functions as well as their **aesthetic** appeal.
스마트폰은 미적인 매력뿐 아니라 다양한 기능 때문에 많이 좋아한다.

2 allegation n. accusation, charge

[æligéiʃən] 혐의, 주장

The **allegations** of wrongdoing were proven to be false.
범법 혐의는 사실이 아닌 것으로 입증되었다.

3 arid adj. dry, parched ↔ moist, humid

[ǽrid] 습기가 없는, 매우 건조한

A cactus can grow even in the most **arid** climates.
선인장은 가장 건조한 기후에서도 자랄 수 있다.

4 committee n. task force, commission

[kəmíti] 위원회

The CEO formed a special **committee** to discuss and plan the new project.
최고 경영자는 새로운 프로젝트를 논의하고 계획하기 위해 특별 위원회를 구성했다.

5 complacent adj. satisfied, unconcerned ↔ worried, distressed

[kəmpléisnt] 자기만족적인, 무관심한

Far too many people are still **complacent** about environmental problems.
지나치게 많은 사람들이 아직도 환경 문제에 대해 무관심한 태도를 취하고 있다.

6 document v. write down, record

[dάkjumènt] 기록하다

Anne Frank **documented** her life of hiding in her famous diary.
안네 프랑크는 자신의 유명한 일기에 은신 생활을 기록했다.

7 economic   adj. financial, business-related   ↔ noncommercial, not-for-profit

[èkənámik] 경제적인, 경제의

The **economic** situations in many poor countries are worsening.
많은 빈곤 국가의 경제 상황이 악화되고 있다.

8 economical   adj. penny-pinching, thrifty   ↔ wasteful, lavish

[èkənámikəl] 알뜰한, 절약적인

Turning off all lights when not in use is an **economical** way to lower your electric bill.
사용하지 않는 전등을 모두 끄는 것은 전기 요금을 낮추기 위한 경제적인 방법이다.

9 fad   n. trend, inthing   ↔ tradition, convention

[fǽd] 일시적 유행

Many people wrongly believed that miniskirts were just a passing **fad**.
많은 사람들이 미니스커트가 단지 일시적인 유행이었다고 잘못 생각했다.

10 garrison   n. sentinels, defense troops

[gǽrəsn] 수비대, 주둔군

A **garrison** was sent in to protect the city until the riots were over.
폭동이 끝날 때까지 도시를 방어하기 위해 수비대가 투입되었다.

11 gist   n. main point, essence, nitty-gritty   ↔ detail

[dʒíst] 요지

John did a quick review of the report to get the **gist** of the main points.
존은 주요 쟁점의 요지를 파악하기 위해 보고서를 신속하게 검토했다.

12 haul   v. drag, transport

[hɔ́ːl] 세게 잡아당기다, 끌어당기다

They **hauled** the heavy boxes across the room.
그들은 무거운 상자를 끌고 방을 지나갔다.

13 indispensable   adj. necessary, crucial   ↔ nonessential, profuse

[ìndispénsəbl] 없어서는 안 되는, 필수적인

With his intelligence and experience, Mr. Carver is an **indispensable** part of the team.
지성과 경험을 겸비한 카버 씨는 팀에서 없어서는 안 될 사람이다.

14 intrigue v. fascinate, captivate

[intríːg] 흥미를 돋우다

The photo of Cambodia **intrigued** him so much that he decided to take his next vacation there.
캄보디아 사진이 그에게 큰 호기심을 불러일으켰기 때문에 그곳에서 다음 휴가를 보내기로 했다.

15 maximize v. boost, amplify ↔ decrease, minimize

[mǽksəmàiz] 극대화하다

The store **maximized** its profits by cutting down on staff hours.
상점은 직원의 근무 시간을 줄여서 수익을 극대화했다.

16 personnel n. staff, employees ↔ management, owners

[pə̀ːrsnél] (조직·군대의) 인원, 요원

Medical **personnel** were called to the crime scene after two wounded men were found.
두 명의 부상자가 발견된 후 의료 요원이 범죄 현장으로 호출되었다.

17 premonition n. apprehension, intuition

[prèmənííʃən] (불길한) 예감

The mother said she had a **premonition** of the accident before it occurred.
어머니는 사건이 발생하기 전에 예감을 느꼈다고 했다.

18 preoccupation n. obsession, fixation ↔ boredom, lack of interest

[priːɑkjupéiʃən] 집착, 몰두

His **preoccupation** with money made him greedy.
돈에 대한 집착이 그를 탐욕스럽게 만들었다.

19 principal[1] n. administrator, head of a school ↔ student, teacher

[prínsəpəl] 교장, 학장

The high school is now run by a new **principal**.
고등학교는 이제 신임 교장이 운영한다.

20 principal[2] adj. foremost, second-to-none ↔ supplementary, secondary

[prínsəpəl] 주요한, 주된

Her constant tardiness was the **principal** reason for her firing.
계속되는 지각이 그녀가 해고된 주된 이유였다.

21 remorse n. repentance, guilty conscience

[rimɔ́ːrs] 후회, 양심의 가책

The families of the victims were angry that the criminal failed to show **remorse** for his violent actions.
희생자들의 가족은 범인이 자신의 폭력 행위에 대해 뉘우침을 보이지 않아 화가 났다.

22 retention n. custody, maintenance ↔ freedom, liberation

[riténʃən] 보유, 유지

Providing longer maternity leaves and a company daycare center may improve **retention** of married female employees.
출산 휴가의 연장과 회사 탁아소 제공은 기혼 여성 직원의 근속에 기여할 것이다.

23 seer n. fortune teller, prophet

[síːər] 선지자, 예언자

As the name suggests, a **seer** can see what will happen in the future.
명칭이 시사하듯이, 예언자는 미래에 일어날 일을 알 수 있다.

24 shroud v. block out, conceal ↔ reveal, uncloak

[ʃráud] 뒤덮다, 가리다

The cars were moving slowly over the road **shrouded** by a thick fog.
자동차들은 짙은 안개에 뒤덮인 도로 위를 천천히 달리고 있었다.

25 status quo phr.

[stǽtəs kwóu] 현재의 상황

People tend to want to maintain the **status quo** when faced with uncertainties about change.
사람들은 변화에 대한 불확실성에 직면하면 현상 유지를 원하는 경향이 있다.

26 strife n. struggle, dissension

[stráif] 갈등, 분쟁

The President's speech created **strife** among the political parties.
대통령의 연설은 정당 간 갈등을 초래했다.

27 taunt v. scoff at, provoke ↔ compliment, pay tribute to

[tɔ́ːnt] 조롱하다, 놀리다

Although they tried to **taunt** him into a fight, he simply turned and walked away.
그들은 그를 놀려서 싸움을 시키려고 했지만 그는 그냥 뒤돌아 가버렸다.

28 vermin   n. noxious animals, pests

[vɘ́ːrmin] 해로운 작은 동물, 해충

Vermin such as rats and mice are difficult to catch.
쥐와 생쥐와 같은 유해 동물은 잡기 어렵다.

29 warrant   n. authorization, order

[wɔ́ːrənt] 영장

A **warrant** was issued for the suspect's arrest.
용의자를 체포하기 위해 영장이 발부되었다.

30 warranty   n. guarantee, promise   ↔ risk, uncertainty

[wɔ́ːrənti] 품질 보증서, 보증

All new cars come with a three-year **warranty** on parts and labor.
모든 신차는 부품과 기술에 대해 3년간 보증이 적용된다.

DAILY QUIZ

1 a selection **committee** •
2 the latest **fad** •
3 military **personnel** •
4 the **principal** city •
5 ethnic **strife** •
6 a revered **seer** •
7 show deep **remorse** •
8 **indispensable** daily necessities •
9 comes with a limited **warranty** •
10 a search **warrant** •

• a repentance
• b struggle
• c trend
• d guarantee
• e crucial
• f authorization
• g prophet
• h staff
• i foremost
• j commission

ANSWERS   1. j   2. c   3. h   4. i   5. b   6. g   7. a   8. e   9. d   10. f

Day 14

1 aboriginal   adj. indigenous, original   ↔ non-native, foreign

[ǽbərídʒənl] 원주(민)의

The **aboriginal** culture and customs have a long history in North America.
북미의 원주민 문화와 풍습은 오랜 역사를 가지고 있다.

2 accumulation   n. build-up, gathering   ↔ dispersion, scattering

[əkjùːmjuléiʃən] 축적

Too much **accumulation** of fat in the body can be dangerous to one's health.
몸에 지방이 너무 많이 축적되면 건강에 해로울 수 있다.

3 adversary   n. opponent, antagonist   ↔ supporter, ally

[ǽdvərsèri] 적수, 상대

There was no **adversary** strong enough to withstand the boxer's famous right hook.
권투 선수의 뛰어난 라이트 훅을 견딜 만큼 강한 적수는 없었다.

4 aeronautics   n.

[ɛ̀ərənɔ́ːtiks] 항공학, 항공술

After receiving his degree in **aeronautics**, he received job offers from both Boeing and Airbus.
항공학 학위를 받은 뒤, 그는 보잉 사와 에어버스 사에서 일자리 제의를 받았다.

5 albeit   conj. although, even though

[ɔːlbíːit] ~(임)에도 불구하고

The team won the game, **albeit** with difficulties.
팀은 어려움에도 불구하고 경기에서 이겼다.

6 bona fide   phr. genuine, authentic   ↔ bogus, counterfeit

[bóunə-fáid] 진정한, 진짜의

He became a **bona fide** singer after he released his first album.
그는 첫 앨범을 발매한 후 진짜 가수가 되었다.

7 commission   n. fee, compensation

[kəmíʃən] 중개료, 수수료

The agent charges a **commission** of 15 percent on all book contracts.
중개상은 모든 서적 계약에 대해 15%의 수수료를 받는다.

8 cryptic   adj. mysterious, enigmatic   ↔ straightforward, clear-cut

[kríptik] 암호 같은, 수수께끼 같은

The intelligence director spent hours reading the **cryptic** messages sent by his spies.
정보 국장은 그의 첩자가 보낸 암호로 된 메시지를 해독하는 데 오랜 시간을 보냈다.

9 custody   n.

[kʌ́stədi] 양육권, 관리권

During the divorce, the husband and wife fought over the **custody** of their children.
이혼 기간 동안 남편과 아내는 자녀 양육권 문제로 싸웠다.

10 demeanor   n. behavior, outward aspect

[dimíːnər] 처신, 행실

Despite his quiet **demeanor**, he was actually a talkative person.
그는 차분한 행실에도 불구하고 실제로는 말이 많은 사람이었다.

11 depict   v. describe, illustrate

[dipíkt] 묘사하다

The senator became angry after the news report **depicted** him as a selfish man.
상원 의원은 뉴스 보도에서 자신을 이기적인 사람으로 묘사하자 화가 났다.

12 dexterity   n. adroitness, deftness   ↔ inability, ineptness

[dekstérəti] 재주, 솜씨

His mental **dexterity** allowed him to solve puzzles and equations quickly.
그는 비상한 머리로 수수께끼와 방정식을 빨리 풀어낼 수 있었다.

13 encounter   v. run across, confront

[inkáuntər] 마주치다, 맞닥뜨리다

Even the best planners often **encounter** unseen problems when traveling abroad.
계획을 아주 잘 짜는 사람들조차도 해외 여행 시 종종 예기치 않은 문제와 마주친다.

14 expanse n. large space, territory

[ikspǽns] 넓은 지역, 광활한 공간

The sailboat looked small in the wide **expanse** of the ocean.
광활한 대양에서 요트는 작아 보였다.

15 generate v. give rise to, propagate ↔ demolish, tear down

[dʒénərèit] 가져오다

The new band **generated** a big crowd on Friday night.
새로운 밴드가 금요일 밤 많은 군중을 모았다.

16 interim adj. temporary, makeshift ↔ permanent, continual

[íntərəm] 임시의, 잠정적인

He served as the **interim** CEO until a new one could be appointed.
그는 새로운 최고 경영자가 임명될 때까지 임시 최고 경영자로 근무했다.

17 invincible adj. indestructible, undefeatable ↔ penetrable, vulnerable

[invínsəbl] 천하무적의

Until he lost the battle at Waterloo, Napoleon believed that he was **invincible**.
나폴레옹은 워털루 전투에서 패배할 때까지 자신이 천하무적이라고 생각했다.

18 manipulate v. control, exploit

[mənípjulèit] 조종하다

She **manipulated** her family and friends into lying for her.
그녀는 자신을 위해 거짓말을 하도록 가족과 친구들을 조종했다.

19 nostalgic adj. longing, recollective ↔ forgetful, oblivious

[nɑstǽldʒik] 향수의, 향수를 불러일으키는

As people get older, they become **nostalgic** for the music they listened to when they were young.
사람은 나이를 먹으면서 어렸을 때 들었던 음악에 향수를 느낀다.

20 obscure adj. inconspicuous, unheard-of ↔ famous, celebrated

[əbskjúər] 무명의, 잘 알려져 있지 않은

Before he became famous, he was just an **obscure** singer in a club.
그는 유명해지기 전에 한 클럽의 무명 가수에 불과했다.

21 peripheral adj. marginal, outlying ↔ paramount, central

[pərífərəl] 중요하지 않은, 지엽적인

At the meeting, people argued about the **peripheral** issues instead of the most pressing ones.
회의에서 사람들은 긴급한 문제가 아닌 지엽적인 문제에 대해 논쟁했다.

22 piecemeal adj. step by step, gradual ↔ complete, cohesive

[pí:smì:l] 조금씩

Unfortunately, environmental policy changes occur gradually and on a **piecemeal** basis.
불행하게도 환경 정책 변화들이 점차 조금씩 나타나고 있다.

23 prudent adj. sensible, wise ↔ careless, absent-minded

[prú:dnt] 신중한

The **prudent** investor is careful and patient in choosing stocks for purchase.
신중한 투자자는 매입할 주식을 선택하는 데 주의하고 인내한다.

24 renegade n. abandoner, dissenter ↔ advocate, supporter

[rénigèid] 변절자, 이탈자

Early Christians were considered religious **renegades** by the Jews.
유태인들은 초기 기독교인들을 종교적 변절자로 여겼다.

25 representative n. agent, delegate

[rèprizéntətiv] 판매 대리인

A group of insurance **representatives** arrived at the scene of the accident to talk to their customers.
한 무리의 보험 판매 대리인들이 고객들과 얘기하려고 사건 현장에 도착했다.

26 secrete v. discharge, emit ↔ absorb, take in

[sikrí:t] 분비하다

Our skin **secretes** more sweat in the summer.
우리 피부는 여름에 더 많은 땀을 배출한다.

27 semiconductor n.

[sèmikəndʌ́ktər] 반도체

Without **semiconductors**, there would be no radios, televisions, or computers.
반도체가 없었다면 라디오도 TV도 컴퓨터도 없었을 것이다.

28 sphere n. scope, bounds

[sfiər] 영역, 범위

For centuries, most of Europe was under the Catholic Church's **sphere** of influence.
수세기 동안 유럽 대부분은 천주교회의 영향 아래 있었다.

29 tamper with phr. play with, mess around with

손대다

The fire alarm was set off after someone **tampered with** the switch.
누군가 스위치를 건드린 후 화재 경보가 울렸다.

30 temper n. angriness, state-of-mind

[témpər] 성질, 성향

Unable to control his bad **temper**, he yelled at the driver of the car in front of him.
고약한 성질을 통제할 수 없었던 그는 앞에 있는 차 운전자에게 고함을 질렀다.

DAILY QUIZ

1. a **cryptic** message
2. **depict** a famous scene
3. **aboriginal** people
4. life without **adversary**
5. **expanse** of the empire
6. **manipulate** the government
7. a lone **renegade**
8. **tamper with** other people's things
9. **sphere** of power
10. show proper **demeanor**

- a describe
- b dissenter
- c control
- d scope
- e play with
- f indigenous
- g opponent
- h mysterious
- i behavior
- j territory

ANSWERS 1. h   2. a   3. f   4. g   5. j   6. c   7. b   8. e   9. d   10. i

COMPREHENSIVE QUIZ — Day 13 & 14

1. Having come back from fighting in a war, he felt that he was a(n) _____ soldier.
   ⓐ aesthetic   ⓑ aboriginal   ⓒ bona fide   ⓓ arid

2. Until the next election, she will serve as _____ president.
   ⓐ cryptic   ⓑ piecemeal   ⓒ peripheral   ⓓ interim

3. The _____ desert has a surprising number of animals living in it.
   ⓐ arid   ⓑ complacent   ⓒ interim   ⓓ indispensable

4. George Washington _____ her so much that she spent three years doing research on him.
   ⓐ encountered   ⓑ depicted   ⓒ intrigued   ⓓ shrouded

5. Cramming for a test the night before does not improve the _____ of information the next day.
   ⓐ commission   ⓑ retention   ⓒ sphere   ⓓ garrison

6. Many people _____ their lives through daily photography and video.
   ⓐ haul   ⓑ document   ⓒ taunt   ⓓ generate

7. He _____ his reaction to the news, so no one knew how he really felt.
   ⓐ hauled   ⓑ maximized   ⓒ shrouded   ⓓ taunted

8. The investigator did not need every detail to get the _____ of it.
   ⓐ gist   ⓑ custody   ⓒ strife   ⓓ principal

9. TV shows about the past make the audience feel _____.
   ⓐ economic   ⓑ principal   ⓒ invincible   ⓓ nostalgic

10. There are many frogs that can _____ poison through their skin.
    ⓐ intrigue   ⓑ depict   ⓒ secrete   ⓓ manipulate

Answers: p.339

Day 15

1. adage n. saying, proverb

[ǽdidʒ] 격언, 속담

Whenever life seemed difficult, he remembered the old **adage**, "There is a light at the end of the tunnel."
삶이 힘들어 보일 때마다 그는 '터널 끝에는 빛이 있다'는 옛 격언을 기억했다.

2. altruistic adj. unselfish, philanthropic ↔ egocentric, self-centered

[æ̀ltruːístik] 이타적인

Can a selfish person be **altruistic** sometimes?
이기적인 사람이 때로는 이타적일 수 있을까?

3. archive n. collection, storage

[ɑ́ːrkaiv] 기록 보관(소)

Maps and photos from a century ago can be found in the city museum's **archives**.
1세기 전의 지도와 사진을 시립 박물관 기록 보관소에서 찾아볼 수 있다.

4. banter v. joke, tease

[bǽntər] 농담을 주고받다

The tourists **bantered** with their guide while they waited for their bus.
여행자들은 버스를 기다리는 동안 가이드와 농담했다.

5. cache n. repository, a hiding place

[kǽʃ] 은닉처, 저장고

A **cache** of money and jewelry was discovered in the basement.
돈과 보석이 들어 있는 저장고가 지하실에서 발견되었다.

6. counterfeit n. forgery, imitation ↔ real thing, genuine

[káuntərfit] 위조품, 가짜

Although the hundred dollar bill was a **counterfeit**, it looked so real that even the experts from the bank were fooled.
100달러짜리 지폐는 위조지폐였지만 너무 진짜 같아서 은행의 전문가들조차 속았다.

7 culmination   n. conclusion, highest point

[kʌ̀lmənéiʃən] 완성, 성취

Kim Yuna's gold medal was a **culmination** of years of practice and experience.
김연아의 금메달은 수년간의 연습과 경험으로 성취한 것이었다.

8 diagnose   v. determine, identify

[dáiəgnòuz] 진단하다

She was **diagnosed** with diabetes during a routine medical checkup.
그녀는 정기 건강 검진에서 당뇨병 진단을 받았다.

9 dissect   v. analyze, cut up

[disékt] 분석하다, 해부하다

In the classroom, the film students **dissected** the movie they had just watched.
교실에서 영화과 학생들은 방금 본 영화를 분석했다.

10 elliptical   adj. egg-shaped, oval

[ilíptikəl] 타원형의

The earth's orbit around the sun is not circular but **elliptical**.
태양 주위를 도는 지구 궤도는 원형이 아니라 타원형이다.

11 empirical   adj. practical, firsthand   ↔ hypothetical, theoretical

[impírikəl] 경험에 의거한, 실증적인

Empirical knowledge through direct experience is as important as ideas gained through books.
직접적인 경험을 통한 실증적인 지식은 책을 통해 얻은 지식만큼이나 중요하다.

12 exhaust   v. use up, consume

[igzɔ́ːst] 다 써버리다, 소모하다

Having **exhausted** all his options, the robber turned himself in to the police.
더 이상의 선택의 여지가 없자 강도는 경찰에 자수했다.

13 exponential   adj. increasing, piling up

[èkspənénʃəl] 기하급수적인

There has been an **exponential** population growth in the satellite cities since the opening of a major highway.
주요 고속 도로가 개통된 이후 위성 도시의 인구가 기하급수적으로 증가하고 있다.

14 **flat** adj.

[flǽt] 김빠진, 맛이 없는

Without carbonation, cola and other soft drinks taste **flat**.
탄산가스가 없으면 콜라와 기타 청량음료는 맛이 없다.

15 **fluctuate** v. vacillate, go up and down

[flʌ́ktʃuèit] 변동하다

Even in the tropics, the weather **fluctuates** from day to day.
열대 지방에서도 날씨는 매일 변한다.

16 **inhabit** v. dwell, populate   ↔ depart, vacate

[inhǽbit] 살다, 서식하다

Over six billion people **inhabit** the earth.
60억 명 이상이 지구에 살고 있다.

17 **inhibit** v. prevent, hold back   ↔ allow, give the green light

[inhíbit] 억제하다

Washing one's hands regularly can help **inhibit** the spread of disease.
손을 규칙적으로 씻으면 질병 확산을 억제하는 데 도움이 된다.

18 **liberal** adj. progressive, open-minded   ↔ conservative, intolerant

[líbərəl] 개방적인

Her **liberal** opinions often made her conservative father angry.
그녀의 개방적인 의견이 종종 보수적인 아버지를 화나게 했다.

19 **maneuver** v. navigate, steer

[mənúːvər] 조종하다, 다루다

He **maneuvered** the big truck carefully over the narrow bridge.
그는 좁은 다리 위에서 대형 트럭을 조심스럽게 운전했다.

20 **migrate** v. move, voyage

[máigreit] 이주하다, 이동하다

The birds in the forest **migrated** south for the winter.
숲 속의 새들은 겨울을 나기 위해 남쪽으로 이동했다.

21. minority n. the outnumbered ↔ majority

[mainɔ́:rəti] 소수, 소수 집단

Women continue to be the **minority** in the workplace dominated by men.
남성이 주도하는 직장에서 여성은 계속 소수 집단이다.

22. nominate v. put down for, designate

[nάmənèit] (후보자로) 지명하다

The Democratic Party **nominated** an Asian-American as its presidential candidate.
민주당은 아시아계 미국인을 대통령 후보로 지명했다.

23. per se phr. essentially, by itself

[pə:r-séi] 그 자체로

The problem was not the price of the computer **per se** but its warranty.
컴퓨터 가격 그 자체가 문제가 아니라 보증이 문제였다.

24. proximity n. closeness, adjacency ↔ distance, remoteness

[prɑksíməti] 가까움, 근접

The retirement homes are in close **proximity** to a major hospital.
노인 전용 주택은 대형 병원 근처에 있다.

25. regime n. leadership, reign

[rədʒí:m] 정권, 정치 제도

The country's military **regime** sent tanks into the streets.
그 나라의 군사 정권은 거리로 탱크를 내보냈다.

26. residue n. leftover, remains

[rézədjù:] 잔여, 찌꺼기

Oil **residue** on a frying pan can be hard to remove.
프라이팬에 남아 있는 기름 찌꺼기는 제거하기 힘들 수 있다.

27. simultaneous adj. concurrent, at the same time ↔ separate, apart

[sàiməltéiniəs] 동시의

Firefighters were busy extinguishing **simultaneous** fires in two buildings.
소방관들은 두 빌딩에서 동시에 난 불을 끄느라 바빴다.

28 sophisticated   adj. complex, highly developed   ↔ simple, crude

[səfístəkèitid] 정교한, 세련된

A design can be both **sophisticated** and simple.
디자인은 정교하면서도 단순할 수 있다.

29 stimulate   v. excite, activate

[stímjulèit] 자극하다

Playing games and solving puzzles are some ways to **stimulate** brain activity.
게임을 하는 것과 퍼즐을 푸는 것은 두뇌 활동을 자극하는 방법이다.

30 tangible   adj. actual, well-grounded   ↔ unsubstantial, indefinite

[tǽndʒəbl] 명백한

There is no **tangible** proof that vampires exist.
뱀파이어가 존재하는지에 대한 명백한 증거는 없다.

DAILY QUIZ

1	**altruistic** tendencies	a closeness
2	**inhabit** the wastelands	b steer
3	a **regime** ruled by a dictator	c dwell
4	**stimulate** growth	d concurrent
5	**maneuver** a boat	e unselfish
6	**simultaneous** events	f designate
7	**proximity** to school	g move
8	**nominate** someone for an award	h use up
9	**exhaust** natural resources	i leadership
10	**migrate** to warmer climates	j activate

ANSWERS   1. e   2. c   3. i   4. j   5. b   6. d   7. a   8. f   9. h   10. g

Day 16

1 abolition   n. elimination, putting an end to   ↔ establishment, legalization

[æ̀bəlíʃən] 폐지

Abraham Lincoln is perhaps best known for the **abolition** of slavery in the United States.
에이브러햄 링컨은 아마 미국 노예 제도의 폐지로 가장 잘 알려져 있을 것이다.

2 agent   n. substance, chemical

[éidʒənt] 약품

Only safe chemicals are allowed for use as coloring **agents** in food.
안전한 화학 물질만이 식용 착색제로 사용 허가된다.

3 aggregate   adj. amassed, cumulative

[ǽgrigət] 총(계의), 모두 합한

The popular actor failed to pay an **aggregate** amount of $12,000,000 in taxes over ten years.
인기 배우는 10년 이상 총 천이백만 달러의 세금을 납부하지 못했다.

4 cardiovascular   adj.

[kὰːrdiouvǽskjulər] 심혈관의

Risks of heart disease and other **cardiovascular** problems can be reduced with regular workout.
심장병과 기타 심혈관 질환의 문제는 규칙적인 운동으로 줄일 수 있다.

5 covet   v. desire, long for   ↔ abjure, give up

[kʌ́vit] 열망하다, 갈망하다

Many high school students **covet** the chance to attend a prominent university.
많은 고등학생이 일류 대학에 다닐 수 있는 기회를 열망한다.

6 credential   n. qualification, certificate

[kridénʃəl] 자격, 자격 증명서

His **credentials** as an FBI agent allowed him to board the plane with his gun.
FBI 요원 자격으로 그는 총을 소지한 채 비행기에 탑승하는 것이 허용되었다.

7 delegate¹ n. representative, envoy

[déligət] 대표(단)

The **delegates** from both countries spent months finalizing the new FTA.
양국의 대표단은 새로운 FTA를 마무리 짓는 데 몇 달을 보냈다.

8 delegate² v. empower, place trust in ↔ keep, hold back

[déligèit] 위임하다

Generally, the CEO **delegates** much of the day-to-day authority to the vice presidents.
일반적으로 최고 경영자는 나날의 권한 중 많은 부분을 부사장에게 위임한다.

9 devout adj. staunch, fervent ↔ insincere, unfaithful

[diváut] 독실한

A **devout** Christian will not work on a Sunday.
독실한 기독교인은 일요일에 일을 하지 않는다.

10 elicit v. bring forth, extract ↔ keep back, repress

[ilísit] (정보, 반응 등을) 끌어내다, 유도해 내다

The violent protests **elicited** an immediate response from the riot police.
격렬한 시위는 폭동 진압 경찰의 즉각적인 대응을 불러왔다.

11 embargo n. prohibition, restriction ↔ allowance, permission

[imbá:rgou] 금지령

The trade **embargo** effectively blocked all shipments to and from the country.
통상 금지령은 모든 선박의 출입을 효과적으로 봉쇄했다.

12 en masse adv. all at once, all together ↔ one at a time, piecemeal

[ɑ:ŋ-mǽs] 일제히

His cheering teammates surrounded him **en masse** after he scored the goal.
그가 점수를 내자 응원 단원들은 일제히 그를 에워쌌다.

13 foreseeable adj. conceivable, predictable ↔ implausible, unexpected

[fɔ:rsí:əbl] 예측 가능한, 장래의

The number of divorces is unlikely to drop in the **foreseeable** future.
이혼하는 부부의 수가 가까운 미래에 감소할 것 같지 않다.

14 funnel v. channel, siphon

[fʌ́nl] (좁은 공간 속을) 이동시키다

Pipes can be used to **funnel** irrigation water to the soil.
파이프를 이용해 관개용수를 토양으로 흘려보낼 수 있다.

15 inadvertently adv. unintentionally, accidentally ↔ purposefully, intentionally

[ìnədvə́ːrtntli] 무심코

He was embarrassed when he **inadvertently** called the wrong number.
그는 무심코 잘못된 번호로 전화를 걸고는 당황했다.

16 indulge v. enjoy, bask in ↔ abstain, resist

[indʌ́ldʒ] 마음껏 하다

Living near a vineyard allowed him to **indulge** in his love of wine.
그는 포도밭 근처에 살았기 때문에 좋아하는 와인을 마음껏 마실 수 있었다.

17 local adj.

[lóukəl] 지역의

The city's **local** media covered the disaster before CNN did.
도시의 지역 언론이 CNN보다 먼저 재난을 보도했다.

18 meltdown n. breakdown, failure

[méltdàun] 붕괴, 몰락

It was the economic crisis in the country that caused the stock market **meltdown**.
주식 시장의 붕괴를 초래한 원인은 국내 경제 위기였다.

19 perpetrate v. carry out, commit ↔ abstain, withhold

[pə́ːrpətrèit] 저지르다

The terrorists have **perpetrated** an attack on an airport.
테러리스트들은 공항에 대한 공격을 감행했다.

20 perpetuate v. carry on, maintain ↔ cease, bring to an end

[pərpétʃuèit] 영구화하다, 영속시키다

While the Internet is a good source of information, it can also be used to **perpetuate** false rumors.
인터넷은 좋은 정보원이지만 허위 소문을 오래 남기는 데에 이용될 수 있다.

21 prevalence n. predominance, popularity   ↔ lack, deprivation

[prévələns] 널리 퍼짐, 유행

Many parents are worried about the **prevalence** of violence in films.
많은 부모들이 영화에 폭력이 만연한 것에 대해 우려한다.

22 punctual adj. on time, prompt   ↔ late, tardy

[pʌ́ŋktʃuəl] 시간을 잘 지키는

Known as a **punctual** person, Jim always tried to be at his appointments on time.
시간을 엄수하는 사람으로 알려졌기 때문에 짐은 항상 제시간에 약속 장소에 나와 있으려고 노력했다.

23 regulation n. rule, order

[règjuléiʃən] 규정

Oil companies did not welcome the government's new environmental **regulations**.
석유 회사들은 정부의 새 환경 규정을 환영하지 않았다.

24 remedy n. medicine, solution   ↔ disease, problem

[rémədi] 해결책, 치료법

According to doctors, an aspirin is not always the best **remedy** for a headache.
의사에 따르면 두통에 아스피린이 항상 최고의 해결책은 아니라고 한다.

25 reputable adj. respectable, well-thought-of   ↔ untrustworthy, notorious

[répjutəbl] 평판이 좋은

Reputable brands can charge high prices because consumers are willing to pay for quality.
고객들은 품질이 좋으면 기꺼이 구입하기 때문에 평판이 좋은 브랜드는 가격을 높게 매길 수 있다.

26 secular adj. non-religious, of this world   ↔ spiritual, chaste

[sékjulər] 세속적인

Religious leaders are known to involve themselves in **secular** issues affecting their community.
종교 지도자들은 지역 사회에 영향을 미치는 세속적인 문제에 연루되어 있는 것으로 알려져 있다.

27 simulation n. trial run, duplication   ↔ reality, like it is

[sìmjuléiʃən] 모의실험, 흉내

The military is known to run war **simulations** on computers.
군대는 컴퓨터로 모의 전쟁을 하는 것으로 알려져 있다.

28 soothe v. calm down, alleviate ↔ agitate, aggravate

[súːð] 달래다. 진정시키다

To **soothe** dry skin, apply the lotion on the affected areas.
건성 피부를 진정시키려면 해당 부위에 로션을 발라야 한다.

29 stigma n. dishonor, shame ↔ dignity, pride

[stígmə] 오명

There is still a social **stigma** against gay marriages.
아직도 동성 결혼에 대해서는 사회적인 오명이 붙는다.

30 tolerant adj. open-minded, receptive ↔ narrow-minded, opinionated

[tálərənt] 관대한

Because he was a **tolerant** man, he was not upset about his son's mistakes.
그는 관대한 사람이기 때문에 아들의 잘못에 대해 속상하지 않았다.

DAILY QUIZ

1 a **devout** follower
2 attack **en masse**
3 **delegate** any power or duty
4 a nuclear **meltdown**
5 **perpetrate** an offense
6 an airplane **simulation**
7 **soothe** a headache
8 a **reputable** used car salesman
9 an oil **embargo**
10 **inadvertently** hit someone

a empower
b duplication
c commit
d accidentally
e respectable
f all together
g breakdown
h fervent
i restriction
j alleviate

ANSWERS 1. h 2. f 3. a 4. g 5. c 6. b 7. j 8. e 9. i 10. d

COMPREHENSIVE QUIZ   Day 15 & 16

1. My relatives always _____ with one another during holiday gatherings.
   ⓐ funnel   ⓑ maneuver   ⓒ nominate   ⓓ banter

2. The detective was able to solve the crime by analyzing the _____ he scraped off of the glass found at the crime scene.
   ⓐ abolition   ⓑ residue   ⓒ adage   ⓓ stigma

3. The mother tried to _____ her crying child.
   ⓐ soothe   ⓑ migrate   ⓒ perpetrate   ⓓ fluctuate

4. A good lawyer will be able to _____ information using indirect questions.
   ⓐ exhaust   ⓑ elicit   ⓒ stimulate   ⓓ delegate

5. Some people think wealth is only about _____ possessions.
   ⓐ liberal   ⓑ cardiovascular   ⓒ elliptical   ⓓ tangible

6. His new book is the _____ of years of research and dedication.
   ⓐ counterfeit   ⓑ embargo   ⓒ culmination   ⓓ minority

7. When you are creating art, do not _____ your imagination!
   ⓐ covet   ⓑ bask in   ⓒ inhibit   ⓓ inhabit

8. Each country will send a(n) _____ to negotiate a peace treaty.
   ⓐ delegate   ⓑ cache   ⓒ proximity   ⓓ archive

9. She _____ lost weight while she was sick.
   ⓐ devoutly   ⓑ en masse   ⓒ altruistically   ⓓ inadvertently

10. The police were afraid that the crime would _____ further copycat crimes.
    ⓐ diagnose   ⓑ perpetuate   ⓒ dissect   ⓓ indulge

Answers: p.339

Day 17

1. abate v. recede, taper off ↔ amplify, build up

[əbéit] 약해지다

The hikers stayed inside a cave to wait for the storm to **abate**.
등산객들은 폭풍이 약해지기를 기다리며 동굴 안에 머물렀다.

2. acquisition n. obtaining, acquirement

[ӕ̀kwəzíʃən] 취득, 습득

With the **acquisition** of ten more cars, it is now the largest rental car agency in town.
자동차를 10대 더 확보함으로써, 그 회사는 이제 도시에서 가장 큰 렌트카 업체이다.

3. ad hoc phr. impromptu, provisional ↔ general, matter-of-course

[æd-hάk] 특별한 목적을 위한, 임시의

The university has formed an **ad hoc** committee to investigate the allegations.
대학은 혐의를 조사하기 위해 임시 위원회를 구성했다.

4. aerodynamic adj. streamlined, sleek

[ɛ̀əroudainǽmik] 공기 역학의

Jeff chose the sports car in lieu of the SUV because the former was more **aerodynamic**.
스포츠카가 더 공기 역학적이었기 때문에 제프는 SUV 대신 스포츠카를 선택했다.

5. anatomy n.

[ənǽtəmi] 해부(학)

All medical school students are required to study the human **anatomy**.
모든 의대생들은 인체 해부학을 공부해야 한다.

6. candid adj. honest, up front ↔ deceitful, underhanded

[kǽndid] 솔직한

Children are more **candid** about their feelings than adults are.
아이들은 성인보다 자기 감정에 더 솔직하다.

7 candidate   n. applicant, competitor

[kǽndidèit] 지원자, 후보자

Of all the **candidates** applying for the position, Charlotte had the most experience.
그 자리에 지원한 모든 후보자 중에서 샬롯이 가장 경험이 많았다.

8 cursory   adj. casual, hit or miss   ↔ meticulous, detailed

[kə́ːrsəri] 서두르는, 대충 하는

The basketball coach gave the tall boy a **cursory** look and agreed to accept him into the team.
농구 코치는 키 큰 소년을 흘깃 보고 팀에 영입하는 데 동의했다.

9 decipher   v. figure out, unravel   ↔ encode, scramble

[disáifər] 해독하다

The experts worked day and night to **decipher** the secret code.
전문가들은 비밀 암호를 풀기 위해 밤낮으로 일했다.

10 dilemma   n. predicament, Catch-22   ↔ resolution, way out

[dilémə] 곤경, 딜레마

John was caught in a **dilemma** in which he had to choose between family and work.
존은 가족과 직장 사이에서 선택을 해야만 하는 곤경에 빠졌다.

11 dividend   n. share, bonus

[dívədənd] 배당금

The past year's unexpected profits allowed the company to pay a small **dividend** to all its shareholders.
작년의 예상하지 않았던 수익으로 회사는 모든 주주에게 소액의 배당금을 지불할 수 있었다.

12 eccentric   adj. bizarre, peculiar   ↔ ordinary, run-of-the-mill

[ikséntrik] 괴짜인, 별난

Throughout history, pioneers in their respective fields were considered **eccentric**.
역사를 통틀어 각 분야의 선구자들은 괴짜로 여겨졌다.

13 emigrate   v. move abroad, migrate   ↔ immigrate

[émigrèit] (타국으로) 이주하다

In Los Angeles, there are quite a few families who have **emigrated** from Asia.
로스앤젤레스에는 아시아에서 이주한 가구가 상당수 있다.

14 immigrate v. come in, settle ↔ emigrate

[íməgrèit] (타국에서) 이주하다

Many Chinese families are **immigrating** to the West to escape the one-child rule.
많은 중국 가정이 1인 자녀 규정을 피해 서구로 이주해 오고 있다.

15 imperative adj. urgent, vital ↔ trivial, insignificant

[impérətiv] 필수적인

It is **imperative** that the gymnasium be completed before the start of the new basketball season.
새 농구 시즌이 시작되기 전에 실내 경기장을 완공하는 것은 필수이다.

16 implement¹ v. execute, put into effect

[ímpləmènt] 실행하다

The new policy allowing longer vacations was **implemented** to improve employee retention.
직원의 이직 방지를 위해 휴가 연장을 허용하는 새로운 정책이 시행되었다.

17 implement² n. tool, device

[ímpləmənt] 도구, 기구

Care should be taken when handling sharp **implements** such as knives or scissors.
칼이나 가위와 같은 날카로운 도구를 다룰 때에는 주의해야 한다.

18 ingredient n. component, part

[ingrí:diənt] 재료, 구성 성분

MSG is an **ingredient** most restaurants no longer use in preparing food.
MSG는 대부분의 식당에서 음식을 준비할 때 더 이상 사용하지 않는 성분이다.

19 junction n. intersection, connection

[dʒʌ́ŋkʃən] 교차로, 연결 지점

The traffic light at the busy **junction** was out again.
혼잡한 교차로의 신호등이 다시 꺼졌다.

20 manifest adj. apparent, crystal clear ↔ ambiguous, vague

[mǽnəfèst] 분명히 나타난

His strong support of the war is **manifest** in his speech.
그의 전쟁에 대한 강한 지지는 연설에 분명히 나타나 있다.

21 merchandise   n. goods, wares

[mə́ːrtʃəndàiz] 상품

The store's **merchandise** includes neckties, handbags, and belts.
상점의 물건에 넥타이와 핸드백, 벨트도 있다.

22 particle   n. fragment, speck

[páːrtikl] 입자

Dust **particles** in the house can cause allergies.
집안의 먼지 입자는 알레르기를 유발할 수 있다.

23 plummet   v. plunge, decline   ↔ shoot up, ascend

[plʌ́mit] 급락하다

During the last recession, the price of most stocks **plummeted**.
지난 불황기에 대부분의 주식 가격이 급락했다.

24 preemptive   adj. preventive, deterrent

[priémptiv] 선제의

A **preemptive** air strike against nuclear facilities in North Korea is an option the U.S. has considered.
북한의 핵 시설에 대한 선제 공습은 미국이 고려했던 선택 사항이다.

25 repression   n. constraint, oppression

[ripréʃən] 억제, 억압

It has been argued that there is connection between **repression** of emotions and certain illnesses.
감정의 억제가 어떤 질병과 관련이 있다는 것이 논란거리가 되어 왔다.

26 scholastic   adj. academic, educational

[skəlǽstik] 학업의

In addition to **scholastic** achievements, volunteer work outside of school is an important part of a student's college application.
학업 성취도 외에도 교외 자원봉사 활동은 학생의 대학 지원서에 있어 중요한 부분이다.

27 startling   adj. frightful, surprising   ↔ expected, familiar

[stáːrtliŋ] 놀랄 만한

The audience became quiet when he presented his **startling** discovery.
그가 놀랄 만한 발견물을 내놓자 청중은 조용해졌다.

28 subjugate   v. overpower, rule over   ↔ liberate, free up

[sʌ́bdʒugèit] 예속시키다, 정복하다

Throughout history, there have been many rulers who invaded and **subjugated** neighboring countries.
역사를 통틀어 이웃 국가를 침략하고 정복한 통치자가 많이 있었다.

29 subterranean   adj. underground, below ground   ↔ earthly, aboveground

[sʌ̀btəréiniən] 지하의

A **subterranean** chamber is located near the bottom of the Great Pyramid.
대 피라미드 바닥 근처에 지하방이 위치하고 있다.

30 transparent   adj. see-through, lucid   ↔ opaque, cloudy

[trænspǽrənt] 투명한

The **transparent** body of the jellyfish is believed to be a form of camouflage.
해파리의 투명한 몸체는 하나의 위장으로 여겨지고 있다.

DAILY QUIZ

1	an **eccentric** artist	a	preventive
2	**repression** of minority groups	b	tool
3	an **imperative** message	c	component
4	meet at the **junction**	d	surprising
5	**preemptive** strategies	e	intersection
6	a main **ingredient**	f	urgent
7	**plummet** into the sea	g	fragment
8	a **startling** announcement	h	oppression
9	a subatomic **particle**	i	bizarre
10	a crude **implement**	j	plunge

ANSWERS   1. i   2. h   3. f   4. e   5. a   6. c   7. j   8. d   9. g   10. b

Day 18

1. abdicate v. step down, renounce ↔ assert, put forward

[ǽbdəkèit] 버리다, 포기하다

King Edward VIII of the United Kingdom **abdicated** his throne in 1936 in order to marry an American woman named Wallis Simpson.
영국의 왕 에드워드 8세는 월리스 심슨이라는 미국 여성과 결혼하기 위해 1936년에 왕위에서 물러났다.

2. acknowledge v. concede, recognize ↔ disavow, deny

[əknálidʒ] 인정하다

The teacher **acknowledged** that she had made a mistake on the fourth question.
교사는 네 번째 문제를 잘못 출제했다고 인정했다.

3. administration n. term, regime

[ædmìnəstréiʃən] 행정부, 집행

He has served as the CIA director in two presidential **administrations**.
그는 연달아 두 명의 대통령을 모시고 CIA 국장으로 근무하고 있다.

4. benign adj. harmless, nonthreatening ↔ tumorous, malignant

[bináin] 양성의, 상냥한

Much to her relief, her tumor was diagnosed as **benign**.
다행히도 그녀의 종양은 양성으로 진단되었다.

5. cartel n. syndicate, consortium

[kɑːrtél] 카르텔, 연합

OPEC is a **cartel** that effectively controls the price of crude oil.
OPEC은 원유 가격을 효과적으로 조절하는 연합체이다.

6. chronological adj.

[krànəládʒikəl] 시간 순서로 된

In a credit card billing statement, transactions are listed in **chronological** order.
신용 카드 요금 청구서에 거래 내역은 시간 순서대로 나열된다.

7 circulation n. distribution, dissemination

[sə̀ːrkjuléiʃən] (신문 · 잡지의) 판매 부수, 순환

The magazine had a monthly **circulation** of 500,000.
잡지의 월 판매 부수는 50만 권이었다.

8 deficit n. shortage, loss ↔ excess, overkill

[défəsit] 부족

Due to the budget **deficit**, many important public projects were cancelled.
예산 부족으로 인해 많은 중요한 공공사업이 취소되었다.

9 dormant adj. inactive, out of action ↔ at work, functioning

[dɔ́ːrmənt] 휴지 상태에 있는

A volcano can lie **dormant** for a long period of time before becoming active.
화산은 활동하기 전에 장기간 휴면 상태로 있을 수 있다.

10 edify v. instruct, enlighten

[édəfài] 교화하다

The purpose of the TV documentary was to **edify** the audience with its hard look at poverty around the world.
TV 다큐멘터리의 목적은 전 세계의 빈곤에 관한 날카로운 시각을 통해 시청자들을 교화시키는 것이었다.

11 emancipation n. freedom, liberation ↔ confinement, imprisonment

[imæ̀nsəpéiʃən] 해방

For Lincoln, the **emancipation** of slaves was a priority.
링컨에게 있어서 노예 해방이 최우선이었다.

12 engulf v. swallow up, overwhelm

[ingʌ́lf] 휩싸다, 집어삼키다

The small wooden building was immediately **engulfed** by fire.
작은 목재 건물이 곧 화염에 휩싸였다.

13 hypocritical adj. deceitful, two-faced

[hìpəkrítikəl] 위선의

It would be **hypocritical** for a liar to call someone else a liar.
거짓말쟁이가 누군가를 거짓말쟁이라고 부르는 것은 위선일 것이다.

14 impairment n. deterioration, damage

[impɛ́ərmənt] 장애

Listening to loud music through earphones can lead to hearing **impairment**.
이어폰을 끼고 시끄러운 음악을 들으면 청력 장애가 될 수 있다.

15 in line with phr. in accordance with, just as ↔ discordant with, in opposition to

~와 긴밀히 관련된

The price of the new computer model is **in line with** consumer expectations.
신형 컴퓨터 모델 가격은 소비자의 기대치와 긴밀하게 관련되어 있다.

16 instinct n. hunch, intuition ↔ intellect, reason

[ínstiŋkt] 본능, 직감

Police officers use their **instincts** when they are investigating a crime.
경찰관은 범죄를 조사할 때 직감을 이용한다.

17 intricate adj. complex, complicated ↔ plain, simple

[íntrəkit] 복잡한

The church chose an **intricate** stained-glass design in lieu of a simpler one.
교회는 간단한 디자인 대신 복잡한 스테인드글라스 디자인을 선택했다.

18 lavish adj. extravagant, excessive ↔ economical, penny-pinching

[lǽviʃ] 호화로운, 아낌없는

Even the bathrooms are **lavish** in a first class hotel suite.
일류 호텔의 스위트룸은 욕실조차 호화롭다.

19 net adj. after taxes, remaining

[nét] (돈의 액수에 대해) 순-

The **net** profit from the land sale was under $20,000 after agent commission and taxes.
토지 매각으로 인한 순이익은 중개 수수료와 세금을 제하고 2만 달러 미만이었다.

20 oath n. promise, sworn statement ↔ breach, noncompliance

[óuθ] 선서, 서약

In many countries, it is traditional for a new head of state to take an **oath** of office in a public ceremony.
많은 나라에서 새로운 국가 수장은 공개 행사에서 취임 선서를 하는 것이 전통이다.

21 pardon   v. forgive, let off   ↔ condemn, denounce

[páːrdn] 사면하다, 용서하다

The President can **pardon** a criminal.
대통령은 범죄자를 사면할 수 있다.

22 phantom   n. ghost, apparition

[fǽntəm] 유령

Several children said they saw a **phantom** walking in the woods at midnight.
몇몇 아이들이 한밤중에 숲 속을 걸어 다니는 유령을 보았다고 말했다.

23 prestigious   adj. preeminent, distinguished   ↔ not worth mentioning, insignificant

[prestídʒəs] 일류의

A degree from a **prestigious** university does not guarantee a high starting salary.
일류 대학의 학위가 높은 초봉을 보장해 주지 않는다.

24 reservation¹   n. arrangement, booking

[rèzərvéiʃən] 예약

Flight **reservations** should be made early during peak seasons.
성수기에는 일찍 항공권을 예약해야 한다.

25 reservation²   n. hesitancy, second thoughts

[rèzərvéiʃən] 주저, 망설임

Because of his prior injury, Stephen had **reservations** about the planned ski trip.
전에 부상을 입은 적이 있는 스티븐은 계획된 스키 여행 가기를 주저했다.

26 reservation³   n. sanctuary, refuge

[rèzərvéiʃən] 보호 구역

Native American tribes have sovereignty over their own Indian **reservations**.
인디언 부족은 자신들의 인디언 보호 구역에 대한 주권을 가지고 있다.

27 revolutionize   v.

[rèvəlúːʃənàiz] 혁명을 일으키다

E-mails have **revolutionized** the way we connect with one another.
이메일은 우리가 서로 연락하는 방식에 혁명을 일으켰다.

28 sequence n. series, order ↔ disorder, chaos

[síːkwəns] 순서, 차례

The instructions for building a model ship must be followed in **sequence**.
모형 선박 건조 지침은 반드시 순서대로 따라야 한다.

29 so to speak phr. a manner of speaking, in such a way that

말하자면

They were drunk with love, **so to speak**.
말하자면, 그들은 사랑에 취했었다.

30 waive v. give up, relinquish ↔ lay claim to, demand

[wéiv] 철회하다, 포기하다

On its opening day, the new zoo **waived** the admission fee.
새 동물원은 개장일에 입장료를 받지 않았다.

DAILY QUIZ

1	animal **instinct**	•	• a	loss
2	make a **reservation**	•	• b	two-faced
3	a drug **cartel**	•	• c	distribution
4	**in line with** the plan	•	• d	syndicate
5	a huge **deficit**	•	• e	arrangement
6	a **hypocritical** leader	•	• f	in accordance with
7	physical **impairment**	•	• g	complex
8	a newspaper **circulation**	•	• h	intuition
9	**intricate** puzzles	•	• i	distinguished
10	a **prestigious** award	•	• j	deterioration

ANSWERS 1. h 2. e 3. d 4. f 5. a 6. b 7. j 8. c 9. g 10. i

COMPREHENSIVE QUIZ — Day 17 & 18

1. Critics praised the movie for its _____ portrayal of the struggles of war refugees.
   ⓐ cursory　　ⓑ candid　　ⓒ so to speak　　ⓓ hypocritical

2. Many people _____ from third world countries for a better life in more developed nations.
   ⓐ pardon　　ⓑ engulf　　ⓒ immigrate　　ⓓ emigrate

3. The President _____ his plan to stop poverty.
   ⓐ implemented　　ⓑ plummeted　　ⓒ pardoned　　ⓓ subjugated

4. The wife's _____ tastes pushed the couple into debt.
   ⓐ dormant　　ⓑ aerodynamic　　ⓒ lavish　　ⓓ subterranean

5. The head of the charity _____ all of the support from donors in a letter.
   ⓐ revolutionized　　ⓑ edified　　ⓒ deciphered　　ⓓ acknowledged

6. The Mayor decided against building a new park because it would increase the city _____.
   ⓐ cartel　　ⓑ deficit　　ⓒ instinct　　ⓓ oath

7. A math formula can be made by looking at the _____ in a set of numbers.
   ⓐ phantom　　ⓑ dilemma　　ⓒ emancipation　　ⓓ sequence

8. His _____ ambition led him to finish two doctorate degrees.
   ⓐ scholastic　　ⓑ benign　　ⓒ imperative　　ⓓ transparent

9. Most stores do not appreciate the customers' touching the displayed _____.
   ⓐ merchandise　　ⓑ repression　　ⓒ ad hoc　　ⓓ anatomy

10. Even though he paid a lot, the art collector was happy with his _____ of a famous Impressionist painting.
    ⓐ candidate　　ⓑ junction　　ⓒ acquisition　　ⓓ impairment

Answers: p.340

Day 19

1. acute adj. sharp, perceptive ↔ insensitive, powerless

[əkjúːt] 예민한, 극심한

Hunters use dogs for their **acute** sense of smell.
사냥꾼들은 예민한 후각 때문에 개를 이용한다.

2. adolescence n. teenage years, period of immaturity

[ædəlésns] 사춘기

Important changes occur in the body during **adolescence**.
사춘기에는 신체에 중요한 변화가 일어난다.

3. bank on phr.

~를 기대하다

There were angry protests after the company failed to pay the bonus that the workers had been **banking on**.
회사가 근로자들이 기대했던 보너스를 지급하지 못하자 성난 항의가 있었다.

4. chaotic adj. disorganized, topsy-turvy ↔ in order, systematic

[keiátik] 혼란스러운, 무질서한

On Friday nights, the kitchen in the restaurant is crowded and **chaotic**.
금요일 밤에 식당의 주방은 혼잡하고 정신없다.

5. chronically adv. incessantly, continually ↔ occasionally, off and on

[kránikəli] 만성적으로

Mr. Johnson is **chronically** late to every meeting.
존슨 씨는 만성적으로 모든 회의에 늦는다.

6. cliché n. overused phrase, platitude ↔ coinage, original phrase

[kliʃéi] 진부한 표현

The phrase "love is blind" has been overused enough to be considered a **cliché**.
'사랑을 하면 눈이 먼다'라는 구절은 상투적인 문구로 여겨질 만큼 남용되어 왔다.

7 demise — n. end, downfall ↔ birth, emergence

[dimáiz] 종말

The 1980s saw the **demise** of communism in Eastern Europe.
1980년대에 동유럽에서 공산주의는 종말을 고했다.

8 erect — v. put up, construct ↔ tear down, raze

[irékt] 세우다, 건립하다

The chicken farmer **erected** a tall fence to keep predators out.
양계장 주인은 포식 동물들이 들어오지 못하도록 높은 울타리를 세웠다.

9 evasion — n. dodging, avoidance ↔ engagement, confrontation

[ivéiʒən] 회피

In the United States, tax **evasion** is a major crime.
미국에서 탈세는 중죄이다.

10 extinguish — v. snuff out, eliminate ↔ create, bring into being

[ikstíŋgwiʃ] 끄다, 진화하다

Helicopters play a key role in **extinguishing** forest fires.
헬리콥터는 산불 진화에 있어 핵심적인 역할을 한다.

11 fragment — n. piece, remnant ↔ whole, entirety

[frǽgmənt] 파편

The explosion was so large that **fragments** of buildings were found a mile away.
폭발은 너무 커서 건물 파편이 1마일 떨어진 곳에서 발견되었다.

12 heir — n. beneficiary, legal inheritor ↔ benefactor, ascendant

[ɛər] 상속인, 후계자

He was the sole **heir** to the family fortune.
그는 가족 재산에 대한 유일한 상속자였다.

13 imagery — n. mental images, representation

[ímidʒəri] 이미지, 형상

A good novel can create vivid **imageries** in the reader's mind.
좋은 소설은 독자의 머릿속에 생생한 이미지를 그리게 한다.

14 impersonate v. imitate, mimic ↔ be original, oppose

[impə́ːrsəneit] 행세하다, 흉내 내다

During the second Gulf War, a lookalike **impersonated** Saddam Hussein.
제2차 걸프전 동안 똑같이 생긴 사람이 사담 후세인 행세를 했다.

15 indigenous adj. native, aboriginal ↔ foreign, from abroad

[indídʒənəs] 토종의, 토착의

Polar bears are **indigenous** to the Arctic region.
북극곰은 북극 지방의 토종 동물이다.

16 laureate n. receiver, winner

[lɔ́ːriət] 수상자

Kim Dae Jung became the first Nobel **laureate** from South Korea.
김대중은 한국 최초의 노벨상 수상자가 되었다.

17 misdemeanor n. minor offense, transgression ↔ good deed, kindness

[mìsdimíːnər] 경범죄

Even for a **misdemeanor**, there can be some jail time involved.
경범죄라도 일정 기간 수감될 수 있다.

18 mitigate v. alleviate, reduce ↔ intensify, build up

[mítəgèit] 경감시키다

The drugs **mitigated** most of his pain but not all.
약은 그의 고통을 대부분 경감시켰지만 완전히 없애지는 못했다.

19 noblesse oblige n.

[noublés əblíːʒ] 노블레스 오블리주 (높은 신분에 따르는 도의상 의무)

The three rich friends donated over $1 million to the charity out of a sense of **noblesse oblige**.
세 명의 부유한 친구들은 노블레스 오블리주 정신으로 백만 달러 이상을 자선 단체에 기부했다.

20 oblivious adj. unaware, ignorant ↔ attentive, heedful

[əblíviəs] 의식하지 못하는

Too many drivers are **oblivious** to the dangers of speeding.
너무 많은 운전자들이 속도위반의 위험에 대해 의식하지 못하고 있다.

21 paradigm   n. model, archetype

[pǽrədàim] 전형적인 본보기, 패러다임

For African-Americans, Barack Obama's success became a **paradigm** of hope.
아프리카계 미국인들에게는 버락 오바마의 성공이 희망의 전형적인 본보기가 되었다.

22 plea   n. appeal, request   ↔ demand, claim

[plíː] 애원, 간청

No one answered the poor man's **plea** for help.
아무도 도움을 요청하는 불쌍한 사람의 애원에 응대하지 않았다.

23 precarious   adj. doubtful, hanging by a thread   ↔ unconcerned, sanguine

[prikɛ́əriəs] 위태로운

His health became more **precarious** during the winter.
겨울 동안 그의 건강은 더욱 위태로워졌다.

24 prejudice   n. intolerance, narrow-mindedness   ↔ tolerance, understanding

[prédʒudis] 편견

Generally, people's **prejudices** are directed against those who are different from them.
일반적으로 편견은 자신과는 다른 사람에게 가지는 것이다.

25 reiterate   v. repeat, stress

[riːítərèit] 반복하다

A point has to be **reiterated** several times before the listener can fully understand it.
듣는 사람이 완전히 이해할 수 있을 때까지 요점을 몇 번 반복해야 한다.

26 resign   v. step down, quit

[rizáin] 사직하다, 사임하다

He **resigned** from the company in order to start his own business.
그는 개인 사업을 시작하기 위해 회사를 사직했다.

27 routine   n.

[ruːtíːn] 규칙적인 일상

Yoga became a part of her daily **routine**.
요가는 그녀의 일상의 한 부분이 되었다.

28 satire n. parody, ridicule

[sǽtaiər] 풍자

Books, movies, or plays that are seen as **satires** on politics are not allowed in countries such as North Korea, Iran, and Cuba.
정치를 풍자하는 것 같은 서적이나 영화, 연극은 북한, 이란, 쿠바와 같은 나라에서는 허용되지 않는다.

29 springboard n. starting point, beginning

[spríŋbɔ̀ːrd] 도약판, 발판

The awards he received for his short film served as a **springboard** to direct Hollywood films.
그가 단편 영화로 받은 상은 할리우드 영화 감독을 맡는 데 발판이 되었다.

30 subscribe v.

[səbskráib] 가입하다, 구독하다

More and more people are **subscribing** to cable or satellite TV.
점점 더 많은 사람들이 케이블 TV나 위성 TV에 가입하고 있다.

DAILY QUIZ

1 the **demise** of cassette players •   • a stress
2 a new **paradigm** •   • b starting point
3 **plea** for mercy •   • c reduce
4 **chronically** ill •   • d piece
5 a **springboard** toward success •   • e perceptive
6 **resign** from a post •   • f step down
7 a glass **fragment** •   • g appeal
8 **reiterate** the importance •   • h downfall
9 an **acute** observation •   • i model
10 **mitigate** the problems •   • j incessantly

ANSWERS 1. h 2. i 3. g 4. j 5. b 6. f 7. d 8. a 9. e 10. c

1 activism n.

[ǽktəvìzm] 행동주의

People often get involved in **activism** in hopes of bringing about a change in society.
사람들은 사회 변화를 가져오기 위해 종종 행동주의에 참여한다.

2 adequate adj. ample, sufficient ↔ lacking, insubstantial

[ǽdikwət] 충분한

No presentation should be made without **adequate** practice.
충분한 연습 없이 어떤 프레젠테이션도 해서는 안 된다.

3 adhere to phr. comply with, abide by ↔ reject, speak against

~을 충실히 지키다

It is prudent to **adhere to** standard English grammar when writing academic papers.
학술 논문을 쓸 때는 표준 영문법을 충실히 지키는 것이 현명하다.

4 corporal adj. bodily, physical ↔ mental, spiritual

[kɔ́ːrpərəl] 신체적인

Corporal punishment in the classroom is seen by its critics as archaic.
비평가들은 교실에서의 체벌을 구식으로 여긴다.

5 curriculum n. course of study, subjects

[kəríkjuləm] 교육 과정

Professor Vogel is famous for including three textbooks in his class **curriculum**.
보겔 교수는 수업 계획에 교과서 3권을 포함시키는 것으로 유명하다.

6 daunting adj. intimidating, formidable ↔ comforting, heartening

[dɔ́ːntiŋ] 힘든, 어려운

Driving in a snowstorm can be a **daunting** experience.
폭설 속에서의 운전은 어려운 경험일 수 있다.

7 excerpt   n. citation, extract   ↔ whole, entirety

[éksə:rpt] 발췌

The famous writer read a short **excerpt** from his new book to the audience.
그 유명한 작가는 자신의 신간에서 발췌한 짧은 내용을 청중에게 읽어 주었다.

8 fluorescent   adj. luminous, resplendent   ↔ dim, poorly lit

[fluərésnt] 형광성의, 화사한

At night or in poor weather conditions, those working on or by the road should wear **fluorescent** clothing.
야간이나 날씨가 안 좋을 때, 도로나 도로 가에서 일하는 사람들은 형광복을 입어야 한다.

9 humble   adj. soft-spoken, modest   ↔ pretentious, pompous

[hʌ́mbl] 겸손한

Brian remained **humble** despite his new fame.
브라이언은 새로 얻은 명성에도 불구하고 겸손했다.

10 impeachment   n. denunciation, reprimand

[impíːtʃmənt] 탄핵, 비난

An **impeachment** of an American president is quite rare.
미국 대통령의 탄핵은 상당히 드문 일이다.

11 inertia   n. inaction, lifelessness   ↔ liveliness, high spirits

[inə́ːrʃə] 무력(증)

Many people experience **inertia** when faced with a difficult decision.
많은 사람들이 어려운 결정에 당면하면 무기력함을 경험한다.

12 investment   n. financing, venture   ↔ divestment, withdrawal

[invéstmənt] 투자(물)

Stocks and real estate can prove to be good **investments**.
주식과 부동산이 좋은 투자인 것이 드러났다.

13 legible   adj. readable, intelligible   ↔ scribbled, hard to make out

[lédʒəbl] 또렷한, 읽기 쉬운

Your writing should be **legible** when you complete a government form.
정부 양식에 기재할 때는 글씨가 또렷해야 한다.

14 meager adj. inadequate, flimsy ↔ substantial, sufficient

[míːgər] 얼마 안 되는, 빈약한

His salary for the first year was **meager**.
그의 첫 1년 월급은 얼마 되지 않았다.

15 opaque adj. muddy, hazy ↔ lucid, transparent

[oupéik] 불투명한

The eyeglasses were so **opaque** that they looked like sunglasses.
안경이 너무 불투명해서 선글라스처럼 보였다.

16 patron n. advocate, supporter

[péitrən] 후원자

Throughout the history of Asia and Europe, musicians and artists found financial support from wealthy **patrons** that included nobles and rulers.
아시아와 유럽의 역사를 통틀어 음악가와 예술가들은 귀족과 통치자를 포함한 부유한 후원자의 재정적 지원을 받았다.

17 pollination n.

[pàlənéiʃən] 수분(꽃가루받이)

Plants depend on bees, butterflies, and even bats for **pollination**.
식물은 수분하기 위해 꿀벌, 나비, 심지어 박쥐에 의존한다.

18 precedent n.

[présədənt] 판례, 전례

The judge's decision set a new **precedent** for similar cases.
판사의 결정은 유사 사건에 대한 새로운 판례를 세웠다.

19 radiation n. radioactive rays

[rèidiéiʃən] 방사선

Experts warn that **radiation** from x-rays, microwaves, and cellular phones are dangerous.
전문가들은 엑스레이, 전자레인지, 휴대 전화에서 나오는 방사선이 위험하다고 경고한다.

20 recommend v. advocate, speak highly of ↔ frown on, disapprove

[rèkəménd] 권장하다, 추천하다

His doctor **recommended** a light cardiovascular workout such as walking, jogging, or cycling.
의사는 걷기, 조깅, 자전거 타기와 같은 가벼운 심혈관계 운동을 권했다.

21 robust adj. vigorous, in good health ↔ frail, feeble

[roubʌ́st] 원기 왕성한

People in their seventies can maintain **robust** health with regular exercise and good eating habits.
70대는 규칙적인 운동과 좋은 식습관으로 원기 왕성한 건강을 유지할 수 있다.

22 salvation n. rescue, deliverance ↔ endangerment, jeopardy

[sælvéiʃən] 구원

Christians believe that humans are in need of **salvation** from sin.
기독교인들은 인류가 죄로부터 구원 받아야 한다고 믿는다.

23 slumber n. sleep, doze ↔ awakening, consciousness

[slʌ́mbər] 잠, 수면

It was the prince who woke Sleeping Beauty from her long **slumber**.
잠자는 미녀를 긴 잠에서 깨운 것은 왕자였다.

24 smuggle v. bootleg, run contraband

[smʌ́gl] 밀수하다

Despite the efforts by the customs officers, large amounts of drugs are successfully **smuggled** into the country every year.
세관원들의 노력에도 불구하고 매년 다량의 마약이 국가로 용케 밀수된다.

25 sophomore n. second year student

[sʌ́fəmɔ̀:r] 2학년생

As a **sophomore** in college, she still had more than two years before graduation.
대학교 2학년인 그녀는 졸업까지 아직도 2년이 더 남았다.

26 successively adv. one after another, continuously ↔ infrequently, irregularly

[səksésivli] 계속해서, 연속으로

She received **successively** higher scores on her TOEIC tests.
그녀는 토익 시험에서 연속해서 높은 점수를 받았다.

27 syllabus n. schedule, outline

[síləbəs] 강의 계획(표)

According to the class **syllabus**, the final exam will be in December.
강의 계획표에 따르면 기말 시험은 12월에 있을 것이다.

28 thrive   v. prosper, flourish   ↔ deteriorate, go downhill

[θráiv] 번성하다

Wild mushrooms **thrive** in the cool and damp floors of forests.
야생 버섯은 서늘하고 축축한 숲 바닥에서 번성한다.

29 unanimously   adv. without dissent, harmoniously   ↔ on the contrary, divergently

[juːnǽnəməsli] 만장일치로

The twelve members in the travel club voted **unanimously** to go to Spain this year.
여행 클럽 회원 12명은 올해 스페인에 가기로 만장일치로 투표했다.

30 vigilant   adj. watchful, with eyes peeled   ↔ off-guard, inattentive

[vídʒələnt] 경계하는

The soldiers at the border remained **vigilant** for any sign of the enemy.
전방에서 복무하는 군인들은 적의 어떠한 조짐에도 경계심을 유지했다.

DAILY QUIZ

1. a **daunting** task
2. **meager** earnings
3. course **syllabus**
4. **smuggle** alcohol
5. **fluorescent** colors
6. a high school **sophomore**
7. **robust** growth in sales
8. a **humble** beginning
9. **thrive** in business
10. vote **unanimously**

- a intimidating
- b luminous
- c second year student
- d vigorous
- e flourish
- f without dissent
- g bootleg
- h inadequate
- i outline
- j modest

ANSWERS   1. a   2. h   3. i   4. g   5. b   6. c   7. d   8. j   9. e   10. f

COMPREHENSIVE QUIZ — Day 19 & 20

1. As the boy's seizures got _____ worse, his parents decided that he needed brain surgery.
   ⓐ unanimously   ⓑ adequately   ⓒ robustly   ⓓ successively

2. Scientists believe that regional outbreaks of the new flu are a(n) _____ for a larger pandemic.
   ⓐ impeachment   ⓑ precedent   ⓒ radiation   ⓓ imagery

3. The fans were allowed to preview a(n) _____ of the new movie being released next month.
   ⓐ excerpt   ⓑ curriculum   ⓒ misdemeanor   ⓓ sophomore

4. The president's mistakes are often the subject of political _____.
   ⓐ syllabus   ⓑ investment   ⓒ laureate   ⓓ satire

5. Their strong relationship meant that he could always _____ his best friend to support him.
   ⓐ smuggle   ⓑ extinguish   ⓒ bank on   ⓓ impersonate

6. Archaeologists marvel at how the Mayans and Egyptians were able to _____ such large pyramids without modern technology.
   ⓐ erect   ⓑ recommend   ⓒ thrive   ⓓ mitigate

7. _____ people were often mistreated by colonists.
   ⓐ Acute   ⓑ Indigenous   ⓒ Corporal   ⓓ Fluorescent

8. The princess was _____ to the hardships of peasant life.
   ⓐ opaque   ⓑ robust   ⓒ sufficient   ⓓ oblivious

9. If the writing in your essay test is not _____, your grade will be reduced.
   ⓐ precarious   ⓑ legible   ⓒ chaotic   ⓓ oblivious

10. The neighborhood was warned to be _____ for any sign of crime.
    ⓐ daunting   ⓑ vigilant   ⓒ humble   ⓓ meager

Answers: p.340

Day 21

1. adamant   adj. unyielding, set in stone   ↔ flexible, malleable

[ǽdəmənt] 강경한, 단호한

Each side in the heated debate was **adamant** about the correctness of its position.
열띤 논쟁에서 양측은 각자 입장의 정당성에 대해 강경했다.

2. alleviate   v. relieve, assuage   ↔ aggravate, provoke

[əlíːvièit] 완화하다

Ecotourism **alleviates** the impact of ordinary tourism on delicate ecosystems.
생태 관광은 민감한 생태계에 일반 관광이 미치는 충격을 덜어준다.

3. antidote   n. remedy, countermeasure   ↔ poison, venom

[ǽntidòut] 해독제

The **antidote** to snake bites is made from the snake's own antibodies.
뱀에 물린 상처에 대한 해독제는 뱀 자체의 항체로 만든다.

4. bursar   n. treasurer, cash keeper

[bə́ːrsər] 회계 담당자

The president of the university had a talk with the **bursar** about the school's finances.
대학교 총장은 회계 담당자와 학교 재정에 대해서 이야기를 나누었다.

5. carcinogenic   adj. cancer-causing, malignant   ↔ benign, harmless

[kɑ̀ːrsənoudʒénik] 발암성의

Asbestos was once popular but now is avoided as a **carcinogenic** building material.
석면은 한때 유행했지만 이제는 발암성 건축 자재로서 기피 대상이다.

6. circumstance   n. situation, condition

[sə́ːrkəmstæns] 정황, 상황

Good historians look at the **circumstances** that brought about an event.
훌륭한 역사가는 사건을 초래했던 정황을 살핀다.

7 come to pass   phr. happen, take place

도래하다, 발생하다

Skeptics did not believe the end of the world would **come to pass**.
회의론자들은 세상의 종말이 올 것이라고 믿지 않았다.

8 compound   n. mixture, combination

[kámpaund] 화합물

A chemical **compound** may have properties different from its individual elements.
화합물은 개별 원소와 다른 성질을 가질 수도 있다.

9 de facto   phr. in reality, actual   ↔ ostensible

[di:-fǽktou] 실질적인, 사실상의

If a ship loses its captain, the second in command becomes the **de facto** leader.
함선에 선장이 없을 경우 2인자가 실질적인 지도자가 된다.

10 depot   n. warehouse, depository

[dí:pou] 창고

Towns in the Old West would have a general **depot** where cowboys bought their supplies.
옛 서부 마을에는 카우보이가 생활용품을 구입했던 일반 창고가 있었다.

11 ecological   adj.

[ì:kəládʒikəl] 생태계의

Ecological balance can be disrupted with the introduction of a new species.
새로운 종의 유입으로 생태 균형이 무너질 수 있다.

12 employ   v. make use of, utilize   ↔ keep away from, shun

[implɔ́i] 이용하다, 고용하다

Modern automobile plants **employ** robots to help in the assembly process.
현대식 자동차 공장에서는 조립 공정을 돕고자 로봇을 사용한다.

13 enchant   v. mesmerize, cast a spell on   ↔ disgust, turn off

[entʃǽnt] 황홀하게 만들다, 마술을 걸다

Particularly beautiful landscapes can **enchant** and delight visitors and tourists.
특히 아름다운 풍경은 방문자나 관광객을 황홀하고 즐겁게 할 수 있다.

14 epidemic   n. outbreak, scourge

[èpədémik] 유행성 전염병

Vaccines are used to prevent the spread of disease and the outbreak of **epidemics**.
백신은 질병의 확산과 전염병의 발생을 막기 위해 사용된다.

15 pandemic   n. worldwide epidemic

[pændémik] 전국[세계]적 유행병

Controls are in place for international travel and commerce to prevent potential **pandemics**.
잠재하는 세계적 유행병을 막기 위해 해외 여행 및 상거래 통제 수단이 마련되어 있다.

16 prerequisite   n. requirement, precondition   ↔ option, choice

[priːrékwəzit] 필요 조건

Beginner's courses are a **prerequisite** to more advanced classes at schools.
초급 과정은 학교에서 더 고급 수준의 수업을 위한 전제 조건이다.

17 prey   n. game, target   ↔ beast of prey, predator

[préi] 먹이

A rich natural environment can offer abundant **prey** for a potential predator.
풍요로운 자연환경은 잠재적인 포식 동물에게 풍부한 먹이를 제공할 수 있다.

18 probe   v. investigate, delve   ↔ ignore, pay no attention to

[próub] 탐색하다, 조사하다

Doctors today can use tiny instruments to **probe** the body for examination or surgery.
오늘날 의사들은 검사나 수술을 위해 몸을 조사하는 작은 기구를 쓸 수 있다.

19 prolific   adj. high-volume, productive   ↔ insufficient, scant

[prəlífik] 다작의, 다산의

Picasso was a **prolific** artist who left thousands of works of art as his legacy.
피카소는 유산으로 수천 점의 예술 작품을 남긴 다작 화가였다.

20 radical   adj. revolutionary, drastic   ↔ conservative, traditional

[rǽdikəl] 급진적인

A **radical** idea shakes up the status quo and challenges accepted notions.
급진적인 사상이 현재 상황을 뒤흔들고 용인된 관념에 도전한다.

21 reconcile v. harmonize, resolve ↔ fall out, clash

[rékənsàil] 조화시키다, 화해하다

Enemies who can **reconcile** their differences can end up as eventual friends.
차이점을 조화시킬 수 있는 적은 결국 친구가 될 수 있다.

22 registrar n. record-keeper, recorder

[rédʒistrɑ̀:r] 기록원, (대학의) 학적 담당 사무원

A school **registrar** maintains all the records and files on its students.
학교 교무 과장은 학생들에 관한 모든 기록과 파일을 보관하고 있다.

23 renovate v. modernize, renew ↔ demolish, tear down

[rénəvèit] 보수하다, 개조하다

The township voted to set aside some money to **renovate** its historic homes.
지역구는 역사적인 집을 보수하기 위해 얼마만큼의 자금을 비축하는 데 가결했다.

24 scant adj. barely sufficient, inadequate ↔ plentiful, abounding

[skænt] 부족한

Scant evidence of a break-in in a robbery led police to suspect an inside job.
경찰은 강도 사건에서 침입의 증거가 부족한 점을 미루어 내부 범죄를 의심했다.

25 spur v. incite, fire up ↔ discourage, cast down

[spə́:r] 자극하다

The promise of a great view at the summit **spurs** mountaineers to continue their hike.
정상에서 장관을 볼 수 있다는 가능성 때문에 등산객들은 등반을 계속해나갈 수 있다.

26 subterfuge n. deception, hoax ↔ honesty, evenhandedness

[sʌ́btərfjùːdʒ] 속임수

Bank robbers employ **subterfuge** to bypass bank security measures.
은행 강도들은 은행의 보안 장치를 피해 가기 위해 속임수를 쓴다.

27 surplus n. oversupply, excess ↔ deficit, scarcity

[sə́:rplʌs] 흑자, 잉여

The talk these days in Washington is about China's trade **surplus** with America.
최근 워싱턴에서 열린 회담은 미국에 대한 중국의 무역 수지 흑자에 관한 것이다.

28 tedious   adj. dreary, monotonous   ↔ stimulating, thought-provoking

[tíːdiəs] 지루한

Workers need something to relieve their boredom if their work is **tedious**.
일이 따분하다면 근로자들에게는 지루함을 달래 줄 무언가가 필요하다.

29 undergraduate   n.

[ʌ̀ndərgrǽdʒuət] 학부생, 대학생

Undergraduates usually have to select a major at a certain point in their studies.
학부생은 보통 재학 중 어떤 시점에 전공을 선택해야 한다.

30 wield   v. put to use, brandish

[wiːld] (무기 등을) 휘두르다, 행사하다

Ancient warriors usually **wielded** a sword and shield during combat.
고대 전사들은 주로 전투에서 검과 방패를 휘둘렀다.

DAILY QUIZ

1 a flu **epidemic**   a warehouse
2 **depot** filled with weapons   b unyielding
3 **antidote** for poison   c make use of
4 **employ** deceitful tactics   d take place
5 an **adamant** tone   e hoax
6 a **de facto** ruler   f actual
7 will soon **come to pass**   g remedy
8 all just a **subterfuge**   h outbreak
9 an office of the **registrar** i excess
10 a trade **surplus**   j record-keeper

ANSWERS   1. h   2. a   3. g   4. c   5. b   6. f   7. d   8. e   9. j   10. i

Day 22

1. abort   v. cancel, call off   ↔ continue, move ahead

[əbɔ́ːrt] 중단되다, 실패하다

Foul weather caused the controllers to **abort** the launch of the rocket.
악천후로 인해 관제사들은 로켓 발사를 중단했다.

2. application[1]   n.

[æ̀pləkéiʃən] 지원서

Recruiters at companies must go through many **applications** to fill a position.
회사의 채용 담당자들은 충원하기 위해 많은 입사 지원서를 검토해야 한다.

3. application[2]   n. utilization, function

[æ̀pləkéiʃən] 적용

Navigation systems are an **application** of satellite technology to driving.
내비게이션 시스템은 운전에 위성 기술을 적용한 것이다.

4. at stake   phr. at risk, jeopardized   ↔ protected, safe

관련이 되어, 위태로워

All parties had much **at stake** in this current round of trade negotiations.
모든 당사자들은 현재 진행 중인 무역 협상과 많이 관련되어 있다.

5. cardinal   n. fundamentally important, principal

[káːrdənl] 가장 중요한

Kathy believed in the **cardinal** rule of never mixing too many styles together.
캐시는 절대로 지나치게 많은 스타일을 함께 섞지 않는다는 가장 중요한 규칙을 믿었다.

6. caricature   n.

[kǽrikətʃùər] 캐리커처

Newspaper cartoonists draw **caricatures** of public figures for humorous effect.
신문 만화가들은 해학적인 효과를 위해 공인들의 캐리커처를 그린다.

7 conduit n. passage, pipeline

[kándwit] 도관, 수로

Pipes act as **conduits** for distributing water or electricity in a building or city.
파이프는 건물이나 도시의 배수 또는 배전을 위한 도관 역할을 한다.

8 deity n. god, celestial being ↔ mortal, human

[díːəti] 신(神)

Apollo was a solar **deity** for the Greeks with equivalents in other cultures.
그리스인에게 아폴로는 다른 문화권의 태양의 신에 해당하는 것이었다.

9 efficacy n. performance, effectiveness ↔ futility, uselessness

[éfikəsi] 효능

Tests are conducted to determine the **efficacy** of a drug before its approval for sale.
판매를 승인하기 전에 약의 효능을 확인하기 위한 검사가 실시된다.

10 emission n. discharge, release

[imíʃən] 방출물, 배기

A contributing cause of urban smog is the accumulation of vehicle **emissions** in the air.
도시 스모그의 주요 원인은 대기 중 차량 배기가스의 축적이다.

11 exhale v. breathe out, let out ↔ breathe in, inhale

[ekshéil] (숨을) 내쉬다

Animals inhale oxygen and **exhale** carbon dioxide into the air.
동물은 산소를 들이쉬고 이산화탄소를 공기 중으로 내쉰다.

12 foreshadow v. indicate, suggest

[fɔːrʃǽdou] ~의 전조가 되다

Protests and riots **foreshadowed** the fall of the unpopular government.
시위와 폭동은 국민의 지지를 얻지 못하는 정부가 몰락할 전조가 되었다.

13 genre n. type, category

[ʒɑ́ːnrə] 장르

Fantasy is a **genre** of literature that appeals especially to the imagination of the young.
판타지는 특히 젊은층의 상상력에 호소하는 문학 장르이다.

14 **hereditary**　adj. inherited, genetic　↔ acquired, learned

[hərédətèri] 유전적인

Some genetic traits are passed on from generation to generation as a **hereditary** feature.
어떤 유전 형질은 유전적 특징으로서 대대로 전해진다.

15 **impending**　adj. at hand, forthcoming　↔ ensuing, subsequent

[impéndiŋ] 임박한

Residents prepared for the **impending** danger of a hurricane striking their area.
주민들은 지역을 강타하는 허리케인의 임박한 위험에 대비했다.

16 **indict**　v. criminate, charge　↔ acquit, exonerate

[indáit] 기소[고발]하다

He was **indicted** on several counts of fraud and will serve some time in jail.
그는 몇 차례의 사기 혐의로 기소되었고 얼마 동안 수감될 것이다.

17 **lukewarm**　adj. slightly heated, tepid

[lúːkwɔ̀ːrm] 미지근한, 열의 없는

Flowers in a vase require **lukewarm** water to avoid extremes in temperature.
꽃병에 있는 꽃은 극단적인 온도를 피하기 위해서 미지근한 물이 필요하다.

18 **meritocracy**　n. merit-based system

[mèritákrəsi] 능력주의

The idea of a **meritocracy** is where the most talented and capable are rewarded.
능력주의는 가장 재능 있고 유능한 사람이 보상을 받는다는 발상이다.

19 **monopoly**　n. corporation with exclusive control

[mənápəli] 독점

Laws are made to illegalize business **monopolies** that limit competition.
법이 경쟁을 제한하는 사업 독점을 불법화하기 위해 제정된다.

20 **ominous**　adj. ill-boding, menacing　↔ promising, auspicious

[ámənəs] 불길한

Ominous clouds on the horizon told everyone that stormy weather was coming.
수평선 위의 불길한 구름이 모두에게 폭풍이 다가오고 있다는 것을 알려주었다.

21. paralyze   v. shut down, immobilize   ↔ animate, set in motion

[pǽrəlàiz] 마비시키다

Snake bites literally **paralyze** the animal victim to allow the snake to swallow it slowly.
뱀에 물린 상처는 말 그대로 뱀이 천천히 삼킬 수 있도록 잡힌 동물을 마비시킨다.

22. perimeter   n. border, outline   ↔ inner parts, interior

[pərímitər] 주변, 주위

Security guards watch the **perimeter** of a building to secure it against attacks.
경비원들은 공격으로부터 건물을 보호하기 위해 건물 주위를 감시한다.

23. pigmentation   n. coloration, tone

[pìgmentéiʃən] 색소

Animal **pigmentation** can act to identify the animal or camouflage it with the background.
동물 색소는 동물을 식별하거나 배경을 이용해 동물을 위장하는 작용을 할 수 있다.

24. postulate   v. put forward, hypothesize

[pástʃəlèi] 가정하다

Scientists **postulate** several theories if they are not completely sure about something.
과학자들은 어떤 것에 대해 완전히 확신하지 않는 경우 몇 가지 이론을 가정한다.

25. proponent   n. advocate, enthusiast   ↔ antagonist, opponent

[prəpóunənt] 지지자

Liberals are **proponents** of minimal government restrictions on individual freedom.
자유주의자란 개인의 자유에 대한 최소한의 정부 규제를 지지하는 자들이다.

26. reactor   n.

[riːǽktər] 원자로, 반응 장치

Balanced and controlled atomic reaction is the function of a nuclear **reactor**.
안정되고 통제된 조건에서 일어나는 핵반응이 원자로의 기능이다.

27. retrieve   v. bring back, recover   ↔ relinquish, hand over

[ritríːv] 되찾다, 회수하다

Hunting dogs can be bred and trained not only to hunt but also to **retrieve** their targets.
사냥개는 사냥뿐만 아니라 사냥감을 물어 오도록 사육하고 훈련시킬 수 있다.

28 statistics   n. figures, data

[stətístiks] 통계 자료

Gathering **statistics** can give us the exact numbers on any given phenomenon.
통계 자료 수집으로 어떤 현상에 대해서도 정확한 수치를 알 수 있다.

29 surveillance   n. watch, scrutiny

[sərvéiləns] 감시

Airport and traffic technology regarding **surveillance** seems to be a rising trend.
감시와 관련된 공항 및 교통관제 기술은 성장 추세인 것 같다.

30 sustainability   n. sustenance, maintenance

[səstéinəbíləti] 지속 가능성

Environmentalists worry about the **sustainability** of any energy resource.
환경론자들은 모든 에너지 자원의 지속 가능성에 대해 우려한다.

DAILY QUIZ

1. **application** of a theory •   • a   suggest
2. a life **at stake** •   • b   coloration
3. **foreshadow** the ending of the story • • c   criminate
4. **retrieve** the lost files •   • d   tepid
5. skin **pigmentation** •   • e   at risk
6. a **lukewarm** response •   • f   recover
7. **indict** offenders •   • g   inherited
8. leaders under **surveillance** •   • h   god
9. **hereditary** disease •   • i   utilization
10. a Roman **deity** •   • j   scrutiny

ANSWERS   1. i   2. e   3. a   4. f   5. b   6. d   7. c   8. j   9. g   10. h

COMPREHENSIVE QUIZ — Day 21 & 22

1. The hatred between them is so deep that there seems to be _____ hope of reconciliation.
   ⓐ scant   ⓑ prolific   ⓒ hereditary   ⓓ radical

2. Clean water is a _____ for cholera eradication.
   ⓐ subterfuge   ⓑ pandemic   ⓒ prerequisite   ⓓ pigmentation

3. The prosecutors asked for a strict _____ of the law for a just and fair trial.
   ⓐ application   ⓑ deity   ⓒ statistics   ⓓ compound

4. The fireman discussed the _____ rules of fire prevention.
   ⓐ prerequisite   ⓑ surveillance   ⓒ meritocracy   ⓓ cardinal

5. The _____ of seatbelts is a hot topic that comes up in every car crash investigation.
   ⓐ efficacy   ⓑ depot   ⓒ bursar   ⓓ surplus

6. Overfishing has caused many countries to enforce policies concerning fish stocks and _____.
   ⓐ registrar   ⓑ undergraduate   ⓒ sustainability   ⓓ antidote

7. _____ is the best system for hiring new employees without discrimination of class or race.
   ⓐ Monopoly   ⓑ Meritocracy   ⓒ Proponent   ⓓ Conduit

8. He is a _____ author who writes several bestselling books every year.
   ⓐ impending   ⓑ hereditary   ⓒ scant   ⓓ prolific

9. Nutritionists say that it is good to eat a diet rich in cancer-fighting fruits and to avoid _____ food.
   ⓐ carcinogenic   ⓑ ecological   ⓒ de facto   ⓓ lukewarm

10. The professor is infamous for his _____ lectures where at least one person falls asleep in every class.
    ⓐ adamant   ⓑ tedious   ⓒ ominous   ⓓ radical

Answers: p.340

1 alchemy n.

[ǽlkəmi] 연금술

Alchemy can be said to be the ancestor of modern chemistry as we know it today.
연금술은 오늘날 알려진 대로 현대 화학의 원형이라고 할 수 있다.

2 apprehend v. capture, take into custody ↔ lose, come up short

[æ̀prihénd] 파악하다, 체포하다

Detectives must **apprehend** all the clues they can find to solve their cases.
수사관들은 사건 해결을 위해서 발견하는 모든 단서를 반드시 파악해야 한다.

3 assume v. presume, take on ↔ grasp, hand over

[əsúːm] 추측하다, 맡다

The former manager now **assumed** the role of CEO in the company.
전임 부장이 현재 회사 최고 경영자의 역할을 맡았다.

4 behavior n. attitude, demeanor

[bihéivjər] 행동

Polite **behavior** always tries to not disturb or offend other people.
공손한 태도란 항상 다른 사람을 방해하거나 불쾌하게 하지 않으려고 하는 것이다.

5 capitalize on phr. cash in on, exploit ↔ forgo, pass up

기회로 삼다

Wise investors **capitalize on** opportunities in the market to earn their money.
현명한 투자자는 돈을 벌기 위해 시장에서의 기회를 이용한다.

6 cavity n. depression, hole ↔ closure, seal

[kǽvəti] 구멍

Brushing is meant to prevent the formation of **cavities** in the teeth.
칫솔질은 치아에 구멍이 생기는 것을 방지하려는 것이다.

7 civil   adj.

[sívəl] 시민의

Civil liberties include the freedom of speech, press, assembly, and religion.
자유권은 언론의 자유, 출판의 자유, 집회·결사의 자유, 종교의 자유를 포함한다.

8 devastate   v. lay waste, demolish   ↔ construct, make strides

[dévəstèit] 완전히 파괴하다

The sudden flood **devastated** the mountainside and valley below.
갑작스런 홍수가 산중턱과 아래에 있는 계곡이 완전히 파괴했다.

9 errand   n. task, assignment

[érənd] 심부름

The boss sent the secretary on an **errand** to buy all the necessary supplies.
상사는 필요한 모든 물품을 구입하기 위해서 비서를 심부름 보냈다.

10 ethnicity   n. cultural group, race

[eθnísəti:] 종족, 민족성

Large countries can have several **ethnicities** living within them.
큰 나라에는 여러 민족이 살 수 있다.

11 financial   adj. economic, fiscal

[fainǽnʃəl] 재정적인

Many Americans are losing their homes because of **financial** problems due to job losses.
많은 미국인이 실업으로 인한 재정적 문제 때문에 집을 잃고 있다.

12 gestation   n. maturation, pregnancy

[dʒestéiʃən] 임신 (기간)

A typical human **gestation** is nine months.
일반적인 인간의 임신 기간은 9개월이다.

13 hegemony   n. predominance, authority   ↔ subordination, servitude

[hédʒəmòuni] 패권

Hitler boasted about his **hegemony** over Europe as he went on to conquer more land.
히틀러는 더 많은 영토를 계속 정복해 나아가면서 유럽에 대한 자신의 패권을 자랑했다.

14 illustrate v. demonstrate, explain

[íləstrèit] 설명하다

Doctor Jackson **illustrated** the importance of hygiene to Zack who refused to take a shower.
의사인 잭슨 선생님은 샤워하기를 거부한 잭에게 위생의 중요성을 설명했다.

15 imperialism n. expansionism, colonialism

[impíəriəlìzm] 제국주의

Imperialism nears its end when it is felt that it has outstayed its welcome.
제국주의는 너무 오래 지속되어 원성을 살 때 종말에 가까워진다.

16 inquiry n. questioning, looking into

[ínkwəri] 조사, 탐구

He was nervous about the **inquiry** into his company's finances by the Internal Revenue Service.
그는 자사의 재정에 대한 국세청의 조사에 불안해 했다.

17 maternal adj. motherly ↔ paternal, fatherly

[mətə́:rnl] 모성의

Raising and nurturing a child is often termed the **maternal** instinct.
아이를 키우고 양육하는 것을 흔히 모성 본능이라 한다.

18 multinational n. international company, transnational

[mÀltinǽʃənl] 다국적 기업

Multinationals do business in and follow the laws of several countries.
다국적 기업은 여러 나라의 법 테두리 내에서 사업을 하고 법을 준수한다.

19 municipal adj.

[mjunísəpəl] 지방 자치의

Municipal codes can sometimes differ from national or state laws.
지방 자치 규정은 때로는 국가나 주의 법과 다를 수 있다.

20 ordain v. anoint, appoint

[ɔːrdéin] 임명하다

The bishop **ordained** a new priest in charge of the congregation at St. Mary's Church.
주교는 신임 사제를 성 마리아 성당의 집회 담당으로 임명했다.

21. partial — adj. incomplete, fragmentary ↔ complete, full

[pá:rʃəl] 불완전한

Some eclipses are **partial** so that the sun or moon is not completely covered up.
어떤 일식이나 월식은 불완전해서 해나 달이 완전히 가려지지 않는다.

22. procedure — n. process, course of action

[prəsí:dʒər] 절차

The school was very strict about following the correct **procedure** in evacuating the building during the fire drill.
학교는 소방 훈련시 정확한 건물 대피 절차 준수에 대해 매우 엄격했다.

23. recede — v. withdraw, move away ↔ advance, forge ahead

[risí:d] (물을) 빼다, 물러가다

When the water finally **receded** after the flood, the people were ready to rebuild their homes.
홍수가 난 후 마침내 물이 빠지자 사람들은 집을 재건할 준비가 되었다.

24. rife — adj. overflowing, teeming ↔ scarce, in short supply

[ráif] 가득 찬

The city is **rife** with homeless people who sleep on the streets and beg for money.
도시는 길에서 잠을 자고 돈을 구걸하는 노숙자로 가득하다.

25. semester — n.

[siméstər] 학기

Tabitha was proud that she succeeded in completing her first **semester** at college.
타비타는 대학 첫 학기를 성공적으로 마친 것에 대해 긍지를 가졌다.

26. succinct — adj. concise, to the point ↔ lengthy, long-winded

[sʌksíŋkt] 간단명료한

With only a few minutes left, each candidate was asked to make a short, **succinct** statement on the issue.
불과 몇 분이 남아 있지 않은 가운데 각 후보자는 쟁점에 대해 간단명료하게 진술하라는 요청을 받았다.

27. theoretical — adj. hypothetical, speculative ↔ factual, verified

[θì:ərétikəl] 이론적인

Sir Isaac Newton's **theoretical** view on gravity was proven by his calculations.
중력에 대한 아이작 뉴턴 경의 이론적인 견해는 그의 계산에 의해 증명되었다.

| 28 | **trigger** | v. activate, give rise to | ↔ halt, bring to an end |

[trígər] 유발하다

A loud noise can sometimes **trigger** an avalanche in snow-covered mountains.
큰 소음은 때때로 눈 덮인 산에서 눈사태를 유발할 수 있다.

| 29 | **usher** | v. guide, escort | ↔ oust, throw out |

[ʌ́ʃər] 안내하다

There was a person at the door to **usher** guests to their tables.
손님들을 테이블로 안내하는 사람이 입구에 있었다.

| 30 | **vanish** | v. disappear, fade away | ↔ materialize, come into view |

[vǽniʃ] 사라지다

Ghosts are said to appear and then **vanish** into thin air.
유령은 나타났다가 흔적도 없이 사라진다고 한다.

DAILY QUIZ

1. **imperialism** of European powers •   • a   overflowing
2. **financial** status •   • b   process
3. **assume** leadership •   • c   withdraw
4. a **succinct** report •   • d   expansionism
5. **recede** into the background •   • e   explain
6. a difficult **procedure** •   • f   take on
7. **maternal** love •   • g   hypothetical
8. **rife** with possibilities •   • h   concise
9. **theoretical** concepts •   • i   economic
10. **illustrate** by using examples •   • j   motherly

ANSWERS   1. d   2. i   3. f   4. h   5. c   6. b   7. j   8. a   9. g   10. e

Day 24

24 | 58

1. abandon   v. leave behind, desert   ↔ retain, cling to

[əbǽndən] 포기하다, 버리다

After some failed experiments, the researcher decided to **abandon** his plan.
실험이 몇 번 실패한 뒤 연구원은 계획을 포기하기로 결정했다.

2. artificial   adj. imitation, synthetic   ↔ natural, raw

[ɑ̀ːrtəfíʃəl] 인공의

Artificial flowers are not as pretty as the real thing but they can last longer.
조화는 생화만큼 예쁘지 않지만 더 오래갈 수 있다.

3. commercial[1]   n. advertisement, endorsement

[kəmə́ːrʃəl] 광고 (방송)

Commercials are made to entertain and inform the viewer about a product.
광고 방송은 시청자를 즐겁게 하고 제품을 알리기 위해서 제작된다.

4. commercial[2]   adj. business-related, industrial   ↔ noncommercial, not-for-profit

[kəmə́ːrʃəl] 상업적인

A mixed-use building offers space for both residential and **commercial** purposes.
주상 복합 건물은 주거 및 상업적 목적을 위한 공간을 제공한다.

5. conform   v. adjust, follow   ↔ deviate from, digress

[kənfɔ́ːrm] 순응하다, 따르다

We all must **conform** to our society to a certain extent.
우리는 모두 어느 정도는 사회에 순응해야 한다.

6. currency   n. legal tender, money

[kə́ːrənsi] 통화

The Euro is the **currency** in many European countries today.
유로화는 오늘날 많은 유럽 국가의 통화이다.

7 denote   adj. indicate, express

[dinóut] 표시하다, 나타내다

In a soccer match, a yellow card **denotes** a warning to a player committing a deliberate foul.
축구 경기에서 옐로카드는 고의적인 반칙을 저지른 선수에게 주는 경고를 나타낸다..

8 diffusion   n. spread, dissemination

[difjú:ʒən] 보급, 전파

Many parents are beginning to worry about the **diffusion** of violent video games.
많은 부모가 폭력적인 비디오 게임의 전파를 걱정하기 시작했다.

9 elastic   adj. pliant, stretchy   ↔ stiff

[ilǽstik] 탄력 있는

Rubber is an **elastic** matter originally made from the sap of the rubber tree.
고무는 원래 고무나무의 수액으로 만든 탄성 물질이다.

10 enlighten   v. elucidate, illuminate   ↔ confound, confuse

[inláitn] 깨우치다, 이해시키다

The lecturer **enlightened** his listeners with clear language and superb explanations.
강사는 명확한 언어와 훌륭한 설명으로 수강생들을 이해시켰다.

11 germinate   v. grow, originate   ↔ halt, take down

[dʒə́ːrmənèit] (생각 등이) 싹트다, 생겨나다

The message of the Buddha **germinated** in India and then spread to the rest of Asia.
부처의 메시지는 인도에서 생겨나 아시아의 나머지 지역으로 전파되었다.

12 hitherto   adv. before then, up until that point

[hìðərtú:] 지금까지

The chemical composition of the planet Mars was **hitherto** unknown until the Mars Rover was sent to transmit the information.
화성 탐사 로버가 정보 전달을 위해 발사될 때까지는 화성의 화학적 구성 요소를 알 수 없었다.

13 influx   n. flow, coming in   ↔ evacuation, taking off

[ínflʌks] 유입, 밀려옴

The United States has an **influx** of immigrants who come with the hope to start a new and prosperous life.
새롭고 부유한 삶을 시작하려는 희망을 품은 이민자들이 미국으로 유입되고 있다.

14 ingenuity n. cleverness, inventiveness ↔ inability, incompetence

[ìndʒənjúːəti] 독창력

The Eiffel Tower is a great symbol of human **ingenuity**.
에펠 탑은 인간의 독창력을 나타내는 위대한 상징이다.

15 mediation n. arbitration, intervention

[mìːdiéiʃən] 중재, 조정

A third party was brought in for **mediation** between the workers and the employer who could not solve their conflict.
노사 갈등을 해결하지 못하는 노동자와 고용주 사이에 중재를 위해서 제3자를 개입시켰다.

16 menial adj. low-status, humble ↔ high-class, eloquent

[míːniəl] 하찮은

Although his **menial** job as a janitor was boring, he was glad that he was able to save up money for his summer trip.
그는 수위로서 하찮은 일이 따분했지만 여름 여행을 위해 돈을 저축할 수 있다는 사실에 기뻤다.

17 microscopic adj. tiny, minuscule ↔ colossal, titanic

[màikrəskápik] 미세한

What looks like lifeless surfaces often harbor life at the **microscopic** level.
생명체가 없는 것으로 보이는 표면에도 종종 미세 단위의 생명체가 살고 있다.

18 native n. inhabitant, national ↔ alien, immigrant

[néitiv] 출신자, 현지인

Steven is a **native** of Canada but grew up in the United States, allowing him to have dual citizenship.
스티븐은 캐나다 출신이지만 미국에서 자랐기 때문에 이중 국적을 가질 수 있다.

19 ostensibly adv. apparently, outwardly

[ɑsténsəbli] 겉치레로, 표면상

Janet **ostensibly** invited Ronald over for a dinner party just so she could introduce him to her sister.
재닛은 표면상으로는 로널드를 만찬회에 초대해서 여동생에게 소개시킬 수 있었다.

20 perennial adj. perpetual, never-ending

[pəréniəl] 다년생의, (오랫동안) 지속되는

The **perennial** flowers were a favorite of the gardener as they blossomed every season on their own.
다년생 화초는 계절마다 스스로 꽃이 피어서 정원사가 가장 좋아하는 꽃이었다.

21 precipitation n. condensation, rainfall ↔ dryness, aridity

[prisìpətéiʃən] 강설, 강수[강우](량)

The **precipitation** made the roads wet and dangerous to drive on because it was slippery.
강우로 인해 도로가 미끄러웠기 때문에 길이 젖어서 운전하기 위험했다.

22 protagonist n. main character, lead ↔ antagonist, rival

[proutǽgənist] 주인공

The **protagonist** of the novel was a hero with a tragic past.
소설의 주인공은 비극적인 과거를 가진 영웅이었다.

23 put up with phr. deal with, bear ↔ shun, have no part of

견디다, 참다

Any great achievement follows after **putting up with** difficulties along the way.
과정의 어려움을 견딘 후에 위대한 성취가 뒤따른다.

24 quell v. put down, squash

[kwél] 진압하다

The riot police were called in to **quell** the violent protest by the factory workers.
공장 근로자들의 폭력적인 시위를 진압하기 위해 폭동 진압 경찰이 호출되었다.

25 relative adj. comparative, with respect to ↔ irrelevant, out of proportion

[rélətiv] 상대적인

It is impressive that ants are able to carry heavy food **relative** to its size.
개미가 몸집에 비해 상대적으로 무거운 먹이를 운반할 수 있다는 점은 인상적이다.

26 scarce adj. insufficient, in short supply ↔ plentiful, well-provided

[skɛ́ərs] 부족한

Food was **scarce** during the war, resulting in starvation for many people.
전쟁 중 식량 부족으로 많은 사람들이 굶주렸다.

27 subsidiary n.

[səbsídièri] 자회사

The movie theater is a **subsidiary** of a larger parent company that controls its finances.
극장은 재정을 관리하는 더 큰 모회사의 자회사이다.

28 transmit   v. convey, pass on   ↔ receive, get hands on

[trænzmít] 옮기다, 전하다

He did not want to **transmit** his flu to his young son who was healthy.
그는 자기가 걸린 독감을 건강한 어린 아들에게 옮기는 것을 원치 않았다.

29 verification   n. evidence, confirmation

[vèrəfikéiʃən] 인증서, 증명

Buying or selling an ancient art object involves **verification** that it is real.
고대 예술품 매매에는 진품 인증서가 필요하다.

30 woe   n. suffering, heartache   ↔ happiness, good spirits

[wóu] 비통

The book can be described as a tale of sorrow and **woe**.
책은 슬프고 비통한 이야기라고 말할 수 있다.

DAILY QUIZ

1 run a **commercial**	a before then
2 **conform** to the rules	b outwardly
3 **enlighten** the students	c main character
4 **hitherto** unseen	d illuminate
5 **ostensibly** visible	e pass on
6 annual **precipitation**	f confirmation
7 **quell** the uprising	g put down
8 the tragic **protagonist**	h rainfall
9 in need of **verification**	i adjust
10 **transmit** information	j advertisement

ANSWERS   1. j   2. i   3. d   4. a   5. b   6. h   7. g   8. c   9. f   10. e

COMPREHENSIVE QUIZ   Day 23 & 24

1. Interning at the local _____ office helped him start his political career.
   ⓐ partial   ⓑ elastic   ⓒ microscopic   ⓓ municipal

2. While he was in the hospital, he was able to hire an assistant to do his _____.
   ⓐ errands   ⓑ currency   ⓒ woe   ⓓ gestation

3. The guide _____ the guests to their seats before the wedding began.
   ⓐ apprehended   ⓑ ushered   ⓒ vanished   ⓓ quelled

4. Rise in taxes is a _____ problem that many people worry about.
   ⓐ maternal   ⓑ theoretical   ⓒ scarce   ⓓ perennial

5. Every fall, there is a(n) _____ of new students on campus.
   ⓐ native   ⓑ imperialism   ⓒ influx   ⓓ alchemy

6. The police were able to _____ the vandals before they could destroy any more property.
   ⓐ apprehend   ⓑ ordain   ⓒ abandon   ⓓ illustrate

7. It is not unusual for a large international company to have many _____ that conduct business in a variety of fields.
   ⓐ mediations   ⓑ subsidiaries   ⓒ ethnicity   ⓓ inquiries

8. She needs to rent a(n) _____ space for her new store.
   ⓐ artificial   ⓑ maternal   ⓒ currency   ⓓ commercial

9. Religious leaders should take _____ over their congregation as a serious responsibility.
   ⓐ semester   ⓑ hegemony   ⓒ cavity   ⓓ ingenuity

10. It was a(n) _____ factory job without much excitement or responsibility, but it was honest work.
    ⓐ theoretical   ⓑ financial   ⓒ menial   ⓓ relative

Answers: p.340

Day 25

25 | 58

1. advertise   v. endorse, make a pitch   ↔ hide, keep secret

[ǽdvərtàiz] 광고하다

Marketers think of many clever ways to **advertise** their products.
마케팅 담당자들은 제품을 광고하기 위해서 여러 가지 기발한 방법을 생각해낸다.

2. apathy   n. lack of interest, indifference   ↔ concern, interest

[ǽpəθi] 무관심

A work done in **apathy** usually suffers from being directionless and half-hearted.
무관심하게 이루어진 일은 보통 방향성이 없고 성의가 없다.

3. aristocracy   n. upper class, nobility   ↔ working class, proletariat

[ærəstákrəsi] 귀족

The **aristocracy** of olden times often had many social and legal privileges.
옛날 귀족들은 많은 사회적, 법적 특권을 자주 누렸다.

4. avid   adj. ardent, fervent   ↔ indifferent, unenthusiastic

[ǽvid] 열렬한

He has been an **avid** collector of insects ever since he was young.
그는 어렸을 때부터 열렬한 곤충 수집가였다.

5. conjecture   n. speculation, hunch   ↔ fact, proof

[kəndʒéktʃər] 추측

It was a **conjecture** based on limited information and facts.
그것은 한정된 정보와 사실에 기초한 추측이었다.

6. detrimental   adj. damaging, harmful   ↔ advantageous, beneficial

[dètrəméntl] 해로운

Unhealthy lifestyle habits can be **detrimental** to our well-being.
건강하지 않은 생활 방식은 우리의 행복에 해가 될 수 있다.

7 dimension n. measurement, size

[diménʃən] 크기, 치수

The king-size bed barely fit into the **dimensions** of the bedroom.
킹사이즈 침대는 침실 크기에 간신히 맞는다.

8 doctrine n. principle, axiom ↔ disbelief, atheism

[dáktrin] 교리, 가르침

Priests are representatives and followers of the **doctrines** of their religion.
사제는 자신이 믿는 종교 교리의 대리인이자 신봉자이다.

9 draft v. formulate, draw up

[dræft] 초안을 만들다

Lawmakers **draft** a bill and then try to convince others to vote for it.
입법자들은 법안의 초안을 만든 다음, 법안에 투표하도록 다른 사람들을 설득시킨다.

10 envelop v. encase, wrap up ↔ unwrap, uncover

[invéləp] 두르다, 감싸다

A winter scarf is used to **envelop** the neck to keep it warm.
겨울 목도리는 목을 따뜻하게 유지하기 위해 목을 감싸는 데 사용된다.

11 evolutionary adj. developmental, transformational

[èvəlú:ʃənèri] 진화의

Recent findings have rewritten the **evolutionary** history of some animals.
최근 연구 결과는 일부 동물의 진화 역사를 다시 썼다.

12 extracurricular adj. additional, supplemental ↔ regular, routine

[èkstrəkəríkjələr] 과외의

Most schools offer **extracurricular** activities, such as sports, for students to enjoy.
대부분의 학교는 학생들이 즐길 수 있도록 스포츠와 같은 과외 활동을 제공한다.

13 feasibility n. practicability, prospect ↔ improbability, unlikelihood

[fi:zəbíliti] 타당성, 가능성

Because of tight schedules, Edward doubted the **feasibility** of his wife's plan to visit both sets of grandparents for the holidays.
빠듯한 일정 때문에 에드워드는 휴일에 양가 조부모를 모두 방문하자는 아내의 계획의 실행 가능성에 의문을 가졌다.

14 formidable   adj. overwhelming, powerful   ↔ manageable, controllable

[fɔ́ːrmidəbl] 가공할 만한, 만만치 않은

The chess player congratulated his **formidable** opponent for winning a difficult game.
체스 선수는 만만찮은 상대 선수가 어려운 게임에 승리한 것을 축하했다.

15 harassment   n. badgering, aggravation   ↔ assistance, helping hand

[hərǽsmənt] 괴롭힘

The employee, verbally abused at work, sued his company for **harassment**.
직장에서 악담을 들은 직원은 회사를 상대로 괴롭힘에 대한 소송을 제기했다.

16 improvise   v. contrive, make up   ↔ premeditate, plan

[ímprəvàiz] 즉흥적으로 하다

After losing his written speech, Alex had to **improvise** what he wanted to say in front of the audience.
연설 원고를 분실한 뒤 알렉스는 청중 앞에서 자신이 말하고자 했던 바를 즉흥적으로 연설해야 했다.

17 inflict   v. administer, cause   ↔ withhold, hold back

[inflíkt] 가하다

The captors **inflicted** torture on the enemy soldiers to gain secret information.
체포자는 비밀 정보를 얻기 위해 적군에게 고문을 가했다.

18 larceny   n. theft, pilfering

[láːrsəni] 절도(죄)

He was accused of **larceny** after being caught stealing an expensive watch and jewelry to give to his girlfriend.
그는 여자 친구에게 주려고 비싼 시계와 보석을 훔치다가 잡혀서 절도죄로 기소되었다.

19 mercenary   n. soldier of fortune, hireling

[mə́ːrsənèri] 용병

A government may hire foreign **mercenaries** to fight its wars.
정부는 전쟁에서 싸워 줄 외국 용병을 고용할 수도 있다.

20 monumental   adj. overwhelming, tremendous   ↔ trivial, of no account

[mànjuméntl] 엄청난

They were not looking forward to tackling the **monumental** task of packing for the big move to their new house.
그들은 새집으로 대대적인 이사를 위해 짐을 꾸려야 하는 엄청난 일과 씨름하는 것을 기대하지 않고 있다.

21 offset v. counterbalance, make up for

[ɔ́:fsèt] 상쇄하다

To **offset** the bookstore's increase in rent, Neil was forced to raise the price of the books.
서점 임대료 인상을 상쇄하기 위해 닐은 책값을 올릴 수 밖에 없었다.

22 patriarchy n. ↔ matriarchy

[péitriɑ̀:rki] 가부장제

England is a society based on **patriarchy** as lineage is only traced through male family members.
영국은 남자 가족 구성원을 통해서만 혈통이 이어지는 가부장제에 기초한 사회이다.

23 phonetically adv.

[fənétikəli] 발음대로

The Roman alphabet allows languages to be written down **phonetically**.
로마 문자는 언어를 발음대로 쓸 수 있다.

24 proportional adj.

[prəpɔ́:rʃənl] 비례적인, 균형 잡힌

The painting was praised for its **proportional** images and sense of dimension.
그림은 균형 잡힌 이미지와 입체감으로 찬사를 받았다.

25 realistic adj. sensible, matter-of-fact ↔ impractical, out of the question

[rì:əlístik] 현실적인, 사실적인

When setting goals it is important to have **realistic** expectations that one can actually achieve.
목표를 정할 때는 실제로 달성할 수 있는 현실적인 기대치를 갖는 것이 중요하다.

26 spontaneous adj. impulsive, free-spirited ↔ deliberate, premeditated

[spɑntéiniəs] 자연히 일어나는

After a hard day at work, he was surprised by his **spontaneous** burst of energy at the party.
직장에서 힘든 하루를 보낸 후 그는 파티에서 에너지가 자연스럽게 분출하는 것에 놀랐다.

27 to and fro phr. back and forth, here and there ↔ unwavering, resolute

앞뒤로, 이리저리

The bell on top of the church moved **to and fro**, making a beautiful sound as it swayed back and forth.
교회 꼭대기에 있는 종은 앞뒤로 왔다 갔다 움직였는데, 그렇게 앞뒤로 흔들릴 때마다 아름다운 소리를 냈다.

28 transcript¹ n. school record, grades

[trǽnskript] 성적 증명서

Students need to submit a **transcript** of their grades when transferring schools.
학생들은 전학할 때 성적표를 제출해야 한다.

29 transcript² n. documentation, paper trail

[trǽnskript] 필기록

Court cases have a **transcript** of their proceedings for recordkeeping purposes.
소송 재판에는 기록 보전을 목적으로 소송 절차에 대한 필기록이 있다.

30 volition n. free will, desire ↔ aversion, having no use for

[voulíʃən] 자유 의지

The travelers decided to leave the tour group of their own **volition**.
여행자들은 자신의 의지로 여행 그룹을 떠나기로 결심했다.

DAILY QUIZ

1. **extracurricular** programs — a school record
2. the **evolutionary** stages — b cause
3. sway **to and fro** — c supplemental
4. a **spontaneous** reaction — d developmental
5. benefits **offset** the disadvantages — e powerful
6. **inflict** pain — f impulsive
7. a **formidable** politician — g back and forth
8. **detrimental** to our health — h hunch
9. a college **transcript** — i counterbalance
10. based only on **conjecture** — j harmful

ANSWERS   1. c   2. d   3. g   4. f   5. i   6. b   7. e   8. j   9. a   10. h

Day 26

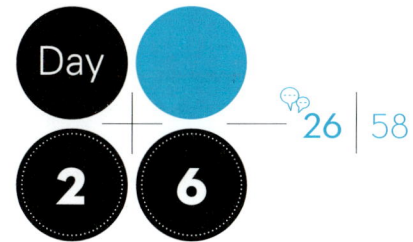

1. accustomed   adj. familiarized, in the habit   ↔ unfamiliar with, not used to

[əkʌ́stəmd] 익숙한

People can become **accustomed** to just about any kind of change.
사람들은 어떠한 종류의 변화에도 익숙해질 수 있다.

2. antecedent   n. predecessor, ancestor   ↔ descendent, progeny

[æ̀ntəsí:dnt] 선행자, 선조

The Roman republic was the **antecedent** to the Roman empire.
로마 공화국은 로마 제국보다 앞서 존재했다.

3. autonomy   n. independence, self-rule   ↔ dependence, reliance

[ɔːtánəmi] 자치권

Most countries try to have independence and practice **autonomy** in their governance.
대부분의 나라는 통치하는 데 있어 독립성을 가지고 자치권을 행사하려고 한다.

4. belated   adj. late, behind time   ↔ ahead of time, punctual

[biléitid] 뒤늦은

The birthday wishes were **belated** but appreciated nonetheless.
생일 소원은 늦었지만 그럼에도 불구하고 환영받았다.

5. caste   n. social class, status   ↔ egalitarianism, fair practice

[kæst] 계층

The Hindu **caste** system is largely hereditary and rigid.
인도의 카스트 제도는 대부분 세습적이고 엄격하다.

6. consensus   n. agreement, understanding   ↔ discord, conflict

[kənsénsəs] 합의, 의견 일치

The community reached a **consensus** on what to do with the unused land.
지역 사회는 사용하지 않는 땅으로 무엇을 할지 합의를 보았다.

7 constraint n. restriction, limitation ↔ allowance, permission

[kənstréint] 제약, 제한

Due to financial **constraints**, the construction was stopped before completion.
재정상의 제약으로 인해 건설 공사는 완공 전에 중단되었다.

8 contaminate v. pollute, defile ↔ purify, clean up

[kəntǽmənèit] 오염시키다

Pollution from factories can **contaminate** the local area.
공장에서 발생하는 공해가 해당 지역을 오염시킬 수 있다.

9 discretion n. judgment, good sense

[diskréʃən] 재량권

They used their **discretion** in deciding which task to do first.
그들은 어떤 일을 먼저 할 것인가 결정하는 데 재량권을 행사했다.

10 discrimination n. bias, prejudice ↔ fair-mindedness, tolerance

[diskrìmənéiʃən] 차별

Employers are careful to avoid **discrimination** of employees based on age, race, or gender.
고용주는 연령, 인종, 혹은 성별을 근거로 직원을 차별하지 않도록 주의한다.

11 disobedience n. defiance, insubordination ↔ conformity, submission

[dìsəbí:diəns] 불복종

Gandhi is well-known for his protest policy of civil **disobedience**.
간디는 시민 불복종 저항 정책으로 유명하다.

12 domestic adj. native, indigenous ↔ overseas, foreign

[dəméstik] 국내의

Foreign ministers deal with international concerns, not **domestic** ones.
외무부 장관은 국내 관계가 아닌, 국제 관계를 다룬다.

13 emphasize v. stress, underscore ↔ depreciate, minimize

[émfəsàiz] 강조하다

Debaters **emphasize** the points that support their side of an argument.
토론자들은 자기 편의 주장을 뒷받침하는 요점을 강조한다.

14 expendable   adj. unimportant, nonessential   ↔ indispensable, fundamental

[ikspéndəbl] 소모해도 되는

Spending less money involves not making **expendable** purchases.
돈을 덜 소비하는 데에는 소모적인 구입을 하지 않는 것이 필요하다.

15 faculty   n. teachers, professors   ↔ students, undergraduates

[fǽkəlti] 교수진

The **faculty** at Harvard Law School was asked to create an exam for incoming students.
하버드 로스쿨의 교수진은 신입생들을 위한 시험을 출제하라는 요청을 받았다.

16 foregone conclusion   phr. certainty, matter of course   ↔ doubt, inconclusiveness

기정사실, 필연적 결론

The huge gap in the score made the outcome of the game a **foregone conclusion**.
큰 점수차로 인해 경기의 결과는 뻔한 결론이 되었다.

17 grievance   n. complaint, objection   ↔ compliment, praise

[grí:vəns] 불만

The renters filed a **grievance** against their landlord who refused to fix the plumbing in their apartment.
세입자들은 아파트의 배관 수리를 거부하는 집주인에게 불만을 제기했다.

18 impart   v. bestow, part with   ↔ hold back, retain

[impá:rt] 주다, 나누어 주다

The Pope made time to **impart** his blessings on the people of Rome during Christmas.
교황은 크리스마스 기간에 로마 시민에게 축복을 나누어 줄 시간을 냈다.

19 inexhaustible   adj. unlimited, tireless   ↔ restricted, enervated

[ìnigzɔ́:stəbl] 없어지지 않는, 지칠 줄 모르는

The mother ran after her **inexhaustible** son, who refused to take a nap.
어머니는 지칠 줄 모르는 아들을 쫓아다니고, 아들은 낮잠을 자려고 하지 않았다.

20 jargon   n. dialect, terminology   ↔ official language, standard language

[dʒá:rgən] 사투리, 전문 용어

The tourists had a hard time understanding the locals because they were not familiar with the **jargon**.
여행객들은 사투리에 익숙하지 않았기 때문에 현지인들을 이해하는 데 어려움을 겪었다.

21 **matriculate** v. enroll, enter ↔ graduate, get a degree

[mətríkjulèit] (대학에) 입학하다

He felt proud that after years of hard work in school he would be **matriculated** into Yale University.
그는 학교에서 수년간 열심히 공부한 후 예일대학교에 입학한다는 것에 대해 자부심을 느꼈다.

22 **nonexistent** adj. fictional, unreal ↔ actual, real

[nànigzístənt] 존재하지 않는

Elves are considered by many to be **nonexistent** but many children still believe in them.
많은 이들은 요정이 존재하지 않는다고 생각하지만, 많은 아이들은 여전히 그 존재를 믿는다.

23 **nuisance** n. annoyance, irritation ↔ delight, pleasure

[njú:sns] 골칫거리

Slippery ice on the roads is one **nuisance** in the winter months.
도로의 미끄러운 얼음은 겨울철의 골칫거리이다.

24 **observe** v. examine, abide by ↔ overlook, fail to notice

[əbzə́:rv] 준수하다

His family **observed** all of the major Jewish holidays by following the required rituals.
그의 가족은 필수 의식에 따라 유대교의 주요 명절을 모두 지켰다.

25 **perplex** v. confuse, confound ↔ clarify, make perfectly clear

[pərpléks] 당황하게 하다

He was **perplexed** by his friend's strange behavior at the party.
그는 파티에서 친구의 이상한 행동에 당황했다.

26 **prescription** n. formula, preparation

[priskrípʃən] 처방전

The doctor wrote Jake a **prescription** to help lessen his migraine headaches.
의사는 제이크에게 편두통 완화에 도움이 되는 처방전을 써주었다.

27 **reliable** adj. trustworthy, dependable ↔ deceptive, unreliable

[riláiəbl] 믿을 수 있는

Edith is a very **reliable** person who can always be counted on to help her friends in need.
이디스는 어려움에 처한 친구를 돕기 위해 항상 의지할 수 있는 매우 신뢰할 만한 사람이다.

28 resistance n. opposition, defiance ↔ compliance, assent

[rizístəns] 내성, 저항성

After taking the medicine for several months, he built up a **resistance** to the virus.
수개월간 약을 복용한 후, 그에게 바이러스에 대한 내성이 생겼다.

29 tactful adj. careful, prudent ↔ absent-minded, inconsiderate

[tǽktfəl] 눈치 있는, 재치 있는

You can always depend on Luke to give a **tactful** response to avoid offending anyone.
어떤 사람도 불쾌하지 않게 재치 있는 답변을 항상 루크에게 기대할 수 있다.

30 virtually adv. in essence, practically ↔ superficially, hardly

[vɚ́ːrtʃuəli] 사실상

All the preparations for the event left **virtually** nothing to chance.
행사의 모든 준비에 사실상 만전을 기했다.

DAILY QUIZ

1. **consensus** among the leaders • • a judgment
2. up to one's own **discretion** • • b independence
3. **discrimination** against a certain group • • c unlimited
4. grant **autonomy** • • d defiance
5. **contaminate** drinking water • • e terminology
6. **impart** knowledge • • f professors
7. a political **jargon** • • g agreement
8. **inexhaustible** resources • • h bestow
9. an outright **disobedience** • • i prejudice
10. a world-class **faculty** • • j pollute

ANSWERS 1. g 2. a 3. i 4. b 5. j 6. h 7. e 8. c 9. d 10. f

COMPREHENSIVE QUIZ

Day 25 & 26

1. The excessive stress from the work project was _____ by a bonus in the month's paycheck.
   ⓐ offset   ⓑ matriculated   ⓒ drafted   ⓓ inflicted

2. Cities often have one international airport and a separate _____ one.
   ⓐ domestic   ⓑ spontaneous   ⓒ belated   ⓓ nonexistent

3. Her _____ approach to the tense situation was the key to a truce between the government and rebel leaders.
   ⓐ detrimental   ⓑ extracurricular   ⓒ tactful   ⓓ nonexistent

4. He left his job of his own _____ to travel the world.
   ⓐ nuisance   ⓑ volition   ⓒ caste   ⓓ transcript

5. Being a(n) _____ reader, her dream is to work in a library.
   ⓐ evolutionary   ⓑ realistic   ⓒ proportional   ⓓ avid

6. The _____ of a manned mission to Mars is still years away because current technology is not developed enough.
   ⓐ feasibility   ⓑ discretion   ⓒ grievance   ⓓ larceny

7. We are going to have to skip dinner and go straight to see the movie because of time _____.
   ⓐ jargon   ⓑ disobedience   ⓒ prescription   ⓓ constraint

8. His mean behavior _____ his friends because he was usually very friendly.
   ⓐ emphasized   ⓑ perplexed   ⓒ improvised   ⓓ drafted

9. Countries _____ their unique cultures to draw in tourists.
   ⓐ contaminate   ⓑ inflict   ⓒ advertise   ⓓ envelop

10. He was a(n) _____ character who could die in the first five minutes of the movie.
    ⓐ expendable   ⓑ avid   ⓒ tactful   ⓓ reliable

Answers: p.341

Day 27

1 abdomen n.

[ǽbdəmən] 복부, 배

Doing sit-ups will strengthen the muscles in one's **abdomen**.
윗몸 일으키기를 하면 복부 근육이 강화될 것이다.

2 account¹ n. report, explanation

[əkáunt] 이야기, 보고

The reporter provided an eyewitness **account** of the recent earthquake.
기자는 최근 발생한 지진에 대한 목격자의 이야기를 제공했다.

3 account² n.

[əkáunt] 계좌

Ken had to open up a new bank **account** upon arriving to live in Korea.
켄은 한국에 거주하기 위해 오자마자 새로운 은행 계좌를 개설해야 했다.

4 affix v. attach, tack on   ↔ detach, tear off

[əfíks] 첨부하다, 붙이다

A couple of nails were used to **affix** the painting to the wall.
그림을 벽에 거는 데 못 두 개가 쓰였다.

5 all the rage phr. fashionable, the latest fad   ↔ out-of-style, old-fashioned

크게 유행하는

Corsets used to be **all the rage** in women's fashion in the West.
코르셋은 서양 여성 패션에서 한때 크게 유행했다.

6 amend v. alter, adjust   ↔ impair, go downhill

[əménd] 수정하다

The contract was **amended** to reflect some recent new developments.
최근 새로운 개발 사항을 반영하기 위해 계약이 수정되었다.

7 condensation   n. water buildup, precipitation   ↔ dehydration, lack of moisture

[kàndənséiʃən] 물방울, 응결

Water droplets on a cold window are an example of **condensation**.
차가운 창에 맺힌 물방울이 응결의 한 예이다.

8 cultivate   v. harvest, produce

[kʌ́ltəvèit] 재배하다, 경작하다

Farmers decide what crops to **cultivate** based on the type of soil available.
농부들은 이용할 수 있는 토양의 종류에 따라 재배할 작물을 결정한다.

9 discipline   n. field of study, specialty

[dísəplin] (학)과목

Universities offer many science **disciplines** for students to study.
대학교는 학생들이 공부할 많은 학과목을 제공한다.

10 dominate   v. rule, conquer   ↔ yield, surrender

[dάmənèit] 지배하다

The increasingly popular brand came to **dominate** its market.
갈수록 인기가 상승하는 브랜드가 시장을 지배하게 되었다.

11 duplicate   v. reproduce, repeat

[djúːplikèit] 복제하다, 두 번 되풀이하다

Famous statues are sometimes **duplicated** and the copies are sent to various museums.
유명 조각상들은 때로 복제되어 모조품들은 여러 박물관으로 보내진다.

12 dwelling   n. home, domicile

[dwélíŋ] 주거(지), 주소

Nomads have to carry their **dwellings** with them on their travels.
유목민은 이동 시 집을 함께 옮겨야 한다.

13 efficient   adj.

[ifíʃənt] 효율적인

Doing two things at once can be **efficient** but not always wise.
동시에 두 가지 일을 하는 것은 효율적일 수 있지만 항상 현명한 것은 아니다.

14 exaggerate　v. overstate, blow out of proportion　↔ minimize, play down

[igzǽdʒərèit] 과장하다

Exaggerating a truth can almost approach the level of telling a lie.
진실을 과장하는 것은 거짓말을 하는 것과 거의 다르지 않다.

15 exceptional　adj. phenomenal, uncommon

[iksépʃənl] 예외적인, 특별한

A genius is a person who possesses **exceptional** talents and abilities.
천재는 특별한 재능과 능력을 소유한 사람이다.

16 fertilize　v. inseminate, nourish

[fə́ːrtəlàiz] 수정시키다, 비료를 주다, 비옥하게 하다

The farmer wanted to make sure his land was **fertilized** so that he could plant corn to sell in the market.
농부는 시장에 팔 수 있는 옥수수를 심을 수 있도록 확실히 땅이 비옥하게 만들고자 했다.

17 functional　adj. working, operational　↔ malfunctioning, in pieces

[fʌ́ŋkʃənl] 기능상의, 가동되는

After dropping his cell phone on the floor, Robert immediately picked it up to check if it was **functional**.
로버트는 휴대 전화를 바닥에 떨어뜨린 후 바로 집어 들어 작동하는지 확인했다.

18 gaze　n. stare, peer

[géiz] 응시하다

The baby **gazed** at the stranger's face.
아기는 낯선 사람의 얼굴을 응시했다.

19 hectic　adj. frantic, chaotic　↔ calm, at a standstill

[héktik] 몹시 바쁜

Ginny was finally able to relax after the **hectic** week of planning for her best friend's birthday party.
지니는 단짝 친구의 생일 파티를 계획하면서 정신 없이 바쁜 한 주를 보낸 후 마침내 휴식을 취할 수 있었다.

20 indefinitely　adv. for a period of time with no fixed end

[indéfənitli] 무기한으로

After the couple's disagreement about having children, the date of their wedding was pushed back **indefinitely**.
아이를 갖는 것에 대해 두 사람의 의견 차이가 있은 후 결혼 날짜는 무기한 뒤로 미뤄졌다.

21. infrastructure n. foundation, framework

[ínfrəstrʌ̀ktʃər] 사회 기반 시설

After the war, England's **infrastructure** was destroyed and had to be rebuilt.
종전 후 영국의 사회 기반 시설은 파괴되었고 재건되어야 했다.

22. myriad adj. countless, innumerable ↔ measurable, quantifiable

[míriəd] 수많은, 무수한

There are a **myriad** kinds of salmon swimming upstream annually in order to breed.
매년 알을 낳기 위해 상류로 헤엄치는 수많은 종류의 연어가 있다.

23. organism n. living thing, entity ↔ inanimate object, lifeless matter

[ɔ́:rgənìzm] 생명체, 유기체

The scientists discovered a new **organism** living at the bottom of the ocean.
과학자들은 해저에 사는 새로운 생명체를 발견했다.

24. permeate v. spread throughout, pervade

[pə́:rmièit] 스며들다, 침투하다

As Dolly entered through the door, her strong perfume **permeated** the room.
돌리가 문으로 들어오자 강한 향수 냄새가 방으로 스며들었다.

25. polarization n. division, divergence ↔ union, convergence

[pòulərizéiʃən] 대립

The **polarization** between the liberals and conservatives grew so large that they could not agree on even the simplest matters.
자유주의자와 보수주의자간의 대립이 매우 심해져서 그들은 가장 간단한 사안에 대해서도 합의할 수 없었다.

26. publicize v. promote, make known ↔ conceal, suppress

[pʌ́bləsàiz] 광고하다, 알리다

The real estate agents used the newspaper to **publicize** the houses that were up for sale.
부동산 중개인은 신문을 이용해서 매물로 나온 집을 광고했다.

27. resourceful adj. imaginative, inventive

[ri:zɔ́:rsfəl] 재치개[수완이] 비상한

June is a **resourceful** young woman who is able to sell her handmade jewelry to support her family.
준은 가족을 부양하기 위해서 수제 장신구를 판매할 수 있는 수완이 좋은 젊은 여성이다.

28 submerge　v. go under, descend　↔ come up, surface

[səbmə́:rdʒ] 물에 잠그다

Anthony **submerged** himself underwater while his friend timed how long he was able to hold his breath.
앤소니는 얼마나 오래 숨을 참을 수 있는지 친구가 시간을 재는 동안 잠수했다.

29 transgress　v. disobey, violate　↔ behave, observe

[trænzgrés] 어기다

He **transgressed** his parent's wishes by enlisting in the army.
그는 군에 입대함으로써 부모님의 바람을 어겼다.

30 vaccinate　v. immunize, inoculate

[vǽksənèit] 예방 접종하다

Elementary schools usually **vaccinate** their students for childhood diseases.
초등학교에서는 어린이 질병에 대비해서 학생들에게 예방 접종을 한다.

DAILY QUIZ

1 **affix** a stamp　　　　　　　　　　　a promote
2 a brief **account**　　　　　　　　　　 b attach
3 **dominate** the world　　　　　　　　 c continually
4 an academic **discipline**　　　　　　 d overstate
5 **publicize** a new product　　　　　　e repeat
6 **polarization** of wealth　　　　　　　f field of study
7 postponed **indefinitely**　　　　　　 g harvest
8 **exaggerate** the importance　　　　 h rule
9 **duplicate** her achievements　　　　i division
10 **cultivate** vegetables　　　　　　　 j report

ANSWERS　1. b　2. j　3. h　4. f　5. a　6. i　7. c　8. d　9. e　10. g

Day 28

28 | 58

1 apprentice   n. student, novice   ↔ teacher, mentor

[əpréntis] 도제, 제자

Apprentices in the old days used to learn how to do a job by assisting a workman.
과거에 견습생들은 장인을 도와 일을 하는 방법을 배우곤 했다.

2 austere   adj. self-denying, plain   ↔ extravagant, indulgent

[ɔːstíər] 소박한, 간소한

An **austere** lifestyle has few possessions and even fewer luxuries.
금욕적인 생활 양식은 소유물이 거의 없고 사치품은 더더욱 소유하지 않는 것이다.

3 biography   n.

[baiɑ́grəfi] 자서전

Famous persons have their life stories told in a **biography**.
유명한 사람들은 자서전에 자신의 삶의 이야기를 기술하게 한다.

4 circa   prep. about, around

[sə́ːrkə] ~경, 약

The primitive sculpture is dated to ancient Greece **circa** 1,300 BC.
초기 조각은 기원전 1300년경 고대 그리스 시대까지 거슬러 올라간다.

5 coherent   adj. understandable, organized   ↔ unclear, incoherent

[kouhíərənt] 논리 정연한, 응집성의

To have a **coherent** argument is to have every point make sense with each other.
논리 정연한 논쟁을 한다는 것은 모든 요점이 서로 의미가 통하게 한다는 것이다.

6 consequence   n. result, effect   ↔ cause, origin

[kɑ́nsəkwèns] 결과

Success is the **consequence** of right planning and proper effort.
성공은 올바른 계획과 타당한 노력의 결과이다.

7 criterion n. standard, measure

[kraitíəriən] 기준

A fair **criterion** is needed to judge anything accurately and objectively.
어떤 것이라도 정확하고 객관적으로 판단하려면 공정한 기준이 필요하다.

8 deft adj. adroit, nimble ↔ clumsy, unskillful

[deft] 날렵한, 재빠른

The expert swordsman displayed **deft** use of his instrument.
전문 검술가는 자신의 날렵한 검 솜씨를 발휘했다.

9 diagonal adj.

[daiǽgənl] 대각선의

The bishop in chess can only move in **diagonal** lines, never forward or sideways.
체스에서 비숍은 절대 앞이나 옆으로 움직일 수 없고 대각선 방향으로만 움직일 수 있다.

10 discount v. ignore, disregard ↔ acknowledge, pay attention to

[dískaunt] 무시하다, 감소시키다

One rule of thumb is to **discount** complex explanations and use the simple ones.
한 가지 경험 법칙은 복잡한 설명을 줄이고 쉬운 설명을 쓰는 것이다.

11 duct n. pipe, passage

[dʌ́kt] 도관

A kitchen fan directs smoke from cooking through a **duct** to the outside.
주방의 송풍기는 조리로 생긴 연기를 도관을 통해 밖으로 내보낸다.

12 eclipse n. concealment, shading

[iklíps] 식(蝕)

A lunar **eclipse** happens when the earth lies between the sun and the moon.
지구가 해와 달 사이에 놓일 때 월식이 일어난다.

13 execute v. perform, carry out ↔ abandon, disregard

[éksikjù:t] 실행하다, 집행하다

The President's main duty is to **execute** the laws made by the national legislature.
대통령의 주된 직무는 국가 입법 기관이 제정한 법을 집행하는 것이다.

14 fallacy n. mistake, misinterpretation

[fǽləsi] 그릇된 생각

The earth being the center of the universe was once believed to be true but is now known as a **fallacy**.
지구가 우주의 중심이라는 것은 한때 진리로 여겨졌지만 이제는 틀린 생각으로 알려져 있다.

15 fiscal adj.

[fískəl] 회계의, 재정상의

The accounting department labored over the annual report that summarized their **fiscal** year.
경리부는 회사의 회계 연도를 요약한 연례 보고서 작업에 힘썼다.

16 gravitational adj. attractive, pulling ↔ repulsive, repelling

[græ̀vətéiʃənl] 중력의

Some people wrongly believe that the **gravitational** pull of the moon produces tsunamis.
어떤 사람들은 달의 인력으로 쓰나미가 발생한다고 잘못 믿고 있다.

17 hire v. use, commission

[háiər] 빌리다

The parents of the groom **hired** a limo service to take the bride to the wedding.
신랑의 부모는 신부를 결혼식장에 데려가기 위해 리무진을 빌렸다.

18 intercept v. hijack, make off with

[ìntərsépt] 가로채다, 차단하다

The soldier **intercepted** the battle plans from the enemy to give to his general.
군인은 전투 계획을 적으로부터 가로채 장군에게 주었다.

19 interlude n. break, interruption

[íntərlùːd] 막간, 사이

The funny **interlude** seemed inappropriate for the serious play.
익살맞은 막간은 진지한 연극에 부적절한 것 같았다.

20 modified adj. changed, adjusted ↔ untouched, unaltered

[mάdəfàid] 변경된, 수정된

George's counselor gave him a **modified** schedule because of his job after school.
조지의 상담 교사는 방과 후 그의 일 때문에 변경된 일정표를 주었다.

21 on the dot phr. right on time, on schedule

정확히 그 시간에

Despite the pouring rain, the annual triathlon started **on the dot**.
폭우에도 불구하고 매년 열리는 3종 경기가 제시간에 시작됐다.

22 pertinent adj. relevant, related ↔ unsuitable, irrelevant

[pə́ːrtənənt] 적절한

The police asked the public to report any **pertinent** information related to the kidnapping of the young boy.
경찰은 어린 소년의 유괴와 관련 있는 적절한 정보가 있으면 경찰에 신고하라고 민중에게 요청했다.

23 placid adj. calm, peaceful ↔ agitated, excited

[plǽsid] 잔잔한, 평온한

The **placid** lake looked beautiful and peaceful under the stars.
평온한 호수는 별빛 아래 아름답고 평화롭게 보였다.

24 predominantly adv. mostly, mainly

[pridámənəntli] 대부분

It was **predominantly** women who attended the fashion show for cocktail dresses.
칵테일 드레스 패션쇼에 참석한 사람들 대부분은 여성이었다.

25 profound adj. deep, emotional ↔ mild, moderate

[prəfáund] 심오한, 깊은

After reaching the top of Mount Everest, Jacob described his achievement as a **profound** experience.
에베레스트 산 정상에 오른 후 제이콥은 자신의 성취를 심오한 경험이라고 기술했다.

26 pullout n. retreat, withdrawal

[púlàut] 철수

After the war ended, the military troops were ordered to begin a **pullout** from the country.
종전 후 군대는 그 나라에서 철수하기 시작하라는 명령을 받았다.

27 reproduce v. copy, duplicate ↔ destroy, erase

[rìːprədjúːs] 복사하다, 복제하다

He was asked to **reproduce** the documents to give to the lawyers because the original had to be kept in the office.
원본을 사무실에 보관해야 했기 때문에, 그는 서류를 복사해서 변호사에게 주라는 요구를 받았다.

28 sedated adj. calm, peaceful ↔ noisy, rowdy

[sidéitid] 차분한

He did not want to do anything exciting for his birthday so he had a small, **sedated** party.
그는 생일날 자극적인 어떤 일도 하고 싶지 않았기 때문에 차분한 작은 파티를 했다.

29 tantamount adj. equal, equivalent

[tǽntəmàunt] 동등한, 같은

Henna's angry glare at her husband was **tantamount** to hitting him in the face.
남편을 쏘아보는 헤나의 화난 눈길이 그의 얼굴을 때리는 것 같았다.

30 unleash v. release, let loose ↔ restrain, confine

[ʌnlíːʃ] (~의 가죽끈을) 풀다, 해방하다

Some towns do not allow dog owners to **unleash** their dogs in public.
어떤 도시에서는 개 주인이 공공장소에서 개를 풀어놓는 것이 허용되지 않는다.

DAILY QUIZ

1	**consequence** of an action	a	release
2	**pertinent** to the investigation	b	carry out
3	the **criterion** used to judge	c	changed
4	**unleash** the caged animals	d	pipe
5	the **placid** sky	e	effect
6	**intercept** the ball	f	standard
7	the **modified** plan	g	make off with
8	**execute** the plans	h	nimble
9	air conditioning **duct**	i	related
10	the **deft** professional	j	calm

ANSWERS 1. e   2. i   3. f   4. a   5. j   6. g   7. c   8. b   9. d   10. h

COMPREHENSIVE QUIZ — Day 27 & 28

1. Her musical skills were so _____ that she was asked to play with symphonies all around the world.
   ⓐ exceptional ⓑ efficient ⓒ functional ⓓ tantamount

2. They were able to keep the whale _____ while they freed it from the net.
   ⓐ resourceful ⓑ coherent ⓒ sedated ⓓ modified

3. His charm attracted people like the _____ pull of a planet.
   ⓐ diagonal ⓑ austere ⓒ fiscal ⓓ gravitational

4. Lawmakers will _____ the bill before they bring the final version to a vote.
   ⓐ hire ⓑ cultivate ⓒ transgress ⓓ amend

5. The family decided to move to the country in order to escape the _____ city life.
   ⓐ hectic ⓑ myriad ⓒ deft ⓓ placid

6. The smell of freshly baked cookies _____ the whole house.
   ⓐ reproduced ⓑ permeated ⓒ unleashed ⓓ fertilized

7. Most scientists _____ the possibility that life could exist on Mars.
   ⓐ duplicate ⓑ discount ⓒ vaccinate ⓓ intercept

8. The people who are watching that action movie are _____ male teenagers who appreciate fancy stunts.
   ⓐ indefinitely ⓑ resourceful ⓒ predominantly ⓓ discipline

9. She was able to set aside time from work to _____ her hobbies such as gardening and painting.
   ⓐ cultivate ⓑ exaggerate ⓒ execute ⓓ transgress

10. They spent a month in training getting to know each other so that they can move as a(n) _____ team.
    ⓐ myriad ⓑ coherent ⓒ austere ⓓ sedated

Answers: p.341

Day 29

1. adroit adj. skillful, expert ↔ unskilled, inept

[ədrɔ́it] 노련한

The seasoned pilot was **adroit** at flying the new plane.
경험이 많은 파일럿은 새 비행기를 조정하는 데 노련했다.

2. alliance n. coalition, federation ↔ separation, falling-out

[əláiəns] 동맹, 연합

The two nations formed an **alliance** for mutual benefit.
두 국가는 상호 이득을 위해 동맹을 맺었다.

3. altitude n. height, elevation ↔ depth, deepness

[ǽltətjùːd] 고도

The plane flew at such a high **altitude** that it was above the clouds.
비행기는 매우 높은 고도로 날아 구름 위에 있었다.

4. annul v. cancel, call off ↔ prolong, lengthen

[ənʌ́l] 취소하다

One of the first acts of the new leader was to **annul** the controversial ban.
새 지도자의 첫 조치 중 하나는 논란이 많은 금지 조항을 폐지하는 것이었다.

5. calligraphy n. artistic writing

[kəlígrəfi] 서예, 캘리그래피

Both beauty and written communication are the aim of **calligraphy**.
아름다움과 글을 통한 의사소통은 둘 다 서예의 목적이다.

6. crack down on phr. go after, quash ↔ sanction, support

엄중히 단속하다

Authorities decided to **crack down on** any illegal gambling going on.
당국은 진행 중인 모든 불법 도박을 엄중히 단속하기로 했다.

7 disperse   v. spread, scatter   ↔ assemble, gather

[dispə́:rs] 흩뜨리다, 해산시키다

Tear gas is used to **disperse** a crowd if the police fear that public safety is at risk.
최루탄은 경찰이 공공의 안전이 위험한 상태라고 염려할 때 군중을 해산시키기 위해 사용된다.

8 divine   adj. godly, heavenly   ↔ worldly, earthly

[diváin] 신성한

Religious books and scriptures talk about the **divine** nature of God.
종교 서적과 성서는 신의 신성에 대해 이야기한다.

9 eddy   n. vortex, swirl

[édi] 회오리, 소용돌이

The rocks in the river caused swirls and **eddies** in the water.
강에 있는 바위가 물에 소용돌이를 일으켰다.

10 enthusiastically   adv. ardently, cheerfully

[inθù:ziǽstikəli] 열광적으로, 열중하여

The crowds **enthusiastically** applauded the politician's call for reform.
군중은 정치인의 개혁 요구에 열렬히 환호했다.

11 filial   adj.   ↔ parental

[fíliəl] 자식의

Parents expect **filial** obedience from their children whose duty is to listen and show respect.
부모는 경청하고 존경을 표해야 하는 의무가 있는 자녀에게 자식으로서의 복종을 기대한다.

12 grossly   adv. overly, downright

[gróusli] 지독히, 극도로

The actress was disappointed by the **grossly** inaccurate media portrayal of her divorce.
여배우는 자신의 이혼에 대한 매체의 대단히 부정확한 기술에 실망했다.

13 herald   v. announce, proclaim

[hérəld] 고지하다, ~의 예고를 하다

According to the Bible, the birth of Jesus was **heralded** by the angels.
성경에 의하면 예수의 탄생은 천사들에 의해 예고되었다.

14 impact n. impression, influence

[ímpækt] 영향

The invention of the car has made a tremendous **impact** on modern society.
자동차의 발명은 현대 사회에 중대한 영향을 미쳤다.

15 infer v. guess, surmise

[infə́ːr] 추론하다, 추측하다

He **inferred** that she was angry after receiving the silent treatment.
그는 그녀가 무시를 당하고 화가 났다고 추측했다.

16 instability n. imbalance, fluctuation ↔ constancy, stability

[ìnstəbíləti] 불안정

For many years, Iraq has suffered **instability** as the people have tried to build a working government.
국민들이 일하는 정부를 세우려 했기 때문에 이라크는 오랫동안 불안정을 겪었다.

17 mobility n. flexibility, adjustability ↔ rigidity, inelasticity

[moubíləti] 유동성, 이동

There is an opportunity for upward **mobility** of class in the United States if one is willing to work hard.
미국에서는 열심히 일하고자 한다면 신분 상승의 기회가 있다.

18 nominal adj. honorary, in name only ↔ actual, real

[námənl] 명목적인, 명목상의

The Queen of England is the **nominal** head of state, but the real power lies with the Prime Minister.
영국 여왕은 명목상 국가 수반이지만 실질적인 권한은 수상에게 있다.

19 noxious adj. toxic, poisonous ↔ healthy, pure

[nákʃəs] 유해한, 불건전한

Sitting in traffic can expose one not only to boredom but also to **noxious** fumes.
차량이 지나다니는 곳에 앉아 있으면 지루할 뿐 아니라 유해한 매연에 노출될 수 있다.

20 overshadow v. eclipse, reduce

[òuvərʃǽdou] 그늘지게 하다, 무색하게 하다

Pamela felt **overshadowed** by her older sister who always had better grades and more friends.
파멜라는 항상 더 좋은 점수를 받고 친구가 더 많은 언니의 그늘에 가려진다고 느꼈다.

21 pervasive adj. common, widespread ↔ limited, restricted

[pərvéisiv] 만연하는

The need to be thin is **pervasive** in American culture where many women have developed eating disorders.
많은 여성들이 섭식 장애를 가진 미국 문화에서는 마르려는 욕구가 만연하다.

22 potential n. possibility, capability

[pəténʃəl] 잠재력

Koby was a good basketball player and was recruited by the university because of his **potential**.
코비는 우수한 농구 선수로, 잠재력으로 인해 대학교에 스카우트되었다.

23 queue n. line, file

[kjúː] (대기하는) 줄

The cashier asked the crowd to form a **queue** so that the purchases could be done in order.
출납원은 구매가 질서 있게 이루어지도록 사람들에게 줄을 서라고 요청했다.

24 remarkably adv. exceptionally, extraordinarily ↔ commonly, insignificantly

[rimáːrkəbli] 두드러지게, 매우

Ellen was praised by her parents for being **remarkably** smart after winning first place at the science fair.
엘렌은 과학 박람회에서 일등을 한 후 부모님으로부터 매우 똑똑하다는 칭찬을 받았다.

25 render v. make, deliver

[réndər] ~을 …하게 하다

Elijah **rendered** the thief unconscious by hitting him over the head with a baseball bat.
일라이저는 야구 방망이로 도둑의 머리를 때려 의식을 잃게 했다.

26 spectrum n. range, scale

[spéktrəm] 범위, 폭넓은 영역

People in the United States hold a broad **spectrum** of political views that are reflected in the votes.
미국인들은 투표에 반영되는 폭넓은 정치적 견해를 가지고 있다.

27 translate v. interpret, decipher

[trænzléit] 번역하다, 해석하다

Juan was hired to **translate** Spanish into English for the ambassador of Mexico.
후안은 멕시코 대사를 위해 스페인어를 영어로 번역하도록 고용되었다.

28 utter¹   v. say, state

[ʌ́tər] 입 밖에 내다, 말하다

Only priests **utter** the words in a sacred text used in religious services.
사제들만이 예배에서 사용되는 성전 본문의 단어를 입 밖에 낼 수 있다.

29 utter²   adj. sheer, absolute

[ʌ́tər] 완전한, 철저한

There was **utter** disappointment when the competition ended too easily.
경쟁이 너무 쉽게 끝났을 때 엄청나게 실망했다.

30 void   adj. useless, invalid   ↔ meaningful, valid

[vɔ́id] 무효의

Coupons after their expiration dates are null and **void** and cannot be used.
만기일이 지난 쿠폰은 무효가 되어 사용할 수 없다.

DAILY QUIZ

1. **herald** the second coming
2. from a high **altitude**
3. the unending **queue**
4. **enthusiastically** play the game
5. huge **impact** on his life
6. the **void** gift certificate
7. a strong **alliance**
8. **remarkably** skilled performance
9. was **grossly** misinformed
10. **instability** of the stock market

- a invalid
- b impression
- c federation
- d exceptionally
- e overly
- f elevation
- g line
- h cheerfully
- i announce
- j fluctuation

ANSWERS   1. i   2. f   3. g   4. h   5. b   6. a   7. c   8. d   9. e   10. j

Day 30

1. allocate v. assign, designate

[ǽləkèit] 할당하다

A company must **allocate** its resources well to maximize its effectiveness.
회사는 효과를 극대화하기 위해 자사의 자원을 잘 할당해야 한다.

2. around the clock phr. continually, nonstop

24시간 내내

The student worked **around the clock** to finish the project on time.
학생은 프로젝트를 제시간에 완료하기 위해 24시간 내내 작업했다.

3. assimilate v. conform, intermix ↔ reject, not adapt

[əsíməlèit] 동화하다

Immigrants to a new country usually start to **assimilate** into the culture.
새로운 나라에 오는 이민자들은 보통 그 나라의 문화에 동화되기 시작한다.

4. bleach v. whiten, lighten ↔ darken, blacken

[bli:tʃ] 표백하다, 바래지게 하다

Long exposure to sunlight can **bleach** and fade the colors of objects.
장시간 햇빛 노출은 물체를 표백해 색을 바래게 할 수 있다.

5. cite v. quote, point out

[sáit] 인용하다, 언급하다

The professor **cited** many examples in the documents to prove his point.
교수는 자신의 주장을 입증하기 위해 문서에 많은 예를 인용했다.

6. colleague n. associate, coworker ↔ enemy, opponent

[káli:g] 동료

The **colleagues** all went out for dinner after work.
퇴근 후 동료들은 모두 저녁 먹으러 나갔다.

7 conspicuous adj. distinct, obvious   ↔ hidden, inconspicuous

[kənspíkjuəs] 이목을 끄는, 현저한

There was a **conspicuous** noise that made everyone pay attention.
모든 사람들을 주목하게 한 튀는 소음이 있었다.

8 declaration n. assertion, pronouncement

[dèkləréiʃən] 선언(문), 발표

The **Declaration** of Independence told England that America wanted to be a free nation.
독립 선언은 미국이 자유 국가가 되길 원한다는 것을 영국에게 알렸다.

9 description n. information, explanation

[diskrípʃən] 설명, 묘사

Online shoppers can learn about a product by reading its **description** on a website.
온라인 쇼핑객들은 웹 사이트에 있는 설명을 읽고 제품에 대해서 알 수 있다.

10 domain n. realm, jurisdiction

[douméin] 영역

The ultimate questions about life are considered not in the **domain** of science.
인생에 대한 궁극적인 질문은 과학의 영역에서 고려 대상이 아니다.

11 emancipate n. set free, liberate   ↔ bind, confine

[imǽsəpèit] 해방시키다

Abraham Lincoln had a difficult time defending his plans to **emancipate** the slaves.
에이브러햄 링컨은 노예를 해방시키려는 계획을 변호하는 데 어려움을 겪었다.

12 entanglement n. complication, involvement   ↔ simplicity, disentanglement

[intǽŋglmənt] 복잡해진 것

They had a long talk to reach an understanding and avoid further **entanglements**.
그들은 타협을 보고 일이 더 복잡해지는 것을 피하기 위해 오랫동안 이야기했다.

13 function n. gathering, party

[fʌ́ŋkʃən] 행사

Martha was excited to see her friends who came to the **function** where she was receiving her award.
마사는 자신이 상을 받는 행사에 온 친구들을 만나 신이 났다.

14 glossary   n. dictionary, word index

[glásəri] 소사전, 용어집

Mrs. Thompson explained to her students that they could find the definition of words they were reading in the **glossary**.
톰슨 선생님은 학생들에게 읽고 있는 단어의 의미를 용어집에서 찾을 수 있다고 설명했다.

15 hail   v. praise, glorify   ↔ condemn, criticize

[héil] 맞이하다, 환영하다

Oprah Winfrey is loved by her audience and **hailed** as the queen of television.
오프라 윈프리는 시청자들로부터 사랑을 받고 있고, TV의 여왕으로 환호받는다.

16 incident   n. episode, event

[ínsədənt] 일어난 일, 사건

Tracy tried to explain to her parents the **incident** that occurred in her class where she got hit.
트레이시는 자신이 매를 맞은 수업 중에 일어난 일에 대해 부모님께 설명하려고 애를 썼다.

17 interpretation   n. explanation, analysis

[intə̀ːrprətèiʃən] 해석

The English teacher asked his students to work on the **interpretation** of the poem.
영어 교사는 학생들에게 시의 해석에 대해 공부하라고 했다.

18 lawsuit   n. accusation, claim

[lɔ́ːsùːt] 소송, 고소

She brought a **lawsuit** against the company that paid her less for the same work done by her male colleagues.
그녀는 남성 동료가 한 것과 동일한 일에 대해 자신에게 급료를 적게 지불한 회사를 상대로 소송을 제기했다.

19 materialistic   adj. greedy, money-oriented   ↔ spiritual, nonphysical

[mətìəriəlístik] 물질주의적인

The Nobel Peace Prize winner thought that people are becoming more and more **materialistic**.
노벨 평화상 수상자는 사람들이 점점 더 물질주의적으로 변해 가고 있다고 생각했다.

20 moral   adj. ethical, righteous   ↔ wicked, corrupt

[mɔ́ːrəl] 도덕적인

When she saw her classmate cheat on the test, she felt a **moral** obligation to tell her teacher.
그녀는 반 친구가 시험에서 부정행위를 하는 것을 보고, 선생님께 말하는 것이 도덕적인 의무라고 생각했다.

21. optimistic   adj. positive, hopeful   ↔ negative, pessimistic

[àptəmístik] 낙관적인

Lenny is a very **optimistic** person who always has something good to say about everyone.
레니는 언제나 모든 사람에 대해서 좋은 말을 하는 아주 낙관적인 사람이다.

22. pious   adj. religious, devoted   ↔ ungodly, sinful

[páiəs] 독실한

He is a very **pious** man who has decided to become a missionary in Africa.
그는 아프리카 선교사가 되기로 결심한 매우 독실한 사람이다.

23. potent   adj. powerful, forceful   ↔ weak, impotent

[póutnt] 강한

She was disgusted at the **potent** smell coming from the public bathroom at the park.
그녀는 공원에 있는 공중 화장실에서 나오는 강한 냄새가 역겨웠다.

24. prevail   v. triumph, overcome   ↔ surrender, succumb

[privéil] 이기다

Scott's basketball team was considered the underdogs going into the game, but they **prevailed** and won the championships.
스콧의 농구 팀은 시합에 참가하는 약체로 여겨졌지만, 승리하여 우승을 차지했다.

25. profitable   adj. successful, money-making   ↔ disadvantageous, unprofitable

[práfitəbl] 수익성이 있는, 이익이 되는

It took over a year for his boutique to become **profitable** and make some money.
그의 양품점이 수익을 내고 돈을 웬만큼 벌기까지는 일년 이상이 걸렸다.

26. respectively   adv. individually, correspondingly

[rispéktivli] 각각

Angela was extremely proud when her sons Steven and Simon got into Stanford and Princeton, **respectively**.
앤젤라는 아들 스티븐과 사이먼이 각각 스탠퍼드와 프린스턴 대학교에 입학했을 때 무척 자랑스러웠다.

27. streamlined   adj. aerodynamic, simplified

[strí:mlàind] 유선형의, 간결한

The company produced **streamlined** cars to make them more affordable and easier to drive.
회사는 좀 더 알맞은 가격에 운전하기 더 쉬운 유선형 자동차를 생산했다.

28 **sustenance** n. food, nourishment

[sʌ́stənəns] 영양, 자양물

Most mothers nurse their newborn babies with their own milk in order to provide **sustenance**.
대부분의 어머니는 영양을 공급하기 위해 신생아에게 모유를 먹인다.

29 **tradeoff** n. compromise, settlement

[trèidɔ́ːf] 타협, 거래

Sonia and Geoff decided to make a **tradeoff** by spending the Thanksgiving holidays with his parents and Christmas with hers.
소니아와 제프는 추수 감사절은 제프의 부모님과, 성탄절은 소니아의 부모님과 함께 보내는 것으로 타협하기로 했다.

30 **vain** adj. useless, pointless ↔ fruitful, successful

[véin] 헛된, 무익한

It was a **vain** effort to try to recover his good name after the scandal.
스캔들이 있은 후 명성을 되찾으려는 그의 노력은 헛된 것이었다.

DAILY QUIZ

1	the lion's **domain**	a	event
2	often **cite** famous authors	b	triumph
3	the **profitable** business	c	coworker
4	a most unusual **incident**	d	quote
5	**allocate** hard drive space	e	realm
6	**optimistic** despite failure	f	claim
7	work with a **colleague**	g	assign
8	good guys always **prevail**	h	successful
9	a **vain** attempt	i	positive
10	a copyright **lawsuit**	j	useless

ANSWERS 1. e   2. d   3. h   4. a   5. g   6. i   7. c   8. b   9. j   10. f

COMPREHENSIVE QUIZ — Day 29 & 30

1. Zack was able to _____ from her smiling face that things went well.
   ⓐ prevail　　ⓑ infer　　ⓒ overshadow　　ⓓ annul

2. Witnesses were able to give a(n) _____ of the bank robber to the police.
   ⓐ altitude　　ⓑ description　　ⓒ glossary　　ⓓ sustenance

3. Even using one drop of this _____ hot sauce is guaranteed to make you cry.
   ⓐ profitable　　ⓑ filial　　ⓒ potent　　ⓓ divine

4. This café imports coffee beans from all over the world, so it offers a broad _____ of flavors.
   ⓐ spectrum　　ⓑ description　　ⓒ queue　　ⓓ colleague

5. With a(n) _____ pull of a rope, the expert was able to guide the sailboat around the rocks.
   ⓐ void　　ⓑ pious　　ⓒ noxious　　ⓓ adroit

6. The dentist will _____ your teeth to make them look whiter and cleaner.
   ⓐ bleach　　ⓑ allocate　　ⓒ assimilate　　ⓓ disperse

7. The company will _____ production to reduce cost and time.
   ⓐ herald　　ⓑ hail　　ⓒ streamline　　ⓓ translate

8. Lions need to _____ a group of prey before they can focus on capturing one.
   ⓐ utter　　ⓑ render　　ⓒ disperse　　ⓓ overshadow

9. I knew he had the _____ to become a professional soccer player ever since I saw him play in elementary school.
   ⓐ domain　　ⓑ potential　　ⓒ eddy　　ⓓ entanglement

10. Everyone had a different _____ of the abstract painting and spent the night arguing about what it meant.
    ⓐ tradeoff　　ⓑ incident　　ⓒ sustenance　　ⓓ interpretation

Answers: p.341

Day 31

1 accountable adj. answerable, liable ↔ blameless, unaccountable

[əkáuntəbl] 책임이 있는

A combination of factors was **accountable** for the failure of the operation.
여러 요인의 결합이 사업 실패의 원인이었다.

2 appointment n. assignment, employment

[əpɔ́intmənt] 임명

Presidents often make **appointments** to their cabinets and close advisors.
대통령은 종종 내각 및 측근 보좌관을 임명한다.

3 argument n. dispute, contention ↔ agreement, peace

[ɑ́ːrgjumənt] 논쟁

A third party can be called in to settle an **argument** if no progress is made.
진척이 없는 경우 논쟁 해결을 위해 제3자를 끌어들일 수 있다.

4 budding adj. beginning, promising ↔ dying, withering

[bʌ́diŋ] 신예의, 싹트기 시작한

The new employees were seen as **budding** talents in the industry.
신입 사원들은 업계에서 신예 인재로 보였다.

5 clout n. authority, influence ↔ ineffectiveness, uselessness

[kláut] 영향력

Politicians use their **clout** to gather support for their causes.
정치인은 자신의 대의에 대한 지지를 얻기 위해 영향력을 행사한다.

6 coalition n. union, alliance ↔ separation, division

[kòuəlíʃən] 연합

It was a **coalition** of various countries that won the war.
전쟁을 승리로 이끈 것은 여러 국가의 연합이었다.

7 component n. part, item ↔ whole, collective

[kəmpóunənt] 부품

They made sure to pack all the **components** of their equipment for the trip.
그들은 출장을 위한 모든 장비의 부품을 확실히 챙겼다.

8 deficiency n. inadequacy, insufficiency ↔ surplus, excess

[difíʃənsi] 부족, 결핍

Vitamin **deficiency** can lead to serious health effects or even death.
비타민 결핍은 심각한 건강 문제나 심지어 죽음까지도 초래할 수 있다.

9 distribution n. dispersal, partitioning ↔ collection, gathering

[dìstrəbjúːʃən] 분배, 배급

Hunger in the world can be blamed on poor **distribution** and not lack of food.
전 세계적인 굶주림은 식량 부족이 아니라 잘못된 식량 분배 때문이라고 할 수 있다.

10 dramatic adj. exciting, sensational ↔ ordinary, dull

[drəmǽtik] 극적인

The last-minute goal led to a **dramatic** win for the underdog team.
막판의 득점은 약체 팀의 극적인 승리로 이어졌다.

11 element n.

[éləmənt] 원소

The number of known chemical **elements** continues to grow.
알려진 화학 원소의 개수는 계속 늘고 있다.

12 exclusively adv. only, solely

[iksklúːsivli] 독점적으로, 오로지

A specialty store **exclusively** sells only one category of item.
전문점에서는 오로지 한 가지 범주에 드는 품목을 판매한다.

13 federal adj. national, central ↔ local, regional

[fédərəl] 연방 정부의

The **federal** government is attempting to pass an immigration policy that would satisfy all of the states.
연방 정부는 모든 주를 만족시킬 이민 정책을 통과시키려 하고 있다.

14 figure   n. character, personage

[fígjər] 인사, 인물

President Obama must always be aware of his actions and words because he is a public **figure**.
오바마 대통령은 공인이기 때문에 자신의 언행에 대해 항상 조심해야 한다.

15 homicide   n. murder, killing

[hάməsàid] 살인

The police investigated the **homicide** of the woman found dead at the park.
경찰은 공원에서 죽은 채로 발견된 여성의 살인 사건을 조사했다.

16 inconsistent   adj. contradictory, incongruent   ↔ steady, consistent

[ìnkənsístənt] 일관성이 없는, 일치하지 않는

Genie did not trust her father when he said he would pick her up after school because his words were often **inconsistent** with his actions.
지니는 아버지의 말이 행동과 자주 달랐기 때문에 방과 후 자신을 데리러 오겠다고 했을 때 믿지 않았다.

17 intensity   n. force, magnitude

[inténsəti] 세기, 강도

The **intensity** of the fire scared the campers who had to back away from the heat.
캠핑객들은 불의 세기에 겁이 나 불에서 물러서야 했다.

18 literally   adv. precisely, actually   ↔ figuratively, loosely

[lítərəli] 문자 그대로, 실제로

Phoebe took the statement **literally** and did not understand that it was a joke.
피비는 그 말을 문자 그대로 받아들여 농담이었다는 것을 이해하지 못했다.

19 measure   n. action, step   ↔ ignorance, inaction

[méʒər] 조치

The principal took the disciplinary **measure** of suspending the students for fighting on campus.
교장은 교내에서 싸움을 한 학생들을 정학시키는 징계 조치를 취했다.

20 negligent   adj. careless, lax   ↔ cautious, attentive

[néglidʒənt] 부주의한, 태만한

The parents were accused of being **negligent** for leaving their young child in the car alone while they went into the store.
부모는 상점에 간 사이 어린 아이를 홀로 차에 남겨 부주의로 기소되었다.

21. personify — v. embody, symbolize

[pərsánəfài] 의인화하다, 상징하다

She tried to be a good person as she strived to **personify** her hero, Mother Teresa.
그녀는 자신의 영웅인 테레사 수녀를 구현하려고 노력하면서 좋은 사람이 되고자 했다.

22. predetermined — adj. preset, prearranged ↔ unplanned, undetermined

[prì:ditə́:rmind] 미리 정해진

He had a **predetermined** answer to the question he knew the lawyer would ask.
그는 변호사가 물을 줄 알고 있었던 질문에 대해 미리 정해진 답변이 있었다.

23. premise — n. assumption, hypothesis ↔ fact, reality

[prémis] 전제

The new secretary took the job under the **premise** that she would have access to the company car and a yearly bonus.
신입 비서는 회사 차를 이용할 수 있고 매년 보너스를 받는다는 전제하에 일을 맡았다.

24. premises — n. property, vicinity

[premisiz] 구내, 부지

The boy was reluctant to go near the **premises** of his angry neighbor because he had been yelled at in the past.
화난 이웃이 예전에 그에게 고함을 친 적이 있기 때문에 소년은 그의 집에 가까이 가는 것을 꺼렸다.

25. prototype — n. sample, model

[próutətàip] 견본

The engineers first created a **prototype** of the robot before presenting it to the public.
엔지니어들은 로봇을 대중에게 선보이기 전에 우선 견본을 만들었다.

26. purchase — v. buy, pay for ↔ sell, put on sale

[pə́:rtʃəs] 구입하다

It is a good idea to **purchase** a gift within your budget.
예산 범위 내에서 선물을 구입하는 게 좋다.

27. rehearse — v. practice, go over

[rihə́:rs] 예행연습을 하다

He **rehearsed** his speech several times to make sure he was prepared to speak in front of the crowd.
그는 대중 앞에서 확실하게 연설할 준비가 되도록 여러 번 예행연습을 했다.

28 restraint   n. restriction, control   ↔ wildness, arousal

[ri:stréint] 자제, 통제

He showed incredible **restraint** when he did not hit back after being attacked.
그는 공격을 받고 되받아치지 않을 때 놀라운 자제력을 보였다.

29 safeguard   n. protection, security

[séifgà:rd] 안전장치

The factory machines have **safeguards** in place that protect workers from harm.
공장 기계에는 작업자들을 위험으로부터 보호하는 안전장치가 적소에 있다.

30 unpredictable   adj. erratic, volatile   ↔ expected, foreseeable

[ʌ̀npridíktəbl] 예측할 수 없는

Unpredictable weather is one reason sports stadiums are covered with a dome.
예측할 수 없는 날씨가 스포츠 경기장이 둥근 지붕으로 덮여 있는 한 가지 이유이다.

DAILY QUIZ

1. the **dramatic** conclusion • • a model
2. eating without **restraint** • • b force
3. a **federal** investigation • • c buy
4. **literally** knocked me out • • d exciting
5. the **intensity** of her voice • • e insufficiency
6. eat **exclusively** raw vegetables • • f control
7. **purchase** a new car • • g national
8. a **budding** relationship • • h actually
9. a protein **deficiency** • • i only
10. the **prototype** stealth jet • • j beginning

ANSWERS   1. d   2. f   3. g   4. h   5. b   6. i   7. c   8. j   9. e   10. a

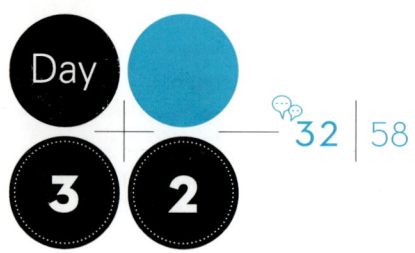

Day 32

1 adjourn   adj. suspend, postpone   ↔ continue, go on

[ədʒə́ːrn] 중단하다, 휴정하다

The case has been **adjourned** until further notice.
사건은 추후 통지가 있을 때까지 중단되었다.

2 approach   n. perspective, method

[əpróutʃ] 접근법, 방법

A rethinking of a problem and a fresh **approach** can help in finding a solution.
문제를 다시 생각하고 새롭게 접근하면 해법을 찾는 데 도움이 될 수 있다.

3 astute   adj. intelligent, perceptive   ↔ ignorant, unintelligent

[əstjúːt] 눈치 빠른

An **astute** person knows the deeper meanings behind the facts.
눈치 빠른 사람은 사실 이면에 있는 더 깊은 의미를 안다.

4 auxiliary   adj. accessory, supplementary   ↔ main, primary

[ɔːgzíljəri] 보조의, 예비의

Computer enthusiasts often use **auxiliary** products that attach to their hardware.
컴퓨터에 열성적인 사람들은 하드웨어에 부착하는 보조 장비를 흔히 사용한다.

5 bemused   adj. confused, absent-minded   ↔ perceptive, clear-headed

[bimjúːzd] 어리벙벙한

He offered a **bemused** smile at all their jokes and humorous comments.
그는 그들의 모든 농담과 해학적인 논평에 어리벙벙한 미소를 보였다.

6 brilliant   adj. excellent, vivid   ↔ normal, dull

[bríljənt] 훌륭한, (색이) 밝은

Pretending to retreat and then attacking was a **brilliant** military strategy.
후퇴하는 척하다가 공격하는 것은 훌륭한 군사 전략이었다.

7 condescend v. lower, demean

[kàndəsénd] (자기를) 낮추다

He did not allow himself to **condescend** to their level in the discussion.
그는 토의에서 자신을 그들 수준으로 낮추는 것을 허용하지 않았다.

8 curb v. reduce, restrict ↔ encourage, foster

[kə́ːrb] 억제하다

Rules and regulations are made to **curb** undesirable behavior.
규칙과 규정은 바람직하지 않은 행동을 억제하기 위해 만들어진다.

9 devoid of phr. empty of, vacant of ↔ full of, filled with

전혀 없는, 결여된

Scientists believe that the other planets are **devoid of** any complex life forms.
과학자들은 다른 행성에는 복잡한 형태의 생물이 없다고 생각한다.

10 dichotomy n. difference, duality

[daikútəmi] 양분, 이분법

The wealth in the world shows a **dichotomy** between countries in the north and south.
세상의 부는 북쪽과 남쪽에 있는 국가들에 양분되어 있다.

11 downsize v. reduce, cut down ↔ expand, grow

[dáunsàiz] 축소하다

Some companies must **downsize** if the scale of their business shrinks.
어떤 회사들은 사업이 축소되면 반드시 규모를 줄여야 한다.

12 equip v. arm, outfit

[ikwíp] 장비를 갖추다

Care was taken to **equip** the boat properly before going out to sea.
바다로 나가기 전에 보트 장비를 제대로 갖추기 위해서 주의를 기울였다.

13 exponent n. supporter, advocate ↔ enemy, opposition

[ikspóunənt] 옹호자

The author was an **exponent** of reducing government spending.
저자는 정부 지출 감축 옹호자였다.

14 famine   n. hunger, starvation

[fǽmin] 기근

Many African countries are suffering from **famine** after a drought that occurred for several years.
수년간 발생한 가뭄으로 인해 많은 아프리카 국가가 기근으로 고생하고 있다.

15 ferocious   adj. violent, vicious   ↔ gentle, tame

[fəróuʃəs] 사나운

The zoo closed its doors to the public after the escape of their most **ferocious** tiger.
가장 사나운 호랑이가 탈출한 뒤 동물원은 일반인 관람을 허용하지 않았다.

16 glacier   n. iceberg, ice mountain

[gléiʃər] 빙하

Some environmentalists worry about the destruction of the **glaciers** because the polar bears are losing their homes.
몇몇 환경 운동가들은 북극곰이 서식지를 잃고 있기 때문에 빙하의 붕괴를 우려하고 있다.

17 icon   n. representation, symbol

[áikɑn] 우상

Simon Bolivar is an **icon** to many people who are struggling to fight for independence.
시몬 볼리바르는 독립을 위해서 투쟁하는 많은 사람들의 우상이다.

18 inflation   n.   ↔ deflation

[infléiʃən] 인플레이션

The generous employer decided to give a raise to his employees to adjust for **inflation**.
관대한 고용주는 인플레이션에 맞추기 위해 직원 급여를 인상하기로 했다.

19 intervene   v. interfere, come between   ↔ ignore, leave alone

[ìntərvíːn] 개입하다

Jill's family felt the need to **intervene** to stop her from abusing drugs.
질의 가족은 그녀가 약을 그만 남용하도록 개입해야 할 필요를 느꼈다.

20 marvel   v. wonder, be amazed   ↔ deride, put down

[mɑ́ːrvəl] 경탄하다, 놀라다

People all over the world come to China to **marvel** at the Great Wall that was built thousands of years ago.
전 세계 사람들은 중국에 와서 수천 년 전에 세워진 만리장성을 보고 경탄한다.

21 obnoxious   adj. offensive, horrid   ↔ pleasant, delightful

[əbnákʃəs] 불쾌한

Stella was irritated by the **obnoxious** man who kept yelling out the window of the bus.
스텔라는 버스 창문 밖으로 계속해서 고함을 지르는 불쾌한 남자 때문에 짜증이 났다.

22 patronize   v. sponsor, support

[péitrənàiz] 단골로 다니다

The couple **patronized** the restaurant every Saturday night where they had a special table reserved for them.
두 사람은 그들을 위한 특별석이 예약된 식당을 매주 토요일 밤 애용했다.

23 premeditated   adj. planned, thought-out   ↔ accidental, unintentional

[pri:médətèitid] 계획적인

Tony was sent to prison for the **premeditated** murder of his neighbor, a crime which he had been planning for months.
토니는 계획적으로 이웃을 살해한 혐의로 수감되었는데, 그는 범죄를 수개월 동안 계획했다.

24 projected   adj. estimated, predicted

[prádʒektid] 예상하는

The company's **projected** profits for their new product exceeded all expectations.
회사 신제품에 대한 예상 수익은 모든 기대치를 능가했다.

25 represent   v. symbolize, play the part

[rèprizént] 묘사하다, 상징하다

In the book, the car **represented** freedom for the main character who used it to drive off to a new life.
책에서 주인공이 새로운 삶을 시작하기 위해 떠나는 데 사용한 자동차는 자유를 상징했다.

26 settlement[1]   n. community, colony

[sétlmənt] 개척지, 정착지

The Jamestown **settlement** was an early British colony in the New World.
제임스타운 개척지는 신세계의 초기 영국 식민지였다.

27 settlement[2]   n. decision, conclusion   ↔ dispute, disagreement

[sétlmənt] 합의

The negotiators reached a compromise **settlement** that pleased everyone.
협상자들은 모든 사람을 만족시키는 합의에 이르렀다.

28 submit v. give, hand in ↔ withdraw, take back

[səbmít] 제출하다

He was told that there was a sales position open at the store, so he **submitted** an application for the job.
그는 상점에 판매직 자리가 났다는 말을 듣고 지원서를 제출했다.

29 trademark n.

[tréidmà:rk] 상표

The inventor made sure to register the **trademark** for his product so that it could not be used by anyone else.
발명가는 다른 사람이 사용할 수 없도록 자신의 제품 상표를 확실하게 등록했다.

30 verbatim adv. word for word, literally

[vəːrbéitəm] 글자 그대로

A transcript tries to record a conversation or dialogue **verbatim**.
필기록은 대화 내용을 글자 그대로 기록하고자 하는 것이다.

DAILY QUIZ

1 a **brilliant** artist
2 an **obnoxious** comment
3 **equip** the soldiers
4 drought and **famine**
5 **represent** the country
6 **intervene** to stop the fight
7 **curb** your enthusiasm
8 a **premeditated** murder
9 **downsize** military operations
10 **marvel** at the monuments

a planned
b restrict
c reduce
d offensive
e arm
f be amazed
g hunger
h excellent
i interfere
j symbolize

ANSWERS 1. h 2. d 3. e 4. g 5. j 6. i 7. b 8. a 9. c 10. f

COMPREHENSIVE QUIZ — Day 31 & 32

1. The policeman put on his bulletproof vest as a _____.
   ⓐ dichotomy ⓑ premise ⓒ restraint ⓓ safeguard

2. Actors must _____ their roles over and over again before important performances.
   ⓐ condescend ⓑ patronize ⓒ rehearse ⓓ curb

3. The mayor decided to take drastic _____ to lower the crime rate in the city.
   ⓐ measures ⓑ prototypes ⓒ trademarks ⓓ inflations

4. It is important to _____ your homework on time.
   ⓐ intervene ⓑ submit ⓒ personify ⓓ downsize

5. Sometimes, even a small puppy could become _____.
   ⓐ premeditated ⓑ ferocious ⓒ federal ⓓ inconsistent

6. The court will _____ until the end of this month.
   ⓐ adjourn ⓑ obnoxious ⓒ bemused ⓓ astute

7. "Be" and "do" are examples of _____ verbs.
   ⓐ negligent ⓑ accountable ⓒ auxiliary ⓓ projected

8. The CSI agents searched the _____ of the crime scene for evidence.
   ⓐ coalition ⓑ clout ⓒ figure ⓓ premises

9. The defense lawyer lost the case because he did not have enough proof to support his _____.
   ⓐ component ⓑ appointment ⓒ argument ⓓ exponent

10. Uneven _____ of wealth could cause a nation's economy to collapse.
    ⓐ distribution ⓑ restraint ⓒ homicide ⓓ element

Answers: p.341

Day 33 | 58

1 abyss   n. depth, chasm

[əbís] 심연

Deep-sea cameras record the conditions of life in the **abyss**.
심해 카메라는 심연에 사는 생물의 환경을 녹화한다.

2 adaptation¹   n. familiarization, adjustment

[ӕdəptéiʃən] 적응(력)

Successful animal species show good **adaptation** to their environments.
성공적으로 생존하는 동물종은 환경에 뛰어난 적응력을 보인다.

3 adaptation²   n.

[ӕdəptéiʃən] 각색

A movie **adaptation** of the best-selling book is in the works.
베스트셀러 도서의 영화 각색이 논의되고 있다.

4 annexation   n. takeover, addition   ↔ subtraction, detachment

[ӕnekséiʃən] 합병

The city considered **annexation** of its surrounding areas to grow in size and population.
시는 규모와 인구를 늘리기 위해 주변 지역의 합병을 고려했다.

5 augment   v. expand, boost   ↔ diminish, lessen

[ɔːgmént] 증대시키다

Machines can either replace or **augment** human capabilities.
기계는 인간의 능력을 대체하거나 증대시킬 수 있다.

6 assess   v. determine, evaluate

[əsés] 평가하다

One can **assess** the type of tree by looking at its characteristics.
나무의 특징을 보고 그 종류를 가늠할 수 있다.

7 board n. committee, council

[bɔːrd] 위원회

The members of the **board** voted to pass the new budget plan for the coming year.
위원회 위원들은 내년 예산 계획을 통과시키기 위해 투표했다.

8 capsize v. overturn, tip over

[kǽpsaiz] 전복하다, 뒤엎다

The storm at sea threatened to **capsize** all ships sailing at the time.
바다에서 폭풍이 당시 항해하는 모든 배를 전복시킬 우려가 있었다.

9 colloquial adj. informal, conversational   ↔ standard, formal

[kəlóukwiəl] 구어의

Colloquial words enter dictionaries only if they become commonly used.
구어체 단어들은 일반적으로 사용되는 경우에만 사전에 기재된다.

10 demonstrate v. show, display   ↔ conceal, hide

[démənstrèit] 보여주다, 발휘하다

The worker **demonstrated** quick thinking and leadership during the project.
작업자는 프로젝트 기간 동안 빠른 사고와 지도력을 발휘했다.

11 despicable adj. appalling, vile   ↔ honorable, respectable

[dispíkəbl] 야비한, 비열한

Hurting or killing a pet is looked upon as a **despicable** act of cruelty.
애완동물을 사냥하거나 죽이는 일은 야비한 학대 행위로 간주된다.

12 divergence n. separation, difference   ↔ merging, convergence

[divə́ːrdʒəns] 차이, 불일치

There was a **divergence** of opinion on the controversial issue.
논란거리에 대해서 의견의 차이가 있었다.

13 eminent adj. outstanding, distinguished   ↔ unimportant, inferior

[émənənt] 걸출한, 저명한

The journalist interviewed an **eminent** scholar in the field to get his opinion.
기자는 전문가의 의견을 구하기 위해 그 분야에서 저명한 학자를 인터뷰했다.

14. expediently   adv. suitably, conveniently   ↔ inappropriately, inexpediently

[ikspíːdiəntli] 쓸모 있게, 알맞게

A shoe box can be **expediently** used as a storage container.
신발 상자는 저장 용기로 쓸모 있게 사용할 수 있다.

15. former   adj. previous, ex-   ↔ following, latter

[fɔ́ːrmər] 이전의

The **former** presidents met with the incumbent head of state.
전직 대통령들은 현직 국가 수장과 만났다.

16. hassle   n. bother, nuisance   ↔ pleasure, delight

[hǽsl] 번거로운 일[상황]

He would not have agreed to babysit his little sister if he knew it would be such a **hassle**.
그는 어린 여동생을 봐주는 일이 그렇게 번거로울 줄 알았다면 승낙하지 않았을 것이다.

17. implicitly   adv. essentially, absolutely   ↔ explicitly, beyond any doubt

[implísitli] 함축적으로, 절대적으로

His employment agreement **implicitly** stated that he would be fired if he stole equipment from his office.
그의 고용 계약에 그가 사무실에서 장비를 훔칠 경우 해고될 것이라는 내용을 함축적으로 명시했다.

18. infringement   n. violation, breach   ↔ defense, protection

[infríndʒmənt] 침해

There are many countries that are being criticized for their **infringement** of human rights because people are being abused by the governments.
정부가 국민을 학대하고 있기 때문에 인권 침해로 비난 받는 나라가 많이 있다.

19. installment   n. part, portion   ↔ whole, entirety

[instɔ́ːlmənt] 분할 불입

The appliance store is offering their customers products that could be paid off in monthly **installments**.
가전 제품 상점은 고객이 월부로 갚을 수 있는 제품을 내놓고 있다.

20. latitude   n. freedom, independence   ↔ limitation, restriction

[lǽtətjùːd] 자유

His parents gave him **latitude** to stay out late because of his good grades.
그의 부모는 좋은 성적 때문에 그가 늦게까지 외출할 수 있는 자유를 주었다.

21 manuscript n.

[mǽnjuskrìpt] 원고

The writer sent the publisher his **manuscript** for his new book.
작가는 새 책의 원고를 출판사에 보냈다.

22 nullify v. cancel, invalidate ↔ affirm, validate

[nʌ́ləfài] 무효로 하다, 파기하다

The Supreme Court of the United States **nullified** the law that was passed by the state.
미국 대법원은 주가 통과시킨 법률을 백지화했다.

23 perilous adj. dangerous, risky ↔ safe, secure

[pérələs] 위험한

The **perilous** mountains are very difficult to climb even for experienced men.
경험이 많은 사람에게도 험한 산은 등반하기 매우 어렵다.

24 precise adj. exact, clear-cut ↔ inaccurate, vague

[prisáis] 정확한

She wanted to know the **precise** amount for the new tires to make sure she had enough cash to pay for it.
그녀는 구입에 필요한 현금이 충분한지 확인하기 위해 새로운 타이어의 정확한 액수를 알기 원했다.

25 qualified adj. equipped, experienced ↔ incapable, unqualified

[kwáləfàid] 자격이 있는

Alice felt she was **qualified** for the job because of her many years of experience.
오랜 경력으로 앨리스는 자신이 그 일에 적임이라고 생각했다.

26 radiant adj. bright, shining ↔ dark, dim

[réidiənt] 빛나는

Cynthia was blinded by the **radiant** sun for a brief moment.
신시아는 눈부신 태양 때문에 잠시 앞이 안 보였다.

27 recognizable adj. identifiable, perceivable ↔ strange, unfamiliar

[rékəgnàizəbl] 알아볼 수 있는

The actor had become so famous that he was easily **recognizable** when out in public.
배우는 매우 유명해져서 대중 속에 있을 때에도 쉽게 알아볼 수 있었다.

28 rekindle v. relight, renew ↔ extinguish, put out

[riːkíndl] 다시 불을 붙이다

The argument with his wife **rekindled** the anger he thought had disappeared.
아내와의 말다툼은 그가 누그러졌다고 생각했던 화를 다시 돋우었다.

29 threshold n. beginning, doorstep

[θréʃhould] 문지방, 발단

The bride stood at the **threshold** of the church, nervous and excited about walking down the aisle to get married.
신부는 결혼하기 위해 통로를 걸어 내려가는 것에 대해 초조하고 들뜬 상태로 교회 문지방에 서 있었다.

30 vanquish v. defeat, overpower ↔ fail, lose

[vǽŋkwiʃ] 완파하다

The French under Joan of Arc were initially able to **vanquish** their British foes.
잔 다르크의 지휘 아래 프랑스인은 적인 영국을 완파할 수 있었다.

DAILY QUIZ

1. the **former** world champion — a. bother
2. **capsize** during the hurricane — b. defeat
3. try to **rekindle** the romance — c. chasm
4. **nullify** his argument — d. exact
5. sink down into the **abyss** — e. previous
6. not worth the **hassle** — f. renew
7. a **perilous** trek in the jungle — g. tip over
8. **augment** his abilities — h. invalidate
9. the **precise** location of the treasure — i. dangerous
10. **vanquish** all the enemies — j. boost

ANSWERS 1. e 2. g 3. f 4. h 5. c 6. a 7. i 8. j 9. d 10. b

Day 34

1 abnormally adv. irregularly, strangely

[æbnɔ́:rməli] 비정상적으로

This summer included some **abnormally** hot weather.
금년 여름에는 비정상적으로 더운 날씨가 몇 번 있었다.

2 ample adj. plenty, enough ↔ insufficient, not enough

[ǽmpl] 충분한

Camping in the mountains allowed for **ample** opportunities to hike.
산에서의 야영은 충분한 등산할 기회를 주었다.

3 apprehensive adj. fearful, anxious ↔ unafraid, confident

[æ̀prihénsiv] 우려하는, 불안한

They were **apprehensive** about entering the dark and unknown cave.
그들은 어두운 미지의 동굴에 들어가는 것이 불안했다.

4 attitude n. position, point of view

[ǽtitʃùːd] 태도, 자세

Cautious optimism is one **attitude** to take in any situation.
조심스러운 낙관주의는 어떤 상황에서라도 가져야 할 태도이다.

5 authentic adj. real, genuine ↔ fake, counterfeit

[ɔːθéntik] 진품의

Historians try to prove that an object or document is **authentic**.
역사학자들은 어떤 물건이나 서류가 진품이라는 것을 입증하고자 한다.

6 borough n.

[bə́ːrou] 자치구

The municipality of New York City consists of five **boroughs**.
뉴욕시의 지방 자치체는 5개의 자치구로 구성된다.

7 coarse adj. rough, unrefined ↔ fine, polished

[kɔːrs] 거친

Using sandpaper turns the surface of wood from **coarse** to smooth.
사포를 사용하면 거친 나무 표면이 매끈해진다.

8 connotation n. implication, nuance ↔ denotation

[kɑ̀nətéiʃən] 함축

Words often carry a **connotation** that goes beyond the dictionary definition.
단어에는 종종 사전적 의미를 넘어서는 함축적 의미가 있다.

9 convene v. assemble, meet together ↔ scatter, disperse

[kənvíːn] 회합하다

The residents all **convened** for a town meeting on the proposal.
주민들은 그 제안에 대한 읍내 회의에 모두 회합했다.

10 cutting-edge adj. latest, newest ↔ outdated, obsolete

최첨단의

The new video game uses **cutting-edge** technology for spectacular gaming.
새로운 비디오 게임은 화려한 게임을 위해 최첨단 기술을 이용한다.

11 devour v. swallow, gulp

[diváuər] 삼켜 버리다

Large sharks can **devour** their prey either whole or in huge bites.
거대한 상어는 먹이를 통째로 또는 커다란 덩어리로 삼켜 버릴 수 있다.

12 dictate v. control, determine ↔ ask, request

[díkteit] 좌우하다, ~에 영향을 주다

Results from the previous year can **dictate** a company's plans for the present year.
전년도의 성과가 금년도의 회사 계획에 영향을 줄 수 있다.

13 engage in phr. participate in, take part in

~에 참여하다

Vacationers at the resort can **engage in** all sorts of activities.
리조트에서 휴가를 보내는 사람들은 모든 종류의 활동에 참여할 수 있다.

14 forensic adj. legal, judicial

[fərénsik] 법의학적인

The detectives of the New York Police Department searched the victim's house for **forensic** evidence that would link the suspected killer to the crime.
뉴욕 경찰서의 수사관들은 살인 용의자와 범죄를 연결할 법의학적인 증거를 찾기 위해 희생자의 집을 수색했다.

15 germ n. bacterium, pathogen

[dʒəːrm] 세균

The daycare cleans their rooms every day to prevent **germs** from spreading.
탁아소에서는 세균이 퍼지는 것을 막기 위해 매일 방을 청소한다.

16 hieroglyphics n.

[hàiərəglífiks] 상형 문자

The anthropology student traveled to Egypt to see the **hieroglyphics** found many years ago.
인류학과 학생은 오래전 발견된 상형 문자를 보기 위해 이집트에 갔다.

17 integrity n. honor, principle   ↔ deceit, treachery

[intégrəti] 진실, 정직

The people of South Africa viewed Nelson Mandela as a man of **integrity** and voted him as the President of the country.
남아프리카 공화국 국민들은 넬슨 만델라를 진실한 사람으로 보고 그를 대통령으로 선출했다.

18 intentional adj. intended, deliberate   ↔ accidental, unintentional

[inténʃənl] 의도적인

The current Prime Minister was criticized for his **intentional** insult towards his oppositional candidate.
현직 수상은 상대 후보에 대한 의도적인 모욕으로 인해 비난 받았다.

19 meteorology n. weather science, climatology

[mìːtiərálədʒi] 기상학

Benjamin loved to watch the weather report on television so he decided to study **meteorology**.
벤자민은 TV로 날씨 보도를 보는 것을 좋아해서 기상학을 공부하기로 했다.

20 overhaul v. redo, reconstruct

[òuvərhɔ́ːl] 점검하다, 수리하다

Ian hired a professional to **overhaul** his office computer system that was not working properly.
이안은 제대로 작동하지 않는 사무실 컴퓨터 시스템을 정비하기 위해 전문가를 고용했다.

21 persecute   v. victimize, pick on

[pə́ːrsikjùːt] 박해하다

The Romans **persecuted** the Christians, who were killed for their beliefs.
로마인들은 기독교도들을 박해했고, 기독교도들은 종교 때문에 죽임을 당했다.

22 preliminary   adj. first, initial   ↔ closing, final

[prilímənèri] 예비의

Moby had to go through a **preliminary** court hearing before going through the trial in front of a jury.
모비는 배심원단 앞에서 재판을 받기 전에 예비 법정 심리를 받아야 했다.

23 prologue   n. beginning, opening

[próulɔːg] 서문, 머리말

The novel was republished with a **prologue** introducing the new edition.
소설은 신판을 소개하는 서문과 함께 재발행되었다.

24 reference   n. connection, quotation

[réfərəns] 언급

The pastor made **references** to the Bible in every sermon.
목사는 매번 설교에서 성경을 언급했다.

25 relentlessly   adv. continuously, tirelessly

[riléntlisli] 가차없이

The police officers **relentlessly** chased the bank robbers through the crowd.
경찰관은 군중을 헤쳐 나가면서 끈질기게 은행 강도를 쫓았다.

26 rivalry   n. competition, opposition

[ráivəlri] 경쟁(의식)

There is a **rivalry** between the two brothers who are competing to get into their high school football team.
고등학교 미식축구 팀에 입단하려고 경쟁하고 있는 두 형제 사이에 경쟁이 있다.

27 scapegoat   n. victim, stooge

[skéipgòut] 희생양

The President fired the Defense Minister, using him as a **scapegoat** to escape public criticism.
대통령은 대중의 비판에서 벗어나기 위한 희생양으로 국방부 장관을 해임했다.

28 submissive   adj. obedient, compliant   ↔ defiant, resistant

[səbmísiv] 순종적인

The servant gave a **submissive** bow as the king walked by.
하인은 왕이 걸어 지나가자 순종적으로 몸을 굽혔다.

29 tactics   n. strategy, plan of attack

[tǽktiks] 전술, 전략

Napoleon Bonaparte was famous for his skills in military **tactics**, which he used to conquer much of Europe.
나폴레옹 보나파르트는 군사 전략 기술로 유명했는데, 그것으로 그는 유럽의 많은 지역을 정복했다.

30 unwavering   adj. consistent, unchanging   ↔ inconsistent, wavering

[ʌ̀nwéivəriŋ] 변함없는

His remarkable dedication to his work was constant and **unwavering**.
일에 대한 그의 변함없는 전념은 꾸준했고 변함이 없었다.

DAILY QUIZ

1. **cutting-edge** military technology
2. his **unwavering** loyalty
3. the council will **convene** today
4. get through the **preliminary** round
5. the **coarse**, rocky salt
6. **ample** time to finish
7. **relentlessly** attack the enemy
8. the **connotation** in her words
9. **overhaul** the entire room
10. a very negative **attitude**

a nuance
b plenty
c continuously
d position
e reconstruct
f unchanging
g assemble
h newest
i first
j rough

ANSWERS   1. h   2. f   3. g   4. i   5. j   6. b   7. c   8. a   9. e   10. d

COMPREHENSIVE QUIZ — Day 33 & 34

1. How effectively a student spends his or her high school years could _____ his or her future.
   ⓐ vanquish   ⓑ nullify   ⓒ convene   ⓓ dictate

2. War sometimes pushes people to commit cruel, _____ acts.
   ⓐ forensic   ⓑ despicable   ⓒ radiant   ⓓ colloquial

3. Albert thought that the film _____ of his favorite book was poorly made.
   ⓐ adaptation   ⓑ threshold   ⓒ hassle   ⓓ borough

4. Mastering _____ words and phrases is the most difficult part in learning a language.
   ⓐ integrity   ⓑ cutting-edge   ⓒ colloquial   ⓓ recognizable

5. The referee took out the yellow card when he saw the _____ foul committed by the player.
   ⓐ forensic   ⓑ ample   ⓒ intentional   ⓓ qualified

6. Children should be _____ to their parents.
   ⓐ submissive   ⓑ despicable   ⓒ precise   ⓓ coarse

7. Hungry athletes _____ the snacks in their locker room after the long game.
   ⓐ rekindled   ⓑ devoured   ⓒ augmented   ⓓ demonstrated

8. Rishi and Pranav searched all day for a(n) _____ Indian restaurant.
   ⓐ unwavering   ⓑ former   ⓒ relentless   ⓓ authentic

9. The admissions officers stayed up all night _____ students' applications.
   ⓐ assessing   ⓑ capsizing   ⓒ persecuting   ⓓ vanquishing

10. Ivy League schools are known for having many _____ professors.
    ⓐ preliminary   ⓑ apprehensive   ⓒ perilous   ⓓ eminent

Answers: p.342

Day 35

1. allegory n.

[ǽləgɔ̀ːri] 우화

An **allegory** tells a story beyond the literal and obvious one.
우화는 있는 그대로의 뻔한 이야기 이상의 이야기를 들려준다.

2. amiable adj. friendly, pleasant ↔ disagreeable, unfriendly

[éimiəbl] 상냥한

He was an **amiable** child who got along with all his classmates.
그는 반 친구 모두와 잘 어울리는 상냥한 아이였다.

3. appropriate¹ adj. proper, suitable ↔ improper, inappropriate

[əpróupriət] 적절한

He always had the **appropriate** thing to say in most situations.
그는 대부분의 상황에서 늘 적절한 말을 하였다.

4. appropriate² v. seize, allot ↔ give, return

[əpróuprièit] 전유하다, 책정하다

Nationalization is the term used when a government **appropriates** a business or industry.
국유화는 정부가 기업이나 산업을 전유할 때 쓰는 용어이다.

5. assortment n. variety, medley

[əsɔ́ːrtmənt] 모음, 여러 가지 물건

The gift basket included an **assortment** of different candies and treats.
선물 바구니에는 여러 가지 사탕과 선물 한 꾸러미가 들어 있었다.

6. boisterous adj. noisy, rowdy ↔ quiet, restrained

[bɔ́istərəs] 명랑하고 떠들썩한

The large party at the restaurant was loud and **boisterous**.
식당에서 열린 대형 파티는 시끄럽고 떠들썩했다.

7 conceal v. hide, mask ↔ show, reveal

[kənsíːl] 숨기다

Celebrities sometimes change their looks to **conceal** their identity in public.
유명인들은 사람들이 있는 곳에서 자신의 정체를 숨기기 위해 때때로 외모를 바꾼다.

8 contentious adj. controversial, quarrelsome

[kənténʃəs] 이론이 분분한

Many voices could be heard being spoken on the **contentious** issue.
이론이 분분한 문제에 대해 많은 의견이 나올 수 있다.

9 corporate adj.

[kɔ́ːrpərət] 기업의

Athletic events are often funded through **corporate** sponsorship.
운동 행사는 종종 기업의 후원을 통해 자금이 조달된다.

10 deplete v. consume, exhaust ↔ fill, increase

[diplíːt] 고갈시키다

Elephants can **deplete** the food resources of their environment rather quickly.
코끼리는 주변 환경의 식량 자원을 다소 빨리 고갈시킬 수 있다.

11 destitute adj. moneyless, down and out ↔ wealthy, well-to-do

[déstətjùːt] 궁핍한, 빈곤한

Homeless people are poor and **destitute** but hopefully can recover.
노숙자들은 가난하고 궁핍하지만 바라건대 그들은 재기할 수 있다.

12 domesticated adj. tamed, trained ↔ wild, undomesticated

[dəméstikèitid] 길들여진

The **domesticated** dog has a long and close history with mankind.
길들여진 개는 인간과 길고 밀접한 역사가 있다.

13 enumerate v.

[injúːmərèit] 열거하다

A good argument **enumerates** clearly all of its supporting evidence.
좋은 주장은 뒷받침하는 모든 증거를 명확하게 열거한다.

14 extraterrestrial   adj. alien, otherworldly

[èkstrətəréstriəl] 외계의

Many people believe humans are not alone in the universe because they are convinced of the existence of **extraterrestrial** life.
많은 사람들은 외계 생명체의 존재에 대해 확신하기 때문에 인간만이 우주에 존재하는 것이 아니라고 믿는다.

15 framework   n. foundation, groundwork

[fréimwə̀:rk] 체제, 뼈대

The **framework** of the American government was set forth by the founding fathers.
미국 정부 체제는 미국 헌법 제정자들에 의해 세워졌다.

16 identical   adj. equal, alike   ↔ different, distinct

[aidéntikəl] 동일한

The little boy had a difficult time telling the differences between the two **identical** toys.
어린 소년은 똑같은 장난감 두 개를 구별하는 데 어려움을 겪었다.

17 indecisive   adj. hesitant, wishy-washy   ↔ determined, decisive

[ìndisáisiv] 우유부단한

Nick was annoyed that he had to wait for his **indecisive** girlfriend to choose an outfit for the party.
닉은 우유부단한 여자 친구가 파티 의상을 고르는 데 기다려야 한다는 것이 짜증났다.

18 inquisition   n. investigation, inquiry

[ìnkwəzíʃən] 심문

After days in the interrogation room without food, he wanted the **inquisition** to end.
그는 먹지도 못하고 취조실에서 며칠을 보낸 후 심문이 끝나기를 바랐다.

19 journalism   n. news, reporting

[dʒə́:rnəlìzm] 저널리즘

The New York Times is well respected for its **journalism** and believed to be reliable by many Americans.
〈뉴욕 타임즈〉는 저널리즘으로 높이 평가받고 있고, 많은 미국인의 신뢰를 받고 있다고 여겨진다.

20 laden   adj. burdened, weighted   ↔ empty, light

[léidn] ~으로 괴로워하는

She was **laden** with guilt after lying to her mother about being at the library when she actually went to a party.
그녀는 실제로 파티에 갔으면서 도서관에 있다고 어머니에게 거짓말을 한 뒤에 죄책감으로 괴로워했다.

21. marine adj. coastal, sea

[mərí:n] 해양의, 바다의

The scuba diver was looking forward to seeing the **marine** life that lived in the ocean.
스쿠버 다이버는 바다에 사는 해양 생명체를 보기를 고대했다.

22. motivation n. inspiration, encouragement ↔ depression, discouragement

[mòutəvéiʃən] 동기

The boy's **motivation** for completing his chores was to get an allowance from his parents.
가사를 끝마치려는 소년의 동기는 부모로부터 용돈을 받는 것이었다.

23. necessitate v. require, compel

[nisésətèit] 필요로 하다

The terrorist attack **necessitated** a change in airline security.
테러리스트의 공격으로 항공 보안상의 변화가 필요해졌다.

24. peculiar adj. unique, specific ↔ typical, conventional

[pikjú:ljər] 특이한, 괴상한

Manuel had a **peculiar** habit of scratching his chin when he was confused.
마누엘은 당황했을 때 턱을 긁는 특이한 습관을 가지고 있었다.

25. predisposition n. likelihood, inclination ↔ unwillingness, disinclination

[prì:dispəzíʃən] 성향, 소인

Agnes had a **predisposition** for cancer because of her family history with the disease.
아그네스는 가족 병력 때문에 암에 걸리기 쉬운 성향이 있었다.

26. retinue n. crew, entourage

[rétənjù:] 수행원

The famous actor was surrounded by a **retinue** who gave him much-needed assistance.
유명 배우는 자신에게 매우 필요한 도움을 준 수행원에게 둘러싸여 있었다.

27. salient adj. noticeable, remarkable ↔ unimportant, unnoticeable

[séiliənt] 핵심적인, 두드러진

After hearing the politician's nonsensical statement, people were impressed with his opponent's **salient** argument.
정치인의 터무니없는 성명을 들은 후 국민들은 상대 정치인의 핵심적인 주장에 감명을 받았다.

28 supervisory adj. regulatory, administrative

[sùːpərváizəri] 관리자의, 감독의

She was asked to take on the **supervisory** role of overseeing the completion of the construction project.
그녀는 건설 프로젝트의 완공을 감독하는 관리자 역할을 맡아 달라는 요청을 받았다.

29 testimony n. confirmation, witness

[téstəmòuni] 증언

Peter was relieved after he gave his **testimony** in court against the accused killer.
피터는 기소된 살인자에 대해 법정에서 증언을 하고 안도했다.

30 variation n. difference, variety ↔ similarity, agreement

[vɛ̀əriéiʃən] 차이, 변화

Butterfly species show a range of **variation** in size, shape, and pattern.
나비 종은 크기 및 모양, 무늬에 있어서 차이의 폭이 있다.

DAILY QUIZ

1. no **motivation** to study
2. great **variation** in the menu
3. **deplete** the energy reserves
4. **domesticated** species
5. will **necessitate** quick action
6. a **peculiar** smell
7. a **destitute** beggar
8. **conceal** the truth
9. the **framework** for success
10. the **amiable** puppy

a. hide
b. moneyless
c. require
d. friendly
e. variety
f. foundation
g. encouragement
h. exhaust
i. unique
j. tamed

ANSWERS 1. g 2. e 3. h 4. j 5. c 6. i 7. b 8. a 9. f 10. d

Day 36

1 affluent adj. rich, wealthy   ↔ poor, impoverished

[ǽfluənt] 부유한

The rows of nice houses showed that it was an **affluent** neighborhood.
열 지어 있는 멋진 주택들이 부유한 동네라는 것을 나타냈다.

2 antibiotics n.

[æ̀ntaibaiάtik] 항생제, 항생 물질

Antibiotics are given to boost the immune system of people at risk of illness.
항생제는 질병에 걸릴 위험이 있는 사람의 면역 체계를 강화하기 위해 주어진다.

3 aphorism n. proverb, maxim

[ǽfərìzm] 격언, 경구

An **aphorism** is a brief saying that sums up years of experience.
격언은 오랜 경험을 집약한 짤막한 말이다.

4 assumption n. belief, expectation

[əsʌ́mpʃən] 추정, 가정

That people grow wiser as they get older is a common **assumption**.
사람은 나이를 먹으면서 더 현명해진다는 것이 일반적인 가정이다.

5 bleak adj. dreary, barren   ↔ appealing, pleasant

[bli:k] 황량한

After a hurricane hits a neighborhood, the landscape can become **bleak**.
허리케인이 마을을 강타한 후, 풍경은 황량해질 수 있다.

6 compilation n. collection, assemblage

[kàmpəléiʃən] 모음집

The CD was a **compilation** of all the biggest hits by the group.
CD는 그룹의 최고 히트곡을 모두 모아 놓은 모음집이었다.

7 confirm v. validate, check ↔ cancel, invalidate

[kənfə́ːrm] 확인하다

He called to **confirm** his reservation at the popular restaurant.
그는 인기 있는 레스토랑에 예약을 확인하려고 전화했다.

8 correspond v. communicate, send word

[kɔ̀ːrəspánd] 연락을 주고받다

The many workers on the project **corresponded** by phone and email.
프로젝트에 참여한 많은 작업자들은 전화와 이메일로 연락을 주고받았다.

9 dampen v. wet, moisten ↔ dry, parch

[dǽmpən] 적시다

The nurse **dampened** a towel with water before giving it to the patient.
간호사는 수건을 환자에게 주기 전에 물로 적셨다.

10 despondent adj. gloomy, hopeless ↔ cheerful, happy

[dispándənt] 의기소침한

The losing team appeared hopeless and **despondent** near the end of the game.
지고 있는 팀은 경기가 종료될 무렵 절망적이고 의기소침해 보였다.

11 disguise v. cover, conceal ↔ reveal, unmask

[disgáiz] 위장시키다

A masquerade is a party where guests **disguise** themselves with masks.
가면 무도회는 손님이 가면으로 변장하는 파티이다.

12 endanger v. risk, put in danger ↔ protect, save

[endéindʒər] 위태롭게 하다

Some enjoy rock climbing while others think it just **endangers** one's life.
어떤 사람들은 암벽 등반을 즐기는 반면 다른 사람들은 그것이 생명을 위태롭게 한다고 생각한다.

13 evidence n. proof, confirmation

[évədəns] 증거

We can guess with **evidence** but we should believe with facts.
증거로 추측할 수 있지만, 사실을 믿어야 한다.

14 flamboyant   adj. colorful, showy   ↔ unflashy, moderate

[flæmbɔ́iənt] 현란한

Philip was mesmerized by the bright lights and **flamboyant** costumes worn by the circus performers.
필립은 밝은 조명과 서커스 공연자들의 현란한 의상에 매료되었다.

15 gesture   n. action, motion

[dʒéstʃər] (의사 표시로서의) 행위

The injured man was touched by the kind **gesture** of the stranger who gave him a ride to the hospital.
부상자는 병원까지 태워 준 낯선 사람의 친절한 행위에 감동했다.

16 hallmark   n. symbol, trademark

[hɔ́:lmɑ̀:rk] 특징

She was impressed by the man who returned her wallet, as he was a **hallmark** of an honest person.
그녀는 자신의 지갑을 돌려준 남자가 정직한 사람의 전형이었기 때문에 감명 받았다.

17 heed   v. follow, bear in mind   ↔ ignore, disregard

[hi:d] 주의를 기울이다

Edith got drenched because she did not **heed** the meteorologist's warning to carry an umbrella.
이디스는 우산을 휴대하라는 기상 캐스터의 예보에 주의를 기울이지 않았기 때문에 흠뻑 젖었다.

18 illegal   adj. banned, wrongful   ↔ lawful, legal

[ilí:gəl] 불법의

It is **illegal** for people under the age of twenty-one to drink or buy alcohol in the United States.
미국에서 21세 미만의 사람이 술을 마시거나 구입하는 것은 불법이다.

19 informative   adj. educational, enlightening   ↔ useless, uninformative

[infɔ́:rmətiv] 유익한

Gabriella went to her college orientation and was glad because she found it very **informative**.
가브리엘라는 대학 오리엔테이션에 가서 매우 유익하다고 여기며 기뻐했다.

20 insufficient   adj. lacking, inadequate   ↔ enough, sufficient

[ìnsəfíʃənt] 부족한, 불충분한

Darren tried to withdraw money from his bank but was rejected because he had **insufficient** funds.
대런은 은행에서 돈을 인출하려 했지만 예금 부족으로 거절당했다.

21 monitor   v. watch, oversee   ↔ ignore, neglect

[mánətər] 감시하다

The teacher **monitored** her students during the test to make sure they were not cheating.
교사는 시험을 볼 동안 확실히 부정행위를 하지 못하도록 학생들을 감독했다.

22 outdated   adj. old, obsolete   ↔ latest, up-to-date

[áutdéitid] 구식의

The boy pleaded with his father to get him a new computer because the one in his room was **outdated**.
그 소년은 자신의 방에 있는 컴퓨터가 구형이라 아버지에게 새 컴퓨터를 사달라고 애원했다.

23 painstakingly   adv. carefully, laboriously   ↔ easily, effortlessly

[péinstèikiŋli] 공들여

She **painstakingly** sewed the numerous individual pearls on the wedding dress.
그녀는 공들여서 웨딩드레스에 수많은 진주를 꿰매어 달았다.

24 pertain to   phr. related to, referred to   ↔ unrelated to, irrelevant to

관련하다

He looked on-line for information that **pertained to** the Vietnam War for his research paper.
그는 보고서를 쓰기 위해 베트남 전쟁과 관련 있는 정보를 온라인에서 조사했다.

25 plaster   v. spread, smear

[plǽstər] 더덕더덕 바르다, 메우다

His wall was **plastered** with posters of his favorite musical band.
그의 벽은 좋아하는 음악 밴드의 포스터로 도배되어 있었다.

26 processed   adj. prepared, refined   ↔ natural, whole

[prásest] 가공한

Nobody wanted to eat the **processed** ham that Laura brought to the dinner party.
아무도 로라가 만찬에 가져온 가공 햄을 먹으려 하지 않았다.

27 retain   v. keep, preserve   ↔ lose, release

[ritéin] 보존하다, 보유하다

Courtney was glad that her shirt **retained** its color despite being washed many times.
코트니는 여러 번 세탁했음에도 셔츠 색이 그대로 보존되어 기뻤다.

28 straightforward   adj. clear, direct   ↔ ambiguous, indirect

[strèitfɔ́:rwərd] 솔직한

Donatella told her son she wanted a **straightforward** answer because she would not tolerate a lie.
도나텔라는 거짓말을 참지 않을 것이니 솔직하게 대답하라고 아들에게 말했다.

29 toxic   adj. poisonous, lethal   ↔ nonpoisonous, harmless

[táksik] 유독성의

There are **toxic** chemicals in many cleaning products that must be kept away from children.
많은 세제 제품에는 반드시 아이들의 손이 닿지 않는 곳에 두어야 하는 독성 화학 물질이 들어 있다.

30 usurp   v. hijack, muscle in   ↔ surrender, give in

[ju:sə́:rp] 빼앗다, 강탈하다

The king's uncle **usurped** power from his young nephew to rule the country.
왕의 숙부는 나라를 통치하기 위해 어린 조카로부터 권력을 빼앗았다.

DAILY QUIZ

1 using **outdated** technology   a keep
2 **heed** my advice   b rich
3 a **bleak**, hopeless future   c conceal
4 **dampen** a washcloth   d smear
5 will **monitor** for changes   e dreary
6 **disguise** his anger   f follow
7 an **illegal** street race   g moisten
8 an **affluent** neighborhood   h obsolete
9 **plaster** the paint on the wall   i banned
10 **retain** her youthful looks   j watch

ANSWERS   1. h   2. f   3. e   4. g   5. j   6. c   7. i   8. b   9. d   10. a

COMPREHENSIVE QUIZ — Day 35 & 36

1. Petunia read a lot of _____ to guide her through difficult times.
   ⓐ inquisitions   ⓑ antibiotics   ⓒ predispositions   ⓓ aphorisms

2. The judge threw the case out of the court for _____ evidence.
   ⓐ insufficient   ⓑ affluent   ⓒ marine   ⓓ amiable

3. Showing _____ behavior is important in front of the elderly.
   ⓐ contentious   ⓑ appropriate   ⓒ bleak   ⓓ corporate

4. The famous actress was _____ with grief when her husband died.
   ⓐ indecisive   ⓑ despondent   ⓒ laden   ⓓ informative

5. Chef Franco _____ the ingredients he needed to his assistants.
   ⓐ enumerated   ⓑ depleted   ⓒ dampened   ⓓ usurped

6. The peacocks displayed their _____ feathers in order to attract the peahens.
   ⓐ domesticated   ⓑ flamboyant   ⓒ toxic   ⓓ destitute

7. It is ridiculous to compare real chunks of steak to _____ meat.
   ⓐ supervisory   ⓑ identical   ⓒ peculiar   ⓓ salient

8. The new CEO inspected the _____ office.
   ⓐ corporate   ⓑ straightforward   ⓒ extraterrestrial   ⓓ processed

9. Some animals rub their noses together as a(n) _____ of friendship.
   ⓐ retinue   ⓑ gesture   ⓒ compilation   ⓓ allegory

10. The principal found it difficult to _____ funds from the school budget for a new science lab.
    ⓐ plaster   ⓑ necessitate   ⓒ appropriate   ⓓ correspond

Answers: p.342

Day 37

1 absurd   adj. ridiculous, foolish   ↔ logical, rational

[əbsə́:rd] 바보 같은, 불합리한

A comedy often contains elements that are **absurd** and nonsensical.
코미디에는 흔히 바보 같고 터무니없는 요소가 포함된다.

2 allegedly   adv. supposedly, professedly

[əlédʒidli] 전해진 바에 의하면

The man was **allegedly** in the area when the incident took place.
전해진 바에 의하면 그 사람은 사건 발생 시 그 지역에 있었다고 한다.

3 ardent   adj. enthusiastic, passionate   ↔ cold, indifferent

[á:rdənt] 열렬한

Ardent supporters of the environment want to limit the damage from man-made pollution.
열렬한 환경 보호 지지자들은 인간이 초래한 공해에 의한 피해를 막고자 한다.

4 atone   v. make up for, compensate

[ətóun] 속죄하다

A spiritual person meditates or prays to **atone** for any sin committed.
영적인 사람은 저지른 죄에 대해 속죄하기 위해 명상을 하거나 기도한다.

5 biofuel   n. biodiesel, organic fuel

[báioufjù(:)əl] 생물 연료

Ethanol made from corn is a common form of **biofuel** used today.
옥수수로 만든 에탄올은 오늘날 사용되는 생물 연료의 흔한 종류이다.

6 catastrophic   adj. disastrous, fatal

[kæ̀təstráfik] 비극적인

A **catastrophic** engine failure is one which makes the engine useless.
비극적인 엔진 고장은 엔진을 무용지물로 만드는 일이다.

7 clutter n. mess, disorder ↔ neatness, order

[klʌ́tər] 잡동사니

A house full of **clutter** is the result of not throwing anything out.
잡동사니로 가득 한 집은 아무것도 버리지 않은 결과이다.

8 collapse v. break, fall apart ↔ build, rise

[kəlǽps] 무너뜨리다

A major earthquake can cause even buildings designed to withstand earthquakes to **collapse**.
대지진은 지진을 버티도록 고안된 건물도 무너뜨릴 수 있다.

9 comprehend v. understand, make out ↔ misinterpret, misunderstand

[kàmprihénd] 이해하다

Background information allows one to fully **comprehend** an event.
배경 지식은 사건을 완전히 이해할 수 있게 해준다.

10 confound v. confuse, bewilder ↔ clarify, enlighten

[kənfáund] 당황케 하다

The surprising results **confounded** even the most experienced scientists.
의외의 결과에 가장 경험이 많은 과학자들마저도 당황했다.

11 decimate v. annihilate, wipe out

[désəmèit] (질병·전쟁 등이) 많은 사람을 죽이다

The army managed to **decimate** the opposing side using superior strategy.
군대는 우수한 전략을 이용해서 가까스로 적군을 대량으로 죽였다.

12 deduct v. subtract, take away ↔ add, increase

[didʌ́kt] 공제하다

Any charge made on a bank's debit card is automatically **deducted** from the account.
은행 현금 카드로 결재한 청구 금액은 계좌에서 자동으로 공제된다.

13 dissertation n.

[dìsərtéiʃən] 박사 논문

Candidates for a PhD are required to write a final **dissertation**.
박사 학위 지원자들은 최종 박사 논문을 써야 한다.

14 enthrall   v. captivate, mesmerize   ↔ bore, dull

[inθrɔ́:l] 마음을 사로잡다

The impressive opening ceremony to the sporting event **enthralled** its viewers.
스포츠 행사의 인상적인 개막식이 보는 이들의 마음을 사로잡았다.

15 exemplify   v. represent, demonstrate

[igzémpləfài] 예증하다, ~의 좋은 예가 되다

The works of Aristotle **exemplify** the philosophy of the ancient Greeks.
아리스토텔레스의 작품은 고대 그리스 철학의 좋은 예이다.

16 freshman   n. beginner, rookie

[fréʃmən] 신입생

Jesse's parents were proud that their son would be attending Duke University as a **freshman** in the fall.
제시의 부모는 아들이 가을에 듀크대학교 신입생으로 입학한다는 것이 자랑스러웠다.

17 impersonal   adj. cold, unfriendly   ↔ friendly, personal

[impə́:rsənl] 냉담한

Xavier was disappointed by the **impersonal** card sent by his girlfriend.
자비어는 여자 친구가 보낸 냉담한 카드에 실망했다.

18 innate   adj. natural, inherited   ↔ acquired, learned

[inéit] 타고난, 선천적인

Cheetahs have the **innate** ability to run up to 110 kilometers per hour to catch their prey.
치타는 먹이를 잡기 위해 시속 110킬로미터까지 달릴 수 있는 타고난 능력이 있다.

19 liability   n. responsibility, disadvantage   ↔ irresponsibility, unaccountability

[làiəbíliti] 책임, 장애

People find that a lack of education is a **liability** to their future goals.
사람들은 교육을 받지 못하면 장래 목표에 장애가 된다는 것을 알고 있다.

20 minimize   v. decrease, shrink   ↔ enlarge, maximize

[mínəmàiz] 최소화하다

The doctor isolated his patient to **minimize** the risk of infecting others in the hospital.
의사는 병원에 있는 다른 사람의 감염 위험성을 최소화하기 위해 자신의 환자를 격리시켰다.

21 navigate v. steer, pilot ↔ get lost, lose the way

[nǽvəgèit] 항해하다

The ship's captain used the map to help him **navigate** the river.
선장은 강을 항해하는 데 도움이 되는 지도를 사용했다.

22 obliterate v. destroy, eliminate ↔ create, build

[əblítərèit] 제거하다, 없애다

The dictator **obliterated** anyone who opposed his power.
독재자는 자신의 정권에 반대하는 자는 누구라도 제거했다.

23 pasture n. field, meadow

[pǽstʃər] 목초지

The farmer let the cows out to graze on the **pasture** and green hills of his family's farm.
농부는 가족 농장의 목초지와 푸른 언덕에서 소들이 풀을 뜯어먹도록 방목했다.

24 pinnacle n. top, peak ↔ base, bottom

[pínəkl] 정점, 절정

The vice-chairman had reached the **pinnacle** of his career after many years of hard work and sacrifice.
부회장은 수년간의 노력과 희생 끝에 성공의 정점에 도달했다.

25 prowess n. skill, mastery ↔ inability, weakness

[práuis] 기량, 솜씨

The baseball player showed his **prowess** for throwing a ball at a very young age.
야구 선수는 아주 어린 나이에 공을 던지는 솜씨를 보였다.

26 reproach v. criticize, find fault with ↔ commend, praise

[ripróutʃ] 꾸짖다

Blair was **reproached** by her mother for hitting her sister.
블레어는 여동생을 때린 이유로 어머니로부터 꾸지람을 들었다.

27 survey n. poll, study

[sə́rvei] 조사

According to the national **survey**, very few teenagers get an adequate amount of sleep.
국가 조사에 따르면 충분한 수면을 취하는 십대는 거의 없다고 한다.

28 symbolic   adj. representative, characteristic

[simbάlik] 상징적인

After the competition, the two opponents shook hands as a **symbolic** act of friendship.
시합이 끝난 후, 두 상대 선수는 우정이라는 상징적 행위로서 악수했다.

29 tout   v. brag, proclaim   ↔ conceal, hide

[tάut] 크게 선전하다

The commercial **touted** that the lotion would create smoother and younger looking skin.
광고는 로션이 더 매끄럽고 젊어 보이는 피부를 만들어 줄 것이라고 크게 선전했다.

30 voluntary   adj. willing, optional   ↔ mandatory, involuntary

[vάləntèri] 자발적인, 임의의

The cleanup effort by the community was strictly **voluntary** and unpaid.
지역 사회의 정화 노력은 순전히 자발적이며 무보수였다.

DAILY QUIZ

1. **enthrall** the crowd
2. cannot walk through the **clutter**
3. **navigate** across the stars
4. a **symbolic** gesture of cooperation
5. **minimize** all the windows
6. roam the **pasture**
7. an **absurd** amount of work
8. conduct a class **survey**
9. **decimate** the population
10. **voluntary** community service

a. optional
b. shrink
c. wipe out
d. ridiculous
e. steer
f. mess
g. captivate
h. field
i. representative
j. study

ANSWERS   1. g   2. f   3. e   4. i   5. b   6. h   7. d   8. j   9. c   10. a

Day 38

1. access n. permission, entry ↔ denial, refusal

[ǽkses] 출입, 접근

Only certain personnel are given **access** to the storage room.
일부 직원들만 창고 출입이 허용된다.

2. appendage n. limb, attachment ↔ body, trunk

[əpéndidʒ] 부속지 (다리 · 꼬리 · 지느러미 등)

Arms, legs, and sometimes tails are **appendages** to an animal's body.
팔, 다리와 간혹 꼬리는 동물 몸체의 부속지이다.

3. archaeology n.

[ὰːrkiálədʒi] 고고학

Recent **archaeology** is revealing new facts about the oldest civilizations.
근대 고고학은 가장 오래된 문명에 대한 새로운 사실을 밝혀내고 있다.

4. attorney n. lawyer, counselor

[ətə́ːrni] 변호사

An **attorney** can speak for a client in a court of law.
변호사는 법원에서 의뢰인을 대변할 수 있다.

5. buttress n. support, reinforcement

[bʌ́tris] 지지대, 버팀

Thick castle walls serve as a **buttress** against enemy attack.
두꺼운 성벽은 적의 공격에 대한 버팀목의 역할을 한다.

6. celebrated adj. famous, notable ↔ unknown, unfamiliar

[sélǝbrèitid] 유명한

The **celebrated** battle is still remembered in the region to this day.
유명한 전투는 오늘날까지 지역에서 여전히 기억되고 있다.

7 character n. symbol, figure

[kǽriktər] 문자

Writing in Chinese requires learning thousands of **characters**.
중국어로 글을 쓰려면 문자 수천 개를 익혀야 한다.

8 compelling adj. irresistible, convincing ↔ optional, unconvincing

[kəmpéliŋ] 강력한, 흥미진진한

Listeners were persuaded by the **compelling** arguments of the speaker.
청중들은 연사의 강력한 주장에 설득되었다.

9 contingency n.

[kəntíndʒənsi] 만일의 사태

The team executed its plan of **contingency** when all else had failed.
팀은 다른 모든 계획이 실패하자 만일의 사태에 대비한 계획을 실행했다.

10 deliberately adv. intentionally, purposely ↔ accidently, unintentionally

[dilíbəritli] 의도적으로

Some felt the new tax was **deliberately** aimed at the middle class.
어떤 사람들은 새로운 세금이 의도적으로 중산층을 겨냥했다고 생각했다.

11 discrepancy n. conflict, inconsistency ↔ agreement, consistency

[diskrépənsi] 차이

There was a **discrepancy** between what they ordered and the bill they received.
그들이 주문한 것과 받은 계산서에는 차이가 있었다.

12 donor n. patron, giver

[dóunər] 기부자

The **donor** of the monetary gift asked to remain anonymous.
금일봉 기부자는 익명으로 남기를 요청했다.

13 elect v. vote, pick ↔ ignore, reject

[ilékt] 선출하다

Democracy allows citizens to **elect** their leaders through voting.
민주주의는 국민이 투표를 통해 지도자를 선출하게 해준다.

14 exquisite   n. elegant, elaborate   ↔ hideous, unsophisticated

[ikskwízit] 매우 아름다운, 정교한

The sculptor's attention to details is simply **exquisite**.
세부 묘사에 대한 조각가의 주의는 아주 정교하다.

15 fill   v. write a prescription

[fil] 조제하다

Leighton went to the pharmacy to **fill** her prescription of Vicodin after her surgery.
레이튼은 수술 뒤 처방전 대로 바이코딘을 조제 받기 위해 약국에 갔다.

16 fundamentally   adv. basically, essentially

[fʌ̀ndəméntəli] 근본적으로

Communism and Capitalism are **fundamentally** different economic principles.
공산주의와 자본주의는 근본적으로 다른 경제 원리이다.

17 grotesque   adj. ugly, misshapen   ↔ beautiful, shapely

[groutésk] 기괴한

The horror movie was so **grotesque** that several members of the audience almost fainted.
공포 영화는 매우 기괴해서 몇몇 관객은 거의 기절할 정도였다.

18 hiatus   n. break, pause   ↔ continuation, continuity

[haiéitəs] 공백

The tired professor decided to take a **hiatus** after a hard year of teaching.
1년간 열심히 가르친 후 지친 교수는 공백을 갖기로 결정했다.

19 interact   v.

[ìntərǽkt] 상호 작용하다

The chemist wanted to test how the two drugs **interacted** before putting it out on the market.
약사는 시판하기에 앞서 두 약이 어떻게 상호 작용하는지 시험하고 싶었다.

20 invade   v. attack, raid   ↔ surrender, leave alone

[invéid] 침략하다

In 1939, Adolf Hitler **invaded** Poland, and it started a large-scale war in Europe.
1939년에 아돌프 히틀러는 폴란드를 침략하고 유럽에서의 대규모 전쟁을 시작했다.

21 mobile adj. movable, portable ↔ fixed, immobile

[móubəl] 이동할 수 있는

Nora was glad she could take her **mobile** phone to Australia to use in case of emergency.
노라는 비상시에 사용할 휴대 전화를 호주에 가져갈 수 있어서 기뻤다.

22 pharmaceutical adj.

[fὰːrməsúːtikəl] 제약의

The **pharmaceutical** company had to pay damages for the tainted drugs.
제약 회사는 부패된 약에 대해 보상금을 지불해야 했다.

23 playwright n. author, dramatist

[pléirὰit] 극작가

The **playwright** was excited about his work being featured on Broadway.
극작가는 자신의 작품이 브로드웨이에서 공연된다는 것에 들떴다.

24 prospective adj. potential, possible ↔ agreed, concurred

[prəspéktiv] 기대되는

In the company's annual report, they published their **prospective** profits for the coming year.
회사 연례 보고서에 그들은 차기 년도의 기대 수익을 게재했다.

25 random adj. arbitrary, chance ↔ definite, specific

[rǽndəm] 무작위의, 임의의

The winner of the lottery was chosen at **random** by a computer.
복권 당첨자는 컴퓨터로 무작위로 선정됐다.

26 refund n.

[rifʌ́nd] 환불

The store offered a **refund** for the damaged toys that were purchased by customers.
상점은 고객이 구입한 파손된 장난감에 대해 환불을 해줬다.

27 reimbursement n. compensation, repayment

[rìːimbə́ːrsmənt] 변제, 상환

He received **reimbursement** from the store for the extra charge to his credit card.
그는 신용 카드에 추가 결제한 상점으로부터 변제받았다.

28 sympathizer n. collaborator, supporter ↔ opponent, detractor

[símpəθàizər] 지지자

Many people were beaten and placed in jail for being communist **sympathizers** in the United States during the 1920s.
1920년대에 미국에서는 많은 사람들이 공산주의 지지자라는 이유로 구타당하고 수감되었다.

29 trample v. stomp, run over

[trǽmpl] 짓밟다

Don was mad at his mother so he **trampled** on her garden, ruining the flowers.
돈은 어머니에게 화가 나서 어머니의 정원을 짓밟아 화초를 망가뜨렸다.

30 velocity n. speed, rate

[vəlásəti] 속도

The meteor traveled through the atmosphere at a high **velocity**.
유성이 빠른 속도로 지구 대기를 통과했다.

DAILY QUIZ

1. the **random** numbers of the lottery •   • a intentionally
2. **reimbursement** of expenses •   • b inconsistency
3. **deliberately** trip the other player •   • c speed
4. the **mobile** homes of nomads •   • d lawyer
5. a **prospective** football player •   • e famous
6. talk to an **attorney** •   • f pick
7. a **discrepancy** in his explanation •   • g arbitrary
8. measure the **velocity** •   • h potential
9. **elect** a new mayor •   • i movable
10. a **celebrated** television actress •   • j repayment

ANSWERS 1. g 2. j 3. a 4. i 5. h 6. d 7. b 8. c 9. f 10. e

COMPREHENSIVE QUIZ　　　Day 37 & 38

1. Insects possess a lot of _____.
   ⓐ appendages　　ⓑ pinnacles　　ⓒ liabilities　　ⓓ reimbursements

2. The coach _____ his players for coming to practice late.
   ⓐ exemplified　　ⓑ interacted　　ⓒ reproached　　ⓓ enthralled

3. Jadelynn was touched by the _____ novel that told the story of an orphaned child.
   ⓐ impersonal　　ⓑ compelling　　ⓒ absurd　　ⓓ voluntary

4. The military government finally _____ after the death of its leader.
   ⓐ confounded　　ⓑ touted　　ⓒ collapsed　　ⓓ filled

5. Quasimodo's _____ physical appearance contrasted sharply with his kind nature.
   ⓐ grotesque　　ⓑ ardent　　ⓒ atone　　ⓓ celebrated

6. One must consider possible side effects before buying a(n) _____ product.
   ⓐ mobile　　ⓑ pharmaceutical　　ⓒ catastrophic　　ⓓ innate

7. Although Joseph was only a high school _____, he looked like a college student.
   ⓐ access　　ⓑ character　　ⓒ donor　　ⓓ freshman

8. The popular author finally wrote another book after a nine-year _____.
   ⓐ survey　　ⓑ biofuel　　ⓒ hiatus　　ⓓ clutter

9. The young male lion displayed his _____ by successfully taking down a huge antelope.
   ⓐ attorney　　ⓑ discrepancy　　ⓒ buttress　　ⓓ prowess

10. The Internet has allowed us to have _____ to a limitless amount of information.
    ⓐ dissertation　　ⓑ access　　ⓒ refund　　ⓓ pasture

Answers: p.342

Day 39

1. accompanied by
phr. joined by, followed by

동반하다, 수반하다

Thunderclouds are often **accompanied by** rain and lightning.
뇌운은 종종 비와 번개를 수반한다.

2. agile
adj. quick, nimble ↔ clumsy, stiff

[ǽdʒəl] 민첩한

The young gymnast was **agile** in her moves and gestures.
젊은 체조 선수는 동작과 몸짓이 민첩했다.

3. anguish
n. torment, suffering ↔ happiness, joy

[ǽŋgwiʃ] 괴로움

Her personal dilemma caused her a lot of worry and **anguish**.
그녀의 개인적인 딜레마는 많은 걱정과 괴로움의 원인이 되었다.

4. apparent
adj. clear, obvious ↔ hidden, uncertain

[əpǽrənt] 명백한, 분명한

What is **apparent** is not always what is real or true.
명백한 것이 항상 사실이거나 진실한 것은 아니다.

5. bankrupt
adj. broke, ruined ↔ rich, wealthy

[bǽŋkrʌpt] 파산한

With rising costs and tough competition, the company went **bankrupt**.
비용 증가와 치열한 경쟁으로 회사가 파산했다.

6. blunt
adj. obtuse, dull ↔ pointed, sharp

[blʌnt] 뭉툭한, 무딘

Hitting something with a **blunt** object can leave a large impact.
뭉툭한 물건으로 때리면 큰 충격을 남길 수 있다.

7. cease v. stop, bring to an end ↔ continue, keep on

[síːs] 중단시키다

Most nations in the world have **ceased** using landmines due to the international agreement.
세계 대부분의 국가는 국제적인 협정 때문에 지뢰 사용을 중단했다.

8. chromosome n. gene, DNA

[króuməsòum] 염색체

Cells hold their DNA and proteins in the form of **chromosomes**.
세포는 염색체 형태로 DNA와 단백질을 보유하고 있다.

9. confederation n. union, alliance

[kənfèdəréiʃən] 연맹

A **confederation** is a looser form of political unity than a federation.
연맹은 연합보다 느슨한 형태의 정치적 개체이다.

10. consumption n. use, ingestion ↔ fasting, starvation

[kənsʌ́mpʃən] 섭취, 소비

Doctors warn of the ill effects of excessive **consumption** of alcohol.
의사들은 지나친 술 섭취의 악영향에 대해 경고한다.

11. depreciate v. devalue, lower ↔ increase, gain value

[diprí:ʃièit] 가치를 저하시키다

Financial policy can raise or **depreciate** the value of a currency.
재정 정책으로 통화 가치를 올리거나 떨어뜨릴 수 있다.

12. diminish v. shrink, become smaller ↔ develop, grow

[dəmíniʃ] 줄다

As the plane flew off, it **diminished** to a small speck in the sky.
비행기가 날아 오르자 하늘의 작은 점으로 작아졌다.

13. disillusioned adj. disappointed, discouraged ↔ enthusiastic, encouraged

[dìsilúːʒənd] 환멸을 느낀

Failure to pass the exam left them **disillusioned** and self-doubting.
시험에 떨어지자 그들은 환멸을 느꼈고 자기 회의에 빠졌다.

14 endeavor v. attempt, make an effort ↔ ignore, be idle

[indévər] 노력하다

The athlete will **endeavor** to do better in the next Olympics.
운동 선수는 다음 올림픽에서 더 잘 하도록 노력할 것이다.

15 ethical adj. moral, righteous ↔ immoral, unethical

[éθikəl] 도덕적인

We face an **ethical** issue whenever an action harms others.
행동이 남에게 피해를 줄 때는 언제나 도덕적인 문제에 직면한다.

16 facet n. part, side

[fǽsit] 면, 측면

Because she wanted to be a good salesperson, she studied every **facet** of the department store.
그녀는 유능한 점원이 되고 싶었기 때문에 백화점을 면밀히 살폈다.

17 indebted adj. accountable, obligated ↔ paid, settled

[indétid] 감사하는, 부채가 있는

Agatha felt **indebted** to her friend for the loan to pay for her mother's hospital bills.
아가사는 어머니의 병원비를 지불하기 위해 받은 대출금에 대해 친구에게 고마움을 느꼈다.

18 indicate v. signal, point out ↔ conceal, hide

[índikèit] 표시하다, 가리키다

The man believed the star on the map **indicated** where the treasure was hidden.
그 사람은 지도상의 별표가 보물이 숨겨진 곳을 표시한 것이라고 믿었다.

19 mutually adv. reciprocally, jointly ↔ distinctly, dissimilarly

[mjúːtʃuəli] 상호간에, 서로

They **mutually** agreed to meet at the café to work on their project.
그들은 프로젝트 작업을 위해 카페에서 만나기로 서로 동의했다.

20 nurture v. raise, care for ↔ ignore, neglect

[nə́ːrtʃər] 양육하다, 키우다

Parents are supposed to **nurture** their children by giving them love and support.
부모는 자녀에게 사랑과 지지를 줌으로써 자녀를 양육하도록 되어 있다.

21 offender n. criminal, wrongdoer

[əféndər] 범죄자

Since Chuck was considered a repeat **offender**, he was sentenced to 20 years in jail for his crime.
척은 상습범으로 간주되었기 때문에 범행에 대해 20년 징역을 선고받았다.

22 persuade v. convince, lead to believe ↔ discourage, dissuade

[pərswéid] 설득하다

Tania tried to **persuade** her son to go to the dentist before the toothache got worse.
타니아는 치통이 심해지기 전에 치과에 가라고 아들을 설득하려 애썼다.

23 prevent v. block, repress ↔ aid, assist

[privént] 예방하다

Putting out campfires properly and following park rules can help **prevent** forest fires.
모닥불을 제대로 끄고 공원 규칙을 지키는 것은 산림 화재 예방에 도움이 될 수 있다.

24 propaganda n. biased support

[pràpəgǽndə] 선전 방법[조직·운동]

The government created **propaganda** to convince people to support the new law.
정부는 국민이 새로운 법을 지지하도록 납득시키기 위해 선전 방법을 만들었다.

25 quagmire n. trouble, predicament ↔ blessing, success

[kwǽgmàiər] 수렁, 궁지

Greg was faced with a **quagmire** to help his friend cheat on a test or to report him to the teacher for breaking the rules.
그렉은 시험에서 부정 행위를 하는 친구를 도울지, 규칙 위반으로 선생에게 보고해야 하는 궁지에 몰렸다.

26 recant v. deny, take back ↔ confirm, emphasize

[rikǽnt] 철회하다

The supporters of the military demanded that the senator **recant** his statement condemning the war.
군대 지지자들은 상원 의원에게 전쟁을 규탄하는 성명을 철회할 것을 요구했다.

27 stellar[1] adj. leading, dominant ↔ poor, minor

[stélər] 우수한

The figure skater awed the audience and brought pride to her country with her **stellar** performance.
피겨 스케이팅 선수는 우수한 연기로 관중에게 경외심을 불러 일으켰고 모국에 긍지를 가져다주었다.

28 stellar²   adj. celestial, astronomical   ↔ earthly, terrestrial

[stélər] 별의

Danny took his son outside the house to see the **stellar** body in the clear evening sky.
대니는 맑은 저녁 하늘의 천체를 보여주기 위해 아들을 집 밖으로 데리고 나갔다.

29 supply   n. stock, inventory   ↔ debt, lack

[səplái] 재고품, 보급품

After the fire destroyed several classrooms, the community donated a **supply** of furniture to the school.
화재로 교실 몇 개가 훼손되자 지역 사회는 가구 재고품을 학교에 기증했다.

30 vertebrate   n. animal with backbone   ↔ invertebrate

[vɚ́ːrtəbrət] 척추동물

Fish were among the first **vertebrates** to appear on earth.
물고기는 지구상에서 최초로 출연한 척추동물 중 하나였다.

DAILY QUIZ

1	the **confederation** works together	a	care for
2	every **facet** of the diamond	b	obvious
3	the **apparent** cause of death	c	union
4	**diminish** in size and strength	d	side
5	killed by a **blunt** object	e	quick
6	**endeavor** to succeed	f	stock
7	lead to **mutually** assured destruction	g	shrink
8	an **agile** fox	h	attempt
9	have a good **supply** of jokes	i	dull
10	**nurture** someone back to health	j	reciprocally

ANSWERS   1. c   2. d   3. b   4. g   5. i   6. h   7. j   8. e   9. f   10. a

Day 40

40 | 58

1. abhor   v. loathe, regard with disgust   ↔ admire, adore

[æbhɔ́ːr] 혐오하다

Park officials **abhor** how some people leave a lot of trash behind.
공원 관리인들은 어떻게 어떤 이들이 많은 쓰레기를 두고 가는지를 혐오한다.

2. acquaintance   n. associate, friend   ↔ stranger, unknown person

[əkwéintəns] 아는 사람

He met an old **acquaintance** from college by coincidence at a café.
그는 대학 시절 알던 사람을 카페에서 우연히 만났다.

3. allot   v. assign, set aside

[əlɑ́t] 배분하다, 할당하다

More money was **allotted** to the local school system this year.
올해는 지역 학제에 더 많은 자금이 할당되었다.

4. ambivalent   adj. conflicting, contradictory   ↔ certain, definite

[æmbívələnt] 상극인

The action was **ambivalent** because it was unlike previous ones.
조치는 이전의 것과 달랐기 때문에 상극이었다.

5. antagonism   n. hatred, opposition   ↔ agreement, understanding

[æntǽgənìzm] 대립

Years of distrust and **antagonism** eventually led to an outbreak of war.
수년간의 불신과 대립은 결국 전쟁의 발발로 이어졌다.

6. binary   adj. double, dual   ↔ lone, singular

[báinəri] 이진법의

The **binary** system uses only 1s and 0s to write any number.
이진법은 오직 1과 0만을 사용해서 숫자를 기록한다.

7 circuit n.

[sə́:rkit] 회로

A computer **circuit** contains transistors and memory chips.
컴퓨터 회로에는 트랜지스터와 메모리칩이 들어 있다.

8 concurrently adv. simultaneously, all at once ↔ separately, singly

[kənkə́:rentli] 동시에

The attack on the fortress was made **concurrently** by land and by air.
요새에 대한 공격이 지상과 공중에서 동시에 이루어졌다.

9 critical adj. life-threatening, grave ↔ settled, stable

[krítikəl] 위기의

The accident victim was rushed to the hospital in **critical** condition.
사고의 피해자는 위독한 상태에서 병원으로 긴급 이송되었다.

10 discharge v. release, let go ↔ hold, keep

[distʃá:rdʒ] 퇴원시키다

The hospital **discharged** him after making sure his condition was stable.
병원은 그의 상태가 안정적이란 것을 확인한 후 퇴원시켰다.

11 disturbance n. commotion, ruckus ↔ peace, quiet

[distə́:rbəns] 교란

Any **disturbance** of a calm surface of water will create ripples or waves.
고요한 수면의 파문이 잔물결이나 파도를 만들어 낸다.

12 dwindle v. decline, waste away ↔ develop, grow

[dwíndl] 감소하다

Continued burning **dwindled** the wood available for the fire.
계속되는 화재로 인해서 땔감용 목재가 줄어들었다.

13 emerge v. arise, come out ↔ disappear, leave

[imə́:rdʒ] 나타나다

Spectators were amazed to see the driver **emerge** from the crash unharmed.
구경꾼들은 운전자가 충돌 사고에서 다치지 않고 모습을 드러내는 것을 보고 놀랐다.

14 encourage   v. stimulate, energize   ↔ depress, discourage

[inkə́:ridʒ] 격려하다

Coaches talk to their teams during a game to **encourage** them to do better.
감독은 팀이 더 잘하도록 격려하기 위해 경기 도중 팀원들에게 이야기한다.

15 expiration   n. finish, termination   ↔ beginning, birth

[èkspəréiʃən] 만기

Bottled juices usually come with a date of **expiration** on them.
병에 든 주스는 대개 병에 유통 만기일을 표시해서 출하한다.

16 formation   n. composition, creation

[fɔ:rméiʃən] 형태, 형성

The geologist was intrigued by the **formation** of the rocks found in Montana.
지질학자는 몬태나에서 발견되는 암석의 형태에 강한 호기심을 가졌다.

17 grumble   v. complain, protest   ↔ compliment, praise

[grʌ́mbl] 투덜거리다

The old man **grumbled** to himself as he walked by the young boys dancing on the street.
노인은 거리에서 춤을 추는 어린 소년들을 지나치며 투덜거렸다.

18 hearsay   n. rumor, gossip   ↔ evidence, proof

[híərsèi] 소문

The lawyer told his client that his claim was **hearsay** and could not be reliable during court proceedings.
변호사는 의뢰인에게 그의 주장은 소문일 뿐이고 소송 과정에서 신뢰 받지 못할 것이라고 말했다.

19 inaugurate   v. install, institute   ↔ end, uninstall

[inɔ́:gjurèit] 취임시키다

Thousands of people watched as the newly-elected president was **inaugurated** into the White House.
새로 선출된 대통령이 백악관으로 취임할 때 수천 명의 사람들이 지켜 보았다.

20 interrogate   v. question, cross-examine   ↔ answer, reply

[intérəgèit] 심문하다

The police **interrogated** the suspect for hours trying to get answers to their questions.
경찰은 질문에 대답을 얻으려고 용의자를 몇 시간 동안 심문했다.

21. loyalty   n. faithfulness, devotion   ↔ unfaithfulness, disloyalty

[lɔ́iəlti] 충성(심)

The king demanded absolute **loyalty** from his subjects, who were expected to follow orders.
왕은 신하들에게 절대적인 충성을 요구했고, 그들은 명령에 따르도록 되어 있었다.

22. millennium   n. a thousand years, turn of the century

[miléniəm] 천 년간

Before the new **millennium** began, it was predicted that there would be a Y2K bug that would disrupt all computer systems.
새로운 천 년이 시작되기 전에 모든 컴퓨터 시스템에 혼란을 줄 Y2K 버그가 있을 것으로 예측되었다.

23. obesity   n. fatness, excess weight

[oubí:səti] 비만

The country has a problem with **obesity** because the citizens do not get enough exercise.
그 나라는 국민들이 충분한 운동을 하지 않기 때문에 비만 문제를 가지고 있다.

24. performance   n. achievement, accomplishment   ↔ failure, defeat

[pərfɔ́:rməns] 성과, 실적

Edward got a promotion based on his excellent **performance** at work.
에드워드는 직장에서의 우수한 근무 성과로 승진했다.

25. precipitate   v. accelerate, push forward   ↔ check, slow

[prisípətèit] 촉발시키다

The government **precipitated** the civil war and closed down the embassies.
정부는 내전을 촉발시켰고 대사관을 폐쇄했다.

26. recruit   v. gather, bring in

[rikrú:t] 보충하다, 모집하다

The army offered college scholarships to **recruit** new men into the military.
육군은 신병 충원을 위해 대학 장학금을 제안했다.

27. rouse   v. stir, wake up   ↔ nap, sleep

[ráuz] 깨우다, 일어나게 하다

He was **roused** from sleep by a loud sound that was made by his roommate.
그는 룸메이트가 내는 큰 소리에 잠에서 깼다.

28 suspension n. pause, interruption ↔ continuation, completion

[səspénʃən] 정지

Clay was charged with drunk driving, which resulted in the **suspension** of his driver's license.
클레이는 음주 운전으로 기소되었고, 이로 인해 운전면허가 정지되었다.

29 ultimate adj. final, last ↔ beginning, first

[ʌ́ltəmət] 궁극적인

The **ultimate** objective of the business strategy was to eliminate any competition.
사업 전략의 궁극적인 목적은 모든 경쟁자를 제거하는 것이었다.

30 verbal adj. oral, spoken

[və́ːrbəl] 구두의, 말에 의한

A **verbal** agreement is not written down but is still somewhat recognized by the law.
구두 합의는 기록된 것은 아니지만 그래도 법에 의해 어느 정도 인정된다.

DAILY QUIZ

1. the **critical** condition of the premature baby
2. a great **disturbance** in the force
3. **abhor** violence on TV
4. the **binary** star system
5. **emerge** as a beautiful butterfly
6. a long-time **acquaintance** of his
7. **antagonism** toward everyone who is different
8. dogs with complete **loyalty**
9. **discharge** the soldiers next month
10. the **ultimate** battle

a. final
b. dual
c. life-threatening
d. commotion
e. loathe
f. faithfulness
g. release
h. friend
i. come out
j. hatred

ANSWERS 1. c 2. d 3. e 4. b 5. i 6. h 7. j 8. f 9. g 10. a

COMPREHENSIVE QUIZ   Day 39 & 40

1. Luxury item _____ is rising as more and more people in the country are becoming richer.
   ⓐ suspension   ⓑ offender   ⓒ consumption   ⓓ obesity

2. The film was very expensive to make because it featured _____ actors and actresses.
   ⓐ critical   ⓑ indebted   ⓒ ethical   ⓓ stellar

3. People should not rely on _____ alone to determine what is true or not.
   ⓐ hearsay   ⓑ antagonism   ⓒ acquaintance   ⓓ millennium

4. The human body has 23 pairs of _____.
   ⓐ facets   ⓑ chromosomes   ⓒ vertebrates   ⓓ supplies

5. The employees who worked for the _____ company were not able to get their wages.
   ⓐ blunt   ⓑ bankrupt   ⓒ agile   ⓓ disillusioned

6. General Clark ordered his men to _____ shooting their weapons immediately.
   ⓐ recruit   ⓑ grumble   ⓒ cease   ⓓ depreciate

7. The intelligence agents _____ the spy who tried to take top government secrets out of the country.
   ⓐ diminished   ⓑ dwindled   ⓒ endeavored   ⓓ interrogated

8. The death of his favorite goldfish caused him great _____.
   ⓐ propaganda   ⓑ acquaintance   ⓒ anguish   ⓓ suspension

9. Gina could not buy anything expensive because of the _____ of her credit card.
   ⓐ disturbance   ⓑ expiration   ⓒ loyalty   ⓓ formation

10. The arrest of the nation's most beloved dissident leader _____ riots across the nation.
    ⓐ precipitated   ⓑ persuaded   ⓒ prevented   ⓓ allotted

Answers: p.342

Day 41 | 58

1 accessory n. ornament, attachment

[æksésəri] 부속품, 장신구

A protective film screen is a popular **accessory** for a cell phone.
화면 보호 필름은 인기 있는 휴대 전화 부속품이다.

2 antiseptic adj. antibacterial, sterile ↔ contaminated, unsanitary

[æ̀ntəséptik] 멸균의, 소독된

Surgeons must use **antiseptic** instruments to conduct surgery.
외과 의사는 수술하는데 반드시 소독된 기구를 사용해야 한다.

3 array n. range, assortment

[əréi] 모음, 집합체

The new product comes with an **array** of features and functions.
그 신제품은 여러 특징과 기능이 있다.

4 assailant n. attacker, assaulter

[əséilənt] 가해자

Witnesses told police that the **assailant** had a gun and was wearing a mask.
목격자들은 가해자가 총을 소지했으며 복면을 쓰고 있었다고 경찰에게 말했다.

5 bereaved adj. ↔ happy, joyful

[birí:vd] 사별한, 가족을 잃은

The **bereaved** parents of the fallen soldier stood silently at the funeral.
전사한 군인의 부모는 장례식에서 말없이 서 있었다.

6 categorize v. classify, sort

[kǽtəgəràiz] 분류하다

Scientists find it useful to **categorize** things into different types to study them.
과학자들은 사물을 여러 가지 종류로 분류해서 연구하는 것이 유용하다는 것을 알고 있다.

7 colony n. community, settlement

[káləni] 집단, 서식지

A bee **colony** usually lives in a beehive but also in caves or trees.
벌떼는 보통 벌집에 살지만 동굴이나 나무에도 산다.

8 considerable adj. large, substantial ↔ insignificant, inconsiderable

[kənsídərəbl] 상당한

A hobby can take up a **considerable** amount of time in a person's day.
취미는 개인 하루의 상당한 시간을 차지할 수 있다.

9 decadence n. corruption, decline of morality ↔ humility, morality

[dékədəns] 타락

Writers talk about **decadence** in society as an indication of the fall of civilization.
작가들은 문명의 몰락에 대한 암시로 사회 타락에 대해 이야기한다.

10 deformation n. distortion, mutilation ↔ beauty, smoothness

[dìːfɔːrméiʃən] 변형, 기형

Two continental plates colliding results in the **deformation** of the land.
두 대륙판 충돌이 육지 변형을 야기한다.

11 disseminate v. spread, distribute ↔ gather, suppress

[disémənèit] 전파하다, 퍼뜨리다

The Internet has been a revolutionary way to **disseminate** information.
인터넷은 정보를 전파하는 혁신적인 방법이 되어 왔다.

12 enterprise n. business, operation

[éntərpràiz] 기업, (민간) 산업

Building a good road system is a big **enterprise** for any government.
좋은 도로망을 건설하는 것은 모든 정부에 있어서 큰 사업이다.

13 evaluate v. judge, grade

[ivǽljuèit] 평가하다

Tests are designed to **evaluate** a person's knowledge in a subject.
시험은 과목에 대한 개인의 지식을 평가하기 위해 고안된 것이다.

14 expertise   n. knowledge, proficiency   ↔ ignorance, inexperience

[èkspə́rtíːz] 전문 지식

Years of study and experience can give one **expertise** in a field.
수년간의 연구와 경험으로 한 분야의 전문 지식을 습득할 수 있다.

15 feminine   adj. womanly, ladylike   ↔ masculine, manly

[fémənin] 여성스러운

She wanted her daughter to dress more **feminine** instead of wearing pants every day.
그녀는 딸이 매일 바지를 입는 대신에 좀 더 여성스러운 옷을 입기를 원했다.

16 flexible   adj. bendable, amenable   ↔ inflexible, stiff

[fléksəbl] 융통성 있는, 유연한

Debbie told her boss she needed a **flexible** schedule because she had to pick up her two children from daycare twice a week.
데비는 두 아이를 일주일에 두 번 탁아소에 데리러 가야 하기 때문에 융통성 있는 일정이 필요하다고 상사에게 말했다.

17 highlight   v. emphasize, draw attention to   ↔ mask, hide

[háilàit] 강조하다

The dentist wanted to **highlight** the importance of brushing and flossing one's teeth to little children who regularly visited his office.
치과 의사는 정기적으로 병원에 오는 꼬마 아이들에게 칫솔질과 치실질의 중요성을 강조하고자 했다.

18 intimidate   v. threaten, frighten   ↔ encourage, assist

[intímədèit] 겁주다, 위협하다

The students were so **intimidated** by their teacher that most of them wanted to drop her class.
교사가 학생들을 매우 겁먹게 했기 때문에 대부분이 그녀의 강의를 취소하고 싶어했다.

19 irregularly   adv. unpredictably, intermittently   ↔ evenly, regularly

[irégjulərli] 비정기적으로, 불규칙하게

She was worried that she would be late to class because the bus came **irregularly**.
그녀는 버스가 불규칙적으로 와서 수업에 늦을까 걱정했다.

20 locomotion   n. movement, travel

[lòukəmóuʃən] 교통 기관, 이동

The train is a great source of **locomotion** because it is quick and the fare is cheap.
열차는 빠르고 요금이 저렴하기 때문에 훌륭한 교통 기관이다.

21. maximum adj. most, greatest   ↔ minimum, lowest

[mǽksəməm] 최고의, 최대의

The freeways in California allow for a **maximum** speed of seventy-five miles per hour.
캘리포니아의 고속 도로에서는 최대 시속 75마일이 허용된다.

22. optical adj. visual, ocular

[áptikəl] 시력의, 광학의

Ally realized that she needed to find an **optical** service to fix her broken eyeglasses.
앨리는 부러진 안경을 고치려면 안경점을 찾아야 한다는 것을 깨달았다.

23. penitentiary n. jail, prison

[pènəténʃəri] 교도소

The neighbors protested against the construction of the **penitentiary** as they did not want a prison in their community.
주민들은 지역 사회에 감옥이 있는 것을 원치 않았기 때문에 교도소 건설에 대해 항의했다.

24. prosperity n. fortune, success   ↔ failure, loss

[prɑspérəti] 번영, 번창

The party guests each wished one another peace, happiness and **prosperity** in the new year.
파티의 손님들은 새해의 평화, 행복, 번영을 서로서로 기원했다.

25. psychological adj. in the mind, cognitive   ↔ bodily, physical

[sàikəláʤikəl] 심리적인

Jared went to see a therapist every week to work on his **psychological** dependence on drugs.
자레드는 약에 대한 심리적인 의존에 관한 문제로 매주 치료사에게 갔다.

26. require v. need, depend upon   ↔ not want

[rikwáiər] 필요하다

He was brought to the emergency room because he **required** medical attention.
그는 치료가 필요했기 때문에 응급실로 이송되었다.

27. septic adj. harmful, toxic   ↔ helpful, curing

[séptik] 부패한

A disgusting smell was coming out of the **septic** tank in the building.
건물의 정화 탱크에서 역겨운 냄새가 풍겨 나왔다.

28 suspicion   n. doubt, distrust   ↔ trust, certainty

[səspíʃən] 의심, 혐의

Keane was under **suspicion** from the police after a witness identified him as the kidnapper.
목격자가 킨을 유괴범으로 지목한 뒤 그는 경찰의 의심을 받았다.

29 tackle   v. attack, take on   ↔ avoid, dodge

[tǽkl] (문제 등을) 다루다

After studying for hours, Marcy was ready to **tackle** the difficult math test.
오랜 시간 공부한 뒤 마시는 어려운 수학 시험을 치를 준비가 되었다.

30 veto   v. reject, refuse permission   ↔ approve, permit

[víːtou] 거부하다

A president has the power to **veto** a law passed by a lawmaking body.
대통령은 입법 기관이 통과시킨 법을 거부할 권한이 있다.

DAILY QUIZ

1	the **maximum** amount of cargo	a	judge
2	**tackle** all his opponents at once	b	distortion
3	**evaluate** his weekly performance	c	bendable
4	**categorize** all his music	d	attack
5	a **deformation** in the structure	e	sort
6	an **array** of solar panels	f	knowledge
7	visit the Martian **colony**	g	threaten
8	rely on her **expertise**	h	settlement
9	**intimidate** the attacker	i	greatest
10	the **flexible** gymnasts	j	assortment

ANSWERS   1. i   2. d   3. a   4. e   5. b   6. j   7. h   8. f   9. g   10. c

Day 42

42 | 58

1. accredited   adj. authorized, certified   ↔ unaccredited, unauthorized

[əkréditid] 인정된, 공인된

There are several **accredited** universities in town from which to choose.
시내에는 선택할 만한 공인된 대학교가 몇 개 있다.

2. adversity   n. hardship, misfortune   ↔ prosperity, fortune

[ædvə́ːrsəti] 역경

A person's character is tested when he or she faces **adversity**.
역경에 직면하면 사람의 성격은 시험을 받는다.

3. aisle   n. path, walkway

[áil] 통로, 복도

Sitting in a seat along the **aisle** allows a person to leave and come back easily.
통로를 끼고 있는 좌석에 앉으면 쉽게 나갔다 돌아올 수 있다.

4. astrology   n. horoscope, astrometry

[əstrálədʒi] 점성학

Leo and Capricorn are examples of birth signs in **astrology**.
사자자리와 염소자리는 점성학에서 탄생궁의 예이다.

5. banish   v. exile, cast out   ↔ welcome, allow

[bǽniʃ] 추방하다

Wrongdoers can be **banished** from their community.
범죄자들은 지역 사회에서 추방될 수 있다.

6. capitulate   v. submit, surrender   ↔ resist, fight

[kəpítʃulèit] 항복하다

The town **capitulated** to the invading army after some brief fighting.
몇 번의 짧은 전투가 있은 후 도시는 침공하는 적에 항복했다.

7 combustion   n. ignition, burning

[kəmbʌ́stʃən] 연소

Automobiles have been using engines run on internal **combustion** for over a century.
자동차는 1세기가 넘도록 내연 기관으로 달리는 엔진을 사용하고 있다.

8 conduct¹   n. behavior, attitude

[kándʌkt] 행동, 처신

The firefighter was thanked for his courageous **conduct** in the rescue.
그 소방관은 구조 작업에서 용감한 행동으로 감사를 받았다.

9 conduct²   v. control, lead

[kəndʌ́kt] 지휘하다

Lots of practice must take place before one **conducts** an orchestra.
관현악단을 지휘하기 전에는 반드시 많은 연습을 해야 한다.

10 conference   n. convention, meeting

[kánfərəns] 회의

Experts from around the world traveled to attend the **conference**.
전 세계의 전문가들이 회의에 참석하기 위해 이동했다.

11 consecrate   v. dedicate, bless   ↔ disrespect, desecrate

[kánsəkrèit] 봉헌하다, 바치다

The new church was **consecrated** by the leaders of the religious group.
종교 집단의 지도자들은 신축된 교회를 봉헌했다.

12 desecrate   v. violate, defile   ↔ honor, consecrate

[désikrèit] 훼손하다

It may be illegal in a certain country to **desecrate** the flag of that country.
어떤 나라에서는 국기 훼손이 불법일 수 있다.

13 disposition   n. character, personality

[dìspəzíʃən] 기질, 성향

People think artists have a **disposition** to passionately pursue beauty in the world.
사람들은 예술가를 세상의 미를 열정적으로 추구하는 기질을 가진 사람으로 여긴다.

14 draw the line   phr. set a limit, fix a limit

한도를 정하다

Because of long and boring acceptance speeches, they **drew the line** at one minute.
길고 지루한 수락 연설 때문에 그들은 연설 한도를 일분으로 정했다.

15 enclave   n. territory, dominion   ↔ outside, outskirts

[énkleiv] 집단 거주지

The area around the college was known as an **enclave** for students.
대학 주변 지역은 학생들을 위한 집단 거주지로 알려졌다.

16 freight   n. goods, cargo

[fréit] 화물 (운송)

The shipping company made sure to charge the man for his **freight** to India.
선적 회사는 그 사람에게 인도행 화물에 대한 운임을 확실히 부과했다.

17 genome   n.

[dʒíːnoum] 게놈

Scientists have worked for years to identify the genes and the chemical base pairs in the human **genome**.
과학자들은 수년간 인간 게놈의 유전자와 화학 염기쌍을 식별하기 위해 연구해 오고 있다.

18 in retrospect   phr. in afterthought, in hindsight

회상해 보면, 되돌아보면

Bernard realized, **in retrospect**, that he should not have driven after drinking alcohol at the party.
회상을 하면서 버나드는 파티에서 술을 마신 후 운전하지 말았어야 했음을 깨달았다.

19 inaccurate   adj. incorrect, false   ↔ accurate, correct

[inǽkjurət] 부정확한

Eyewitness testimony is often **inaccurate** and as a result, not reliable in court.
목격자의 증언은 종종 부정확하기 때문에, 결과적으로 법정에서 신뢰할 만한 것이 못된다.

20 interpersonal   adj.   ↔ private

[ìntərpə́ːrsnəl] 대인 관계의

Josh is benefitting from the **interpersonal** relationship he has with his mentor who helps guide him in difficult situations.
조쉬는 역경 속에서 그를 인도하는 멘토와의 대인 관계로 득을 보고 있다.

21 mutiny n. defiance, revolt ↔ obedience

[mjúːtəni] 폭동, 반란

The ship's captain was worried after he heard rumors of a possible **mutiny** among his crew.
선장은 선원들 사이에 폭동이 일어날 가능성이 있다는 소문을 듣고 걱정했다.

22 obstruct v. block, prevent ↔ aid, promote

[əbstrʌ́kt] 방해하다

He was placed in jail for **obstructing** justice after refusing to tell the police where his friend was hiding.
그는 친구가 숨은 곳을 경찰에 말하기를 거부한 후 사법 집행을 방해한 혐의로 수감되었다.

23 paranoid adj. suspicious, unreasonable ↔ rational, reasonable

[pǽrənɔ̀id] 편집증의, 피해망상의

The **paranoid** king believed that there were assassins following his every move.
편집증이 있는 왕은 자신의 모든 움직임을 뒤쫓는 암살자가 있다고 믿었다.

24 promote v. help, advance ↔ hurt, demote

[prəmóut] 증진시키다, 촉진하다

The United Nations is an organization that has a goal of **promoting** peace and unity among countries.
유엔은 국가 간 평화와 화합을 증진하기 위한 목적을 가진 기구이다.

25 regurgitate v. vomit, throw up

[rigə́ːrdʒətèit] 토하다, 게우다

After eating tainted meat at the restaurant, Joshua **regurgitated** his food in the bathroom.
조슈아는 식당에서 부패한 고기를 먹고 욕실에서 음식을 토했다.

26 reservoir n. reserve, basin

[rézərvwàːr] 저장고, 저수지

The city is concerned that the **reservoir** is being depleted too quickly and will soon run out of drinking water.
시는 저수지가 너무 빠르게 고갈되어 식수가 곧 떨어질 것을 우려했다.

27 sacrificial adj. surrendering ↔ beneficial

[sæ̀krəfíʃəl] 제물의

The Aztecs made a **sacrificial** altar to offer humans to the gods in order to gain favor from them.
아즈텍족은 신들의 호의를 얻기 위해서 인간을 제물로 바치는 제단을 만들었다.

28 sorority   n. sisterhood, organization   ↔ fraternity

[sərɔ́:rəti] 여학생 클럽

In order to make friends in college, female students join **sororities** on campus.
대학에서 여학생들은 친구를 사귀기 위해 교내 여학생 클럽에 가입한다.

29 tentative   adj. temporary, conditional   ↔ definite, certain

[téntətiv] 불확실한, 모호한

She was not sure if she could get time off from work, so she made **tentative** plans to go home for Christmas.
그녀는 직장에서 시간을 낼 수 있을지 확신하지 못해 성탄절에 집에 갈 불확실한 계획을 세웠다.

30 venerate   v. admire, revere   ↔ hate, disrespect

[vénərèit] 공경하다, 숭배하다

People **venerate** the elderly for their wisdom and experience.
사람들은 지혜와 경험으로 인해 노인을 공경한다.

☀ DAILY QUIZ

1	**banish** the traitors	a throw up
2	the need to **draw the line** somewhere	b revere
3	a water **reservoir**	c suspicious
4	**venerate** the teachers	d cargo
5	Protesters **obstruct** traffic	e defile
6	becoming **paranoid** about privacy	f set a limit
7	**regurgitate** fish bones	g lead
8	**desecrate** the holy grounds	h exile
9	**conduct** a debate	i reserve
10	an air **freight**	j block

ANSWERS   1. h   2. f   3. i   4. b   5. j   6. c   7. a   8. e   9. g   10. d

COMPREHENSIVE QUIZ — Day 41 & 42

1. The disciples of the prophet went around the world to _____ his important messages.
   ⓐ intimidate   ⓑ disseminate   ⓒ capitulate   ⓓ tackle

2. The queen _____ her son from the kingdom for trying to take the throne away from her.
   ⓐ consecrated   ⓑ evaluated   ⓒ promoted   ⓓ banished

3. The student body president is responsible for _____ many of the school meetings.
   ⓐ desecrating   ⓑ regurgitating   ⓒ conducting   ⓓ intimidating

4. A single idea can affect a(n) _____ number of people.
   ⓐ considerable   ⓑ interpersonal   ⓒ psychological   ⓓ optical

5. The notorious crime boss was sent to a maximum security _____.
   ⓐ sorority   ⓑ penitentiary   ⓒ disposition   ⓓ freight

6. The bride and groom practiced walking down the _____ before tomorrow's wedding.
   ⓐ aisle   ⓑ enterprise   ⓒ assailant   ⓓ penitentiary

7. Kumar had a(n) _____ that his little sister was stealing his CDs.
   ⓐ deformation   ⓑ array   ⓒ combustion   ⓓ suspicion

8. Although the ship lost all the _____ when she capsized, luckily, no one on board was hurt.
   ⓐ expertise   ⓑ conference   ⓒ freight   ⓓ adversity

9. The mother bird fed her chicks by _____ the food that she had swallowed earlier.
   ⓐ conducting   ⓑ regurgitating   ⓒ obstructing   ⓓ venerating

10. There is a myth going around that anyone who _____ a tomb of a pharaoh will be cursed for life.
    ⓐ desecrates   ⓑ consecrates   ⓒ highlights   ⓓ requires

Answers: p.343

Day 43

1 absolve v. excuse, liberate ↔ blame, convict

[æbzálv] 무죄를 선고하다, 면제하다

The jury **absolved** the suspect of any wrongdoing.
배심원단은 범행에 대해서 용의자에게 무죄를 선고했다.

2 accident n. chance, fluke ↔ plan, intent

[æksədənt] 우연

He ran into her by **accident** when he was not looking.
그는 보지 않고 있을 때 그녀와 우연히 마주쳤다.

3 anesthetic n. analgesic, sedative

[æ̀nəsθétik] 마취제

The surgery required **anesthetic** to prevent pain to the patient.
환자의 고통을 방지하기 위해 수술에 마취제가 필요했다.

4 appease v. satisfy, calm ↔ upset, annoy

[əpíːz] 달래다, 진정시키다

The candidate offered many promises to **appease** his skeptics and to win votes.
후보자는 자신을 의심하는 사람들을 달래서 표를 얻기 위해 많은 약속을 제안했다.

5 biochemical adj.

[báioukémikəl] 생화학의

The chemistry of what happens in living organisms is the nature of **biochemical** research.
생체 내에서 일어나는 일에 대한 화학적 작용이 생화학 연구의 본질이다.

6 census n. demographics, population count

[sénsəs] 인구 조사

Governments take a **census** every few years to gather statistics on their citizens.
정부는 시민에 대한 통계 자료를 모으기 위해 몇 년마다 인구 조사를 실시한다.

247

7 compatible   adj. agreeable, fitting   ↔ incompatible, different

[kəmpǽtəbl] 뜻이 맞는

Two people get along if they are **compatible** with each other.
서로 뜻이 맞는다면 두 사람은 잘 어울리게 된다.

8 conditional   adj. dependent, limited   ↔ unrestricted, unconditional

[kəndíʃənl] 조건부의

The promise to return them home was part of their **conditional** surrender.
그들을 귀가시킨다는 약속은 그들의 조건부 항복의 일부였다.

9 congestion   n. blockage, jam   ↔ opening, emptiness

[kəndʒéstʃən] 혼잡

A huge increase in the number of automobiles led to more **congestion** on the roads.
자동차 수가 크게 증가해 도로 혼잡이 더 심해졌다.

10 custom   n. tradition, habit   ↔ departure, irregularity

[kʌ́stəm] 관습, 풍습

Shopping for gifts is a holiday **custom** during the Christmas season.
선물 쇼핑은 크리스마스 시즌의 명절 관습이다.

11 deceptive   adj. dishonest, fake   ↔ truthful, honest

[disép

tiv] 속이는, 오해를 사는

Judging a person only based on outer appearance can be **deceptive**.
외모만으로 사람을 판단하는 것은 오해를 살 수 있다.

12 deliver   v. give, convey

[dilívər] 전달하다, 연설하다

She **delivered** her speech with a confidence that could be felt by all.
그녀는 모두가 느낄 수 있을 것이라는 확신을 가지고 연설했다.

13 discordance   n. conflict, difference   ↔ agreement, harmony

[diskɔ́:rdəns] 불일치, 부조화

The public was upset with the **discordance** between his words and his actions.
대중은 그의 말과 행동이 일치하지 않아 심기가 불편했다.

14 enhance   v. improve, upgrade   ↔ reduce, downgrade

[inhǽns] 향상시키다

Technology can only **enhance**, not replace, human intelligence.
기술은 향상될 수 있지만 인간의 지능을 대체할 수는 없다.

15 exile   v. ban, expel   ↔ welcome, import

[égzail] 추방하다

Political enemies can be **exiled** by a ruler to faraway lands.
정적들은 통치자에 의해 먼 곳으로 유배될 수 있다.

16 furnish   v. decorate

[fə́ːrniʃ] 들여놓다, 비치하다

The newlyweds were excited to **furnish** their apartment with a new sofa and other household items.
신혼부부는 아파트에 새 소파와 다른 살림살이를 들여놓고 기분이 들떴다.

17 humility   n. humbleness, modesty   ↔ arrogance, pride

[hjuːmíləti] 겸손

She was ashamed of her son's arrogance and wished that he had more **humility**.
그녀는 아들의 오만함을 부끄러워했고 좀 더 겸손하기를 바랐다.

18 inflate   v. expand, blow up   ↔ deflate, compress

[infléit] 팽창시키다

He started feeling dizzy after having to **inflate** three swimming tubes for his young daughters.
그는 어린 딸들을 위해 수영 튜브 3개를 불어 놓고 어지럼증을 느끼기 시작했다.

19 intrude   n. trespass, infringe

[intrúːd] 침범하다

Modern technology has made it easier for us to **intrude** upon other people's privacy.
현대 기술은 타인의 사생활을 침해하기 쉽게 했다.

20 junta   n. committee, council

[húntə] 군사 정부

Myanmar is ruled by a **junta**, where the military group rules without the people's approval.
미얀마는 군사 정부의 지배를 받는데, 그곳에서는 군사 집단이 국민의 승인 없이 통치한다.

21 lament v. mourn, grieve ↔ celebrate

[ləmént] 비탄하다

Zack **lamented** over the loss of his wife and could not go to work.
잭은 아내를 잃은 것을 비탄한 나머지 출근할 수 없었다.

22 malnourished adj. starving, underfed ↔ overweight, fat

[mælnə́ːriʃt] 영양실조의

There are many poor countries that have **malnourished** children begging for food on the streets.
영양실조에 걸린 아이들이 거리에서 음식을 구걸하는 빈국이 많이 있다.

23 monologue n. speech, address ↔ dialogue

[mánəlɔ̀ːg] 독백

The famous theater actor had an incredible **monologue** at the end of the play.
유명한 연극배우는 연극 막바지에 훌륭한 독백을 했다.

24 passive adj. inactive, quiet ↔ active, lively

[pǽsiv] 순순히 따르는, 활기 없는

She appeared **passive** as her mother scolded her for coming home late.
그녀는 어머니가 집에 늦게 온 이유로 야단을 쳐서 기가 죽어 보였다.

25 plethora n. plenty, surplus ↔ lack, scarcity

[pléθərə] 과다, 다양성

The buffet offered a **plethora** of dishes and cuisines from which to choose.
뷔페에는 많고 다양한 가운데 선택할 수 있는 요리가 나왔다.

26 provoke v. arouse, incite ↔ prevent, calm

[prəvóuk] 자극하다, 화나게 하다

When dealing with a dangerous animal, it is important to be calm and not to **provoke** it in any way.
위험한 동물을 다룰 때는 침착하고 어떻게든 동물을 자극하지 않는 것이 중요하다.

27 resilient adj. flexible, strong ↔ inflexible, rigid

[rizíliənt] 회복력 있는, 탄력 있는

Anthony is a **resilient** young man who was able to recover quickly after being hit by a car.
앤소니는 차에 치인 후 빠르게 회복할 수 있었던 회복이 빠른 젊은이다.

28 strikingly adv. noticeably, conspicuously ↔ vaguely, indistinctly

[stráikiŋli] 두드러지게

The artist's style was **strikingly** similar to the earlier works of Pablo Picasso.
그 작가의 스타일은 파블로 피카소의 초기 작업과 눈에 띄게 비슷하다.

29 toil v. work, labor ↔ idle, neglect

[tɔ́il] 힘써 일하다

Jordan **toiled** for many hours under the hot sun helping his father with farm work.
조던은 아버지의 농장 일을 도우며 뜨거운 태양 아래 오랜 시간 힘써 일했다.

30 vendor n. seller, merchant

[véndər] 행상인

Street **vendors** sell simple snacks to pedestrians walking around.
노점상들은 다니는 보행자들에게 간단한 간식류를 판매한다.

DAILY QUIZ

1. an **anesthetic** for a sick patient • • a tradition
2. practicing hard to **enhance** one's skills • • b dishonest
3. observe an important **custom** • • c jam
4. **provoke** anger • • d calm
5. **compatible** computer parts • • e improve
6. a **deceptive** official • • f excuse
7. **absolve** all sins • • g noticeably
8. **appease** the excited mob • • h sedative
9. a **strikingly** attractive woman • • i arouse
10. traffic **congestion** • • j fitting

ANSWERS 1. h 2. e 3. a 4. i 5. j 6. b 7. f 8. d 9. g 10. c

Day 44

1. acrid   adj. bitter, sour   ↔ delicious, sweet

[ǽkrid] 매운, 쓴

People can find unfamiliar and strong spices **acrid** and difficult to eat.
사람들은 익숙지 않고 강한 맛이 나는 양념이 맵고 먹기 어렵다고 느낀다.

2. alternative   n. substitute, back-up

[ɔːltə́ːrnətiv] 대체, 대안

Tofu burgers are a vegetarian **alternative** to hamburgers with meat.
두부 버거는 고기가 든 햄버거에 대한 채식주의자의 대체 식품이다.

3. applaud   v. praise, clap   ↔ disapprove

[əplɔ́ːd] 박수하다, 손뼉을 치다

The audience **applauded** wildly to the artful performance.
관객은 기교가 뛰어난 연주에 박수갈채를 보냈다.

4. arouse   v. excite, alert   ↔ calm

[əráuz] 자극하다

Any strange behavior can **arouse** the looks and suspicions of others.
이상한 행동은 다른 사람의 눈초리와 의심을 불러일으킬 수 있다.

5. asset   n. resource, treasure   ↔ disadvantage, drawback

[ǽset] 자산

The **assets** of a company include its leadership, workers, properties, and capital.
회사의 자산에는 지도력, 근로자, 자산 및 자본이 포함된다.

6. brisk   adj. refreshing, invigorating

[brísk] 상쾌한

The climbers were able to enjoy the **brisk** air at the summit of the mountain.
등산객들은 산 정상에서 상쾌한 공기를 마실 수 있었다.

7. blemish n. flaw, defect ↔ decoration, ornament

[blémiʃ] 흠, 결점

There was hardly a **blemish** in his entire career at the office.
그의 전체적인 사무 경력에는 흠이 거의 없었다.

8. cavernous adj. large, open ↔ small, cramped

[kǽvərnəs] 휑한, 동굴 같은

The **cavernous** streets of downtown are always cool and shaded in the summer.
휑한 도심의 거리는 여름에도 항상 서늘하고 그늘져 있다.

9. commitment n. promise, obligation ↔ denial, refusal

[kəmítmənt] 약속, 헌신

The business deal required a long-term **commitment** from both parties.
사업 거래에는 장기적인 쌍방의 헌신이 필요했다.

10. confine v. limit, enclose ↔ free, release

[kənfáin] 한정하다, 제한하다

Thanks to their efforts, the fire was **confined** to a small area.
그들의 노력 덕분에 화재는 좁은 지역에 제한되었다.

11. containment n. control, regulation ↔ release

[kəntéinmənt] 봉쇄, 견제

Much care is taken for the proper **containment** of radioactive waste.
방사능 폐기물을 적절히 봉쇄하기 위해 주의를 많이 기울여야 한다.

12. credible adj. believable, trustworthy ↔ incredible, unbelievable

[krédəbl] 믿을 만한

Reporters have to decide whether a news source is **credible** or not.
기자는 뉴스 출처가 믿을 만한지 아닌지 결정해야 한다.

13. curse n. misfortune, tribulation ↔ blessing, fortune

[kə́:rs] 저주, 악담

The failure turned out to be more of a blessing than a **curse**.
실패는 저주보다는 오히려 축복으로 나타났다.

14 decoy n. lure, trap

[dikɔ́i] 유인물, 미끼

Duck hunters are known to use **decoys** to attract ducks to a particular spot.
오리 사냥꾼은 특정 장소로 오리를 유인하기 위해 미끼를 사용하는 것으로 알려져 있다.

15 delineate v. describe, outline

[dilínièit] 설명하다, 서술하다

In his speech, the president **delineated** his plans for the future of the company.
연설에서 사장은 회사의 미래에 대한 자신의 계획을 자세히 설명했다.

16 disdain n. hate, scorn ↔ respect, admiration

[disdéin] 경멸

He showed **disdain** for mass popular forms of entertainment.
그는 연예의 대중적 인기 형태를 경멸했다.

17 extinction n. annihilation, disappearance ↔ birth, creation

[ikstíŋkʃən] 멸종

It is well known that dinosaurs used to roam the earth until they suffered **extinction**.
공룡들은 멸종될 때까지 지구를 돌아다닌 것으로 잘 알려져 있다.

18 forlorn adj. hopeless, unhappy ↔ cheerful, happy

[fərlɔ́ːrn] 쓸쓸한, 절망적인

The couple gave each other **forlorn** glances across the room.
두 사람은 방 맞은편에서 쓸쓸하게 서로를 힐끗 쳐다보았다.

19 genocide n. holocaust, slaughter

[dʒénəsàid] 대량[집단] 학살

The survivors of the **genocide** continue to remember their suffering and the death of their loved ones.
집단 학살의 생존자들은 자신들이 겪은 고통과 사랑했던 이들의 죽음을 끊임없이 기억한다.

20 humiliate v. ridicule, embarrass ↔ praise, compliment

[hjuːmílièit] 창피를 주다

Agnes was **humiliated** in front of all her friends.
아그네스는 모든 친구들 앞에서 창피를 당했다.

21. integral adj. essential, indispensable ↔ unnecessary, unneeded

[íntigrəl] 필수적인

The smartphone is now an **integral** part of people's lives.
이제 일상 생활에서 스마트폰은 필수적이다.

22. muster v. gather, collect ↔ separate, remove

[mʌ́stər] 모으다, (용기 등을 최대한) 내다

He was able to **muster** the strength to get out of bed and go to work after being sick all night.
그는 밤새 앓은 후, 자리에서 일어나 출근할 힘을 낼 수 있었다.

23. outrageous adj. unbelievable, shocking ↔ delightful, magnificent

[autréidʒəs] 터무니없는

He was angry at the **outrageous** accusation made by his boss that he was stealing money from the cash register.
그는 자신이 금전 등록기에서 돈을 훔치고 있었다는 상사의 터무니없는 고발에 화가 났다.

24. parochial adj.

[pəróukiəl] 교구의

The best schools in town were all **parochial** schools run by the local churches.
도시에 있는 최고의 학교는 모두 지역 교회가 운영하는 교구 학교였다.

25. petroleum n. oil, fossil fuel

[pətróuliəm] 석유

The oil company invested a large sum of money to dig for **petroleum** in Saudi Arabia.
석유 회사는 사우디 아라비아에서 석유 시추를 위해 많은 돈을 투자했다.

26. pose v. advance, extend ↔ withhold

[póuz] 제기하다, 가하다

The rebels **posed** a threat to the stability of the government.
반역자들은 정부의 안정에 위협을 가했다.

27. rebuttal n. refutation, counterstatement

[ribʌ́tl] 반박, 반증

The debate partners hastily prepared a **rebuttal** to the argument of the opposing team.
토론 파트너들은 상대 팀의 논거에 대한 반박을 서둘러 마련했다.

28 request n. plea, appeal ↔ answer, reply

[rikwést] 요청, 요구

Jim made a **request** to the hostess of the restaurant to seat them by the window.
짐은 식당의 여주인에게 창가 쪽 자리를 달라고 요청했다.

29 shatter v. break, explode ↔ fix, mend

[ʃǽtər] 산산조각 나다

The glass cup **shattered** onto the floor after being accidently dropped.
우연히 떨어진 유리컵은 바닥에서 산산조각 났다.

30 unilateral adj. one-sided, biased ↔ bilateral, many-sided

[jùːnəlǽtərəl] 일방적인, 한편(만)의

A nation may adopt a **unilateral** decision without consulting other countries.
국가는 타국과 상의 없이 일방적인 결정을 채택할 수 있다.

DAILY QUIZ

1 **arouse** the audience •   • a essential
2 use a **decoy** to trick the enemy • • b one-sided
3 an **integral** part of any human society • • c unbelievable
4 import **petroleum** from the Middle East • • d annihilation
5 a **unilateral** contract •   • e trap
6 reject a **request** •   • f trustworthy
7 an **outrageous** rumor •   • g excite
8 information from a **credible** source • • h oil
9 **extinction** of a rare animals • • i substitute
10 margarine as an **alternative** to butter • • j appeal

ANSWERS 1. g 2. e 3. a 4. h 5. b 6. j 7. c 8. f 9. d 10. i

COMPREHENSIVE QUIZ Day 43 & 44

1. The restaurant manager tried to _____ the angry customers who complained that their food was coming out way too late.
   ⓐ appease   ⓑ confine   ⓒ shatter   ⓓ lament

2. The newspaper claimed that it received the story from a(n) _____ source.
   ⓐ deceptive   ⓑ acrid   ⓒ credible   ⓓ cavernous

3. Hermes had the responsibility of _____ the messages of the Greek gods.
   ⓐ delivering   ⓑ appeasing   ⓒ exiling   ⓓ applauding

4. It is important to remember that love should never be _____.
   ⓐ brisk   ⓑ compatible   ⓒ malnourished   ⓓ conditional

5. The _____ that controlled the country was finally overthrown by the citizens.
   ⓐ congestion   ⓑ census   ⓒ junta   ⓓ decoy

6. A serious leg injury _____ Joseph's dream of getting an athletic scholarship to college.
   ⓐ mustered   ⓑ shattered   ⓒ aroused   ⓓ furnished

7. Without _____, friendships do not last and can be easily broken.
   ⓐ commitment   ⓑ monologue   ⓒ blemish   ⓓ discordance

8. The people of the clan respected and loved their leader because he treated them with _____.
   ⓐ containment   ⓑ disdain   ⓒ humility   ⓓ request

9. A _____ attitude toward education can ruin a student's future.
   ⓐ passive   ⓑ biochemical   ⓒ compatible   ⓓ resilient

10. The _____ survivor of the plane crash had to live on eating wild berries and nuts.
    ⓐ acrid   ⓑ plethora   ⓒ conditional   ⓓ malnourished

Answers: p.343

Day 45

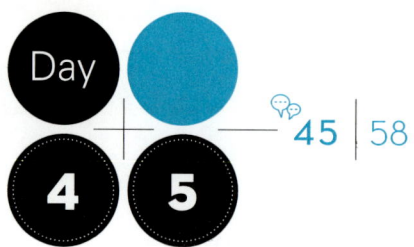

45 | 58

1 abrogate v. abolish, revoke ↔ approve, legalize

[ǽbrəgèit] 폐지하다

The city law was **abrogated** after much public complaint.
대중의 불만이 크게 있은 후 도시법이 폐지되었다.

2 affiliation n. association, connection

[əfìliéiʃən] (정치적인) 관계, 제휴

The independent candidate had no **affiliation** with any political party.
그 무소속 후보는 어떤 정당과도 정치적인 관계를 맺지 않았다.

3 anthropologist n.

[æ̀nθrəpάlədʒist] 인류학자

An **anthropologist** studies people and cultures in a scientific manner.
인류학자는 과학적인 방법으로 사람과 문화를 연구한다.

4 attain v. achieve, acquire ↔ abandon, lose

[ətéin] 습득하다, 달성하다

Lots of study and practice are required to **attain** skills in any field.
어떤 분야에서든 기술을 습득하려면 많은 공부와 실습이 필요하다.

5 bubble n. inflated speculation

[bʌ́bl] 일시적인 호황, 거품

A rise in prices followed by a sudden drop is a sign of an economic **bubble**.
가격이 오른 후 갑자기 떨어지는 것이 경제적 거품의 징후이다.

6 captivating adj. enchanting, engrossing ↔ boring, uninteresting

[kǽptəvèitiŋ] 매혹적인

Science fiction movies often have **captivating** special effects.
공상 과학 영화는 흔히 매혹적인 특수 효과가 있다.

7 compliance n. agreement, consent ↔ defiance, dissent

[kəmpláiəns] 준수, 순응

Good citizens exercise **compliance** with the law at all times.
선량한 시민은 언제나 법을 준수한다.

8 consent n. permission, agreement ↔ denial, disapproval

[kənsént] 동의, 찬성

The workers went ahead on the idea with the **consent** of their boss.
직원들은 상사의 동의를 받은 계획을 추진했다.

9 conspiracy n. plot, collusion

[kənspírəsi] 음모, 모의

The men were jailed for **conspiracy** to cover up the crime.
그 사람들은 죄를 덮으려는 공모죄로 투옥되었다.

10 contribute v. donate, provide ↔ take, withdraw

[kəntríbjuːt] 기부하다

Graduates are often asked to **contribute** money to their former schools.
졸업생들은 종종 모교에 돈을 기부하라는 요청을 받는다.

11 cylinder n.

[sílindər] 원통

Glasses for drinking water are usually in the form of a **cylinder**.
물잔은 보통 원통 형태이다.

12 deluge n. flood, barrage

[déljuːdʒ] 쇄도

We live in an age when there is a potential **deluge** of information available to us.
우리는 가용 정보 쇄도가 가능한 시대에 살고 있다.

13 demand n. request, need ↔ supply, offer

[dimǽnd] 수요, 요구

The **demand** for an item can influence its price in the marketplace.
물품에 대한 수요는 시장 가격에 영향을 미칠 수 있다.

14 determine v. figure out ↔ miss, overlook

[ditə́:rmin] 알아내다

The hikers **determined** their location by using the position of the sun.
등산객들은 태양의 위치를 이용해 자신의 위치를 알아냈다.

15 entitled to phr. deserving of, privileged ↔ no right to

권리가 있다, 자격이 있다

The law says that everyone is **entitled to** a fair trial in a court of law.
법에 모든 사람은 법정에서 공정한 재판을 받을 권리가 있다고 명시되어 있다.

16 estimated adj. approximated, supposed ↔ accurate, precise

[éstəmèitid] 추측의

An **estimated** 7 billion people live on earth.
70억 명으로 추산되는 인구가 지구에 살고 있다.

17 fragile adj. delicate, breakable ↔ durable, sturdy

[frǽdʒəl] 깨지기 쉬운

The two countries worried that their **fragile** peace agreement would not last and lead to an outbreak of war.
양국은 깨지기 쉬운 평화 협정이 지속되지 않고 전쟁 발발로 이어질 것을 우려했다.

18 gross v. earn, make

[gróus] 수익을 올리다

Mr. Barnes found out from his accountant that he had **grossed** one million dollars last year from his export business.
반즈 씨는 회계사로부터 자신이 작년에 수출업으로 백만 달러의 수입을 올린 것을 알게 되었다.

19 horrendous adj. terrible, horrible

[hɔːréndəs] 무서운, 끔찍한

The reporter was disgusted to learn the details of the **horrendous** crimes committed by the serial killer.
기자는 연쇄 살인범이 저지른 끔찍한 범죄의 내용을 알고 역겨움을 느꼈다.

20 insolvent adj. bankrupt, broke ↔ solvent, in the black

[insάlvənt] 파산한

Some companies actually make money by buying **insolvent** businesses.
어떤 회사들은 실제로 파산한 사업을 사들여 돈을 번다.

21 instrumental adj. important, vital ↔ useless, unhelpful

[ìnstrəméntl] 중요한, 도움이 되는

He was **instrumental** in negotiating the terms of the peace treaty.
그는 평화 협정 조건을 협상하는 데 있어 중요한 역할을 했다.

22 maintenance n. support, repairs ↔ abandonment, negligence

[méintənəns] 정비, 유지

Paul's car broke down because he did not keep proper **maintenance** of his car over the years.
폴이 수년간 자동차를 제대로 정비하지 않았기 때문에 차가 고장 났다.

23 mechanical adj. machinelike, automated ↔ manual, physical

[məkǽnikəl] 기계적인

Paul was late for the meeting because he was also having **mechanical** problems with his car.
폴은 자동차에 기계상 문제도 있었기 때문에 회의에 늦었다.

24 neutral adj. impartial, unbiased ↔ subjective, prejudiced

[njú:trəl] 중립의

Switzerland managed to remain a **neutral** country as war occurred around its borders during World War II.
스위스는 제2차 세계 대전 동안 자국 국경선 주위에서 전쟁이 일어났을 때 가까스로 중립국으로 남았다.

25 pioneer n. founder, explorer

[pàiəníər] 선구자, 개척자

Galileo was a **pioneer** in the field of astronomy and is well known for stating that the sun was the center of the solar system, not the earth.
갈릴레오는 천문학 분야에서 선구자였고, 지구가 아닌 태양이 태양계의 중심이라고 말한 것으로 잘 알려져 있다.

26 practical adj. realistic, pragmatic ↔ improbable, idealistic

[prǽktikəl] 현실적인

While her friends considered her very **practical** and full of common sense, Susan sometimes wished she could be more spontaneous and reckless.
친구들은 수잔을 매우 현실적이고 상식이 풍부하다고 여긴 반면, 그녀는 때때로 자신이 좀 더 자발적이고 무모하길 바랐다.

27 rapport n. relationship, affinity

[ræpó:r] (친밀한) 관계

Establishing a strong **rapport** between the coach and the players is crucial in winning the league games.
리그 경기에서 승리하는데 있어서 코치와 선수 간의 긴밀한 관계가 중요하다.

28 stock   v. store, put away   ↔ remove, deplete

[sták] 비축하다, 저장하다

They **stocked** their shelves with canned goods and water in case of an emergency.
그들은 비상시를 대비해 통조림과 물을 선반에 비축해 두었다.

29 tacitly   adv. quietly, silently   ↔ loudly, audibly

[tǽsitli] 암암리에, 무언으로

The husband **tacitly** agreed with his wife who scolded their daughter for stealing makeup at the store.
남편은 상점에서 화장품을 훔친 딸을 꾸짖는 아내에게 무언으로 동의했다.

30 undergo   v. experience, go through

[ʌ̀ndərɡóu] 겪다, 경험하다

Reaching success may require one to **undergo** many failures beforehand.
사전에 많은 실패를 겪어야 성공에 이를 수 있을지도 모른다.

DAILY QUIZ

1. **conspiracy** against the state
2. an **estimated** value of an apartment
3. take a **neutral** stance
4. the **pioneer** of the new movement
5. an **affiliation** with the radical group
6. **undergo** difficult times
7. **stock** products in a warehouse
8. **gross** millions of dollars
9. **determine** the cause of an accident
10. **captivating** CG effects

a. earn
b. founder
c. connection
d. engrossing
e. plot
f. store
g. impartial
h. figure out
i. approximated
j. experience

ANSWERS   1. e   2. i   3. g   4. b   5. c   6. j   7. f   8. a   9. h   10. d

Day 46

1. acclaimed   adj. praised, lauded   ↔ unknown, ordinary

[əkléimd] 찬사를 받은

The **acclaimed** actor has won numerous awards over the years.
찬사를 받은 그 배우는 수년 동안 많은 상을 받았다.

2. allegiance   n. loyalty, duty   ↔ treason, unfaithfulness

[əlíːdʒəns] 충성

Singing a national anthem demonstrates an **allegiance** to a country.
국가를 부르는 것은 국가에 대한 충성을 보여준다.

3. apocalyptic   adj.

[əpɑ̀kəlíptik] 종말적인, 종말론적

The age of dinosaurs saw an **apocalyptic** end when a giant meteor struck our planet.
거대한 유성이 지구를 강타했을 때 공룡 시대는 종말을 맞았다.

4. appendix   n. supplement, attachment

[əpéndiks] 부록

Most books have an **appendix** that lists additional information.
대부분 책에는 추가 정보를 기재한 부록이 있다.

5. assertion   n. declaration, statement   ↔ denial, rejection

[əsə́ːrʃən] 주장

The **assertion** he made was later found to be incorrect and premature.
후에 그의 주장은 부정확하고 시기상조인 것으로 밝혀졌다.

6. bewildered   adj. confused, stumped   ↔ composed, oriented

[biwíldərd] 어리둥절한, 당황한

The shocking incident left them confused and **bewildered**.
충격적인 사건이 그들을 혼란스럽고 어리둥절하게 만들었다.

7 capricious adj. unpredictable, fickle ↔ steady, dependable

[kəpríʃəs] 변덕스러운

Being **capricious** does not inspire the trust and confidence of others.
변덕스러운 사람은 다른 사람에게 믿음과 신뢰를 주지 못한다.

8 circumspect adj. cautious, discreet ↔ careless, direct

[sə́ːrkəmspèkt] 신중한, 주의 깊은

He was **circumspect** in his behavior so as not to offend any of his guests.
그는 어떤 손님이라도 불쾌하게 하지 않도록 행동에 신중을 기했다.

9 composition n. arrangement, creation

[kàmpəzíʃən] 작곡, 작품

Famous musicians sometimes leave behind unfinished **compositions**.
유명한 음악가는 때로 미완성 작품을 남긴다.

10 derive v. originate, come from

[diráiv] (단어·관습 등이) 파생하다, 유래하다

Words can **derive** from older forms of a language or even other languages.
단어는 언어의 오래된 형태나 다른 언어에서도 파생할 수 있다.

11 detract v. divert, draw away ↔ help, clarify

[ditrǽkt] 딴 데로 돌리다

Minor issues often **detract** us from the main goal we have in mind.
사소한 문제는 염두에 두고 있는 주된 목적에서 종종 우리의 주의를 다른 곳으로 돌린다.

12 disruptive adj. disturbing, distracting ↔ calming, settling

[disrʌ́ptiv] 지장을 주는

Talking loudly or using a cell phone can be **disruptive** in a movie theater.
극장에서 크게 말하거나 휴대 전화를 사용하는 것은 방해가 될 수 있다.

13 encumber v. bother, burden ↔ help, assist

[inkʌ́mbər] 방해하다

Furthermore, using a cell phone while driving can also **encumber** a driver.
뿐만 아니라, 운전 중 휴대 전화 사용 또한 운전자를 방해할 수 있다.

14 experience   v. encounter, undergo   ↔ avoid, evade

[ikspíəriəns] 경험하다

Works of art allow us to **experience** more of the world.
예술 작품으로 우리는 세상을 더 많이 체험할 수 있다.

15 fulfillment   n. completion, accomplishment   ↔ disappointment, failure

[fulfílmənt] 성취, 실현

Many people search for jobs that can give them a sense of **fulfillment**.
많은 사람들이 성취감을 줄 수 있는 직업을 찾는다.

16 genetically   adv. inherently, innately

[dʒənétikəli] 유전적으로

The young mother refused to feed her baby **genetically** modified food because she believed that it was harmful to his body.
젊은 엄마는 유전자 조작 식품이 몸에 해롭다고 믿었기 때문에 아기에게 먹이려고 하지 않았다.

17 infection   n. disease, contamination

[infékʃən] 감염

The young mother was also worried that her baby would get an **infection** from the cut on his arm.
젊은 엄마는 또 아기가 팔에 베인 상처로 인해 감염될 것을 걱정했다.

18 intuitive   adj. instinctive, perceptive   ↔ calculated, reasoned

[intʃúːətiv] 직관에 의한

Most psychics use their **intuitive** powers to help their customers with their problems.
대부분의 심령술사들은 문제가 있는 고객들을 돕기 위해 직관력을 사용한다.

19 irreversible   adj. unstoppable, unchangeable   ↔ temporary, transitory

[ìrivə́ːrsəbl] 돌이킬 수 없는

Although we try everything to stop aging, it is **irreversible**.
우리는 노화 방지를 위해 무엇이든 시도하지만, 그것은 돌이킬 수 없다.

20 marginal   adj. slight, insignificant   ↔ definite, significant

[máːrdʒinl] 미미한

Despite the hard work, the company produced only **marginal** results of economic gain.
고된 작업에도 불구하고 회사는 미미한 수준의 경제적 이득을 보았을 뿐이다.

21. maxim   n. proverb, motto

[mǽksim] 격언, 금언

Many people agree with the **maxim** that money does not buy happiness.
많은 사람들이 돈으로 행복을 살 수 없다는 격언에 동의한다.

22. outright   adv. absolutely, utterly   ↔ hesitantly, reluctantly

[áutráit] 철저히, 완전히

Nick's parents punished him after he refused **outright** to clean his room.
닉의 부모는 닉이 철저히 방 청소를 거부하자 벌을 주었다.

23. paradoxically   adv. contrarily, oppositely

[pærədáksikəli] 역설적으로

Certain forms of poison can **paradoxically** improve one's health.
역설적이지만 어떤 형태의 독극물은 건강을 개선시킬 수 있다.

24. perspiration   n. sweat, secretion

[pə̀ːrspəréiʃən] 땀

There was **perspiration** on the faces of the runners who were crossing the finish line.
결승선을 지나는 주자들의 얼굴에는 땀이 있었다.

25. hoist   v. lift, raise   ↔ drop, lower

[hɔ́ist] 올리다

The citizens **hoisted** the national flag to commemorate Independence Day.
시민들은 독립 기념일을 기념하기 위해 국기를 게양했다.

26. retail   adj.   ↔ general, wholesale

[ríːteil] 소매의, 소매상의

The **retail** price of the HDTV has gone down significantly in the last few years.
지난 몇 년 동안 HDTV 소매가가 크게 내렸다.

27. sensual   adj. arousing, pleasing

[sénʃuəl] 관능적인

She decided to buy the candle for its **sensual** smell in order to mask the bad odor in the kitchen.
그녀는 주방의 악취를 감추기 위해 관능적인 향이 나는 양초를 구입하기로 했다.

28 summit   n. meeting of leaders, peak   ↔ base, bottom

[sʌ́mit] 정상[수뇌] 회담

Several world leaders had a meeting at the **summit** to discuss possible solutions to the problems of global warming.
몇몇 세계 지도자들이 지구 온난화 문제에 대해 가능한 해결책을 논의하기 위해 정상 회담을 가졌다.

29 voyage   n. travel, journey

[vɔ́iidʒ] 여행

For their next vacation, the Waltons decided to take an ocean **voyage**.
월튼 가족은 다음 휴가에 바다 여행을 가기로 결정했다.

30 wholesale   adj. bulk, large-scale   ↔ partial, retail

[hóulsèil] 도매의, 도매상의

Only stores usually pay the **wholesale** price for items.
상점들만이 물건 가격을 도매가로 지불한다.

DAILY QUIZ

1. an **appendix** of a book   a innately
2. suffer from an **infection**   b loyalty
3. **genetically** fit to survive   c journey
4. a **disruptive** noise   d disturbing
5. pledge **allegiance** to the flag   e large-scale
6. Sinbad's first **voyage**   f sweat
7. **wholesale** stores   g disease
8. **perspiration** during exercise   h lift
9. **hoist** the cargo on to the ship   i supplement
10. a **maxim** to live by   j proverb

ANSWERS   1. i   2. g   3. a   4. d   5. b   6. c   7. e   8. f   9. h   10. j

COMPREHENSIVE QUIZ — Day 45 & 46

1. Everyone was surprised when the rookie player opposed the coach's directions _____.
   ⓐ genetically   ⓑ outright   ⓒ marginally   ⓓ instrumentally

2. A parent's _____ is needed for a student to leave early from school.
   ⓐ allegiance   ⓑ deluge   ⓒ consent   ⓓ maxim

3. The explorers used their _____ abilities to survive in the wild.
   ⓐ bewildered   ⓑ irreversible   ⓒ fragile   ⓓ intuitive

4. Edison thought that genius was one percent inspiration and ninety-nine percent _____.
   ⓐ conspiracy   ⓑ perspiration   ⓒ rapport   ⓓ affiliation

5. Economists warn that the current real estate _____ could burst at any time.
   ⓐ bubble   ⓑ voyage   ⓒ infection   ⓓ allegiance

6. The nobles swore _____ to their new king.
   ⓐ composition   ⓑ summit   ⓒ demand   ⓓ allegiance

7. _____ chain stores are popping up everywhere these days.
   ⓐ Apocalyptic   ⓑ Neutral   ⓒ Retail   ⓓ Estimated

8. The national soccer team _____ rigorous training to prepare for the finals.
   ⓐ underwent   ⓑ abrogated   ⓒ detracted   ⓓ encumbered

9. The villagers _____ the invading barbarians by setting the surrounding forest on fire.
   ⓐ hoisted   ⓑ detracted   ⓒ stocked   ⓓ grossed

10. Within a year, the coffee shop _____ enough money to cover the cost of opening business.
    ⓐ abrogated   ⓑ bewildered   ⓒ grossed   ⓓ acclaimed

Answers: p.343

Day 47

1. adverse — adj. unfavorable, negative ↔ advantageous, favorable

[ædvə́ːrs] 불운한, 불리한

Businesses can fail when they are faced with **adverse** economic conditions.
기업은 불리한 경제 환경에 당면하면 파산할 수 있다.

2. arson — n. burning, incineration

[áːrsn] 방화

The police determined that the fire was deliberately set and therefore was **arson**.
경찰은 화재가 고의로 일어났으므로 방화라는 결론을 내렸다.

3. audiovisual — adj.

[ɔ̀ːdiouvíʒuəl] 시청각의

An **audiovisual** presentation gives people information in different forms.
시청각 발표는 사람들에게 여러 가지 형태로 정보를 제공한다.

4. bureaucracy — n. officials, administration

[bjuərάkrəsi] 관료 제도, 관료주의

People complain that a complicated **bureaucracy** can prevent things from getting done.
사람들은 복잡한 관료주의가 일 처리를 방해할 수 있다고 불평한다.

5. carnivore — n. predator, meat-eater

[káːrnəvɔ̀ːr] 육식 동물

Pandas are actually **carnivores**.
팬더는 사실 육식 동물이다.

6. compassionate — adj. kind, sympathetic ↔ cruel, merciless

[kəmpǽʃənət] 동정적인, 인정 많은

The **compassionate** side of people shows when they help others in a crisis.
사람의 동정적인 면은 위기에 처한 타인을 도와줄 때 나타난다.

7 console v. cheer, comfort ↔ depress, hurt

[kənsóul] 위로하다

True friends **console** each other in times of sadness.
진정한 친구는 슬플 때 서로 위로한다.

8 crusade n. mission, expedition

[kruːséid] 개혁 운동[활동]

He was on a one-man **crusade** to stop crime in his neighborhood.
그는 동네의 범죄 방지를 위한 1인 개혁 활동을 펼쳤다.

9 culpable adj. responsible, guilty ↔ innocent, inculpable

[kʌ́lpəbl] 과실이 있는, 책임이 있는

On the other hand, his neighbors thought that he was **culpable** of the recent crime.
반면, 이웃 사람들은 그가 최근 범죄 사건에 책임이 있다고 생각했다.

10 date v. record, measure

[déit] 연대를 매기다

Archaeologists **dated** the recently discovered skull all the way back to the Stone Age.
고고학자들은 최근 발견된 두개골의 연대를 석기 시대로 잡았다.

11 discard v. abandon, throw away ↔ retain, hold onto

[diskάːrd] 버리다

Recycling **discards** objects according to the category of its material.
재활용은 재료의 종류에 따라서 물건을 버리는 것이다.

12 display v. show, indicate ↔ conceal, hide

[displéi] 보이다, 드러내다

The student early on **displayed** signs of high academic potential.
그 학생은 초기에 수준 높은 학문적 잠재력의 조짐을 보였다.

13 dynamic adj. active, forceful ↔ dull, apathetic

[dainǽmik] 역동적인

The energetic and **dynamic** performer kept the fans entertained.
정력적이고 역동적인 연주자는 계속해서 팬들을 즐겁게 해주었다.

14 essence   n. foundation, soul

[ésns] 정수

A proverb contains the **essence** of many people's experiences.
속담에는 많은 사람의 경험의 정수가 들어 있다.

15 expense   n. cost, payment

[ikspéns] 경비

Expenses by businessmen are sometimes covered by the company.
사업가의 경비는 때때로 회사가 지불한다.

16 felony   n. crime, offense

[féləni] 중죄, 흉악 범죄

Josh was placed in custody after being accused of murder, which was a **felony** in New York.
조쉬는 살인 혐의로 고소 당한 후 구금 상태에 있었는데, 살인은 뉴욕에서 중죄이다.

17 hospitable   adj. friendly, cordial   ↔ mean, alienating

[háspitəbl] 친절한, 쾌적한

The visitors to the island were encouraged by the **hospitable** smiles of the local people.
섬 방문객들은 현지인들의 상냥한 미소에 고무되었다.

18 imprisonment   n. confinement, incarceration   ↔ freedom, liberty

[impríznmənt] 수감, 투옥

The innocent man suffered **imprisonment** for a crime he did not commit.
무고한 사람이 저지르지 않은 범죄로 수감되었다.

19 introspective   adj. contemplative, self-examining   ↔ shallow, unreflective

[ìntrəspéktiv] 자기 성찰적인

Psychologists require that their patients be **introspective** about their feelings.
심리학자들은 환자들에게 자기 감정에 대해 자기 성찰적이기를 요구한다.

20 linguistic   adj. lingual, semantic

[liŋgwístik] 언어의

My friend has great **linguistic** abilities as she is able to learn a language very easily.
내 친구는 언어를 아주 쉽게 배울 수 있을 만큼 대단한 언어 능력을 가지고 있다.

21. malfunction   v. crash, break down   ↔ run, function

[mælfʌ́ŋkʃən] 제대로 작동하지 않다

The computers **malfunctioned**, causing panic among the workers in the technology company.
컴퓨터가 제대로 작동하지 않아 기술 회사 직원들끼리 우왕좌왕하는 일이 있었다.

22. morale   n. confidence, self-esteem

[mərǽl] 사기

The coach believed that the only way to win the game was to increase the team's **morale**.
감독은 경기에서 이기는 유일한 방법은 팀의 사기를 올리는 것이라고 믿었다.

23. pneumonia   n. respiratory disease

[njumóunjə] 폐렴

He took his grandmother to the hospital because he was worried that she was suffering from **pneumonia**.
그는 할머니가 폐렴을 앓고 계신 것이 걱정되어 병원으로 모셔 갔다.

24. provincial   adj. country, rural   ↔ modern, metropolitan

[prəvínʃəl] 시골의

The peasants in the country enjoyed their **provincial** and sheltered life.
시골의 농부들은 세상 풍파로부터 격리된 시골 생활을 즐겼다.

25. reactive   adj. responsive, susceptible   ↔ insensitive, placid

[riǽktiv] 민감한, 반응을 보이는

Since she started meditating, Gloria has learned to stay calm and not become **reactive** to negative criticism.
글로리아는 명상을 시작한 후 평정심을 유지하고 부정적인 비판에 대응하지 않는 법을 배웠다.

26. scramble   v. rush, scurry

[skrǽmbl] 서로 다투다

One of the baseball players hit a ball into the stands and the crowd **scrambled** to catch it.
야구 선수 중 한 명이 관중석으로 공을 쳤고, 군중은 공을 잡으려고 서로 다투었다.

27. shrink   v. shrivel, contract   ↔ enlarge, expand

[ʃríŋk] 줄어들다

Adrienne was worried that her newly bought expensive jeans would **shrink** and no longer fit if they were put in the dryer.
애드리언은 새로 산 비싼 청바지를 건조기에 넣으면 줄어들어 더 이상 맞지 않을까 걱정했다.

28 transplant   v. transfer, relocate   ↔ preserve, save

[trænsplǽnt] 이식하다

Danielle offered one of her kidneys to be **transplanted** into her sick sister.
대니얼은 자신의 신장 중 하나를 아픈 언니에게 이식하도록 기증했다.

29 volume   n. measure, amount

[válju:m] 양, 용량

The same **volume** of liquid can look greater or smaller depending on the container.
동일한 양의 액체가 통에 따라서 더 많게 또는 더 적게 보일 수 있다.

30 zoologist   n.

[zouálədʒist] 동물학자

Zoologists are consulted in planning and designing a new zoo.
새로운 동물원의 기획과 설계는 동물학자들과 상담한다.

DAILY QUIZ

1	cause **adverse** effects	a	crime
2	**date** the fossils	b	friendly
3	jailed for a **felony**	c	throw away
4	live in a **hospitable** environment	d	kind
5	boost a person's **morale**	e	active
6	**compassionate** volunteers	f	transfer
7	**discard** trash	g	negative
8	a **dynamic** economy	h	confidence
9	**transplant** a body organ	i	measure
10	a religious **crusade**	j	mission

ANSWERS   1. g   2. i   3. a   4. b   5. h   6. d   7. c   8. e   9. f   10. j

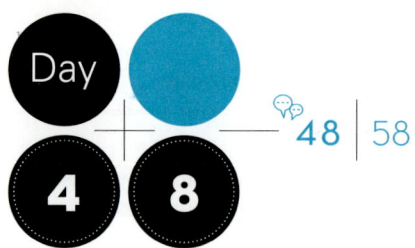

1. accuse   v. charge, implicate   ↔ absolve, vindicate

[əkjúːz] 비난하다, 고발하다

The child **accused** his playmate of cheating in the game.
아이는 게임에서 속임수를 썼다고 같이 노는 친구를 비난했다.

2. analogous   adj. comparable, parallel   ↔ dissimilar, unrelated

[ənǽləgəs] 유사한

The CPU in a computer is **analogous** to the brain of an animal.
컴퓨터 CPU는 동물의 뇌와 유사하다.

3. appeal   v. contest, petition   ↔ deny, disclaim

[əpíːl] 항소하다

The lawyer wanted to **appeal** the case to a higher court.
변호사는 그 사건을 상급 법원에 항소하고자 했다.

4. associate   v. link, correlate   ↔ dissociate, separate

[əsóuʃièit] 관련시키다

People usually **associate** having a lot of money with an easy life.
사람들은 대개 돈을 많이 소유하는 것을 안락한 생활과 관련시킨다.

5. atmosphere   n. air, sky

[ǽtməsfìər] 대기

The upper **atmosphere** has a different nature from that of the lower.
상층 대기는 하층 대기와 다른 성질이 있다.

6. banquet   n. feast, reception

[bǽŋkwit] 만찬

They gave a huge **banquet** to host all the guests who came.
그들은 방문한 모든 손님을 접대하기 위해 성대한 만찬을 열었다.

7 calamity n. disaster, tragedy ↔ fortune, blessing

[kəlǽməti] 재앙, 재난

The war was a **calamity** in terms of damage to property and loss of life.
그 전쟁은 재산 피해와 인명 손실 면에서 재앙이었다.

8 coffer n. treasury, chest

[kɔ́:fər] 금고

The empty city **coffers** led to calls for budget cuts.
고갈된 시의 금고가 예산 삭감 요구로 이어졌다.

9 convict v. sentence, adjudge ↔ free, exonerate

[kənvíkt] 유죄 판결을 내리다

The trial **convicted** the suspect of numerous crimes.
재판에서 많은 범죄의 용의자에게 유죄 판결을 내렸다.

10 denomination¹ n. group, sect

[dinɑ̀mənéiʃən] 교파

Some churches do not belong to any one **denomination** but embrace all.
일부 교회는 어느 한 교파에 속하지 않고 모든 교파를 받아들인다.

11 denomination²

[dinɑ̀mənéiʃən] 화폐 단위, 액면가

American paper money comes in **denominations** of 1, 5, 10, 20, 50, and 100 dollars.
미국 지폐는 1, 5, 10, 20, 50, 100달러의 화폐 단위로 발행된다.

12 distorted adj. crooked, deformed ↔ honest, straight

[distɔ́:rtid] 왜곡된

Looking at too few examples gives one a **distorted** picture of reality.
사례를 너무 적게 보면 현실을 왜곡해서 보게 된다.

13 embezzlement n. theft, misappropriation ↔ compensation, reimbursement

[imbézlmənt] 횡령

The accountant was charged with **embezzlement** of the company funds.
회계사는 회사 자금을 횡령한 혐의로 기소되었다.

14 encrypt   v. scramble, encode   ↔ crack, make sense of

[enkrípt] 암호화하다

Secret military messages are **encrypted** to prevent the enemy from reading them.
비밀 군사 메시지는 적이 판독할 수 없도록 암호화된다.

15 flagrant   adj. obvious, blatant   ↔ secret, subtle

[fléigrənt] 명백한

The prisoners, who were beat without reason, were shocked by the guards' **flagrant** abuse of power.
이유 없이 구타를 당한 수감자들은 교도관의 노골적인 권한 남용에 충격을 받았다.

16 generation   n. era, age group

[dʒènəréiʃən] 세대

Many people worry that we are destroying the earth and that the next **generation** will suffer the consequences.
많은 사람들이 우리가 지구를 파괴하고 있으며, 다음 세대가 그 영향으로 고통 받을 것을 우려하고 있다.

17 hesitate   v. pause, think twice   ↔ continue, persevere

[hézətèit] 망설이다

He **hesitated** before tasting the soup because his girlfriend was a terrible cook.
여자 친구가 요리를 못하기 때문에 그는 수프를 맛보기 전 망설였다.

18 illiterate   adj. uneducated, ignorant   ↔ learned, erudite

[ilítərət] 문맹의

Joseph avoided situations where he had to read because he was ashamed that he was **illiterate**.
조셉은 자신이 문맹이라는 것이 부끄러워 읽어야 하는 상황을 피했다.

19 infinite   adj. boundless, never-ending   ↔ limited, countable

[ínfənət] 무한한

While camping, Abby was in awe of the **infinite** amount of stars that she saw at night.
캠핑하면서 애비는 밤에 본 무한한 수의 별에 경외심을 느꼈다.

20 invariably   adv. customarily, consistently   ↔ occasionally, irregularly

[invɛ́əriəbli] 변함없이

Invariably, Jill gets really expensive presents from her parents every Christmas.
질은 늘 성탄절마다 부모로부터 아주 고가의 선물을 받는다.

21 **mechanism** n. component, device

[mékənìzm] 장치

The motor is an essential **mechanism** used to run the air conditioner.
모터는 에어컨 작동에 사용되는 필수적인 장치이다.

22 **nutrient** n. nourishment, nutriment

[njúːtriənt] 영양분

The pediatrician told Margaret to feed her infant steamed broccoli because it was full of **nutrients**.
소아과 의사는 마가렛에게 브로콜리가 영양분이 풍부하니 아기에게 찐 브로콜리를 먹이라고 말했다.

23 **omnivore** n. plant and meat eater

[ámnivɔ̀ːr] 잡식 동물

It is believed that bears are **omnivores** that can attack humans when they are hungry.
곰은 배가 고프면 사람을 공격할 수 있는 잡식 동물로 여겨진다.

24 **politics** n. government affairs, civics

[pálətiks] 정치

Sheila did not like to talk about **politics** and international news at the dinner table.
셰일라는 저녁 식사 중에 정치와 국제 뉴스에 대해 이야기하는 것을 좋아하지 않았다.

25 **proliferation** n. spread, expansion ↔ suppression, containment

[prəlìfəréiʃən] 확산

All leaders agree that stopping the threat of nuclear **proliferation** is a top priority.
모든 지도자들은 핵 확산 조짐을 막는 것이 최우선이라는 데 동의한다.

26 **retard** v. hinder, delay ↔ advance, help

[ritáːrd] 지체시키다, 방해하다

Many people believe that smoking cigarettes will **retard** the growth of young adolescents.
많은 사람들은 흡연이 어린 청소년의 성장을 방해할 것이라고 생각한다.

27 **tremendous** adj. immense, magnificent ↔ small, dreadful

[triméndəs] 엄청난, 대단한

The sad news story prompted a **tremendous** show of sympathy from viewers.
슬픈 보도 기사가 시청자들의 엄청난 연민을 불러일으켰다.

28 trite adj. unoriginal, commonplace ↔ unique, imaginative

[tráit] 진부한

Critics called the dialogue in the TV show **trite** and unoriginal.
평론가들은 TV쇼의 대화가 진부하고 독창성이 없다고 했다.

29 vacillate v. sway, waver ↔ remain, stay

[vǽsəlèit] 망설이다

To **vacillate** too much on an issue may mean the window of opportunity is lost.
한 문제에 대해 너무 망설인다는 것은 기회의 창이 닫힌다는 것을 의미할지도 모른다.

30 withhold v. conceal, hold back ↔ release, provide

[wiθhóuld] 주지 않고 두다, 보류하다

To **withhold** important or relevant information as a witness is a crime.
목격자로서 중요하거나 관련 있는 정보를 알려 주지 않는 것은 범죄이다.

DAILY QUIZ

1	**associate** heart with love	a	theft
2	a **distorted** truth	b	contest
3	**accuse** the defendant	c	spread
4	**appeal** a decision	d	unoriginal
5	**embezzlement** of public property	e	charge
6	**proliferation** of the Internet	f	immense
7	a **trite** storyline	g	deformed
8	the **infinite** sky	h	sway
9	a **tremendous** effort	i	boundless
10	**vacillate** back and forth	j	link

ANSWERS 1. j   2. g   3. e   4. b   5. a   6. c   7. d   8. i   9. f   10. h

COMPREHENSIVE QUIZ — Day 47 & 48

1. The rundown shack was _____ enough for the homeless.
   ⓐ distorted   ⓑ hospitable   ⓒ analogous   ⓓ adverse

2. The conqueror has _____ outstanding leadership abilities since childhood.
   ⓐ consoled   ⓑ accused   ⓒ malfunctioned   ⓓ displayed

3. Jake spent all afternoon trying to find the _____ that could start the complicated machine.
   ⓐ denomination   ⓑ felony   ⓒ mechanism   ⓓ arson

4. Complimenting your children too much can actually create _____ effects.
   ⓐ adverse   ⓑ linguistic   ⓒ analogous   ⓓ illiterate

5. The new car model received a(n) _____ response from younger consumers.
   ⓐ audiovisual   ⓑ culpable   ⓒ tremendous   ⓓ introspective

6. People of all _____ gathered together to pray for world peace.
   ⓐ embezzlements   ⓑ denominations   ⓒ omnivores   ⓓ nutrients

7. A severe case of _____ can kill a person.
   ⓐ pneumonia   ⓑ mechanism   ⓒ denomination   ⓓ politics

8. The excited students _____ to take the best seats in the school auditorium.
   ⓐ encrypted   ⓑ consoled   ⓒ scrambled   ⓓ dated

9. Bill thought that studying for the law exam was _____ to running in a marathon.
   ⓐ hospitable   ⓑ provincial   ⓒ trite   ⓓ analogous

10. The new condo was designed to withstand any natural _____.
    ⓐ coffer   ⓑ calamity   ⓒ politics   ⓓ generation

Answers: p.343

Day 49

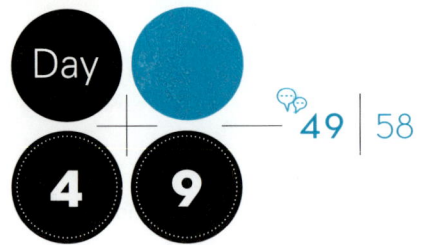

49 | 58

1 aggravate   v. exacerbate, inflame   ↔ alleviate, relieve

[ǽgrəvèit] 악화시키다

Stress can **aggravate** any illness a person suffers from.
스트레스는 사람이 앓고 있는 어떠한 병이든 악화시킬 수 있다.

2 apt   adj. tending, prone   ↔ disinclined, inapt

[ǽpt] ~하는 경향이 있는

Some animals are **apt** to play dead when in danger.
어떤 동물들은 위험에 처했을 때 죽은 척하는 경향이 있다.

3 architecture   n. building, construction

[ɑ́:rkətèktʃər] 건축(학)

Designing a structure and a space for people to use is the concern of **architecture**.
사람이 사용하는 건물과 공간을 설계하는 것이 건축학의 관심사이다.

4 ascertain   v. check up on, determine

[æ̀sərtéin] 확인하다

The detective looked for clues to **ascertain** exactly what happened.
수사관은 정확히 무슨 일이 있었는지 확인하기 위한 단서를 찾았다.

5 auspicious   adj. favorable, promising   ↔ ominous, unlucky

[ɔːspíʃəs] 상서로운, 행운의

Many friends came together to celebrate the **auspicious** occasion.
상서로운 일을 축하하기 위해 많은 친구들이 모였다.

6 biodiversity   n.

[bàioudivə́:rsəti] 생물의 다양성

Biodiversity is the number of plants and animals coexisting in an environment.
생물의 다양성은 한 환경에서 공존하는 동식물 수이다.

7 complimentary adj. gratuitous, free of charge ↔ for sale, purchasable

[kàmpləméntəri] 무료의

There were **complimentary** snacks for everyone at the meeting.
회의에 참석한 모든 사람들을 위한 무료 간식이 있었다.

8 condemn v. punish, sentence ↔ pardon, set free

[kəndém] 유죄 판결을 내리다

The guilty criminal was **condemned** to a sentence of life in prison.
범죄자는 종신형을 선고 받았다.

9 contrived adj. artificial, strained ↔ natural, genuine

[kəntráivd] 부자연스러운, 꾸며낸

The awkward dialogue between the characters seemed **contrived**.
등장인물 간의 어색한 대화는 부자연스러워 보였다.

10 cremate v. burn, incinerate

[krí:meit] 화장하다

Funeral homes offer the choice to **cremate** or to bury the dead.
장례식장은 고인을 화장할 것인지 매장할 것인지에 대한 선택권을 준다.

11 dainty adj. delicate, refined ↔ heavy, rough

[déinti] 맛 좋은, 섬세한

The bakery had **dainty** pastries that looked as good as they tasted.
제과점에는 맛만큼이나 모양이 좋아 보이는 맛 좋은 페이스트리가 있었다.

12 decry v. condemn, denounce ↔ applaud, compliment

[dikrái] 비난하다, 헐뜯다

Older people **decry** the behavior of the young, sometimes forgetful of their own past.
노인들은 때로 자신의 과거는 잊고 젊은이들의 행동을 비난한다.

13 degenerate v. deteriorate, go downhill ↔ develop, improve

[didʒénərèit] 퇴화하다

Muscles shrink and **degenerate** if they are not used for a long time.
근육은 장기간 사용하지 않으면 수축하고 퇴화한다.

14 elude v. evade, escape ↔ clear up, meet

[ilúːd] ~에게 이해되지 않다, 피하다

The answer **eluded** investigators until a breakthrough finally came.
마침내 돌파구가 마련되기까지 수사관들은 해결책을 찾지 못했다.

15 expatriate n. emigrant, expat

[ekspéitrièit] 국외 거주자

Hemingway was a famous American **expatriate** living in Europe.
헤밍웨이는 유럽에 거주했던 유명한 미국인 국외 거주자였다.

16 fraternity n. brotherhood, fellowship

[frətə́ːrnəti] 형제애, 남학생 사교 클럽

The soldiers in Afghanistan have built a **fraternity** by looking out for one another during dangerous situations.
아프가니스탄에 있는 군인들은 위험한 상황에서 서로를 보살핌으로써 형제애를 다졌다.

17 heretic n. nonconformist, dissenter ↔ adherent, loyalist

[hérətik] 이교도

Martin Luther was considered a **heretic** when he criticized the Roman Catholic Church.
마틴 루터는 로마 천주교회를 비난했을 때 이교도로 여겨졌다.

18 inanimate adj. inactive, motionless ↔ alive, animated

[inǽnəmət] 죽은, 죽은 것 같은

Tiffany realized that the **inanimate** shell was a hermit crab when it began to move.
티파니는 죽은 것 같은 조개 껍질이 움직였을 때 그것이 소라게라는 것을 알았다.

19 intermediate adj. middle, median

[ìntərmíːdiət] 중급의, 중간의

Nadia was ready for the **intermediate** yoga class after months of taking the entry level courses.
나디아는 입문 과정을 수개월 동안 들은 후 중급 요가반에 들어갈 준비가 되었다.

20 literacy n. the ability to read and write ↔ ignorance, illiteracy

[lítərəsi] 글을 읽고 쓸 줄 아는 능력

The rate of **literacy** is lower in some countries that are very poor.
매우 가난한 몇몇 나라에서는 글을 읽고 쓸 줄 아는 국민의 비율이 더 낮다.

21 machinery   n. system, organization

[məʃíːnəri] 조직, 기구

The rich men profited from the corrupt political **machinery** that gave them power to control the government.
부자들은 자신에게 정부를 통제할 권력을 준 부패한 정치 조직으로부터 득을 보았다.

22 mundane   adj. day-to-day, humdrum   ↔ exciting, extraordinary

[mʌndéin] 일상적인, 단조로운

Fran decided to go skydiving to add excitement to her otherwise **mundane** life.
프랜은 달리 단조로운 생활에 자극을 주기 위해 스카이다이빙을 하기로 결심했다.

23 obsolete   adj. ancient, out-of-date   ↔ current, up-to-date

[àbsəlíːt] 한물간, 구식의

Latin is an **obsolete** language that was once used in ancient Rome but is not spoken today.
라틴어는 예전에 고대 로마에서 사용된 적이 있지만 오늘날에는 사용되지 않는 한물간 언어이다.

24 pathological   adj. unhealthy, unwholesome   ↔ proper, decent

[pæθəládʒikəl] 병적인

Cindy was starting to suspect that her new roommate was a **pathological** liar who had serious mental problems.
신디는 새로운 룸메이트가 심각한 정신적 문제가 있는 병적인 거짓말쟁이라고 의심하기 시작했다.

25 pollutant   n. impurity, contaminant

[pəlúːtnt] 오염 물질

After many people got sick from the drinking water, the scientists tried to isolate the **pollutant** that was causing the problem.
식수로 인해 많은 사람들이 병들자, 과학자들은 문제를 일으키고 있는 오염 물질을 분리하려 노력했다.

26 prolong   v. draw out, continue   ↔ abbreviate, shorten

[prəlɔ́ːŋ] 연장하다

He was enjoying the time with his family and wanted to **prolong** his visit with them.
그는 가족과의 시간을 즐기고 있었고, 방문 기간을 연장하고자 했었다.

27 reckless   adj. irresponsible, wild   ↔ careful, responsible

[réklis] 무모한

Many teenagers engage in **reckless** behavior like skipping classes and drinking alcohol.
많은 십대가 수업에 빠지거나 음주와 같은 무모한 행동에 관여한다.

28 sluggish   adj. slow, indolent   ↔ active, energetic

[slʌ́giʃ] 느린, 굼뜬

After eating a heavy meal, most people move in a **sluggish** manner.
과식 후에는 대부분의 사람들이 둔하게 움직인다.

29 tumultuous   adj. turbulent, chaotic   ↔ harmonized, organized

[tjumʌ́ltʃuəs] 소란스러운

People living in a war-torn country live in **tumultuous** and unpredictable times.
전쟁으로 파괴된 나라에 사는 사람들은 소란스럽고 예측할 수 없는 시기를 산다.

30 undertake   v. begin, take on   ↔ abstain, forego

[ʌ̀ndərtéik] 착수하다, 맡다

The group decided to **undertake** the renovation project in its own hands.
그 단체는 자체적으로 혁신 프로젝트를 착수하기로 결정했다.

DAILY QUIZ

1. **ascertain** the exact cause •   • a slow
2. a **reckless** driver •   • b determine
3. just another **mundane** routine •   • c out-of-date
4. **aggravate** ethnic tension •   • d evade
5. a **pathological** gambler •   • e free of charge
6. **complimentary** wine and cheese •   • f unwholesome
7. **elude** punishment •   • g exacerbate
8. an **obsolete** model •   • h condemn
9. **decry** the injustice done •   • i day-to-day
10. a **sluggish** economy •   • j irresponsible

ANSWERS   1. b   2. j   3. i   4. g   5. f   6. e   7. d   8. c   9. h   10. a

Day 50

1. absorb v. soak up, take in ↔ emit, disperse

[æbzɔ́ːrb] 흡수하다

A dry sponge will **absorb** a lot more than a wet one.
마른 스폰지는 젖은 스폰지 보다 더 많이 흡수한다.

2. anoint v. bless, sanctify ↔ condemn, curse

[ənɔ́int] 성유(聖油)를 바르다

The church **anointed** a new priest to lead the congregation.
교회는 신도를 이끌 새로운 목사에게 성유를 발라 주었다.

3. apathetic adj. emotionless, uninterested ↔ caring, responsive

[æ̀pəθétik] 무관심한

To be **apathetic** is to have no particular interest or opinion on something.
무관심하다는 것은 어떤 것에 대해 특별한 관심이나 의견을 갖지 않는 것이다.

4. ascetic adj. abstinent, disciplined ↔ greedy, gluttonous

[əsétik] 금욕적인

An **ascetic** monk would not eat rich foods or have many comforts.
금욕적인 수도사는 기름진 음식을 먹거나 편의 도구를 많이 갖지 않는다.

5. atheist n. pagan, agnostic ↔ believer, devotee

[éiθiist] 무신론자

An **atheist** would support the separation of religion from politics.
무신론자들은 정치와 종교를 분리하는 것을 지지할 것이다.

6. barter v. swap, trade

[báːrtər] 물물 교환하다

In the days before coins or money, people used to **barter** one item for another.
동전이나 화폐가 생기기 전에 사람들은 하나의 상품을 다른 상품으로 바꾸는 물물 교환을 했다.

7 commodity   n. asset, ware

[kəmádəti] 상품

A handmade item is always a rare **commodity** in the marketplace.
수공예품은 언제나 시장에서 귀한 상품이다.

8 conjure   v. raise, summon

[kʌ́ndʒər] 마음 속에 그려내다, 생각해 내다.

The language in the novel **conjured** up images of mythology and fantasy.
소설에 사용된 언어는 신화와 환상의 이미지를 떠올리게 했다.

9 counteract   v. check, offset   ↔ aid, support

[kàuntərǽkt] 대응하다

A second medicine can be given to **counteract** the side effects of the first.
첫 번째 약의 부작용에 대응하기 위해 두 번째 약을 받을 수 있다.

10 decapitate   v. behead, guillotine

[dikǽpətèit] 참수하다

Stories of ancient warfare sometimes include the **decapitating** of the heads of enemies.
고대 전쟁 이야기에는 때때로 적의 머리를 참수하는 내용이 나온다.

11 delinquent   n. criminal, felon

[dilíŋkwənt] 불량배, 범죄자

Laws are slightly different for a juvenile **delinquent** than for an adult criminal.
법은 성인 범죄자보다는 비행 소년에 대해 약간 다른 입장을 가진다.

12 distinguish   v. categorize, identify

[distíŋgwiʃ] 구분하다, 구별하다

Morality is a system that **distinguishes** between right and wrong.
도덕은 옳고 그름을 구분하는 체계이다.

13 epic   adj. colossal, monumental   ↔ insignificant, small

[épik] 대규모의, 광범위한

World War I was the first to use war machines on an **epic** scale.
제1차 세계 대전에서 최초로 대규모로 전쟁 기계를 사용했다.

14 firsthand   adj. direct, eyewitness   ↔ hearsay, impersonal

[fə́:rsthǽnd] 직접의

The police went in search of the man who witnessed the shooting of the victim in order to get a **firsthand** account of the incident.
경찰은 사건에 대한 직접적인 정보를 얻기 위해 희생자의 피격을 목격한 사람을 찾아 나섰다.

15 garnish   n. decoration, trimming

[gá:rniʃ] 장식물, 고명

The chef added **garnish** to his pork chops to make it more appealing.
주방장은 더 먹음직스러워 보이도록 돼지 갈비에 고명을 얹었다.

16 incidental   adj. accidental, unintentional   ↔ intended, planned

[ìnsədéntl] 우연히 일어나는

Although the crowd thought it was **incidental** contact, the referee still gave the soccer player a red card.
관중들은 그것이 우발적인 접촉이었다고 생각했지만, 그럼에도 불구하고 심판은 그 축구 선수에게 레드카드를 주었다.

17 legitimacy   n. legality, lawfulness   ↔ illicitness, illegitimacy

[lidʒítəməsi] 합법성, 적법성

The protesters questioned the **legitimacy** of the new military government.
시위대는 새 군사정부의 합법성에 이의를 제기했다.

18 magnificent   adj. brilliant, splendid   ↔ poor, unimpressive

[mægnífəsnt] 웅장한, 멋진

The Taj Mahal is a **magnificent** structure that was built and dedicated by an emperor for his deceased wife.
타지마할은 황제가 건설해서 죽은 아내에게 바쳤던 웅장한 건축물이다.

19 matriarchal   adj. matricentric   ↔ patriarchal, patricentric

[méitrià:rkəl] 모계 중심의

There are several **matriarchal** societies in Africa where the lineage is traced through the mother.
아프리카에는 어머니를 통해 혈통이 이어지는 모계 중심 사회가 몇 있다.

20 novice   n. beginner, rookie   ↔ expert, professional

[návis] 초보자

Since he was a beginner, Theo was placed into the fencing class for **novices**.
테오는 초보자였기 때문에 초보자를 위한 펜싱반에 배정되었다.

21 pedestrian n. walker, passerby

[pədéstriən] 보행자

He slammed on his brakes in order to avoid hitting the **pedestrian** crossing the street.
그는 길을 건너는 보행자를 치는 것을 피하기 위해 급브레이크를 밟았다.

22 plague¹ n. epidemic, pestilence

[pléig] 전염병

Europe was hit by a highly contagious **plague** that killed many people.
많은 사람을 죽인 전염성이 매우 강한 전염병이 유럽을 강타했다.

23 plague² v. bother, vex

[pléig] 괴롭히다, 들끓다

Corruption **plagued** the nation as political officials bribed people for their votes.
정치인들이 표를 얻기 위해 사람들에게 뇌물을 줌으로써 부패가 전국에 들끓었다.

24 plaintiff n. accuser, litigant ↔ the accused, defendant

[pléintif] 원고, 고소인

The judge ruled in favor of the **plaintiff** who was satisfied that his lawsuit was successful.
판사는 성공적인 소송에 만족해 하는 원고에게 승소 판결을 내렸다.

25 philanthropy n. charity, contribution

[filǽnθrəpi] 자선 활동

The celebrated actress is also known for her **philanthropy**.
그 유명 여배우는 자선 활동으로도 잘 알려져 있다.

26 prosecutor n. indicter, district attorney

[prásikjùːtər] 검사

The District Attorney established his career as a **prosecutor** who sent some of the most violent criminals in the state to jail.
지방 검사는 주에서 가장 흉악한 범죄자 몇 명을 감옥에 보낸 검사로서 경력을 쌓았다.

27 receptacle v. vessel, container

[riséptəkl] 그릇, 저장소

Radioactive waste **receptacles** must be handled with extra care.
방사능 쓰레기 저장소는 특별히 주의해서 취급해야 한다.

28 sensation n. feeling, touch

[senséiʃən] 느낌

After brushing his teeth, he realized that the toothpaste left a tingling **sensation** in his mouth.
이를 닦은 후 그는 치약이 입안에 얼얼한 느낌으로 남은 것을 알았다.

29 trait n. attribute, quality

[tréit] 특성

The zebra's most noticeable **trait** is its stripes.
얼룩말의 두드러진 특성은 줄무늬이다.

30 via prep. by, through

[váiə] ~을 통하여, 경유하여

The shortest flight path going east or west is **via** an arched line on the globe.
동쪽이나 서쪽으로 가는 최단 비행 항로는 지구상의 아치형 라인을 거쳐가는 것이다.

DAILY QUIZ

1. a numb **sensation**
2. **plaintiff** filing a lawsuit
3. send letter **via** airmail
4. **absorb** water
5. of **epic** proportions
6. **barter** goods and services
7. a noble **trait**
8. spells to **conjure** spirits
9. a **pedestrian** on the roadway
10. **incidental** results

a. by
b. summon
c. colossal
d. feeling
e. unintentional
f. walker
g. soak up
h. quality
i. trade
j. accuser

ANSWERS   1. d   2. j   3. a   4. g   5. c   6. i   7. h   8. b   9. f   10. e

COMPREHENSIVE QUIZ — Day 49 & 50

1. The riot police was sent to break up the _____ crowd protesting the unpopular trade agreement.
   ⓐ obsolete   ⓑ dainty   ⓒ sluggish   ⓓ tumultuous

2. A team of medical investigators were assigned to _____ the cause of the flu outbreak.
   ⓐ degenerate   ⓑ ascertain   ⓒ aggravate   ⓓ anoint

3. The magician amazed his audience by moving _____ objects without touching them.
   ⓐ incidental   ⓑ matriarchal   ⓒ inanimate   ⓓ pathological

4. Airlines usually provide _____ meals on board.
   ⓐ complimentary   ⓑ reckless   ⓒ apathetic   ⓓ incidental

5. Mr. Brandon had problems _____ the twins apart.
   ⓐ decapitating   ⓑ cremating   ⓒ distinguishing   ⓓ undertaking

6. Student violence continues to _____ the schools.
   ⓐ conjure   ⓑ plague   ⓒ barter   ⓓ ascertain

7. The leaders of the ethnic minority groups _____ the abuse of their people.
   ⓐ decried   ⓑ absorbed   ⓒ degenerated   ⓓ prolonged

8. Working as an intern at the hotel allowed Peter to gain _____ experience in the hospitality industry.
   ⓐ tumultuous   ⓑ ascetic   ⓒ obsolete   ⓓ firsthand

9. People often do wild things when they want to get away from their _____ lives.
   ⓐ magnificent   ⓑ epic   ⓒ mundane   ⓓ intermediate

10. The principal was very unpopular because he was _____ to the need of the students.
    ⓐ complimentary   ⓑ apathetic   ⓒ dainty   ⓓ auspicious

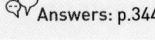
Answers: p.344

Day 51

51 | 58

1. accomplice   n. partner, collaborator

[əkámplis] 공범자

He was convicted to a year in prison as an **accomplice** to the crime.
그는 범죄의 공범자로 1년 징역의 유죄 판결을 받았다.

2. agitate   v. disturb, disconcert   ↔ calm, soothe

[ædʒitèit] 교란하다

The continuous noise **agitated** the nerves of those who heard it.
끊임없는 소음이 듣는 사람들의 마음을 교란시켰다.

3. algae   n.

[ǽldʒiː] 조류

Small creatures and even bacteria can feed on the **algae** in the water.
작은 생물과 박테리아조차도 물속의 조류를 먹고 살 수 있다.

4. astonishing   adj. amazing, beyond belief   ↔ expected, dull

[əstɑ́niʃiŋ] 놀라운

Coral reefs allow an **astonishing** number of fish to live among them.
놀라운 수의 물고기가 산호초에서 서식할 수 있다.

5. auditorium   n. assembly hall, reception hall

[ɔ̀ːdətɔ́ːriəm] 강당

The students gathered together at the school **auditorium**.
학생들은 학교 강당에 모였다.

6. brace (oneself) for   phr. prepare for, steel oneself against

대비하다

We should **brace** ourselves **for** any surprises along the way.
우리는 도중에 있을 수 있는 기습에 대비해야 한다.

7. conviction n. belief, view

[kənvíkʃən] 신념, 확신

The manager showed his **conviction** that the new product would succeed.
매니저는 신제품이 성공할 것이라는 확신을 보였다.

8. corps n. crew, squadron

[kɔ́ːr] 단체

A **corps** of volunteers helped in the relief effort after the disaster.
재난이 있은 후 한 자원 단체가 구호 활동을 도왔다.

9. corpse n. body, remains

[kɔ́ːrps] 시체

Police found the **corpse** of the victim after days of searching.
경찰은 며칠 간의 수색 후에 희생자의 시체를 발견했다.

10. cumbersome adj. burdensome, unmanageable

[kʌ́mbərsəm] 번거로운

Using large scissors to cut small designs is **cumbersome**.
작은 도안을 자르기 위해 큰 가위를 사용하면 번거롭다.

11. defunct adj. expired, obsolete ↔ functioning, inexistence

[difʌ́ŋkt] 없어져 버린

Customers could no longer repair their products after the company became **defunct**.
회사가 없어져 버리자 고객들은 더 이상 제품을 수리할 수 없었다.

12. desolate adj. bare, vacant ↔ populated, used

[désələt] 황량한

The lands near the North Pole can often be empty and **desolate**.
북극 근처의 육지는 종종 생물이 살지 않고 황량할 수 있다.

13. doctorate n. doctoral degree, PhD

[dɑ́ktərət] 박사 학위

Acquiring a **doctorate** usually takes many years of advanced study.
박사 학위 취득은 보통 수년간의 고등 연구 활동을 필요로 한다.

14 excess   adj. extra, surplus   ↔ insufficient, meager

[ékses] 과잉의, 초과한

Cutting out the **excess** fat from meat can improve the taste and nutrition.
육류에서 과잉 지방을 떼어 내면 맛과 영양을 향상시킬 수 있다.

15 extensive   adj. comprehensive, lengthy   ↔ limited, short

[iksténsiv] 광범위한

The study was published after **extensive** research materials had been collected.
광범위한 조사 자료를 수집한 후 연구 결과가 발표되었다.

16 frivolous   adj. flippant, light   ↔ sensible, thoughtful

[frívələs] 하찮은, 사소한

The President was criticized for spending time on **frivolous** matters rather than on important issues that would help his country.
대통령은 자국에 도움이 될 중요한 문제보다는 사소한 문제에 시간을 보내고 있다는 비판을 받았다.

17 halt   v. cease, come to an end   ↔ initiate, get underway

[hɔ́ːlt] 중단하다, 멈추다

The construction workers signaled the cars to **halt** when they attempted to get through the road that was being fixed.
건설 인부들은 자동차들이 보수 중인 도로를 지나가려 하자 정지하라는 신호를 보냈다.

18 incurable   adj. fatal, terminal   ↔ curable, operable

[inkjúərəbl] 불치의

Chelsea was told by her doctor that she had an **incurable** disease.
첼시는 의사로부터 그녀에게 불치병이 있다고 들었다.

19 invigorating   adj. energizing, refreshing   ↔ tiring, exhausting

[invígərèitiŋ] 활기를 북돋우는, 기운 나게 하는

Andrew went swimming every morning before work because he found it **invigorating**.
앤드류는 수영이 활기를 북돋는다는 것을 알았기 때문에 매일 아침 출근 전에 수영하러 갔다.

20 juxtapose   v. set side by side, examine in contrast

[dʒʌ́kstəpóuz] 나란히 놓다

The professor **juxtaposed** Picasso's work with da Vinci's to teach his students about the different styles of art.
교수는 학생들에게 서로 다른 예술 방식에 대해 가르치려고 피카소의 작품과 다빈치의 작품을 나란히 놓았다.

21 | mainstream adj. common, typical ↔ unusual, unconventional

[méinstrì:m] 주류의

Many teenagers listen to **mainstream** American music, which is popular and is often played on the radio.
많은 십대가 인기 있고 종종 라디오에 나오는 미국의 주류 음악을 듣는다.

22 | multitude n. assembly, collection ↔ handful, single

[mʌ́ltətjùːd] 다수

There were a **multitude** of brands and styles to choose from at the shoe store.
신발 가게에는 선택할 수 있는 다수의 브랜드와 스타일이 있었다.

23 | originate v. start, come from ↔ end, terminate

[ərídʒənèit] 유래하다, 시작되다

It is believed that the earliest man **originated** in Africa and spread to other continents.
초기 인간은 아프리카에서 유래해 다른 대륙으로 퍼졌다고 여겨진다.

24 | posture n. attitude, pose

[pástʃər] 태도, 자세

After being picked on by his classmates, Andrew took on an aggressive **posture**.
반 친구들에게 괴롭힘을 당한 뒤 앤드류는 공격적인 태도를 취했다.

25 | protrude v. bulge, jut out ↔ depress, sink

[proutrúːd] 튀어나오다

After falling from the roof, Willy cried out in pain as his bones **protruded** out from his shoulder.
윌리는 지붕에서 떨어진 후, 어깨에서 뼈가 튀어나와 통증으로 비명을 질렀다.

26 | resuscitate v. revive, restore

[risʌ́sətèit] 소생시키다

The life guard attempted to **resuscitate** a little boy who was found unconscious in the pool.
구조대원은 수영장에서 의식을 잃은 상태로 발견된 어린 소년을 소생시키려고 시도했다.

27 | security n. guard, protection ↔ danger, trouble

[sikjúərəti] 경비, 보안

He needed to hire **security** to protect his new property.
그는 새로운 재산을 보호하기 위해 경비를 고용해야 했다.

28 spate n. outpouring, rush ↔ dab, little

[spéit] 연발, 터져 나옴

The family members experienced a **spate** of grief when they were told that their father was killed in an accident.
식구들은 아버지가 사고로 죽었다는 소식을 듣고 슬픔이 터져 나오는 것을 경험했다.

29 tabloid n. synopsis, summary

[tǽblɔid] 타블로이드 (신문), 요약

The **tabloid** claimed that the movie star was involved in a drunk driving accident.
타블로이드 신문은 그 영화배우가 음주 운전 사고에 연루되었다고 주장했다.

30 unimaginable adj. inconceivable, unknowable ↔ believable, thinkable

[ʌ̀nimǽdʒinəbl] 상상할 수 없는

Today's technology is progressing at a level **unimaginable** even a few years ago.
최신 기술은 몇 년 전에는 상상조차 할 수 없는 수준으로 진보하고 있다.

DAILY QUIZ

1	the **cumbersome** space suit	a light
2	**originate** from an unknown planet	b amazing
3	always make **frivolous** purchases	c disturb
4	the **astonishing** wonders of Egypt	d burdensome
5	survive in the **desolate** wasteland	e come from
6	**agitate** the sleeping walrus	f bulge
7	**halt** the spread of the tumor	g bare
8	an **invigorating** cold shower	h prepare for
9	**brace** themselves **for** the collision	i cease
10	**protrude** from under the cover	j energizing

ANSWERS 1. d 2. e 3. a 4. b 5. g 6. c 7. i 8. j 9. h 10. f

Day 52

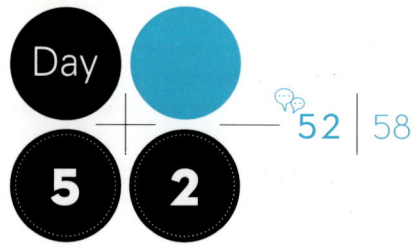 52 | 58

1 addiction   n. dependence, habit

[ədíkʃən] 중독

It is said that any habit that one cannot control is an **addiction**.
통제할 수 없는 습관은 어느 것이든 중독이라고 한다.

2 affirmation   n. confirmation, testimonial   ↔ rejection, denial

[æ̀fərméiʃən] 확인, 확언

The excellent grades gave the students an **affirmation** of their hard work.
우수한 성적은 학생이 열심히 공부했다는 확인이었다.

3 assassinate   v. kill, gun down

[əsǽsənèit] 암살하다

The congressman was behind the sinister plot to **assassinate** political enemies.
하원 의원은 정적을 암살하는 사악한 음모의 배후에 있었다.

4 autocratic   adj. absolute, tyrannical   ↔ democratic, representative

[ɔ́:təkrǽtik] 독재적인

Autocratic leaders tell others what to do without listening to any feedback.
독재적인 지도자는 어떠한 의견에도 귀를 기울이지 않고, 다른 사람에게 해야 할 일을 말한다.

5 bypass   v. circumvent, get around

[báipæ̀s] 우회하다

A highway can act as a shortcut that **bypasses** smaller local streets.
고속 도로는 작은 지방 도로를 우회하는 지름길 역할을 할 수 있다.

6 concave   adj. curved in, scooped   ↔ convex

[kɑnkéiv] 오목한

Any dinner plate must be **concave** in order to contain the food.
모든 정찬용 접시는 음식을 담을 수 있도록 오목해야 한다.

7. conditioning   n. practice, workout

[kəndíʃəniŋ] (심신의) 조절

Marathon runners go through training and **conditioning** to stay lean and fit.
마라톤 주자들은 늘씬하고 건강한 몸을 유지하기 위해 훈련과 조절을 한다.

8. consecutive   n. continuous, sequential   ↔ broken, interrupted

[kənsékjutiv] 연이은, 계속적인

The national festival went on for five **consecutive** days.
그 전국 제전은 5일 연속 계속됐다.

9. convex   adj. curved out, arched   ↔ concave

[kɑnvéks] 볼록한

A **convex** lens can focus light traveling through it into a single point.
볼록 렌즈는 한 지점으로 통과하는 빛에 초점을 맞출 수 있다.

10. convey   v. communicate, get across   ↔ refrain, withhold

[kənvéi] (소식·용건을) 전달하다

Language can **convey** our thoughts and feelings to others.
언어는 우리의 생각과 느낌을 타인에게 전달할 수 있다.

11. cynical   adj. sarcastic, skeptical   ↔ respectful, believing

[sínikəl] 냉소적인

Being **cynical** means that a person does not take an issue seriously.
냉소적이라는 것은 그 사람이 문제를 진지하게 받아들이지 않는다는 것을 의미한다.

12. deduce   v. conclude, reason

[didjú:s] 추론하다

Answers to mathematical problems can be **deduced** from mathematical principles.
수학 문제의 해답은 수학 원리에서 추론할 수 있다.

13. deportation   n. exile, expulsion

[dì:pɔːrtéiʃən] 국외 추방

A person without permission to live in a country can face **deportation** by the authorities.
나라에서 허가 없이 거주하는 사람은 관계 당국에 의해 국외 추방 당할 수 있다.

14 disoriented   adj. confused, unsettled   ↔ balanced, clear-headed

[disɔ́:riéntid] 혼란에 빠진

Future shock comes when one feels **disoriented** and overwhelmed by change.
미래의 충격은 변화에 의해 혼란에 빠지고 압도 당한 느낌을 받을 때 온다.

15 egoistic   adj. narcissistic, selfish   ↔ modest, humble

[ì:gouístik] 이기주의의

People have to balance being **egoistic** with thinking of others.
사람은 이기적인 것과 남을 배려하는 것 사이의 균형을 맞춰야 한다.

16 executive   n. director, manager

[igzékjutiv] 경영자

An **executive** is in a high position within a company with high responsibility.
경영자는 큰 책임을 맡아 회사 고위직에 있다.

17 fidelity   n. loyalty, true-heartedness   ↔ faithlessness, treachery

[fidéləti] 충실, 정절

Ashley hired a private detective to follow her husband because she doubted his **fidelity**.
애슐리는 남편의 정절을 의심해 그를 뒤쫓기 위해 개인 탐정을 고용했다.

18 fission   n. splitting, breaking up   ↔ fusion, union

[fíʃən] 분열

Albert Einstein is famous for his theory of nuclear **fission** which was later used to develop a deadly and dangerous weapon.
앨버트 아인슈타인은 후에 치명적이고 위험한 무기 개발에 이용된 핵분열 이론으로 유명하다.

19 garner   v. assemble, pick up   ↔ disperse, spread

[gá:rnər] 모으다

The politician went around the country to **garner** support for his campaign.
정치인은 그의 선거 운동에 대한 지지를 얻기 위해 전국을 돌아다녔다.

20 inappropriate   adj. ill-fitted, unseemly   ↔ fitting, proper

[ìnəpróupriət] 부적절한

Mr. Smith yelled at his daughter to change her clothes because her outfit was **inappropriate** for school.
스미스 씨는 딸의 복장이 등교에 적당하지 않자 옷을 갈아입으라며 소리질렀다.

21. offensive adj. disgusting, insulting ↔ pleasant, courteous

[əfénsiv] 불쾌한

He thought the comedian's joke was **offensive** rather than funny.
그는 코미디언의 농담이 재미있기보다는 불쾌하다고 생각했다.

22. portfolio n. briefcase, list

[pɔːrtfóuliòu] 서류첩, (특정 회사의) 상품 목록[범위]

Gus frantically searched for his **portfolio**, which contained important documents.
거스는 중요한 서류가 든 서류첩을 미친 듯이 찾았다.

23. precondition n. arrangement, stipulation

[prìːkəndíʃən] 전제 조건

The **precondition** to his divorce settlement was to give up half his assets to his ex-wife.
그의 이혼 문제 해결을 위한 전제 조건은 전처에게 재산의 절반을 주는 것이었다.

24. proactive adj. preemptive, preventive

[prouǽktiv] 사전 대비적인, 사전 대책을 강구한

The police chief made a **proactive** decision to hire more cops to patrol the streets in high crime areas.
경찰서장은 우범 지대의 거리를 순찰을 위해 더 많은 경찰을 고용한다는 사전 대비적인 결정을 내렸다.

25. remuneration n. compensation, payment

[rimjùːnəréiʃən] 보수

The contractor received **remuneration** for his tireless work on the old abandoned bridge.
토건업자는 낡아 버려진 교량을 꾸준히 작업한 보수를 받았다.

26. revitalize v. breathe new life into, revive ↔ exhaust, wear out

[riːváitəlaiz] 활력을 주다[불어 넣다]

The President attempted to **revitalize** the economy by creating new jobs and giving tax breaks.
대통령은 새로운 일자리를 창출하고 감세 조치를 함으로써 경제를 소생시키려 했다.

27. souvenir n. memento, token

[sùːvəníər] 기념품

Brandon purchased a **souvenir** so that he would always remember his summer trip in Australia.
브랜든은 호주에서의 여름 여행을 늘 기억하도록 기념품을 구입했다.

28 tract   n. tube, corridor

[trǽkt] 관(管), 계(系)

After having stomach pain, Rosemary went to see her doctor, who told her she had problems with her digestive **tract**.
로즈메리는 배가 아파 병원에 갔는데, 그녀의 소화관에 문제가 있다고 했다.

29 vindictive   adj. vengeful, malicious   ↔ forgiving, kind

[vindíktiv] 앙심을 품은, 보복적인

It was suspected that these were **vindictive** rumors spread by his enemies.
이것은 그의 적들이 앙심을 품고 퍼뜨린 소문으로 짐작되었다.

30 withstand   v. hold off, resist   ↔ surrender, yield

[wiθstǽnd] 저항하다, 견디어 내다

Cars today are designed to **withstand** collisions by absorbing the impact.
최신 자동차는 충격을 흡수함으로써 충돌에 견딜 수 있도록 설계된다.

DAILY QUIZ

1. the top **executive** • • a revive
2. an **inappropriate** laughter • • b get across
3. an **addiction** to chocolate • • c unsettled
4. **convey** all the important ideas • • d manager
5. **deduce** what caused the accident • • e dependence
6. **assassinate** the religious leaders • • f selfish
7. a **proactive** move against the enemy • • g conclude
8. **disoriented** after getting punched • • h kill
9. an **egoistic** ruler • • i ill-fitted
10. **revitalize** your mind, body, and spirit • • j preemptive

ANSWERS   1. d   2. i   3. e   4. b   5. g   6. h   7. j   8. c   9. f   10. a

COMPREHENSIVE QUIZ Day 51 & 52

1. Candice could not _____ enough votes to win the student council presidency.
   ⓐ halt   ⓑ garner   ⓒ agitate   ⓓ deduce

2. Many buildings in San Francisco are engineered to _____ earthquakes.
   ⓐ revitalize   ⓑ originate   ⓒ withstand   ⓓ convey

3. Only the toughest and the bravest are accepted to the Marine _____.
   ⓐ Algae   ⓑ Corps   ⓒ Auditorium   ⓓ Addiction

4. People were shocked to hear that the president of the bank himself acted as a(n) _____ to the infamous robbery.
   ⓐ spate   ⓑ accomplice   ⓒ deportation   ⓓ multitude

5. The workers felt that the _____ did not reflect their hours of labor.
   ⓐ remuneration   ⓑ fidelity   ⓒ tract   ⓓ tabloid

6. Not even the heads of states were able to _____ the strict security policy during the summit meeting.
   ⓐ refrain   ⓑ juxtapose   ⓒ assassinate   ⓓ bypass

7. The tourists were upset about having to pay extra money for _____ baggage.
   ⓐ proactive   ⓑ excess   ⓒ frivolous   ⓓ incurable

8. CPR is a procedure that can _____ people who have cardiac arrests.
   ⓐ protrude   ⓑ initiate   ⓒ resuscitate   ⓓ depress

9. Scientists could not explain the reason for the _____ of dead dolphins that filled the beach.
   ⓐ corpses   ⓑ doctorates   ⓒ corps   ⓓ deportations

10. Kate picked up a pretty seashell that she found on the beach to take home as a(n) _____.
    ⓐ souvenir   ⓑ precondition   ⓒ posture   ⓓ executive

Answers: p.344

Day 53

1. adept adj. accomplished, proficient ↔ incompetent, unskilled

[ədépt] 능숙한

The veteran player was skilled and **adept** at his game.
노련한 선수는 기량이 뛰어났고 시합에 능숙했다.

2. announcement n. declaration, statement

[ənáunsmənt] 발표

Reporters gathered at the press conference to hear the big **announcement**.
기자들은 중대한 발표를 듣기 위해 기자 회견에 모였다.

3. attribute n. characteristic, trait

[ǽtrəbjùːt] 자질, 속성

Well-developed muscles and a strong heart are **attributes** of athletes.
잘 발달된 근육과 튼튼한 심장은 운동 선수의 속성이다.

4. attribute to phr. be due to, caused by ↔ have nothing to do with, no connection with

~의 탓으로 하다

The financial collapse was **attributed to** various causes.
재정 붕괴는 여러 가지 원인에 기인했다.

5. breakout n. burst, outbreak

[bréikàut] (병 등의) 급속한 만연

This season saw a huge **breakout** of the flu in the city.
이번 계절은 도시에서 독감이 만연했다.

6. coastal adj. seaside, shoreline

[kóustəl] 해안의, 연안의

High winds and sea storms are dangers found in **coastal** environments.
센 바람과 바다 폭풍은 해안 환경에서 발견되는 위험이다.

7 coded adj. encoded, concealed ↔ deciphered, revealed

[kóudid] 암호화된

The frontline soldiers sent a **coded** message to headquarters.
최전방의 군인들은 본부로 암호화된 메시지를 보냈다.

8 commensurate adj. proportionate, in accord ↔ inadequate, unbalanced

[kəménsərət] 상응하는, 액수가 알맞은

The pay was **commensurate** with the amount of work put into it.
급여는 투입된 작업량에 상응했다.

9 confrontation n. dispute, conflict ↔ peace, calm

[kànfrəntéiʃən] 대립, 대결

News crews reported on the **confrontation** between the police and the protestors.
취재진은 경찰과 시위자들 사이의 대립을 보도했다.

10 contemplate v. observe, mull over ↔ disregard, neglect

[kántəmplèit] 곰곰이 생각하다

Reading is a great way for us to **contemplate** the world around us.
독서는 우리가 주변 세상을 바라보는 훌륭한 방법이다.

11 credit n. acknowledgement, tribute ↔ disapproval, discredit

[krédit] 인정

Everyone agreed to give **credit** to the new employee for a job well done.
모두 좋은 업무 성과에 대해 그 신입 사원의 공로를 인정해 주기로 했다.

12 decrepit adj. run-down, wasted ↔ clean, tidy

[dikrépit] 낡은, 노후한

The abandoned factory district looked old and **decrepit** due to years of neglect.
버려진 공장 지역은 수년간의 방치로 인해 오래되고 노후해 보였다.

13 devote v. allot, dedicate

[divóut] 할애하다, 기울이다

A good novel **devotes** much of its space to developing its characters.
좋은 소설은 등장인물을 전개하는 데 많은 지면을 할애한다.

14 at one's disposal phr. ready for use, at hand

마음대로 이용할 수 있는

Libraries offer many resources **at one's disposal** for research or entertainment.
도서관은 연구나 오락을 위해 마음대로 이용할 수 있는 여러 자원을 제공한다.

15 enforce v. impose, apply ↔ disregard, neglect

[infɔ́ːrs] 시행하다

Cameras on the roads are sometimes set up to **enforce** traffic laws.
도로상의 카메라는 간혹 교통법을 시행하기 위해 설치된다.

16 equitable adj. fair, nondiscriminatory ↔ biased, partial

[ékwətəbl] 공정한

Teachers should be **equitable** in their treatment of students.
교사는 학생을 다루는 데 있어 공정해야 한다.

17 fossil n. petrifaction, remnant

[fásəl] 화석

Archaeologists are excited about the **fossil** found in Asia, which they believe dates back to over 40,000 years.
고고학자들은 아시아에서 발견된 화석에 들떠 있는데, 그 시기가 4만년 전 이상으로 거슬러 올라간다고 본다.

18 horizontal adj. level, parallel to the horizon ↔ upright, vertical

[hɔ́ːrəzántl] 수평의

The first aid instructor asked a volunteer to lie down in a **horizontal** position to demonstrate rescue breathing.
응급 치료 강사는 구조 호흡 시범을 보이기 위해 지원자에게 똑바로 누우라고 요청했다.

19 involuntary adj. unintentional, spontaneous ↔ conscious, intentional

[inváləntèri] 본의 아닌

The man accidentally killed another driver and was charged with **involuntary** manslaughter.
그 남자는 사고로 다른 운전자를 죽였기 때문에 과실 치사로 기소되었다.

20 manufacture v. assemble, turn out ↔ disassemble, break up

[mæ̀njəfǽktʃər] 제작하다, 제조하다

The company **manufactures** computer components.
그 회사는 컴퓨터 부품을 제조한다.

21 mollify   v. placate, calm down   ↔ agitate, upset

[málǝfài] 진정시키다, 달래다

Harry tried to **mollify** his friend Rupert who was about to yell at a classmate for taking his lunch.
해리는 자기의 점심을 먹는다고 반 친구에게 소리 지르려는 친구 루퍼트를 진정시키려고 했다.

22 numb   v. immobilize, stun

[nʌ́m] 마비시키다

The dentist needed to **numb** her patient's gums to perform oral surgery.
치과 의사는 구강 수술을 하기 위해 환자의 잇몸을 마비시켜야 했다.

23 olfactory   adj. related to the sense of smell

[ɑlfǽktǝri] 후각의

Her **olfactory** sense was temporarily damaged when she broke her nose.
그녀의 후각은 코가 부러졌을 때 일시적으로 훼손되었다.

24 pesticide   n. insect repellent, insecticide

[péstǝsàid] 살충제

Henry is very careful in buying his vegetables because many farmers spray their crops with **pesticides** that can be very harmful.
많은 농부가 무척 해로울 수 있는 살충제를 농작물에 뿌리기 때문에 헨리는 야채를 구입하는 데 매우 신중하다.

25 predicament   n. dilemma, tight spot

[pridíkǝmǝnt] 곤경

Alice experienced a **predicament** when her boss asked her to stay late for work when she was expected to be at her daughter's birthday party.
앨리스는 딸의 생일 파티에 있어야 할 때 상사가 늦게까지 남아서 일하라고 해서 곤경을 겪었다.

26 produce   n. crop, harvest

[prǝdjúːs] 농산물

The small grocery store sold **produce** that was grown at a nearby farm.
작은 식료 잡화점은 근처 농장에서 재배한 농산물을 판매했다.

27 respondent   n. answerer, responder

[rispándǝnt] 응답자

According to the questionnaire, 10 percent of the **respondents** agreed that they were unhappy with their jobs.
설문지에 따르면, 응답자의 10%가 자신의 직업에 만족하지 않는다는 데 동의했다.

28 specialize   v. focus, practice

[spéʃəlàiz] 전공하다, 전문으로 삼다
The couple brought their sick child to Doctor Kim because he **specializes** in pediatrics.
김 선생님은 소아과 전문이기 때문에 부부는 아픈 아이를 그에게 데려갔다.

29 tension   n. strain, anxiety   ↔ looseness, relaxation

[ténʃən] 불안, 긴장
Phil felt **tension** from his parents who were worried about their finances after his father lost his job.
필은 아버지가 직장을 잃은 후 재정을 걱정하는 부모로부터 불안감을 느꼈다.

30 yearn   v. desire, wish for

[jə:rn] 갈망하다
City dwellers sometimes **yearn** to see the nature and beauty of a scenic countryside.
도시 거주자들은 때때로 경치가 아름다운 전원의 자연과 미를 보기를 갈망하기도 한다.

DAILY QUIZ

1	**equitable** for all members of the deal	a	strain
2	an **involuntary** muscle movement	b	impose
3	an **adept** professional poker player	c	crop
4	police **enforce** the law	d	focus
5	not fully **contemplate** the consequences	e	fair
6	stuck in quite the **predicament**	f	proficient
7	**credit** for his honor and service	g	spontaneous
8	**tension** between the neighboring countries	h	mull over
9	**specialize** in dealing with spies	i	acknowledgement
10	buy fresh **produce**	j	dilemma

ANSWERS   1. e   2. g   3. f   4. b   5. h   6. j   7. i   8. a   9. d   10. c

Day 54

54 | 58

1. acquainted   adj. accustomed, used to   ↔ unfamiliar, ignorant

[əkwéintid] 안면이 있는, 아는 사이인

The guest was already **acquainted** with almost everyone at the party.
손님은 파티에 온 거의 모든 사람들과 이미 안면이 있었다.

2. aggressive   adj. hostile, antagonistic   ↔ calm, laid-back

[əgrésiv] 공격적인, 저돌적인

The team practiced an **aggressive** offensive maneuver to score many points.
팀은 점수를 많이 얻기 위해 저돌적인 공격 책략을 연습했다.

3. amicable   adj. harmonious, cordial   ↔ unfriendly, hostile

[ǽmikəbl] 원만한, 우호적인

They finally came to an **amicable** agreement in the divorce.
그들은 마침내 이혼에 원만하게 합의했다.

4. appliance   n. device, mechanism

[əpláiəns] 기구

Household **appliances** most people take for granted are refrigerators and washers.
대부분의 사람들이 당연시하는 가정용 기구는 냉장고와 세탁기이다.

5. attest   v. verify, confirm   ↔ deny, disavow

[ətést] 증명하다

Friends can **attest** to our personality traits as well as character flaws.
친구를 보면 사람의 성격적 결함뿐만 아니라 인격도 알 수 있다.

6. bait   n. lure, enticement

[béit] 미끼

Fishermen use worms for **bait** when they try to catch fish.
낚시꾼은 고기를 잡을 때 벌레를 미끼로 사용한다.

7 certification   n. license, endorsement

[sə̀:rtəfikéiʃən] 인증(서)

A **certification** may be earned by taking a test or by taking a class.
시험을 보거나 강의를 들어서 자격증을 받을 수 있다.

8 compromise¹   v. jeopardize, imperil   ↔ protect, look after

[kámprəmàiz] ~을 위태롭게 하다

The sniper's mistake **compromised** the whole operation.
저격수의 실수는 작전 전체를 위태롭게 했다.

9 compromise²   n. concession, trade-off   ↔ disagreement, dissention

[kámʃprəmàiz] 양보, 타협

Disagreements are often resolved when everyone offers a little **compromise**.
모든 사람들이 조금씩 양보하면 의견 차이가 종종 해결될 수 있다.

10 dean   n. president, department head

[di:n] 학과장

University students can talk to their **dean** about any questions regarding their graduation.
대학생은 졸업과 관련해서 어떠한 질문이라도 학장에게 할 수 있다.

11 destination   n. goal, journey's end   ↔ source, beginning point

[dèstənéiʃən] 목적지

Passengers get off when their train arrives at their particular **destination**.
승객들은 기차가 특정 목적지에 도착하면 내린다.

12 didactic   adj. edifying, instructive

[daidǽktik] 교훈적인, 남을 가르치고 싶어하는

A **didactic** speaker makes an effort to educate and instruct the audience.
가르치려 드는 연설가는 청중을 교육하고 지시하려는 노력을 한다.

13 embryo   n. beginning, conception

[émbriòu] 배아

An unborn mammal is first an **embryo** and then turns into a fetus before birth.
아직 태어나지 않은 포유동물은 처음에는 배아였다가 출생 전에 태아로 변한다.

14 entail   v. involve

[intéil] 수반하다

Raising a child **entails** commitment and responsibility.
아이를 키우는 데는 헌신과 책임을 수반한다.

15 erode   v. abrade, wear down   strengthen, fortify

[iróud] 서서히 손상시키다

Scandals can **erode** the public's confidence in a famous figure.
스캔들은 유명 인사에 대한 대중의 신뢰를 손상시킬 수 있다.

16 eruption   n. explosion, discharge   ↔ implosion, cave-in

[irʌ́pʃən] 폭발

The **eruption** of Vesuvius is one of the most famous events in history.
베수비오 화산 폭발은 역사상 가장 유명한 사건 중 하나이다.

17 garment   n. clothing, apparel

[gáːrmənt] 의상, 옷

The fashion designer was hired to create several **garments** for the famous actress.
패션 디자이너는 유명 여배우를 위한 의상을 몇 가지 제작하기 위해 고용되었다.

18 haunt   v. preoccupy, trouble   ↔ pacify

[hɔ́ːnt] 머리에서 떠나지 않다, 괴롭히다

He was **haunted** by the memories of his wife and children who were killed during the war.
전쟁 중에 죽은 아내와 아이들에 대한 기억이 그의 머리에서 떠나지 않았다.

19 insensitive   adj. uncaring, aloof   ↔ mindful, concerned

[insénsətiv] 몰이해한, 무신경한

Mr. Brown's **insensitive** comments about Leroy's poor test score made the students in the classroom uncomfortable.
르로이의 낮은 시험 점수에 대한 브라운 선생님의 무신경한 말로 교실의 학생들이 불편해했다.

20 itinerary   n. travel plan, schedule

[aitínərèri] 여행 일정(표)

The travel agent sent Alex his **itinerary** after booking his flight to Japan.
여행사 직원은 알렉스의 일본행 항공권을 예약한 뒤 그에게 여행 일정을 보내 주었다.

21 merchant n. trader, vendor ↔ purchaser, customer

[mə́ːrtʃənt] 상인

The **merchant** made a large profit by trading goods at the port.
상인은 항구에서 상품을 매매하여 큰 수익을 올렸다.

22 outweigh v. surpass, prevail over ↔ fall behind, be less important than

[àutwéi] ~보다 중대하다

When faced with a problem, it is important to see if the pros **outweigh** the cons.
문제에 당면했을 때에는 장점이 단점보다 큰지 살펴보는 것이 중요하다.

23 preservation n. conservation, protection ↔ harm, endangerment

[prèzərvéiʃən] 보존, 보호

The national museum was dedicated to the **preservation** of historical and cultural artifacts.
국립 박물관은 역사적이고 문화적인 공예품 보존에 전념했다.

24 quench v. relieve, alleviate

[kwéntʃ] 갈증을 해소하다

Drinking a bottle of water instead of a soft drink is the best way to **quench** the thirst after doing vigorous exercise.
격렬한 운동 후에 갈증을 해소하는 방법으로 청량음료 대신 물을 마시는 것이 가장 좋다.

25 refine v. improve, hone ↔ impair, tarnish

[riːfáin] 세련되게 하다, 개선하다

The news reporter wanted to **refine** his speaking skills, so he practiced in front of the mirror every day.
뉴스 기자는 화술을 세련되게 하고자 매일 거울 앞에서 연습했다.

26 retribution n. vengeance, retaliation ↔ forgiveness, pardon

[rètrəbjúːʃən] 보복

The eyewitness to the incident did not testify at the court because he feared **retribution** from the criminals.
사건의 증인은 범인들의 보복이 두려워 법정에서 증언하지 않았다.

27 supernatural adj. unearthly, paranormal ↔ earthly, mundane

[sùːpərnǽtʃərəl] 초자연의

The psychic claimed he could predict the future because he had **supernatural** powers.
심령술사는 자신이 초자연적인 힘을 가지고 있기 때문에 미래를 예언할 수 있다고 말했다.

28 treatment n. care, consideration ↔ disregard, neglect

[tríːtmənt] 대접, 대우

The celebrity who came to the basketball championship game received VIP **treatment**.
농구 결승전 때 경기장을 찾은 유명 인사는 VIP 대접을 받았다.

29 vocational adj. technical, occupational

[voukéiʃənl] 직업상의

Even his hobbies were related to his **vocational** training as a programmer.
그의 취미마저도 프로그래머로서의 그의 직업 훈련과 관련이 있었다.

30 xerox v. photocopy, replicate

[zíəraks] 복사하다

Office workers frequently **xerox** important documents for future reference.
사무실 직원들은 나중에 참고하기 위해 중요한 서류를 자주 복사한다.

DAILY QUIZ

1 **haunt** her for the rest of her life — a cordial
2 a dishonest **merchant** — b vengeance
3 **erode** the enamel of your teeth — c hostile
4 can **attest** to his generosity — d trader
5 **retribution** for all his evil deeds — e lure
6 the **aggressive** mother bear — f verify
7 **insensitive** to her situation — g trouble
8 the **amicable** party guests — h uncaring
9 **bait** the naïve customers — i travel plan
10 keep track of your **itinerary** — j wear down

ANSWERS   1. g   2. d   3. j   4. f   5. b   6. c   7. h   8. a   9. e   10. i

COMPREHENSIVE QUIZ   Day 53 & 54

1. After watching the rock concert, Max _____ to learn to play the guitar.
   ⓐ eroded   ⓑ yearned   ⓒ attested   ⓓ mollified

2. The famous film director had thirty-five assistants at his _____.
   ⓐ credit   ⓑ didactic   ⓒ tension   ⓓ disposal

3. The devastating flood was _____ the record rainfall.
   ⓐ attributed to   ⓑ contemplated   ⓒ enforced   ⓓ specialized

4. Chief Blackhawk oversaw the _____ between the two warring factions.
   ⓐ preservation   ⓑ destination   ⓒ pesticide   ⓓ compromise

5. The ability to negotiate is an important _____ for anyone wishing to become a diplomat.
   ⓐ retribution   ⓑ attribute   ⓒ itinerary   ⓓ announcement

6. Dr. Alexander successfully extracted stem cells from animal _____.
   ⓐ certifications ⓑ respondents   ⓒ treatments   ⓓ embryos

7. The smoke rising from their campfire _____ their hideout.
   ⓐ compromised   ⓑ devoted   ⓒ refined   ⓓ xeroxed

8. Dennis thought that acquiring a(n) _____ skill was more practical than going to college.
   ⓐ aggressive   ⓑ vocational   ⓒ coastal   ⓓ involuntary

9. Jacob stopped teasing Linda because he wanted to avoid _____ with her big brother.
   ⓐ confrontation   ⓑ appliance   ⓒ fossil   ⓓ bait

10. The commander believes that the benefit of taking the fort _____ the cost of losing several of his men.
    ⓐ manufactures   ⓑ numbs   ⓒ outweighs   ⓓ haunts

Answers: p.344

Day 55

55 | 58

1. adoration   n. reverence, ardor   ↔ disrespect, abhorrence

[ӕdəréiʃən] 흠모, 동경

The singer received the **adoration** of many fans all around the world.
그 가수는 전 세계적으로 많은 팬의 흠모를 받았다.

2. affliction   n. illness, suffering   ↔ fortune, blessing

[əflíkʃən] 고통

Society must deal with the **affliction** of poverty in its public policies.
사회는 공공 정책에 있어서 빈곤의 고통을 반드시 다뤄야 한다.

3. applicable   adj. relevant, pertinent   ↔ improper, unrelated

[ӕplikəbl] 적용할 수 있는

Good study skills are **applicable** in almost any job setting or workplace.
좋은 학습 기술은 대부분의 직업 환경이나 직장에서 적용할 수 있다.

4. barren   adj. desolate, bleak   ↔ fertile, productive

[bǽrən] 메마른

Deserts can appear lifeless and **barren** but they are actually not completely so.
사막은 활기 없고 메말라 보일 수 있지만 실제 완전히 그렇지는 않다.

5. burrow   v. excavate, dig out   ↔ fill, cover

[bə́:rou] 〈굴을〉 파다, 굴에 살다[숨다]

Groundhogs will **burrow** into the earth to make their home and to hide from danger.
마멋은 집을 만들고 위험으로부터 몸을 숨기기 위해 땅을 파고 굴에 살 것이다.

6. censorship   n. suppression   ↔ permission, allowance

[sénsərʃip] 검열

Not allowing certain ideas to reach the public is **censorship**.
어떤 생각이 대중에게 미치지 않게 하는 것이 검열이다.

313

7 characteristic n. trait, attribute

[kæ̀riktərístik] 특징

Beauty and readability are **characteristics** of good handwriting.
아름다움과 가독성은 잘 된 필적의 특징이다.

8 collide v. crash, slam into ↔ miss, avoid

[kəláid] 충돌하다, 부딪치다

Drivers in car races must take care not to **collide** with any object or car on the road.
자동차 경주 선수는 도로 위에 있는 물체나 차와 충돌하지 않기 위해 반드시 조심해야 한다.

9 commendable adj. admirable, praiseworthy ↔ shameful, loathsome

[kəméndəbl] 칭찬할 만한, 훌륭한

A selfless action that helps others is praised as **commendable** behavior.
남을 돕는 이타적 행위는 훌륭한 행동으로 칭찬 받는다.

10 consolidate v. integrate, tie up with ↔ separate, disperse

[kənsálədèit] 통합하다

The company decided to **consolidate** all its offices into one building.
회사는 모든 사무실을 하나의 건물 안으로 통합하기로 결정했다.

11 contagious adj. infectious, transmittable

[kəntéidʒəs] 전염성의

Precautions can prevent the spread of **contagious** diseases.
예방 조치로 전염병 확산을 막을 수 있다.

12 convert v. modify, transform ↔ retain, sustain

[kənvə́:rt] 개조하다, 전환하다

Old buildings can be **converted** into new spaces for new uses.
오래된 건물은 새로운 용도를 위한 새 공간으로 개조될 수 있다.

13 defect v. leave, abscond ↔ join, come in

[difékt] 떠나다, 망명하다

Citizens who do not agree with their own governments try to **defect** to other countries.
자국 정부와 의견이 일치하지 않는 국민은 타국으로 떠나려 한다.

14 disorder n. affliction, malady

[disɔ́:rdər] 장애, 병

Diabetes is a **disorder** affecting millions and a major public health concern.
당뇨병은 수백만 명이 앓고 있고, 대중의 주요 건강 관심사인 병이다.

15 dissuade v. discourage, deter ↔ persuade, talk into

[diswéid] 만류하다, 단념시키다

Friends tried to **dissuade** him from taking any action without careful thought.
친구들은 그가 신중한 생각 없이 행동하지 않도록 만류하려 했다.

16 encode v. encrypt, convert ↔ crack, decipher

[inkóud] 부호화하다

Whenever we type words into our computers, it **encodes** them into 1s and 0s.
우리가 단어를 컴퓨터에 입력할 때는 언제나 입력 내용을 항상 0과 1로 부호화한다.

17 eulogy n. tribute, high praise ↔ criticism, denigration

[júːlədʒi] 추도 연설, 찬미

The president delivered a **eulogy** at the funeral of the fallen soldiers.
대통령은 전사자들에 대한 장례식에서 추도 연설을 했다.

18 formula n. method, blueprint

[fɔ́ːrmjulə] 법칙, 처리 방안

There is no correct **formula** for breaking up with someone.
누군가와 헤어지는 것에 대한 옳은 처리 방법은 없다.

19 grant v. permit, consent to ↔ deny, refuse

[grǽnt] 승인하다, 허락하다

The bank **granted** a loan to the newlyweds who wanted to buy a new home.
은행은 새집을 사고자 하는 신혼부부에게 대출을 해 주었다.

20 headline n. front page, caption

[hédlàin] 머리기사, 주요 뉴스

The engagement of Prince William to Kate Middleton was the **headline** on every newspaper in the country.
윌리엄 왕자와 케이트 미들턴의 약혼은 나라의 모든 신문 1면에 머리기사로 실렸다.

21 imitation n. fake, replica ↔ original, archetype

[ìmətéiʃən] 모조품

Helen was thrilled that her name brand purse was such a good **imitation** that it even fooled her picky friends.
헬렌은 자신의 메이커 지갑이 까다로운 친구들까지 속였을 정도로 훌륭한 모조품이라는 것에 신이 났다.

22 invaluable adj. priceless, precious ↔ worthless, inferior

[inváeljuəbl] 매우 귀중한

The boss thanked his employees for their **invaluable** assistance in completing the paperwork by the deadline.
상사는 마감일까지 서류 작업을 마치는 데 귀중한 도움을 준 부하 직원들에게 감사를 표했다.

23 petrify v. terrify, frighten

[pètrəfài] 질겁하게 하다

He thought he was home alone and was **petrified** when he heard sounds coming from the next room.
그는 집에 혼자 있다고 생각했는데 옆방에서 나는 소리를 듣고 겁에 질렸다.

24 prioritize v. give precedence to, arrange

[praiɔ́:rətàiz] 우선 순위를 매기다

Sandra made sure to **prioritize** her errands because she was not sure she had time to complete them.
산드라는 맡은 일을 끝낼 수 있는 시간이 있다고 확신하지 못했기 때문에, 일에 확실한 우선 순위를 두었다.

25 pronounced adj. noticeable, obvious ↔ indistinct, vague

[prənáunst] 뚜렷한

Gary tried not to stare at his neighbor's **pronounced** birthmark, which covered the entire left side of her face.
게리는 이웃의 뚜렷한 모반을 빤히 쳐다보지 않으려 애썼는데, 그녀의 모반은 왼쪽 얼굴 전체를 덮고 있었다.

26 revolve v. spin, orbit

[riválv] 돌다, 회전하다

It is a well-known fact that the earth as well as other planets **revolves** around the sun.
다른 행성뿐만 아니라 지구도 태양 주위를 돈다는 것은 잘 알려진 사실이다.

27 scenic adj. picturesque, spectacular ↔ gloomy, dreary

[sí:nik] 경치가 아름다운

He thought his guests would enjoy the **scenic** drive overlooking the ocean.
그는 손님들이 바다가 보이는 경치 좋은 드라이브를 즐길 거라 생각했다.

28 sponsorship n. endorsement, patronage ↔ opposition, antagonism

[spánsərʃip] 후원

The athletes sought **sponsorship** from various companies that could help fund their team at the World Cup.
선수들은 월드컵 경기에서 팀의 자금 조달을 도와줄 수 있는 여러 회사에 후원을 청했다.

29 treacherous adj. hazardous, perilous ↔ harmless, secure

[trétʃərəs] 위험한

He carefully walked on the **treacherous** road that was full of slippery rocks.
그는 미끄러운 바위가 가득한 위험한 길을 조심스럽게 걸었다.

30 vestige n. trace, remnant

[véstidʒ] 흔적

The outdated laws were **vestiges** of a time and an age long past.
시대에 뒤진 그 법은 오래된 과거의 흔적이었다.

DAILY QUIZ

1 **adoration** for our grandparents • • a terrify
2 a **treacherous** journey into the woods • • b crash
3 **grant** access to the next level of security • • c transform
4 the **barren** desert • • d reverence
5 **imitation** crab meat • • e hazardous
6 **burrow** under the garden • • f spin
7 **revolve** around the center • • g bleak
8 **collide** into the moon • • h fake
9 **convert** between kilometers and miles • • i permit
10 **petrify** with chicken • • j excavate

ANSWERS 1. d 2. e 3. i 4. g 5. h 6. j 7. f 8. b 9. c 10. a

Day 56

56 | 58

1 alternate   v. change, fluctuate   ↔ remain, persist

[ɔ́ltərnèit] 교차하다, 번갈아 하다

The weather this week will **alternate** between warm and cold days.
이번 주 날씨는 따뜻한 날과 추운 날이 교차할 것이다.

2 anecdote   n. tale, narrative

[ǽnikdòut] 일화

Anecdotes give insight into how people dealt with situations in the past.
일화는 사람들이 과거에 상황을 다루었던 방법에 대한 통찰력을 제공한다.

3 audience   n. meeting, reception

[ɔ́:diəns] 접견

The ambassadors were given an **audience** with the king.
대사들은 왕을 접견했다.

4 avert   v. turn away, divert   ↔ face, maintain

[əvə́:rt] 돌리다, 피하다

We usually **avert** our eyes when we see something embarrassing.
우리는 보통 무언가 당황스러운 것을 보면 눈을 돌린다.

5 bailout   adj. relief, easing

[béilàut] 긴급 구제의

The government decided on a **bailout** plan for the failing business.
정부는 파산하는 기업을 위한 긴급 구제 계획을 결정했다.

6 carbohydrate   n.

[kɑ̀:rbəháidreit] 탄수화물

Some people want to reduce **carbohydrates** in their diet in order to lose weight.
어떤 사람들은 체중 감량을 위해 탄수화물 섭취를 줄이려 한다.

7. conquistador   n. conqueror, subjugator

[kɑnkwístədɔ́ːr] 정복자

The Spanish **conquistadors** moved into Mexico in the sixteenth century.
스페인 정복자들은 16세기에 멕시코로 이동했다.

8. conscience   n. ethics, sense of right and wrong   ↔ unconscionable, unprincipled

[kánʃəns] 양심

Saying those harsh words bothered his **conscience** for a long time.
그런 거친 말을 한 것이 오랫동안 그의 양심을 괴롭혔다.

9. conscious   adj. aware, vigilant   ↔ indifferent, senseless

[kánʃəs] 의식하고 있는

Animals must stay **conscious** of their surroundings to avoid danger.
동물은 위험을 피하기 위해 반드시 주위 환경을 의식하고 있어야 한다.

10. consummate   adj. gifted, accomplished   ↔ incomplete, inept

[kənsʌ́mət] 완벽한, 훌륭한

The museum displayed many masterpieces by **consummate** artists.
박물관은 훌륭한 예술가들의 걸작을 많이 전시했다.

11. convection   n. heat transfer, circulatory movement

[kənvékʃən] 대류

The second story of a house is partially heated by **convection** from below.
집의 2층은 아래층에서 오는 대류에 의해 부분적으로 난방이 된다.

12. decade   n. ten years

[dékeid] 10년간

People separated by a **decade** or more can have differing views on life and society.
10년 이상 떨어져 산 사람들은 인생과 사회에 대해 견해가 다를 수 있다.

13. determined   adj. strong-minded, resolved   ↔ wavering, irresolute

[ditə́ːrmind] 굳게 결심한

The driver was **determined** to look for a free parking space no matter what.
그 운전자는 무슨 일이 있어도 무료 주차 공간을 찾겠다고 결심했다.

14 dictatorship   n. autocracy, totalitarian   ↔ democracy, republic

[diktéitərʃìp] 독재 정부, 독재 국가

There is little freedom or dialogue among the citizenry in a **dictatorship**.
독재 국가에서는 국민들 간의 자유나 대화가 거의 없다.

15 diplomatic   adj. political, ambassadorial

[dìpləmǽtik] 외교상의

It was a **diplomatic** answer designed so as not to offend the British ambassador.
그것은 영국 대사를 불쾌하게 하지 않기 위한 목적의 외교적인 답변이었다.

16 epitaph   n. inscription, dedication

[épitæ̀f] 묘비명

The tombs of famous people can have **epitaphs** written on them.
유명인의 무덤에는 그들에 대해 쓴 묘비명이 있을 수 있다.

17 exhibition   n. display, presentation   ↔ concealment, cover

[èksəbíʃən] 전시(회)

Museums occasionally put on **exhibitions** of the works of famous artists.
박물관은 이따금 유명 예술가의 전시회를 연다.

18 fabricate   v. construct, put together   ↔ destroy, break apart

[fǽbrikèit] 조립하다, 만들다

The construction company won a contract to **fabricate** several houses in a new neighborhood.
건설 회사는 새로운 동네에 집 몇 채를 짓는 계약을 수주했다.

19 hybrid   n. combination, cross-breed   ↔ pure, homogeneous

[háibrid] 잡종, 혼성물, 〈자동차가〉 하이브리드의

In Greek mythology, Centaurs were feared by humans because they were a **hybrid** of man and horse.
그리스 신화에서 켄타우로스는 인간과 말의 혼성이었기 때문에 인간이 두려워했다.

20 intimately   adv. closely, confidentially   ↔ unfriendly, remotely

[íntəmətli] 친밀히

Janette and Anthony were **intimately** related but wanted to keep it secret at their work because it was unprofessional.
재닛과 앤소니는 친밀한 관계였지만, 아마추어처럼 보일까 봐 직장에서는 비밀로 하기를 원했다.

21. longitude n. ↔ latitude

[lándʒətjùːd] 경도

The students were asked to find the **longitude** of several different cities in their Geography class.
지리 수업 시간에 몇몇 도시의 경도를 찾으라는 요구가 있었다.

22. mysticism n. magic, witchcraft

[místəsìzm] 신비주의

Many scientists view **mysticism** with skepticism and scorn its practices and rituals.
많은 과학자들은 신비주의를 의심의 눈초리로 보며 그것의 관행과 의식을 경멸한다.

23. opponent n. adversary, antagonist ↔ supporter, ally

[əpóunənt] 반대자

She believes in non-violence and is a strong **opponent** of the death penalty.
그녀는 비폭력이 좋다고 생각하며 강경한 사형 반대자이다.

24. principle n. rule, belief

[prínsəpl] 원칙, 신념

The priest has always been respected for acting on his moral **principles**.
사제는 자신의 도덕적인 신념에 따른 행동으로 항상 존경을 받았다.

25. procrastinate v. put off, postpone ↔ accelerate, complete

[proukrǽstənèit] 질질 끌다

Ryan **procrastinated** in writing his 100-page thesis.
라이언은 100장짜리 학위 논문 작성을 질질 끌었다.

26. rectify v. repair, amend ↔ damage, impair

[réktəfài] 바로잡다

Hank attempted to **rectify** his relationship with his wife by giving her jewelry.
행크는 아내에게 보석을 주어서 그녀와의 관계를 바로잡으려 했다.

27. rhythmically adv.

[ríðmikəli] 율동적으로

The guests of the night club danced **rhythmically** to the music.
나이트클럽의 손님들은 음악에 맞춰 율동적으로 춤을 추었다.

28 specimen   n. example, sample

[spésəmən] 견본, 표본

The scientists examined the **specimen** of a rare insect very carefully.
과학자들은 희귀 곤충의 표본을 매우 조심스럽게 조사했다.

29 structure   n. architecture, construction

[strʌ́ktʃər] 구조

Jonathan, an architecture student, was amazed by the **structure** of the Empire State Building.
건축학도인 조나단은 엠파이어 스테이트 빌딩의 구조에 놀랐다.

30 underlying   adj. hidden, latent   ↔ obvious, apparent

[ʌ́ndərlàiiŋ] 뒤에 숨은

Children's stories often have an **underlying** moral lesson or message.
동화에는 흔히 숨어 있는 도덕적 교훈이나 메시지가 있다.

DAILY QUIZ

1. **fabricate** custom parts for the motorcycle
2. **procrastinate** right before the due date
3. the toughest **opponent**
4. the **structure** of the beehive
5. gasoline electric **hybrid** vehicles
6. an excellent **exhibition** of talent
7. implement **bailout** measures
8. **intimately** related
9. **rectify** your mistakes
10. **alternate** between left and right

a. change
b. display
c. relief
d. closely
e. postpone
f. amend
g. construction
h. adversary
i. put together
j. combination

ANSWERS   1. i   2. e   3. h   4. g   5. j   6. b   7. c   8. d   9. f   10. a

COMPREHENSIVE QUIZ — Day 55 & 56

1. Important scientific projects occasionally receive government _____.
   ⓐ convection   ⓑ sponsorship   ⓒ adoration   ⓓ affliction

2. The leaders of the two conflicting nations met to _____ possible war.
   ⓐ avert   ⓑ prioritize   ⓒ grant   ⓓ encode

3. Fortunately for people, cancer is not a _____ disease.
   ⓐ invaluable   ⓑ consummate   ⓒ bailout   ⓓ contagious

4. _____ is sometimes needed to ensure the safety of our youths.
   ⓐ Epitaph   ⓑ Censorship   ⓒ Specimen   ⓓ Eulogy

5. David _____ his friends from picking a fight with the bullies.
   ⓐ burrowed   ⓑ dissuaded   ⓒ fabricated   ⓓ collided

6. Many believed that there must have been a(n) _____ reason behind his refusal to accept the prestigious award.
   ⓐ barren   ⓑ scenic   ⓒ underlying   ⓓ treacherous

7. One of the first things young children learn in a geography class is that the prime meridian is the line of _____ at zero degrees.
   ⓐ exhibition   ⓑ longitude   ⓒ characteristic   ⓓ hybrid

8. The farmer could not shoot the suffering horse because taking a life went against his _____.
   ⓐ conscience   ⓑ opponent   ⓒ vestige   ⓓ headline

9. The _____ of the common good argues that sacrificing few to save many can be justified.
   ⓐ carbohydrate   ⓑ disorder   ⓒ imitation   ⓓ principle

10. Although the boxer was still _____, he could not get up to fight again.
    ⓐ applicable   ⓑ commendable   ⓒ conscious   ⓓ diplomatic

Answers: p.344

Day 57

1 accounting   n. bookkeeping

[əkáuntiŋ] 회계

A company's division of accounting keeps track of revenue and spending.
회사의 회계부는 수입과 지출 내역에 대해 끊임없이 정보를 얻는다.

2 aftermath   n. consequence, result

[ǽftərmæ̀θ] 여파, 결과

Cleaning crews repaired the damage in the aftermath of the storm.
청소 담당 직원들이 폭풍의 여파로 인한 피해를 수습했다.

3 aspiration   n. goal, ambition

[æ̀spəréiʃən] 포부

Helping the less fortunate in society was his childhood aspiration.
사회의 불행한 사람을 돕는 것이 그의 어린 시절 포부였다.

4 asteroid   n.

[ǽstərɔ́id] 소행성

Unlike watery comets, asteroids are mostly hard and dry rocks.
물이 존재하는 혜성과 달리 소행성은 대부분 단단하고 건조한 암석이다.

5 bourgeoisie   n. upper class, nobility   ↔ working class, proletariat

[bùərʒwɑ:zí:] 부르주아

Bourgeoisie is the old-fashioned term for the wealthy landowners of Europe.
부르주아는 유럽의 부유한 지주를 일컫는 옛 용어이다.

6 capture   v. catch, snare   ↔ free, liberate

[kǽptʃər] 붙잡다, 포획하다

The trap managed to capture a few animals during the night.
밤 사이에 덫으로 간신히 동물 몇 마리를 잡을 수 있었다.

7 charitable   adj. humanitarian, philanthropic   ↔ selfish, unsacrificing

[tʃǽrətəbl] 자선의

Taxes are often not collected on **charitable** contributions.
자선 기부금에 대해서는 종종 세금이 부과되지 않는다.

8 condolence   n.

[kəndóuləns] 애도

Friends and relatives offered their **condolences** at the funeral.
친구들과 친척들은 장례식에서 애도를 표했다.

9 confident   adj. assured, undaunted   ↔ uncertain, apprehensive

[kánfədənt] 자신만만한

She seemed **confident** that things would work out fine.
그녀는 일이 잘 될 것으로 자신만만하고 있는 것 같았다.

10 constitution   n. charter, code

[kànstətjúːʃən] 헌법

Most nations have a **constitution** that outlines their basic laws.
대부분의 국가는 기본법을 나타내는 헌법이 있다.

11 cordial   adj. warm, affable   ↔ unpleasant, hostile

[kɔ́ːrdʒəl] 진심 어린

He received a **cordial** invitation to the grand opening of the gallery.
그는 화랑의 개관식에 진심 어린 초대를 받았다.

12 dedicate   v. commit, devote   ↔ disregard, ignore

[dédikèit] 헌정하다, 바치다

Authors often **dedicate** their books to someone who is special to them.
저자들은 종종 자신에게 특별한 사람에게 책을 헌정한다.

13 deforestation   n. forest destruction

[diːfɔ́ːristéiʃən,] 삼림 벌채, 산림 파괴

Environmentalists worry about too much **deforestation** in the world today.
환경론자들은 오늘날 전 세계의 지나친 삼림 벌채에 대해 우려하고 있다.

14 desertification — n. the gradual transformation into desert

[dezə̀ːrtəfikéiʃən] 사막화

People living near deserts often have to fight against **desertification** of their land.
사막 근처에 사는 사람들은 종종 토지의 사막화와 싸워야 한다.

15 environmental — adj. ecological, green

[invàiərənméntl] 환경의

Quality of life can partly depend on **environmental** factors.
삶의 질은 부분적으로 환경 요인에 달려 있다.

16 expedite — v. accelerate, speed up ↔ hinder, get in the way of

[ékspədàit] 신속히 처리하다

Using a map can **expedite** finding the location of a store.
지도를 이용하면 상점의 위치를 신속하게 찾을 수 있다.

17 flourish — v. prosper, blossom ↔ wane, deteriorate

[fləˊːriʃ] 번창하다, 활약하다

Kenny did poorly in high school, but he **flourished** as an outstanding student once he got to college.
케니는 고등학교 때 성적이 형편없었으나, 일단 대학에 진학하고 나서는 우수한 학생으로 활약했다.

18 immaculate — adj. tidy, flawless ↔ filthy, imperfect

[imǽkjulət] 청결한

The nuns at the convent like to keep their room **immaculate** by cleaning it daily.
수도원의 수녀들은 매일 방을 청소해서 청결하게 유지하기를 좋아한다.

19 intensive — adj. concentrated, serious

[inténsiv] 집중적인

The patient was moved to **intensive** care after the difficult surgery.
힘든 수술 후 환자는 집중 치료실로 옮겨졌다.

20 makeshift — adj. temporary, provisional ↔ permanent, complete

[méikʃift] 임시변통의

While waiting for his couch to be delivered, he made **makeshift** chairs out of paper boxes.
그는 소파가 배달되기를 기다리는 동안 종이 상자로 임시 의자를 만들었다.

21 nursery — n. day care, preschool

[nə́ːrsəri] 놀이방, 탁아소

Don dropped his son at the **nursery** before going into his office.
돈은 출근하기 전에 아들을 놀이방에 맡겼다.

22 participate — v. engage, partake ↔ observe, watch

[pɑːrtísəpèit] 참여하다, 관여하다

He was asked to **participate** in a panel discussion at the university.
그는 대학교에서 열리는 공개 토론회에 참여해 달라는 요청을 받았다.

23 present — v. award, bestow ↔ take, withhold

[prizént] 수여하다, 주다

The mayor **presented** the police officers with medals for their years of honorable service.
시장은 수년간의 훌륭한 노고를 기려서 경찰관들에게 훈장을 수여했다.

24 privilege — n. honor, right ↔ burden, obligation

[prívəlidʒ] 영광, 특권

The children felt it was a **privilege** to be invited to the White House to meet the President.
아이들은 대통령을 만나기 위해 백악관에 초대된 것을 영광으로 생각했다.

25 professional — adj. specialized, expert ↔ amateur, unskillful

[prəféʃənl] 전문직의

Sylvia went shopping to find **professional** attire for her new job interview.
실비아는 새 면접에 대비해 전문직에 맞는 옷을 찾으려고 쇼핑하러 갔다.

26 regiment — n. squad, company ↔ single, individual

[rédʒəmənt] 연대

The army formed a **regiment** to be sent overseas to fight in the war.
군대는 전쟁에서 싸우기 위해 해외로 파병될 연대를 구성했다.

27 subversive — adj. rebellious, treasonous ↔ loyal, obedient

[səbvə́ːrsiv] 전복하는, 파괴하는

He was accused of being a spy after writing **subversive** literature against the government.
그는 정부에 대해 전복적인 글을 쓴 후 간첩 혐의로 기소되었다.

28 tremble   v. recoil, cringe   ↔ calm, steady

[trémbl] 벌벌 떨다

Soldiers on foot are trained not to **tremble** at the sight of enemy tanks.
보병들은 적의 탱크를 보고 벌벌 떨지 않도록 훈련을 받는다.

29 vulgar   adj. offensive, obscene   ↔ decent, refined

[vʌ́lgər] 비속한

Vulgar language is never welcomed in a polite conversation.
정중한 대화에서 비속어는 결코 환영받지 못한다.

30 yield   v. give way, accede   ↔ challenge, defy

[jíːld] 양보하다

Defensive driving is always being ready to **yield** to pedestrians and other cars.
방어 운전이란 항상 보행자와 다른 자동차에게 양보할 준비가 되어 있는 것이다.

DAILY QUIZ

1	a **nursery** full of excited children	a	ambition
2	revolt against the **bourgeoisie**	b	consequence
3	raise **environmental** concerns	c	concentrated
4	the national **constitution**	d	ecological
5	the **aspiration** to become someone famous	e	devote
6	an **intensive** effort	f	accelerate
7	**present** the certificate of appreciation	g	charter
8	**aftermath** of the holocaust	h	preschool
9	**expedite** the passing of an important bill	i	award
10	**dedicate** one's life to combating poverty	j	nobility

ANSWERS   1. h   2. j   3. d   4. g   5. a   6. c   7. i   8. b   9. f   10. e

Day 58

1. agricultural   adj. rural, agrarian   ↔ industrial, urban

[ægrikʌ́ltʃərəl] 농업의

Agricultural products are the main source of income in the region.
농산품은 지역의 주요 수입원이다.

2. ailment   n. sickness, malady   ↔ health, well-being

[éilmənt] 병

The doctor diagnosed the exact nature of the patient's **ailment**.
의사는 환자의 질병의 정확한 종류를 진단했다.

3. analytical   adj. rational, logical   ↔ chaotic, disorganized

[ænəlítikəl] 분석적인

The informative news report was **analytical** and objective on the issue.
정보를 제공하는 뉴스 보도는 사안에 대해 분석적이고 객관적이었다.

4. ballot   n. vote, ticket

[bǽlət] 투표

Voters use a box for **ballots** to cast their votes.
유권자들은 투표하기 위해 투표함을 이용한다.

5. carcass   n. remains, corpse

[ká:rkəs] 시체

Vultures are birds that feed on the **carcass** of dead animals.
독수리는 동물의 시체를 먹고 사는 새이다.

6. cluster   v. gather, assemble   ↔ scatter, disperse

[klʌ́stər] 모이다, 무리를 이루다

The children **clustered** together to see what their teacher was holding.
아이들은 교사가 들고 있는 것을 보기 위해 모여들었다.

7 commencement   n. graduation, ceremony

[kəménsmənt] 졸업식

College graduates receive their diplomas in a ceremony of **commencement**.
대학 졸업자들은 졸업식에서 학위를 받는다.

8 concentration   n. attentiveness, vigilance   ↔ distraction, negligence

[kὰnsəntréiʃən] 집중

Solving a difficult problem takes attention to detail and a lot of **concentration**.
어려운 문제를 해결하는 데는 세부 내용에 주목하고 집중을 많이 해야 한다.

9 conduction   n. transmission, conveyance

[kəndʌ́kʃən] 전도

Electricity is the **conduction** of electrons through a medium.
전기는 매체를 통해 전자가 전도되는 것이다.

10 congenial   adj. friendly, affable   ↔ disagreeable, surly

[kəndʒíːnjəl] 친절한, 마음이 맞는

The ministers were polite and **congenial** toward their foreign guests.
장관들은 외국 손님들에게 정중하고 친절했다.

11 constructive   adj. helpful, effectual   ↔ hurtful, useless

[kənstrʌ́ktiv] 건설적인

She welcomed any **constructive** criticism to improve her plan.
그녀는 자신의 계획을 개선하기 위해 어떠한 건설적인 비판이라도 환영했다.

12 contract¹   n. agreement, deal

[kάntrækt] 계약(서)

The terms of the deal were all written out in the **contract**.
거래 조건은 모두 계약서에 명기되었다.

13 contract²   v. catch, acquire

[kəntrǽkt] (병)에 걸리다

Maintaining good health can help one not **contract** a disease.
건강 유지는 병에 걸리지 않는 데 도움이 된다.

14 corruption   n. immorality, exploitation   ↔ honesty, decency

[kərʌ́pʃən] 부패

Citizens groups rallied to eliminate **corruption** in the government.
시민 단체들이 정부 내의 부패를 제거하기 위해 단결했다.

15 culprit   n. offender, perpetrator   ↔ victim, casualty

[kʌ́lprit] 범인

The detective helped catch the **culprit** by investigating some clues.
형사는 몇 가지 단서를 조사해서 범인을 잡는 데 도왔다.

16 dab   v. pat, tap

[dǽb] 가볍게 문지르다, 가볍게 두드리다

People **dab** their mouths with napkins when eating at restaurants.
사람들은 식당에서 식사할 때 냅킨으로 입을 가볍게 문지른다.

17 decorate   v. enhance, embellish   ↔ spoil, mar

[dékərèit] 장식하다

Interior designers **decorate** a room with careful selection of furniture and accessories.
실내 디자이너는 신중하게 선택한 가구와 부속품으로 방을 장식한다.

18 discourse   n. discussion, colloquy

[dískɔːrs] 담론, 토론

The article featured a **discourse** between two experts in the field.
기사는 그 분야의 전문가 두 명의 담론을 다루고 있다.

19 extract   v. take out, extricate   ↔ put in, insert

[ikstrǽkt] 뽑다, 뽑아내다

He had to go to the dentist to **extract** a loose tooth.
그는 흔들리는 치아를 뽑기 위해 치과에 가야 했다.

20 haphazardly   adv. carelessly, arbitrarily   ↔ carefully, systematically

[hæphǽzərdli] 아무렇게나, 우연히

Vivian yelled at her husband for **haphazardly** throwing his shirt on the bed.
비비안은 셔츠를 침대 위에 아무렇게나 벗어 던진다고 남편에게 큰 소리를 질렀다.

21. irreparable adj. beyond repair, irreversible ↔ fixable, mendable

[irépərəbl] 회복할 수 없는

After slapping her daughter in the face, Agatha felt that she had done **irreparable** damage to their relationship.
애거서는 딸의 뺨을 때린 후, 그들의 관계에 회복할 수 없는 손상을 줬다고 느꼈다.

22. magistrate n. judge, arbitrator

[mǽdʒəstrèit] 치안 판사

The **magistrate** dismissed the case because he thought that the charges made were unfounded.
치안 판사는 기소가 근거가 없다고 생각했기 때문에 그 사건을 기각했다.

23. parole n. liberation, probation ↔ imprisonment, incarceration

[pəróul] 가석방

The thief was released from prison after receiving **parole** for good behavior.
절도범은 모범수로 가석방을 받고 감옥에서 풀려났다.

24. proscribe v. ban, get rid of ↔ permit, maintain

[prouskráib] 금지하다

The citizens wanted to **proscribe** the law that would allow young children to buy cigarettes.
시민들은 어린이의 담배 구입을 허용하는 법을 금지하고자 했다.

25. recurring adj. repeating, reappearing ↔ occasional, temporary

[rikə́:riŋ] 재발하는

He had a **recurring** pain in his lower back that caused problems every month.
그는 매달 허리에 문제를 일으키는 재발성 고통을 겪었다.

26. sizable adj. ample, hefty ↔ small, insignificant

[sáizəbl] 상당한, 꽤 큰

The Andersons earned a **sizable** income, so they were able to send their children to expensive private schools.
앤더슨 부부는 상당한 수입을 올렸기 때문에 아이들을 비용이 많이 드는 사립 학교에 보낼 수 있었다.

27. striking adj. outstanding, dazzling ↔ homely, unimpressive

[stráikiŋ] 매력적인, 두드러진

He was told that he could be a male model because he had **striking** features.
그는 매력적인 특징이 있기 때문에 남자 모델이 될 수 있다는 말을 들었다.

28 superintendent n. administrator, supervisor

[sùːpərinténdənt] 관리자

The teachers had to negotiate a new contract with the superintendent of the school district.
교사들은 교육감과 새로운 계약에 대해 협상해야 했다.

29 sympathetic adj. sensitive, compassionate ↔ uncaring, callous

[sìmpəθétik] 동정심 있는

Suzie considers Joanne a sympathetic friend who is willing to listen and give support during difficult times.
수지는 어려운 시기에 기꺼이 이야기를 들어주고 지지해주는 조앤을 동정심 있는 친구라고 생각한다.

30 zenith n. pinnacle, apex ↔ bottom, nadir

[zíːniθ] 천정(天頂)

The sun or moon at the point of zenith always looks far away.
천정에 있는 태양이나 달은 항상 멀리 있어 보인다.

DAILY QUIZ

1. a **recurring** nightmares •   • a   deal
2. sign a **contract** •   • b   rural
3. arrest the **culprit** •   • c   probation
4. the **agricultural** industry •   • d   repeating
5. **congenial** host and hostess •   • e   take out
6. released on **parole** after many years in prison •   • f   sickness
7. **extract** juice from fruits •   • g   immorality
8. suffer from an **ailment** •   • h   offender
9. combat political **corruption** •   • i   friendly
10. public **discourse** on an important issue •   • j   discussion

ANSWERS   1. d   2. a   3. h   4. b   5. i   6. c   7. e   8. f   9. g   10. j

COMPREHENSIVE QUIZ — Day 57 & 58

1. The miners spent several weeks just to _____ a handful of gold from the deep cave.
   ⓐ extract ⓑ participate ⓒ tremble ⓓ decorate

2. Schools must initiate educational programs that could help prevent students from _____ contagious diseases.
   ⓐ dedicating ⓑ inserting ⓒ contracting ⓓ proscribing

3. The collective power of the _____ almost equaled that of the king.
   ⓐ ailment ⓑ bourgeoisie ⓒ deforestation ⓓ carcass

4. The count _____ his daughter to the duke.
   ⓐ clustered ⓑ presented ⓒ dabbed ⓓ captured

5. The mayor asked for more federal agents to _____ the search for the serial killer still at large in the city.
   ⓐ flourish ⓑ yield ⓒ mar ⓓ expedite

6. The popular singer was sued for not following the _____.
   ⓐ conduction ⓑ contract ⓒ accounting ⓓ desertification

7. Without having dreams and _____, one has little chance of succeeding in life.
   ⓐ aspirations ⓑ aftermaths ⓒ superintendents ⓓ regiment

8. A surveillance camera was secretly installed in order to catch the _____ responsible for stealing people's personal items.
   ⓐ parole ⓑ corruption ⓒ culprit ⓓ nursery

9. Love and betrayal are _____ themes in romance novels.
   ⓐ immaculate ⓑ cordial ⓒ charitable ⓓ recurring

10. At the _____ of his power, Genghis Khan ruled about a fifth of the world's total land area.
    ⓐ privilege ⓑ zenith ⓒ condolence ⓓ constitution

Answers: p.345

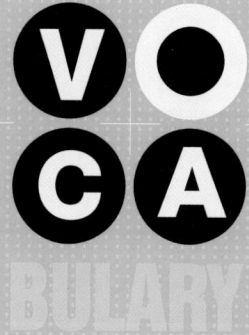

Answer Keys

1 ⓑ. 국가 방위는 싸울 만한 가치가 있는 신념이다.
2 ⓒ. 비관적인 사람은 인생에서 행복을 얻기 어렵다.
3 ⓑ. 기자들은 전 세계에서 일어나고 있는 시사 문제를 파악하기 위해 노력한다.
4 ⓐ. 많은 개발 도상국이 자국 경제를 보호하기 위해 관세를 부과한다.
5 ⓒ. 일류 대학교는 실력 있는 학생들을 모집하려고 한다.
6 ⓓ. 재정적으로 어려운 시기에는 검소한 것이 중요하다.
7 ⓐ. 존슨 씨는 너무 바빠서 세세한 내용까지 듣고 싶지 않았다.
8 ⓒ. 교수는 교재를 가득 채운 애매모호한 용어들을 상세히 설명해야 했다.
9 ⓑ. 그날은 매우 청명해서 사람들이 육안으로 협곡을 볼 수 있었다.
10 ⓐ. 작은 마을은 엄청난 수의 침략군에게 굴복하지 않았다.

1 ⓑ. 변동이 심한 주식 시장은 투자자들을 혼란스럽게 했다.
2 ⓒ. 최우수 감독상 수상자는 시상식에 온 사람들에게 감사를 표했다.
3 ⓓ. 대학생은 학비 충당을 거들기 위해 방학 동안 취직했다.
4 ⓐ. 시장은 노조 지도자에게 파업을 중단하라고 강요했다.
5 ⓑ. 상여금 제도는 종업원들이 더 열심히 일하도록 독려하기 위한 장려책으로 이용되었다.
6 ⓑ. 모든 선수는 반드시 경기 규칙을 준수해야 한다.
7 ⓒ. 대립 중인 양당 간 분쟁에 마침내 돌파구가 마련되었다.
8 ⓑ. 버스를 놓쳤다는 것이 지각 출근에 대한 그럴싸한 이유가 될 수는 없다.
9 ⓒ. 캔디스는 외동딸이었기 때문에 항상 형제자매를 원했다.
10 ⓐ. 권투 선수는 약물 검사에서 걸린 후 챔피언 벨트 포기를 선언할 수 밖에 없었다.

1 ⓑ. 생분해 제품은 오염 수준을 낮추는 데 도움이 될 수 있다.
2 ⓒ. 연사는 공산주의 이론에 내재된 결함에 대해 의논했다.
3 ⓐ. 현대식 집안 장식은 보통 매우 단순하고 현대적이다.
4 ⓑ. 아무도 감히 장군의 명령에 이의를 제기할 엄두를 내지 못했다.
5 ⓑ. 최근 경제 불황 시기에 부동산 거래가 실질적으로 얼어붙었다.
6 ⓓ. 다양한 TV 프로그램을 시청하려면 케이블 설치가 필요하다.
7 ⓒ. 백화점 소유주는 엘리베이터 공포증이 있기 때문에 에스컬레이터를 탔다.
8 ⓑ. 열대 지방의 섬은 습도가 특히 높다.
9 ⓒ. 북한의 핵 시설을 조사하기 위해 국제 원자력 기구 사찰단이 파견되었다.
10 ⓐ. 아무도 전설적인 마이클 잭슨의 독창적인 댄스 동작을 결코 모방할 수 없을 것이다.

1 ⓓ. 콘서트 기획자들은 열광하는 팬들로 스타디움이 가득 찰 것으로 자신만만하게 예상하고 있다.
2 ⓒ. 작곡가는 자신의 노래를 표절했다는 이유로 유명한 록그룹을 고소했다.
3 ⓑ. 빌 & 멜린다 게이츠 재단에 10억 달러를 기부한 비밀스러운 사람은 익명으로 남기를 원했다.
4 ⓒ. 국민들은 해외 망명 지도자의 의기양양한 귀국을 환영했다.
5 ⓑ. 목동은 우르르 몰려오는 물소들로부터 가까스로 피신했다.
6 ⓓ. 총선에서 양당 모두 정확히 50%씩 득표했기 때문에 정치적인 교착 상태가 초래되었다.
7 ⓑ. 환경주의자들은 계속되고 있는 천연자원 개발에 대해 우려하고 있다.
8 ⓐ. 보통의 지능을 가진 사람이 천재의 마음을 헤아리는 것은 거의 불가능하다.
9 ⓐ. 팀은 전반전에 9점을 허용한 뒤 조기에 패배를 인정해야 했다.
10 ⓒ. 피고는 직접적인 답변을 피하기 위해 비유적인 언어를 많이 사용했다.

1 ⓑ. 부동산 거품 붕괴가 국가의 재정 위기를 초래한 기폭제로 작용했다.
2 ⓓ. 유권자였던 많은 남성은 또한 여성의 참정권을 위해 싸웠다.
3 ⓒ. 탈옥수가 아직 체포되지 않았기 때문에 경찰서장은 시민들에게 문을 걸어 잠그라고 권고했다.
4 ⓒ. 도시 박물관 가까이에 거대한 자유의 여신상 모형이 있다.
5 ⓑ. 카페인에 둔감한 사람들은 커피를 몇 잔 마셔도 밤에 숙면을 취할 수 있다.
6 ⓓ. 아마도 허파는 호흡기계에서 가장 중요한 부위일 것이다.
7 ⓐ. 기록적인 폭설로 직장을 통근해야 하는 시민들이 큰 어려움을 겪었다.
8 ⓓ. 보건 당국은 유아와 노인이 신종 독감 바이러스에 더 취약할 수 있다고 경고했다.
9 ⓑ. 많은 심판 판정이 대부분 임의적이었다.
10 ⓒ. 럭비 팀은 지난 밤 승리로 마침내 10연속패에 종지부를 찍었다.

1 ⓐ. 자신의 생각을 분명히 표현할 수 있다는 것은 다른 사람들과 함께 일하기 위한 훌륭한 자산이다.
2 ⓑ. 선물 가게는 기념품, 문구류 및 기타 액세서리를 판매한다.
3 ⓓ. 그의 상사는 일을 잘했다며 그를 칭찬했다.
4 ⓑ. 많은 고등학생이 과도한 대학 등록금에 대해 항의하려 계획하고 있다.
5 ⓓ. 시민들은 새로운 법으로 인해 십대들이 부당한 혐의를 받게 될 것으로 믿고 있다.
6 ⓐ. 연설이 너무 열정적이어서, 끝난 뒤 모든 사람들이 일어나 박수를 쳤다.
7 ⓐ. 반복해서 뇌 손상을 입으면 인지 기능이 떨어질 수 있다.
8 ⓑ. 체계적인 논의를 하기 위해 팀의 대변인을 지명하십시오.
9 ⓓ. 쌀은 많은 아시아인의 주식이다.
10 ⓐ. 저조한 수익으로 인해 식품부는 내년까지 폐지될 것이다.

1 ⓒ. 그는 전쟁에서 돌아와 자신이 진정한 군인이었다고 생각했다.
2 ⓓ. 다음 선거 때까지 그녀가 임시 대통령직을 수행할 것이다.
3 ⓐ. 건조한 사막에는 놀랄 만큼 많은 동물이 살고 있다.
4 ⓒ. 그녀는 자신에게 강한 호기심을 불러일으킨 조지 워싱턴에 대해 연구하며 3년을 보냈다.
5 ⓑ. 시험 전날 밤의 벼락공부는 다음 날 정보 기억력을 향상시켜 주지 않는다.
6 ⓑ. 많은 사람들이 나날이 찍은 사진과 영상을 통해 자신의 삶을 기록한다.
7 ⓒ. 그는 뉴스에 대한 반응을 숨겼기 때문에 아무도 그가 실제로 느끼는 바를 알지 못했다.
8 ⓐ. 조사관은 요점을 파악하는 데 모든 정보를 필요로 하지 않았다.
9 ⓓ. 과거에 대한 TV쇼는 시청자들이 향수를 느끼게 한다.
10 ⓒ. 피부를 통해 독을 분비할 수 있는 개구리가 많다.

1 ⓓ. 내 친척들은 명절 모임에서 항상 서로 농담을 주고받는다.
2 ⓑ. 수사관은 범죄 현장에서 발견된 유리에서 긁어낸 잔여물을 분석해서 범죄를 해결할 수 있었다.
3 ⓐ. 어머니는 우는 아이를 달래려 했다.
4 ⓑ. 실력 있는 변호사는 간접적인 질문으로 정보를 도출할 수 있을 것이다.
5 ⓓ. 어떤 사람들은 부가 단지 유형의 소유물 정도라고 생각한다.
6 ⓒ. 그의 신간은 수년간의 연구와 헌신의 결정체이다.
7 ⓒ. 예술품을 창조할 때는 상상력을 억제하지 마십시오!
8 ⓐ. 각국은 평화 조약을 협의하기 위해 대표를 파견할 것이다.
9 ⓓ. 그녀는 병을 앓는 동안 의도하지 않게 체중이 줄었다.
10 ⓑ. 경찰은 범죄가 추가로 모방 범죄를 영속시킬까봐 우려했다.

1 ⓑ. 평론가들은 전쟁 피난민의 몸부림을 솔직하게 묘사했다고 영화에 찬사를 보냈다.
2 ⓓ. 많은 사람들이 선진국에서 더 나은 삶을 살기 위해 제3세계 국가에서 이주한다.
3 ⓐ. 대통령은 빈곤을 막기 위한 계획을 시행했다.
4 ⓒ. 아내의 호사스런 취향은 부부를 빚더미로 내몰았다.
5 ⓓ. 자선 단체장은 서신에서 기부자들의 모든 후원에 감사를 표했다.
6 ⓑ. 시장은 시의 재정 적자를 악화시킬 것이라는 이유로 새로운 공원 건설에 반대하는 결정을 내렸다.
7 ⓓ. 일단의 숫자에서 순서를 살펴보면 수학 공식을 만들 수 있다.
8 ⓐ. 그는 학업에 대한 야망으로 2개의 박사 학위 과정을 마쳤다.
9 ⓐ. 대부분의 상점에서는 고객이 상품을 손으로 만지는 것을 좋아하지 않는다.
10 ⓒ. 미술품 수집가는 많은 돈을 지불했지만 유명한 인상파 화가의 그림을 손에 넣어 기뻤다.

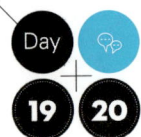

1 ⓓ. 소년의 발작이 계속해서 악화되자, 그의 부모는 뇌수술이 필요하다는 결정을 내렸다.
2 ⓑ. 과학자들은 신종 독감이 국지적 발병에 광범위한 지역에서 대규모로 유행한다고 믿고 있다.
3 ⓐ. 팬들이 다음 달에 개봉하는 신작 영화의 일부를 미리 보는 것이 허용되었다.
4 ⓓ. 대통령의 실수는 흔히 정치적 풍자의 주제가 된다.
5 ⓒ. 그들의 끈끈한 유대는 그가 가장 친한 친구가 자신을 지지해 줄 것이라고 항상 믿을 수 있음을 의미했다.
6 ⓐ. 고고학자들은 마야인과 이집트인이 현대 기술 없이 어떻게 그렇게 큰 피라미드를 세울 수 있었는지 경탄한다.
7 ⓑ. 토착민들은 종종 식민지 개척자들에 의해 혹사당했다.
8 ⓓ. 공주는 소작농 생활의 어려움을 의식하지 못했다.
9 ⓑ. 논술 시험에서 글씨를 알아볼 수 없는 경우 점수가 떨어질 것이다.
10 ⓑ. 지역 주민들은 어떠한 범죄 조짐에 대해서도 경계를 게을리 하지 말라는 경고를 받았다.

1 ⓐ. 그들 사이에 증오의 골이 너무 깊어서 화해의 희망이 희박한 것으로 보인다.
2 ⓒ. 깨끗한 물은 콜레라 박멸의 필요조건이다.
3 ⓐ. 검사들은 공명정대한 재판을 위해 엄격한 법의 적용을 요구했다.
4 ⓓ. 소방관이 화재 예방의 중요한 규칙에 대해 말했다.
5 ⓐ. 안전벨트의 유효성은 모든 차 충돌사고 조사가 있을 때마다 나오는 큰 화젯거리이다.
6 ⓒ. 물고기 남획으로 인해 많은 나라가 어류 자원과 개체수 유지에 관한 정책을 강행하고 있다.
7 ⓑ. 능력주의는 계층이나 인종 차별 없이 신입 사원을 채용하기 위한 최고의 제도이다.
8 ⓓ. 그는 매년 몇 권의 베스트셀러를 쓰는 다작 작가이다.
9 ⓐ. 영양학자들은 항상 과일이 풍부한 식사를 하고 발암 식품을 피하는 것이 좋다고 말한다.
10 ⓑ. 교수는 매 수업마다 최소한 한 사람을 잠자게 하는 지루한 강의로 악명 높다.

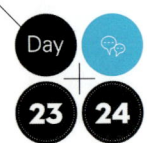

1 ⓓ. 지방 시청에서의 인턴 근무가 그가 정치 경력을 시작하는 데에 도움이 되었다.
2 ⓐ. 그는 입원해 있는 동안 심부름을 해 줄 도우미를 쓸 수 있었다.
3 ⓑ. 안내원은 결혼식이 시작되기 전에 하객들을 자리로 안내했다.
4 ⓓ. 세금 인상은 많은 사람들이 우려하는 계속 반복되는 문제이다.
5 ⓒ. 매년 가을마다 신입생들이 대거 입학한다.
6 ⓐ. 경찰은 공공 기물 파괴자들이 더 많은 재산을 더 파괴하기 전에 체포할 수 있었다.
7 ⓑ. 다국적 대기업이 다양한 분야에서 사업을 하는 자회사를 많이 거느리는 것이 드문 일은 아니다.
8 ⓓ. 그녀는 새로 상점을 내기 위해 상업 공간을 임대해야 한다.
9 ⓑ. 종교 지도자들은 중대한 책임로서 신도들에 대한 주도권을 장악해야 한다.
10 ⓒ. 그것은 아주 신나지도 책임이 막중하지도 않은 하찮은 공장 일이었지만 정직한 일이었다.

1 ⓐ, 작업 프로젝트로 인한 과도한 스트레스가 월급에 포함된 보너스로 상쇄되었다.
2 ⓐ, 도시에는 흔히 국제공항 하나와 별도의 국내선 공항 하나가 있다.
3 ⓒ, 긴박한 상황에 대한 그녀의 요령 있는 접근법이 정부와 반군 지도자들간 휴전의 비결이었다.
4 ⓑ, 그는 세계 여행을 하기 위해서 자의로 사직했다.
5 ⓓ, 독서광인 그녀의 꿈은 도서관에서 일하는 것이다.
6 ⓐ, 현재 기술이 충분히 발달하지 않았기 때문에 화성 유인 탐사 실현은 아직도 몇 년 더 있어야 한다.
7 ⓓ, 시간 제약으로 우리는 식사를 거르고 바로 영화를 보러 가야 한다.
8 ⓑ, 그는 보통 매우 친절했기 때문에 친구들은 그의 짓궂은 행동에 당혹해 했다.
9 ⓒ, 국가들은 관광객을 유치하기 위해 자국의 고유 문화를 선전한다.
10 ⓐ, 그는 영화 시작 5분 만에 죽을 수 있는 소모성 인물이었다.

1 ⓐ, 그녀의 음악적 기교는 매우 특출해서 전 세계적 교향악단과 함께 공연해 달라는 요청을 받았다.
2 ⓒ, 그들은 고래를 그물에서 놓아주는 동안 진정시킬 수 있었다.
3 ⓓ, 그의 매력은 행성의 인력처럼 사람들의 마음을 끌어당겼다.
4 ⓓ, 입법자들은 최종 안을 표결에 부치기 전에 의안을 수정할 것이다.
5 ⓐ, 가족은 정신없이 바쁜 도시 생활에서 벗어나기 위해 시골로 이사하기로 했다.
6 ⓑ, 갓 구운 쿠키 냄새가 온 집안에 스며들었다.
7 ⓑ, 대부분의 과학자들은 화성에 생명체가 존재할 수 있다는 가능성을 무시한다.
8 ⓒ, 그 액션 영화를 보고 있는 사람들은 대부분 화려한 스턴트를 좋아하는 십대 남자 아이들이다.
9 ⓐ, 그녀는 정원 가꾸기와 그림 그리기 같은 취미를 개발하기 위해 업무 외 시간을 낼 수 있었다.
10 ⓑ, 그들은 서로를 알아가는 훈련을 한 달 동안 받아 혼연일체의 팀으로 움직일 수 있었다.

1 ⓑ, 잭은 그녀의 미소 짓는 얼굴에서 일이 잘 되었음을 추측할 수 있었다.
2 ⓑ, 목격자들은 경찰에게 은행 강도에 대해 묘사할 수 있었다.
3 ⓒ, 매운 맛이 강한 소스를 한 방울만 넣어도 틀림없이 눈물을 흘릴 것이다.
4 ⓐ, 이 카페는 전 세계에서 원두를 수입하기 때문에 가지각색의 풍미를 제공한다.
5 ⓓ, 전문가는 노련하게 밧줄을 한 번 당겨서 바위 주위로 범선을 인도할 수 있었다.
6 ⓐ, 치과 의사는 당신의 치아가 더 희고 깨끗하게 보이도록 미백할 것이다.
7 ⓒ, 회사는 비용과 시간을 절감하기 위해 생산 공정을 간소화할 것이다.
8 ⓒ, 사자는 한 마리를 포획하는 데 집중하기 전에 사냥감 무리를 분산시켜야 한다.
9 ⓑ, 나는 그가 초등학교 시절 경기하는 것을 본 후 프로 축구 선수가 될 가능성이 있다는 것을 알았다.
10 ⓓ, 모두가 추상화를 각자 다르게 해석했고, 그림의 의미에 대해 논의하며 밤을 보냈다.

1 ⓓ, 경찰관은 안전장치로 방탄조끼를 착용했다.
2 ⓒ, 배우들은 중요한 공연 전에 반드시 자신의 역할을 반복해서 예행연습해야 한다.
3 ⓐ, 시장은 도시의 범죄율을 낮추기 위해 과감한 조치를 취하기로 했다.
4 ⓑ, 숙제를 제때 제출하는 것이 중요하다.
5 ⓑ, 때로는 작은 강아지도 사나워질 수 있다.
6 ⓐ, 공판은 3월 말까지 휴정할 것이다.
7 ⓒ, 조동사의 예로 'be'와 'do'가 있다.
8 ⓓ, 과학 수사대 요원들은 증거를 찾기 위해 범죄 현장 구역을 수색했다.
9 ⓒ, 피고측 변호인은 자신의 주장을 뒷받침할 충분한 증거가 없었기 때문에 패소했다.
10 ⓐ, 균등하지 않은 부의 분배는 국가 경제 몰락을 초래할 수 있다.

1 ⓓ. 고등학교 시절을 얼마나 효과적으로 보내느냐에 따라 장래가 좌우될 수 있다.
2 ⓑ. 전쟁은 때로 사람들이 잔인하고 비열한 행위를 저지르게 내몬다.
3 ⓐ. 앨버트는 자신이 좋아하는 책의 영화 각색본이 형편없이 만들어졌다고 생각했다.
4 ⓒ. 구어체 단어와 구를 익히는 것이 언어 학습에서 가장 어려운 부분이다.
5 ⓒ. 심판은 선수가 의도적으로 저지른 반칙을 보고 옐로카드를 꺼냈다.
6 ⓐ. 자식은 부모에게 순종해야 한다.
7 ⓑ. 긴 경기 뒤 허기진 운동선수들이 탈의실에서 간식을 게걸스럽게 먹어 치웠다.
8 ⓓ. 리시와 프라나프는 하루 종일 정통 인도 식당을 찾아 다녔다.
9 ⓐ. 입학 사정 담당자들은 학생들의 지원서를 평가하면서 밤을 지새웠다.
10 ⓓ. 아이비리그 학교에는 저명한 교수가 많이 있다.

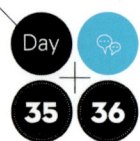

1 ⓓ. 피튜니아는 어려운 시기에 길잡이가 될 경구를 많이 읽었다.
2 ⓐ. 판사는 증거 불충분을 이유로 사건을 기각했다.
3 ⓑ. 연장자 앞에서는 적절한 행동을 보여주는 것이 중요하다.
4 ⓒ. 유명 여배우는 남편이 죽자 슬픔에 괴로워했다.
5 ⓐ. 주방장 프랭코는 필요한 재료를 보조에게 나열했다.
6 ⓑ. 수공작은 암공작을 유인하기 위해 화려한 깃털을 드러냈다.
7 ⓓ. 진짜 스테이크 살코기를 가공육과 비교하는 것은 바보 같다.
8 ⓐ. 신임 최고 경영자는 본사를 시찰했다.
9 ⓑ. 어떤 동물들은 우호의 몸짓으로 코를 서로 비빈다.
10 ⓒ. 교장은 학교 예산으로 과학 실험실 신축 자금을 책정하기 어렵다는 것을 깨달았다.

1 ⓐ. 곤충은 많은 부속지가 있다.
2 ⓒ. 감독은 연습에 늦게 온 이유로 선수들을 꾸짖었다.
3 ⓑ. 제이드린은 고아에 관한 이야기인 흥미진진한 소설에 감동받았다.
4 ⓒ. 지도자의 사망 뒤 군사 정부는 마침내 붕괴되었다.
5 ⓐ. 콰시모도의 기괴한 외모는 그의 친절한 본성과 뚜렷한 대조를 보였다.
6 ⓑ. 약을 구입하기 전에 있을 수 있는 부작용에 대해 반드시 고려해야 한다.
7 ⓓ. 조셉은 고등학교 신입생에 불과했지만 대학생처럼 보였다.
8 ⓒ. 인기 작가는 9년의 공백 기간을 보낸 뒤 마침내 또 한 권의 책을 썼다.
9 ⓓ. 어린 수사자는 커다란 영양을 성공적으로 쓰러뜨려 용맹성을 보였다.
10 ⓑ. 인터넷으로 무한한 정보를 찾아볼 수 있게 되었다.

1 ⓒ. 나라의 점점 더 많은 사람들이 더 부유해지면서 사치품 소비가 늘고 있다.
2 ⓓ. 영화는 일류 남녀 배우들을 주연시켰기 때문에 제작 비용이 아주 많이 들었다.
3 ⓐ. 소문만을 근거로 진위를 판단해서는 안 된다.
4 ⓑ. 인체에는 23쌍의 염색체가 있다.
5 ⓑ. 파산한 회사에서 일했던 직원들은 임금을 받을 수 없었다.
6 ⓒ. 클라크 장군은 부하들에게 즉시 사격을 중지하라고 명령했다.
7 ⓓ. 정부 요원들은 일급 정부 비밀을 국외로 빼내려고 했던 간첩을 심문했다.
8 ⓒ. 아끼던 금붕어가 죽자 그는 아주 슬퍼했다.
9 ⓑ. 지나는 신용 카드가 만기가 되어서 비싼 것은 아무 것도 살 수 없었다.
10 ⓐ. 나라에서 가장 사랑 받는 반체제 지도자가 체포되어 전국에서 폭동을 촉발했다.

Day 41+42

1 ⓑ. 예언자의 제자들은 예언자의 중요한 메시지를 전파하기 위해 전 세계를 누볐다.
2 ⓓ. 여왕은 왕위 탈취를 시도했다는 이유로 아들을 왕국에서 추방했다.
3 ⓒ. 학생회장은 많은 학교 집회를 주최해야 할 책임이 있다.
4 ⓐ. 하나의 사상이 상당수의 사람들에게 영향을 줄 수 있다.
5 ⓑ. 악명 높은 범죄 집단의 두목은 경비가 가장 삼엄한 교도소에 수감되었다.
6 ⓐ. 신부와 신랑은 내일 결혼식에 앞서 통로를 행진해 내려가는 연습을 했다.
7 ⓓ. 쿠마는 여동생이 자신의 CD를 훔치고 있다고 의심했다.
8 ⓒ. 배가 전복되어 모든 화물을 잃었지만, 다행히 승선자 중에 다친 사람은 없었다.
9 ⓑ. 어미 새는 먼저 삼켰던 먹이를 다시 뱉어서 새끼들을 먹였다.
10 ⓐ. 누구라도 파라오의 무덤을 훼손하는 자는 평생 저주를 받을 것이라는 떠도는 이야기가 있다.

Day 43+44

1 ⓐ. 식당 지배인은 음식이 너무 늦게 나온다고 불평하는 화난 손님들을 달래기 위해 애를 썼다.
2 ⓒ. 신문사는 믿을 만한 출처로부터 소식을 입수했다고 주장했다.
3 ⓐ. 헤르메스는 그리스 신들의 메시지를 전달하는 책임이 있었다.
4 ⓓ. 사랑은 결코 조건부가 아니라는 것을 기억하는 게 중요하다.
5 ⓒ. 국가를 통치했던 군사 정부는 국민에 의해 마침내 타도되었다.
6 ⓑ. 심한 다리 부상으로 인해 대학 입학을 위한 선수 장학금을 받으려 했던 조셉의 꿈이 산산조각 났다.
7 ⓐ. 신뢰가 없다면, 우정은 지속되지 못하고 쉽게 깨질 수 있다.
8 ⓒ. 씨족 사람들은 겸손으로 자신들을 대우해 준 지도자를 존경하고 사랑했다.
9 ⓐ. 교육에 대한 수동적인 태도는 학생의 장래를 망칠 수 있다.
10 ⓑ. 비행기 추락 사고 후 영양실조에 걸린 생존자는 산딸기와 견과를 먹고 살아야 했다.

Day 45+46

1 ⓑ. 신인 선수가 감독의 지시를 노골적으로 반대하자 모든 사람들이 놀랐다.
2 ⓒ. 학생이 조퇴를 하려면 부모의 동의가 필요하다.
3 ⓓ. 탐험가들은 야생에서 생존하기 위해 직감을 이용했다.
4 ⓑ. 에디슨은 천재란 1%의 영감과 99%의 땀으로 만들어진다고 생각했다.
5 ⓐ. 경제학자들은 현재의 부동산 거품이 언제라도 터질 수 있다고 경고한다.
6 ⓓ. 귀족들은 새로운 왕에게 충성을 맹세했다.
7 ⓒ. 요즘 갑자기 소매 체인점이 도처에 생겨나고 있다.
8 ⓐ. 국가 대표 축구팀은 결승전에 대비해 혹독한 훈련을 받았다.
9 ⓑ. 마을 사람들은 주위 숲에 불을 질러서 쳐들어오는 야만인들의 주의를 딴 데로 돌렸다.
10 ⓒ. 1년 만에 커피숍은 개업 비용을 충당할 만큼 충분한 수익을 올렸다.

Day 47+48

1 ⓑ. 노숙자들에게는 허름한 판잣집이 충분히 쾌적했다.
2 ⓓ. 정복자는 어린 시절부터 뛰어난 지도력을 보였다.
3 ⓒ. 제이크는 오후 내내 복잡한 기계를 작동시킬 수 있는 장치를 찾으려고 애썼다.
4 ⓐ. 자녀를 너무 많이 칭찬하면 사실 역효과가 날 수 있다.
5 ⓒ. 신형 차 모델이 젊은 고객들로부터 대단한 반응을 얻었다.
6 ⓑ. 모든 교파의 사람들이 세계 평화를 기원하기 위해 함께 모였다.
7 ⓐ. 심한 폐렴으로 사람이 죽을 수 있다.
8 ⓒ. 흥분한 학생들은 학교 강당에서 가장 좋은 자리를 차지하기 위해 서로 다퉜다.
9 ⓓ. 빌은 사법 고시 공부가 마라톤을 달리는 것과 유사하다고 생각했다.
10 ⓑ. 신축 콘도는 어떠한 자연 재해에도 견디도록 설계되었다.

Day 49+50

1 ⓓ 지지를 얻지 못하는 무역 협정에 시위하는 격앙된 군중을 해산시키기 위해서 폭동 진압 경찰이 투입되었다.
2 ⓑ 독감 발병 원인을 확인하기 위해 역학 조사팀이 파견되었다.
3 ⓒ 마술사는 무생물체를 만지지 않고 움직여 관객을 놀라게 했다.
4 ⓐ 보통 항공사는 기내에서 무료 식사를 제공한다.
5 ⓒ 브랜드 씨는 쌍둥이를 구별하는 데 문제가 있었다.
6 ⓑ 학교는 학교 폭력에 계속 시달리고 있다.
7 ⓐ 소수 민족 단체의 지도자들은 자국 민족에 대한 학대를 비난했다.
8 ⓓ 피터는 호텔에서 인턴으로 근무하면서 서비스 업계에서 직접적인 경험을 할 수 있었다.
9 ⓒ 사람들은 일상적인 생활에서 벗어나고 싶을 때 종종 엉뚱한 일을 저지른다.
10 ⓑ 교장은 학생들의 요구에 무관심했기 때문에 매우 인기가 없었다.

Day 51+52

1 ⓑ 캔디스는 학생 회장 당선에 필요한 충분한 투표를 얻을 수 없었다.
2 ⓒ 샌프란시스코의 많은 건물이 지진을 견디도록 설계되었다.
3 ⓑ 가장 강인하고 용감한 자만이 해병대 입대가 허용된다.
4 ⓑ 사람들은 은행장 자신이 악명 높은 강도 사건의 공범이었다는 소식에 충격을 받았다.
5 ⓐ 근로자들은 급료가 노동 시간을 반영하지 않았다고 생각했다.
6 ⓓ 정상 회담 기간에는 국가 원수들조차도 엄격한 보안 정책을 비켜갈 수 없었다.
7 ⓑ 여행객들은 초과 수하물에 대해 추가 요금을 내야 한다는 것에 속상했다.
8 ⓒ 심폐소생술은 심장 마비가 일어난 사람을 소생시킬 수 있는 방법이다.
9 ⓐ 과학자들은 해안을 가득 메운 돌고래 사체의 원인을 설명할 수 없었다.
10 ⓐ 케이트는 해변에서 발견한 예쁜 조개 껍질을 기념품으로 집에 가져가려고 주웠다.

Day 53+54

1 ⓑ 맥스는 록 콘서트를 보고 난 뒤 기타를 몹시 배우고 싶어했다.
2 ⓓ 그 유명한 영화 감독은 자신이 마음대로 부릴 수 있는 조수 35명을 두었다.
3 ⓐ 기록적인 폭우가 엄청난 홍수의 원인이었다.
4 ⓓ 블랙호크 추장은 교전 중인 두 파벌 간의 화해를 지켜보았다.
5 ⓑ 외교관이 되고자 하는 사람에게 중요한 자질은 협상 능력이다.
6 ⓓ 알렉산더 박사는 성공적으로 동물 배아에서 줄기세포를 추출했다.
7 ⓐ 야영 모닥불에서 피어오르는 연기로 그들의 은신처가 위태로워졌다.
8 ⓑ 데니스는 대학 진학보다 직업 기술을 습득하는 것이 더 실용적이라고 생각했다.
9 ⓐ 제이콥은 린다의 오빠와 대결하는 것을 피하기 위해 그녀를 괴롭히는 것을 그만두었다.
10 ⓒ 지휘관은 요새를 차지함으로써 얻는 이득이 부하 몇 명을 잃는 대가보다 더 크다고 믿는다.

Day 55+56

1 ⓑ 중요한 과학 프로젝트는 때때로 정부의 후원을 받는다.
2 ⓐ 대립 중인 양국의 지도자들은 발발 가능성이 있는 전쟁을 피하기 위해 만났다.
3 ⓓ 다행스럽게도 암은 전염병이 아니다.
4 ⓑ 청년들의 안전을 지키기 위해 때로 검열이 필요하다.
5 ⓑ 데이빗은 깡패에게 싸움을 걸지 말라고 친구들을 만류했다.
6 ⓒ 많은 사람들은 그가 명망 있는 상의 수상을 거부한 데에는 틀림없이 숨겨진 이유가 있을 거라 믿었다.
7 ⓑ 어린이들이 지리 수업에서 처음 배우는 것 중 하나는 본초 자오선은 경도 0도 선이라는 것이다.
8 ⓐ 농부는 생명을 빼앗는 것이 자기 양심과 맞지 않기 때문에 고통스러워 하고 있는 말을 총으로 쏠 수 없었다.
9 ⓐ 공익의 원리가 내세우는 바는 소수를 희생해서 다수를 구하는 것이 정당화될 수 있다는 것이다.
10 ⓒ 권투 선수는 여전히 의식이 있었지만 다시 싸우기 위해 일어날 수 없었다.

1 ⓐ. 광부들은 깊은 동굴에서 한 줌의 금을 채굴하기 위해 몇 주를 보냈다.
2 ⓒ. 학교는 학생들의 전염병 예방에 도움이 되는 교육 프로그램을 반드시 실시해야 한다.
3 ⓑ. 부르주아의 집단 세력은 왕의 세력과 거의 맞먹었다.
4 ⓑ. 백작은 자신의 딸을 공작에게 바쳤다.
5 ⓓ. 시장은 도시에서 아직 체포되지 않은 연쇄 살인범을 신속하게 수색할 수 있도록 연방 정부 요원을 더 많이 요청했다.
6 ⓑ. 그 인기 가수는 계약을 이행하지 않은 것으로 고소되었다.
7 ⓐ. 꿈과 포부가 없이는 인생에서 성공할 기회가 거의 없다.
8 ⓒ. 사람들의 개인 용품을 훔친 범인을 잡기 위해 감시 카메라가 비밀리에 설치되었다.
9 ⓓ. 사랑과 배신은 연애 소설에서 반복되는 주제이다.
10 ⓑ. 권력의 절정기에 징기스칸은 세계 육지 전체의 약 1/5을 통치했다.

Voca Plus

표제어에 실리지 않은 고난도 필수 어휘 확장 학습

VOCA PLUS

A

- **abundant** [əbʌ́ndənt] 풍부한
- **acclimate** [ǽkləmèit] 순응시키다
- **acquiesce** [ækwiés] 잠자코 따르다
- **acupuncture** [ǽkjupʌ́ŋktʃər] 침술
- **adhesive** [ædhíːsiv] 접착제
- **adorn** [ədɔ́ːrn] 장식하다
- **affront** [əfrʌ́nt] 과감히 맞서다
- **afloat** [əflóut] 물 위에 떠서
- **agonize** [ǽgənàiz] 몹시 괴롭히다
- **agoraphobia** [ægərəfóubiə] 광장 공포증
- **agriculture** [ǽgrikʌ̀ltʃər] 농업
- **almighty** [ɔːlmáiti] 전능한
- **ambivalence** [æmbívələns] 서로 다른 감정이 병존
- **amenity** [əménəti] 오락 시설
- **amnesty** [ǽmnəsti] 사면
- **ample** [ǽmpl] 풍부한
- **anesthesia** [ænəsθíːʒə] 마취
- **annihilate** [ənáiəlèit] 무력하게 하다
- **antipathy** [æntípəθi] 반감
- **appetite** [ǽpitàit] 식욕
- **applause** [əplɔ́ːz] 박수갈채
- **armistice** [áːrməstis] 휴전
- **arrogant** [ǽrəgənt] 거만한
- **arsenal** [áːrsənl] 무기고
- **aspire** [əspáiər] 열망하다
- **as follows** 다음과 같은
- **as it were** 말하자면
- **as of** ~부터
- **as[so] far as I concerned** 나로서는
- **astronomer** [əstrʌ́nəmər] 천문학자
- **at any rate** 어쨌든
- **atrocity** [ətrásəti] 흉악
- **attend of** ~을 처리하다
- **audacious** [ɔːdéiʃəs] 대담한
- **auditing** [ɔ́ːditiŋ] 회계, 감사
- **auditory** [ɔ́ːdətɔ̀ːri] 귀의
- **aura** [ɔ́ːrə] 독특한 분위기
- **autonomous** [ɔːtánəməs] 자치권이 있는
- **avalanche** [ǽvəlæ̀ntʃ] 눈사태
- **avian** [éiviən] 새

B

- **back up** (사실 등을) 뒷받침하다
- **backlash** [bǽklæ̀ʃ] 격렬한 반발
- **barely** [bɛ́ərli] 거의 ~않다, 간신히
- **bargain** [báːrgən] 싸게 산 물건
- **barometer** [bərámətər] 기압계, 표준
- **be acquainted with** ~을 익히다, ~에 익숙하다
- **be mired in** ~의 수렁에 빠져 있다
- **be replete with** ~으로 가득하다

- beneath [biníːθ] ~보다 낮은
- benevolent [bənévələnt] 자비로운
- bill of rights 권리 장전
- bite the bullet 고통을 참다
- black-out 정전
- blade [bléid] 칼날
- blast [blǽst] 돌풍
- blizzard [blízərd] 심한 눈보라
- blur [bləːr] 흐림
- boil down to ~이 핵심이다
- bout [báut] 한차례, 발작
- bow [báu] 절하다
- breed [bríːd] 새끼를 낳다
- brevity [brévəti] 간결
- bring down ~을 낮추다, 줄이다
- brink [bríŋk] 가장자리
- brisk [brísk] 활기찬
- burglar [bə́ːrglər] 절도범
- by the book 규정대로
- bygone [báigɔ̀ːn] 과거의

C

- cabinet [kǽbənit] 내각
- call for ~을 요구하다
- callous [kǽləs] 무감각한
- canvass [kǽnvəs] 유세하다
- canyon [kǽnjən] 협곡
- capacity [kəpǽsəti] 수용력
- capitalism [kǽpətəlìzm] 자본주의
- captive [kǽptiv] 포로
- carefree [kɛ́ərfrìː] 무사태평한
- carnivorous [kɑːrnívərəs] 육식 동물의
- cash cow 고수익 상품
- casualty [kǽʒuəlti] 사상자
- catastrophe [kətǽstrəfi] 큰 재해
- catchy [kǽtʃi] 사람의 마음을 끄는
- cave in 설득 당하다
- centigrade [séntəgrèid] 섭씨온도
- cherish [tʃériʃ] 소중히 여기다
- chip in 돈을 갹출하다
- chop [tʃáp] 절단하다
- circulate [sə́ːrkjulèit] 순환하다
- citizenship [sítəzənʃip] 시민권
- civil law 민법
- clandestine [klændéstin] 은밀한
- clasp [klǽsp] 꽉 쥐다
- claustrophobic [klɔ́ːstrəfóubik] 폐쇄 공포증의
- clergy [klə́ːrdʒi] 성직자
- clip [klíp] 자르다
- clog [klág] 방해하다
- close the book on ~에 대한 일을 중단하다
- coed [kóuéd] 남녀공학의
- coincide [kòuinsáid] 동시에 일어나다
- collocation [kàləkéiʃən] 연어 관계
- colossal [kəlásəl] 거대한
- come a long way 크게 발전하다
- come down on ~를 호되게 나무라다
- come down with ~에 걸리다

- come in handy 쓸모가 있다
- come to a standstill 교착 상태에 빠지다
- complicity [kəmplísəti] 연루
- composure [kəmpóuʒər] 침착
- comprise [kəmpráiz] 구성되다
- conceit [kənsíːt] 자만
- conceive [kənsíːv] 상상하다, 임신하다
- concord [kánkɔːrd] 일치
- concourse [kánkɔːrs] 중앙 홀, 넓은 길
- condense [kəndéns] 요약하다
- congregate [káŋgrigèit] 모이다
- consonant [kánsənənt] 자음
- contempt [kəntémpt] 경멸
- context [kántekst] 문맥
- contraband [kántrəbænd] 밀수품
- correspondent [kɔ̀ːrəspándənt] 특파원
- corridor [kɔ́ːridər] 복도
- courier [kə́ːriər] 급송 택배
- courteous [kə́ːrtiəs] 예의 바른
- covert [kóuvərt] 은밀한
- cozy [kóuzi] 아늑한
- crackdown [krǽkdaun] 일제 단속
- crack-handed 서투른
- cramp [krǽmp] 경련
- crescent [krésnt] 초승달
- crouch [kráutʃ] 쭈그리다
- crude [krúːd] 거친, 날것의
- crutch [krʌ́tʃ] 목발
- cuisine [kwizíːn] 요리법
- curtail [kərtéil] 단축하다

- decent [díːsnt] 점잖은
- decimal [désəməl] 십진법
- deference [défərəns] 존경
- dehydrate [diːháidreit] 탈수하다
- deposit [dipázit] 예금하다
- descendant [diséndənt] 자손
- despair [dispɛ́ər] 절망하다
- detach [ditǽtʃ] 분리시키다
- detain [ditéin] 감금하다
- detergent [ditə́ːrdʒənt] 세정제
- dexterous [dékstərəs] 솜씨 좋은
- diagram [dáiəgræm] 도표
- differentiate [dìfərénʃièit] 구별 짓다
- diffuse [difjúːz] 퍼뜨리다
- dilapidate [dilǽpədèit] (건물 등을) 헐다
- dilate [dailéit] 팽창하다
- dilute [dilúːt] 묽어지다
- disabled [diséibld] 신체 장애의
- discern [disə́ːrn| -zə́ːrn] 식별하다
- disclaim [diskléim] 거부하다
- dismal [dízməl] 음침한
- dismay [disméi] 실망시키다
- dismiss [dismís] 해고하다
- disparity [dispǽrəti] 서로 다름
- dispatch [dispǽtʃ] 급파하다
- dispel [dispél] 쫓아 버리다
- dispense [dispéns] 분배하다
- dispose [dispóuz] 처분하다
- dissipate [dísəpèit] 흩뜨리다

- dissolve [dizálv] 녹이다
- distress [distrés] 비통
- do one's utmost 최선을 다하다
- do wonders 큰 효과가 있다
- docile [dásəl] 유순한
- dose [dóus] (약의) 1회 복용량
- downside [dáunsàid] 부정적인 면
- down-to-earth 현실적인
- dwarf [dwɔ́:rf] 소형의
- dynasty [dáinəsti] 왕조

E

- earmark [íərmà:rk] 지정하다
- edible [édəbl] 먹을 수 있는
- edict [í:dikt] 포고령
- efface [iféis] 말소하다
- embark [imbá:rk] 착수하다
- emblem [émbləm] 상징
- embroil [imbrɔ́il] 뒤얽히게 하다
- encompass [inkʌ́mpəs] 둘러싸다
- encroach [inkróutʃ] 침입하다
- endow [indáu] 부여하다
- en route [ɑ:n-rú:t] 도중에
- ensue [insú:] 뒤이어 일어나다
- envisage [invízidʒ] 마음에 그려보다
- ephemeral [ifémərəl] 일시적인
- epoch [í:pɔk] 신기원
- equinox [í:kwənɑ̀ks] 춘분, 추분
- equivocal [ikwívəkəl] 모호한

- era [íərə] 시대
- euphemism [jú:fəmìzm] 완곡어법
- evaporate [ivǽpərèit] 증발시키다
- exalt [igzɔ́:lt] 칭찬하다
- excrement [ékskrəmənt] 배설물
- exempt [igzémpt] 면제하다
- exert [igzə́:rt] 열심히 노력하다
- exhilarate [igzíləréit] 유쾌하게 하다
- explicit [iksplísit] 명백한
- exposition [èkspəzíʃən] 박람회
- extort [ikstɔ́:rt] 무리하게 강요하다
- extraction [ikstrǽkʃən] 추출
- extrovert [ékstrəvə̀:rt] 외향적인

- face the music 잘못을 인정하다
- Fahrenheit [fǽrənhàit] 화씨온도
- fall back on ~에 의지하다
- fall for ~에 속아 넘어가다
- fallacious [fəléiʃəs] 허위의
- faraway [fá:rəwèi] 먼
- far-fetched [fá:rféʃt] 부자연스러운
- fatality [feitǽləti] 사망자
- fauna [fɔ́:nə] 동물군
- facility [fəsíləti] 재주
- feat [fi:t] 위업, 재주
- fiancé [fi:ɑ:nséi] (남자) 약혼자
- file for ~소송을 제기하다
- flora [flɔ́:rə] 식물군

- folk story 설화
- forbear [fɔːrbɛ́ər] 삼가다
- forebear [fɔ́ːrbɛ̀ər] 조상
- for the sake of ~을 위해서
- foul [fául] 부정한
- fraction [frǽkʃən] 파편
- fragrant [fréigrənt] 향기로운
- fraud [frɔ́ːd] 사기
- fugitive [fjúːdʒətiv] 도망자

- gaiety [géiəti] 명랑함
- gain [géin] 얻다
- gainsay [gèinséi] 이의를 제기하다
- gateway [géitwèi] 관문, 입구
- genial [dʒíːnjəl] 다정한
- get down on 진지하게 ~을 하다
- give off (빛 등을) 내다, (냄새 등을) 풍기다
- glacial period [gléiʃəl píəriəd] 빙하기
- gladiator [glǽdièitər] 검투사
- go all out 전력을 다하다
- go downhill 악화되다
- go Dutch (돈을) 각자 내다
- go through the roof 치솟다, 급등하다
- governor [gʌ́vərnər] 주지사
- gratitude [grǽtətjùːd] 감사
- grief [gríːf] 큰 슬픔

- hand down ~을 물려주다
- hangover [hǽŋòuvər] 숙취
- harbor [háːrbər] 생각을 품다
- harsh [háːrʃ] 거친, 가혹한
- herd [hə́ːrd] (가축의) 한 떼
- hilarious [hilɛ́əriəs] 유쾌한
- hold on to ~을 계속 갖고 있다
- hold out for ~을 위해 보류하다
- hostage [hástidʒ] 인질
- hover [hʌ́vər] 공중을 맴돌다
- hypertension [hàipərtènʃən] 고혈압
- hypocrite [hípəkrit] 위선자

- immature [ìmətʃúər] 미숙한
- immerse [imə́ːrs] 담그다
- in accordance with ~에 따라서
- in the dark 아무것도 모르는
- in the wake of ~이후로, ~의 결과로
- incarnate [inkáːrneit] 인간의 모습을 한
- incorporation [inkɔ́ːrpəréiʃən] 법인 단체
- incur [inkə́ːr] 손실을 입다
- inclined [inkláind] ~하고 싶어하는
- ingenious [indʒíːnjəs] 독창적인
- initially [iníʃəli] 본래
- inquisitive [inkwízətiv] 알고 싶어하는
- insolent [ínsələnt] 건방진

- **insomnia** [insámniə] 불면증
- **intestine** [intéstin] 창자
- **irresolute** [irézəlùːt] 우유부단한
- **livestock** [láivstàk] 가축
- **loquacious** [loukwéiʃəs] 수다스러운
- **lose track of** ~을 모르다
- **lunatic** [lúːnətik] 미친 사람

J

- **jot** [dʒát] 간단히 적어두다
- **justly** [dʒʌ́stli] 정당하게

K

- **keep pace with** ~와 보조를 맞추다
- **keynote** [kíːnòut] 기조, 주안점
- **knowingly** [nóuiŋli] 고의로

L

- **landfill** [lǽndfil] 쓰레기 매립지
- **lavatory** [lǽvətɔ̀ːri] 화장실
- **lease** [líːs] 임대하다
- **legend** [lédʒənd] 전설
- **lenient** [líːniənt] 너그러운
- **level with** ~에게 솔직하게 털어놓다
- **liaison** [lìːeizɔ́ːŋ] 연락
- **lineage** [líniidʒ] 혈통
- **lingering** [líŋgəriŋ] 우물쭈물하는
- **litigate** [lítəgèit] 소송을 제기하다
- **live up to** ~에 부응하다
- **livelihood** [láivlihùd] 생계

M

- **manifold** [mǽnəfòuld] 가지각색의
- **mar** [máːr] 훼손하다
- **martial** [máːrʃəl] 전쟁의
- **masculine** [mǽskjulin] 남자의
- **massacre** [mǽsəkər] 대학살
- **material** [mətíəriəl] 중요한
- **maxim** [mǽksim] 격언
- **meddling** [médliŋ] 간섭하는
- **merciless** [məːrsilis] 무자비한
- **medieval** [mìːdíívəl] 중세의
- **metamorphosis** [mètəmɔ́ːrfəsis] 변형
- **meticulous** [mətíkjuləs] 세심한
- **mind your p's and q's** 행동을 조심하다
- **miser** [máizər] 구두쇠
- **mishap** [míshæp] 재난, 불운
- **moan** [móun] 신음하다
- **mute** [mjúːt] 무언의

- naïve [nɑːív] 천진난만한
- Neolithic [nìːəlíθik] 신석기 시대의
- notwithstanding [nùtwiðstǽndiŋ] ~에도 불구하고
- novel [nával] 새로운
- numerous [njúːmərəs] 수많은

O

- obese [oubíːs] 매우 뚱뚱한
- odor [óudər] 악취
- omnivorous [ɑmnívərəs] 잡식성의
- on alert 경계 태세 중인
- on the horizon 가까운 장래에, 곧
- on the line 위태로운
- on the point of 막 ~하려는 중인
- on the road 여기저기를 옮겨 다니는
- opulent [ápjulənt] 부유한
- ordeal [ɔːrdíːl] 시련
- outskirt [áutskə̀ːrt] 교외
- overrule [òuvərrúːl] 파기하다

- paralysis [pərǽləsis] 마비
- parliament [páːrləmənt] 의회
- parsimony [páːrsəmòuni] 인색
- pass the buck (책임을) 떠넘기다

- pathetic [pəθétik] 불쌍한
- peer [píər] 또래
- percussion [pərkʌ́ʃən] 충격
- periphery [pərífəri] 주변
- perspicuous [pərspíkjuəs] 명료한
- pillar [pílər] 기둥
- pick up on ~을 알아채다
- pivotal [pívətl] 중추적인
- plagiarism [pléidʒərìzm] 표절
- play it by ear 그때그때 상황에 따라 처신하다
- pliable [pláiəbl] 고분고분한
- plight [pláit] 곤경
- ponder [pándər] 깊이 생각하다
- posterity [pɑstérəti] 자손
- posthumous [pástʃuməs] 사후의
- preliminary [prilímənèri] 예비의
- prelude [préljuːd] 서곡
- preposterous [pripástərəs] 비상식적인
- preside [prizáid] 사회를 보다
- pretext [príːtekst] 핑계
- primeval [praimíːvəl] 원시적인
- proceed [prəsíːd] 앞으로 나아가다
- projecting [prədʒéktiŋ] 돌출한
- proposal [prəpóuzəl] 제안
- prosaic [prouzéiik] 무미건조한
- protocol [próutəkɔ̀ːl] 의정서
- psychiatrist [saikáiətrist] 정신과 의사

R

- ransom [rǽnsəm] (포로의) 몸값
- ratify [rǽtəfài] 비준하다
- rear [ríər] 기르다
- redundant [ridʌ́ndənt] 여분의, 말이 많은
- referee [rèfərí:] 심판원
- referendum [rèfəréndəm] 국민 투표
- rejoice [ridʒɔ́is] 기뻐하다
- reminiscent [rèmənísnt] 상기시키는
- rendezvous [rá:ndəvù:] 회합
- renown [rináun] 명성
- renunciation [rinʌ̀nsiéiʃən] 포기
- replenish [ripléniʃ] 보충하다
- reptile [réptail] 파충류
- requisite [rékwəzit] 필수품
- residual [rizídʒuəl] 남은 것
- resent [rizént] 분개하다
- resolute [rézəlù:t] 단호한
- retaliate [ritǽlièit] 보복하다
- retract [ritrǽkt] 철회하다
- resurrection [rèzərékʃən] 부활
- reverent [révərənt] 숭배하는
- rhetoric [rétərik] 미사여구
- ripe [ráip] 잘 익은
- rip-off [rípɔ́:f] 도둑질
- roam [róum] 배회하다
- roar [rɔ́:r] 으르렁거리다
- rust [rʌ́st] 녹슬다

S

- sabotage [sǽbətà:ʒ] 파괴 행위
- sanitation [sæ̀nətéiʃən] 공중위생
- sarcasm [sá:rkæzm] 빈정거림
- savor [séivər] 맛
- savvy [sǽvi] 이해하다
- scope [skóup] 특종 기사, 푸다
- scrap [skrǽp] 파편
- scrutinize [skrú:tənàiz] 철저히 검사하다
- seasoning [sí:zəniŋ] 양념
- seclude [siklú:d] 격리하다
- seduce [sidjú:s] 유혹하다
- segregate [ségrigèit] 분리하다
- sensory [sénsəri] 감각의
- serene [sərí:n] 잔잔한
- setback [-bæ̀k] 퇴보
- set off 출발하다
- sever [sévər] 나누다
- sewage [sú:idʒ] 오수
- shabby [ʃǽbi] 초라한
- shed light on 밝히다
- shred [ʃréd] 갈기갈기 찢다
- shrewd [ʃrú:d] 예리한
- side with ~편을 들다
- sinister [sínəstər] 불길한
- sip [síp] 조금씩 마시다
- slander [slǽndər] 명예 훼손
- sleet [slí:t] 진눈깨비
- smack [smǽk] 찰싹 때리다
- snatch [snǽtʃ] 잡아채다

- **snooze** [snúːz] 잠깐 자다
- **soar** [sɔ́ːr] 높이 치솟다
- **solemn** [sáləm] 엄숙한
- **solitude** [sálətjùːd] 고독
- **solstice** [sálstis] 하지, 동지
- **sonic** [sánik] 음의
- **spell** [spél] (날씨 등이 계속되는) 기간, 잠깐
- **spice up** ~의 흥미를 돋우다
- **spinach** [spínitʃ] 시금치
- **spouse** [spáus] 배우자
- **stack** [sték] 더미
- **stale** [stéil] 김빠진
- **stealthy** [stélθi] 몰래 하는
- **steep** [stiːp] 가파른, 비싼
- **step aside** (공직 등에서) 물러나다
- **string** [stríŋ] 줄, 일련
- **stingy** [stíndʒi] 인색한
- **stone's throw** 가까운 거리
- **strain** [stréin] 잡아당기다
- **stray** [stréi] 길을 잃고 헤매다
- **stroll** [stróul] 산책하다
- **stumble** [stʌ́mbl] 비틀거리다
- **sturdy** [stə́ːrdi] 튼튼한
- **successor** [səksésər] 후임자
- **suction** [sʌ́kʃən] 빨아들임
- **suffocate** [sʌ́fəkèit] 질식시키다
- **suit oneself** 마음대로 하다
- **surge** [sə́ːrdʒ] 급등하다
- **surreal** [səríːəl] 초현실적인
- **swamp** [swámp] 습지
- **sweep aside** ~을 무시하다
- **synchronize** [síŋkrənàiz] 동시에 일어나다

T

- **temperate** [témpərət] 절제하는
- **tend** [ténd] 돌보다
- **terrain** [təréin] 지역
- **thesis** [θíːsis] 학위 논문
- **thorough** [θə́ːrou] 철저한
- **titanic** [taiténik] 거대한
- **topnotch** [tápnàtʃ] 최고점
- **torture** [tɔ́ːrtʃər] 고문
- **trifle** [tráifl] 사소한 것
- **trilogy** [trílədʒi] 3부작
- **trim** [trím] 깎아 다듬다
- **twilight** [twáilàit] 황혼
- **tyrant** [táiərənt] 독재자

U

- **umpire** [ʌ́mpaiər] 심판
- **undercover** [ʌ̀ndərkʌ́vər] 비밀로 행해지는
- **undo** [ʌ̀ndúː] 원상태로 돌리다
- **uneasy** [ʌ̀níːzi] 불안한
- **unjust** [ʌ̀ndʒʌ́st] 부당한
- **unveil** [ʌ̀nvéil] 공개하다
- **up in arms** 들고일어나는
- **upkeep** [ʌ̀pkìːp] 유지, 보존

- vandalism [vǽndəlìzm] 야만적 파괴 행위
- ventilate [véntəlèit] 환기하다
- vocal [vóukəl] 목소리의
- voracious [vɔːréiʃəs] 탐욕적인
- voucher [váutʃər] 상품권, 할인권
- vowel [váuəl] 모음

- wander [wándər] 길을 잃고 헤매다
- wary [wɛ́əri] 조심하는
- width [wídθ] 폭, 너비
- wind up ~하게 되다
- wither [wiðər] 말라 죽게 하다
- wreck [rék] 난파시키다
- wretched [rétʃid] 비참한

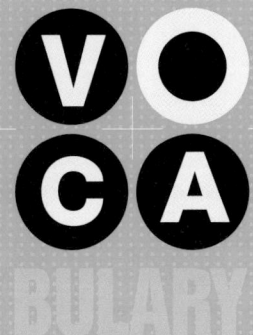

Index
A to Z

A

abandon	35, 142, 165, 258, 270	
abandoner	90	
abandonment	261	
abate	104	
abbreviate	27, 283	
abdicate	109	
abdomen	159	
abhor	29, 230	
abhorrence	313	
abide by	32, 72, 120, 156	
abjure	98	
abnormally	197	
abode	43	
abolish	258	
abolition	98	
aboriginal	87, 117	
abort	131	
abounding	69, 129	
about	164	
aboveground	108	
abrade	309	
abridge	17, 27	
abrogate	258	
abrupt	32	
abscond	314	
absent-minded	90, 157, 186	
absolute	174, 194, 266, 296	
absolve	247, 274	
absorb	90, 285	
absorption	51	
abstain	38, 100, 284	
abstinent	285	
abstract	54	
absurd	214	
abundant	24, 69	
abyss	192	
academic	107	
accede	328	
accelerate	38, 233, 321, 326	
accent	61	
accept	17, 43, 49, 50	
acceptable	50	
access	219	
accessibility	32	
accessory	186, 236	
accident	247	
accidental	100, 189, 199, 220, 287	
acclaimed	263	
accompanied by	225	
accompany	76	
accomplice	291	
accomplished	35, 302, 319	
accomplishment	233, 265	
account	159	
accountable	181, 227	
accounting	324	
accredited	241	
accumulation	22, 87	
accurate	243, 260	
accusation	82, 177	
accuse	274, 288	
accuser	288	
accustomed	153, 307	
achieve	258	
achievement	233	
acknowledge	109, 165	
acknowledgement	303	
acquaintance	230	
acquainted	307	
acquire	258, 330	
acquired	34, 45, 133, 216	
acquirement	104	
acquisition	104	
acquit	133	
acrid	252	
action	183, 210	
activate	97, 141	
active	38, 51, 250, 270, 284	
activism	120	
actual	54, 97, 127, 156, 172, 183	
acumen	51	
acute	115	
ad hoc	104	
adage	93	
adamant	126	
adaptation	192	
add	215	
addiction	296	
addition	192	
additional	149	
address	27, 250	
adept	302	
adequate	120	
adhere to	120	
adherent	282	
adjacency	96	
adjacent	76	
adjourn	186	
adjudge	275	
adjust	142, 159	
adjustability	172	
adjusted	166	
adjustment	192	
administer	150	
administration	109, 269	
administrative	207	
administrator	84, 333	
admirable	314	
admiration	254	
admire	230, 245	
admonish	76	
adolescence	115	
adopt	35	
adoration	313	
adore	29, 230	
adroit	22, 165, 170	
adroitness	88	
advance	140, 244, 255, 277	
advancement	32	

advantageous	148, 269	ailment	329	amazement	38
advent	43	air	274	amazing	291
adversary	321	aisle	241	ambassadorial	320
adversary	87	albeit	87	ambiance	49
adverse	269	alchemy	137	ambiguous	16, 106, 212
adversity	241	alert	252	ambition	324
advertise	148	algae	291	ambivalent	230
advertisement	142	alias	19	ambulate	53
advocate	71, 90, 122, 134, 187	alien	144, 205	ambulatory	74
aerodynamic	104, 178	alienate	43	amenable	238
aeronautics	87	alienating	271	amend	159, 321
aesthetic	82	alike	205	amiable	203
affable	325, 330	alive	282	amicable	307
affected	64	all-knowing	73	amount	78, 273
affiliation	258	all-powerful	73	ample	120, 197, 332
affinity	67, 261	all-purpose	25	amplify	84, 104
affirm	195	all at once	99, 231	analgesic	247
affirmation	296	allegation	82	analogous	274
affix	159	allegedly	214	analogy	65, 73
affliction	313, 315	allegiance	263	analysis	16, 177
affluent	208	allegory	203	analytical	329
aftermath	324	alleviate	29, 102, 117, 126, 280, 310	analyze	94
age	276	alliance	170, 181, 226	anarchy	60
agent	45, 90, 98	allocate	175	anatomy	104
aggravate	102, 126, 280	allot	203, 230, 303	ancestor	153
aggravation	150	allotment	30	ancestral	32
aggregate	98	allow	27, 95, 241	ancient	19, 283
aggressive	307	allowance	30, 99, 154, 313	anecdote	318
agile	225	ally	87, 321	anesthetic	247
agitate	102, 291, 305	aloof	309	angle	62
agitated	167	alter ego	77	angriness	91
agnostic	285	alter	34, 159	anguish	225
agrarian	329	alternate	69, 318	animal	229
agree	44	alternative	51, 252	animate	134
agreeable	39, 248	although	87	animated	53, 282
agreed	222	altitude	170	annexation	192
agreement	153, 181, 207, 220, 230, 248, 259, 330	altruistic	93	annihilate	215
		amassed	98	annihilation	254
agricultural	329	amateur	18, 327	announce	171
ahead	153	amazed	188	announcement	302
aid	228, 244, 286				

annoy	247	applicable	313	arousal	185
annoyance	156	applicant	105	arouse	44, 250, 252
annul	170	application	131	arousing	266
anoint	139, 285	apply	304	arrange	316
anonymous	49	appoint	139	arrangement	43, 112, 264, 299
answer	232, 256	appointment	181	array	236
answerable	181	apprehend	137	arrogance	249
answerer	305	apprehension	45, 84	arson	269
antagonism	67, 230, 317	apprehensive	197, 325	artful	82
antagonist	76, 87, 134, 145, 321	apprentice	164	articulate	71
antagonistic	307	approach	27, 41, 186	artificial	142, 281
antecedent	35, 153	approaching	72	artistic	170
anthropologist	258	appropriate	78, 203	ascend	107
antibacterial	236	approve	39, 42, 240, 258	ascendant	116
antibiotics	208	approximated	260	ascertain	280
anticipate	49	apt	280	ascetic	285
anticipation	61	aptitude	21	ask	198
antidote	126	arbitrarily	331	asked	74
antique	74	arbitrary	60, 222	aspiration	324
antiseptic	236	arbitration	144	assailant	236
anxiety	41, 306	arbitrator	332	assassinate	296
anxious	197	archaeology	219	assaulter	236
apart	96	archaic	65	assemblage	208
apathetic	270, 285	arched	297	assemble	171, 198, 298, 304, 329
apathy	75, 148	archetype	118, 316	assent	109, 157
apex	333	architecture	280, 322	assertion	176, 263
aphorism	208	archive	93	assess	192
apocalyptic	263	ardent	148, 171, 214	asset	252, 286
appalling	193	ardor	313	assign	175, 230
apparel	309	arduous	21	assignment	138, 181
apparent	106, 144, 225, 322	argue	71	assimilate	175
apparition	112	argument	181	assimilation	29
appeal	118, 256, 274	arid	82	assist	228, 238, 264
appealing	208	aridity	40, 51, 145	assistance	52, 150
appearance	43	arise	231	associate	175, 230, 274
appease	247	aristocracy	148	association	258
appendage	219	arithmetic	65	assortment	203, 236
appendix	263	arm	187	assuage	126
applaud	252, 281	around the clock	175	assume	137
appliance	307	around	164	assumption	40, 184, 208

assure	18	
assured	325	
asteroid	324	
astonishing	291	
astrology	241	
astrometry	241	
astronomical	229	
astute	186	
asymmetrical	52	
at a standstill	161	
at hand	133, 304	
at large	60	
at one's disposal	304	
at risk	131	
at stake	131	
atheism	149	
atheist	285	
atmosphere	49, 71, 274	
atone	214	
attach	159	
attachment	219, 236, 263	
attack	221, 240	
attacker	236	
attain	258	
attempt	227	
attentive	117, 183	
attentiveness	330	
attest	307	
attitude	137, 197, 242, 294	
attorney	219	
attractive	166	
attribute	289, 302, 314	
audibly	262	
audience	318	
audiovisual	269	
auditorium	291	
augment	192	
aura	71	
auspicious	133, 280	
austere	164	

authentic	17, 87, 197	
authenticate	42	
author	222	
authority	72, 138, 181	
authorization	28, 86	
authorize	27	
authorized	241	
autocracy	320	
autocratic	296	
automated	261	
autonomy	57, 153	
autonym	19	
auxiliary	186	
availability	32	
average	41	
aversion	152	
avert	318	
avid	148	
avoid	27, 240, 264, 314	
avoidance	116	
awakening	123	
award	49, 327	
aware	319	
awe	38	
axiom	149	

B

back-up	252	
back and forth	151	
back out	44	
backbone	229	
backward	32	
bacterium	199	
badgering	150	
baffle	21	
bailout	318	
bait	307	
balanced	52, 298	
ballot	329	
ban	249, 332	

banish	241	
bank on	115	
bankrupt	225, 260	
banned	210	
banquet	274	
banter	93	
bare	292	
barely	129	
barrage	259	
barren	208, 313	
barter	285	
base	40, 217, 267	
basically	221	
basin	244	
bask in	100	
beacon	43	
beam	43	
bear	72, 145, 210	
beast	128	
beauty	82, 221, 237	
begetter	45	
begin	52, 284	
beginner	216, 287	
beginning	41, 44, 119, 181, 196, 200, 232, 234, 308	
behave	163	
behavior	88, 137, 242	
behead	286	
behind time	153	
belated	153	
belief	16, 61, 208, 292, 321	
believable	253, 295	
believer	285	
believing	297	
below ground	108	
bemused	186	
bendable	238	
benefactor	65, 76, 116	
beneficial	73, 148, 244	
beneficiary	30, 65, 116	
benign	109, 126	

bequeath	49	blossom	326	breakthrough	32
bereaved	236	blow out of proportion	161	breathe	40, 132, 299
beside the point	78	blow up	249	breathing	68
bestow	49, 71, 155, 327	blueprint	315	briefcase	299
bewilder	215	blunder	54	bright	23, 195
bewildered	263	blunt	225	brilliant	186, 287
beyond any doubt	194	board	193	bring	16, 28, 72, 99, 100, 116, 134, 141, 226, 233
beyond belief	291	bodily	62, 120, 239		
beyond range	72	body	219, 292	bring up the rear	31
beyond repair	332	bogus	87	brisk	252
bias	154	boisterous	203	broad	21
biased support	228	bolster	54, 71	broke	225, 260
biased	256, 304	bona fide	87	broken	297
bilateral	60, 256	bonus	105	brotherhood	282
bill of sale	77	booking	112	brutal	46
binary	230	bookkeeping	324	bubble	258
bind	176	boom	52, 63	budding	181
biochemical	247	boost	84, 192	budget	38
biodegradable	38	bootleg	123	buffer	27
biodiesel	214	border	134	build-up	87, 104, 117
biodiversity	280	bore	216	build	20, 215, 217
biofuel	214	boredom	84	building	280
biography	164	boring	68, 258	built-in	45
biological	62	borough	197	bulge	294
birth	116, 232, 254	bother	194, 264, 288	bulk	267
bitter	252	bottom	217, 267, 333	bulwark	72
bizarre	105	boundless	276	bumble	71
blacken	175	bounds	91	buoyant	30
blame	247	bourgeoisie	324	burden	264, 327
blameless	181	brace (oneself) for	291	burdened	205
blatant	276	brag	218	burdensome	292
bleach	175	branch out	33	bureaucracy	269
bleak	208, 313	brandish	130	burn	281
blemish	253	breach	72, 111, 194	burning	242, 269
bless	242, 285	break apart	320	burrow	313
blessing	228, 253, 275, 313	break	45, 166, 215, 221, 256, 272, 304	bursar	126
bliss	43	breakable	260	burst	302
block out	85	breakdown	100	business-related	83, 142
block	17, 228, 244	breaking up	298	business	237
blockage	65, 248	breakout	302	businessperson	72
				bustling	38

busy	38	careful	31, 157, 211, 283, 331	certificate	98
buttress	54, 219	careless	90, 183, 264, 331	certification	308
buy	184	cargo	243	certified	241
buzzword	16	caricature	131	chain of command	67
by itself	96	caring	285	challenge	17, 44, 328
bypass	296	carnivore	269	chamber	54
byproduct	32	carry out	100, 165	chance	16, 17, 222, 247, 318
		cartel	109	changed	166
C		cash in on	137	changeover	35
cache	93	cash keeper	126	changing	75
calamity	275	cast a spell on	127	channel	100
calculate	49, 265	cast	129, 241	chaos	60, 113
caliber	60	caste	153	chaotic	115, 161, 284, 329
call off	78, 131, 170	casual	105	character	183, 220, 242
calligraphy	170	casualty	331	characteristic	218, 302, 314
callous	333	catalyst	65	charge	57, 82, 133, 274
calm down	102, 305	catastrophic	214	charitable	325
calm	161, 167, 168, 247, 250, 252, 291, 303, 307, 328	catch	216, 307, 324, 330	charity	288
		Catch-22	105	chart	60
calming	264	catchphrase	21	charter	325
camouflage	39	catchword	16	chasm	192
cancel	131, 170, 195, 209, 78	categorize	236, 286	chaste	101
cancer-causing	126	category	132	check	209, 233, 280, 286
candid	104	cater to	54	cheer	270
candidate	105	cause	16, 150, 164, 302	cheerful	30, 171, 209, 254
capability	21, 173	cautious	183, 264	chemical	78, 98
capable	21	cave-in	309	chest	275
capitalize on	137	cavernous	253	chief	74
capitulate	241	cavity	137	child	45
capitulation	57	cease	100, 226, 293	childish	67
capricious	264	celebrate	250	choice	128
capsize	193	celebrated	56, 89, 219	chromosome	226
caption	315	celestial	33, 132, 229	chronically	115
captivate	84, 216, 258	censorship	313	chronological	109
capture	137, 324	censure	66	circa	164
carbohydrate	318	census	247	circuit	231
carcass	329	central	90, 182	circulation	110
carcinogenic	126	ceremony	24, 330	circulatory movement	319
cardinal	131	certain	34, 230, 245	circumspect	264
cardiovascular	98	certainty	17, 22, 155, 240	circumstance	126
care	227, 311				

circumvent	27, 296	collaborate	54	commonplace	278
citation	121	collaborator	223, 291	commotion	231
cite	175	collapse	215	communicate	55, 209, 297
civics	277	colleague	175	community	189, 237
civil	138	collect	255	commute	65
claim	113, 118, 177	collection	93, 182, 208, 294	company	327
clap	252	collective	182	comparable	274
clarify	17, 156, 215, 264	collide	314	comparative	19, 145
clash	129	colloquial	193	comparison	65
classify	236	colloquy	331	compartment	54
clean	77, 154, 303	collusion	259	compassionate	80, 269, 333
clear-cut	88, 195	colonialism	139	compatible	248
clear-headed	186, 298	colony	189, 237	compel	27, 206
clear	16, 21, 46, 75, 212, 225, 282	coloration	134	compelling	220
cleverness	144	colorful	53, 210	compensate	33, 214
cliché	115	colorless	53	compensation	88, 222, 275, 299
climatology	199	colossal	144, 286	competent	21
cling to	142	combination	127, 320	competition	200
closely	320	combustion	242	competitor	105
closeness	96	come between	188	compilation	208
closing	200	come	25, 39, 106, 163, 231, 264, 294, 314, 293	complacent	82
closure	137			complain	232
clothing	309	come into view	141	complaint	155
cloudy	108	come to pass	127	complement	76
clout	181	come to the fore	39	complementary	57
clumsy	22, 165, 225	come up short	137	complete	90, 140, 321, 326
cluster	329	comfort	270	completion	41, 44, 234, 265
clutter	215	comforting	120	complex	54, 97, 111
coalition	170, 181	coming in	143	compliance	157, 259
coarse	198	commencement	41, 330	compliant	201
coastal	206, 302	commend	39, 217	complicated	111
code	325	commendable	314	complication	176
coded	303	commensurate	303	compliment	76, 85, 155, 232, 254, 281
coerce	27	commercial	142		
coffer	275	commission	82, 88, 166	complimentary	281
cognitive	71, 239	commit	100, 325	comply with	32, 120
coherent	164	commitment	253	component	106, 182, 277
cohesive	90	committee	82, 193, 249	composed	263
coinage	115	commodity	286	composition	232, 264
cold	214, 216	common	80, 173, 294	compound	127
		commonly	173	comprehend	55, 215

comprehensive 21, 293	confidential 71, 320	consideration 311
compress 24, 249	configuration 43	consistency 16, 36, 220
compromise 76, 179, 308,	confine 56, 168, 176, 253	consistent 33, 44, 183, 201, 276
compulsory 34, 61	confined 25, 60, 80	console 270
computation 65	confinement 110, 271	consolidate 314
compute 49	confirm 209, 228, 307	consortium 109
concave 296, 297	confirmation 146, 207, 209, 296	conspicuous 176, 251
conceal 68, 85, 162, 193, 204, 209, 218, 227, 270, 278	confiscate 71	conspiracy 259
	conflict 153, 220, 248, 303	constancy 172
concealed 303	conflicting 230	constitution 325
concealment 39, 66, 165, 320	conform 142, 175	constraint 107, 154
concede 44, 49, 109	conformity 154	construct 20, 116, 138, 320
conceivable 99	confound 21, 143, 156, 215	construction 280, 322
concentrated 326	confront 27, 88	constructive 330
concentration 330	confrontation 116, 303	consumable 17
conception 308	confuse 143, 156, 215	consume 94, 204
conceptual 54	confused 186, 263, 298	consummate 319
concern 148	confusing 16	consumption 226
concerned 309	congenial 330	contact 55
concession 76, 308	congestion 248	contagious 314
concise 140	conglomerate 61	container 288
conclude 297	congruence 50	containment 253, 277, 283
conclusion 41, 44, 94, 189	conjecture 148	contaminate 154
concrete 54	conjure 286	contaminated 77, 236
concurred 222	connection 67, 106, 200, 258	contamination 265
concurrent 44, 96, 231	connotation 198	contemplate 303
condemn 39, 112, 177, 281, 285, 281	conquer 160	contemplative 271
condensation 145, 160	conqueror 319	contemporary 44
condense 24	conquistador 319	contempt 38
condescend 187	conscience 319	contention 181
condition 126	conscious 304, 319	contentious 39, 204
conditional 79, 245, 248	consciousness 123	contest 44, 274
conditioning 297	consecrate 242	contiguous 76
condolence 325	consecutive 297	contingency 220
condone 66	consensus 153	contingent on 79
conduct 242	consent 259, 315	continual 89, 115, 175
conduction 330	consequence 164, 324	continuation 45, 221, 234
conduit 132	conservation 310	continue 72, 131, 186, 226, 276, 283
confederation 226	conservative 95, 128	continuity 221
conference 242, 272	considerable 63, 237	continuous 123, 200, 297
confident 24, 197, 325		

contour	50	correspondingly	178	criterion	165
contract	272, 330	corridor	300	critical	79, 231
contradict	17	corrupt	177	criticism	315
contradictory	183, 230	corruption	237, 331	criticize	39, 71, 76, 177, 217
contrarily	266	cosmic	33, 79	crooked	275
contribute	259	cost	271	crop	305
contribution	288	council	193, 249	cross-breed	320
contributor	76	counselor	219	cross-examine	232
contrive	150	countable	276	crowded	57
contrived	281	counteract	286	crucial	83
control	89, 185, 198, 242, 253	counterbalance	151	crude	97
controllable	150	counterfeit	87, 93, 197	cruel	269
controlled	62	countermeasure	126	crusade	73, 270
controversial	39, 204	counterpart	77	cryptic	88
convection	319	counterstatement	255	crystal clear	106
convene	198	countless	162	culmination	94
conveniently	194	country	272	culpable	270
convention	83, 242	course	64	culprit	331
conventional	22, 50, 206	courteous	299	cultivate	160
convergence	162, 193	cover	209, 313, 320	cultural group	138
conversational	193	covering	67	cumbersome	292
convert	314, 315	covet	98	cumulative	98
convex	296, 297	coworker	175	curable	293
convey	146, 248, 297	crack	66, 170, 276, 315	curb	187
conveyance	330	cramped	253	curing	239
convict	247, 275	crash	272, 314	currency	142
conviction	292	create	116, 217	current	283
convince	228	creation	232, 254, 264	curriculum	120
convincing	220	creative	34	curse	253, 285
cooperate	54	credential	98	cursory	105
copy	56, 167	credible	29, 253	curved	296, 297
copyright	68	credit	303	custody	55, 85, 88
cordial	271, 307, 325	creed	61	custom	66, 248
corporal	120	cremate	281	customary	22, 276
corporate	204	crevice	66	customer	310
corps	292	crew	206, 292	cut	94, 187
corpse	292, 329	crime	271	cutting-edge	50, 198
correct	54, 243	criminal	228, 286	cylinder	259
correlate	274	criminate	133	cynical	24, 30, 297
correspond	209	cringe	328		

D

dab	295, 331
dainty	281
damage	111, 321
damaging	148
dampen	28, 209
dampness	40
danger	294
dangerous	56, 195
dark	23, 195
darken	175
data	135
date	270
daunting	120
day-to-day	283
day care	327
dazzling	332
de facto	127
deadlock	57
deal	27, 47, 145, 330
dean	308
debris	39
debt	57, 229
decade	319
decadence	237
decapitate	286
deceit	199
deceitful	110, 104
decelerate	38
decency	331
decent	283, 328
deception	22, 129
deceptive	17, 156, 248
decimate	215
decipher	105, 173, 315
deciphered	303
decision	53, 189
decisive	205
declaration	176, 263, 302
declare	68
decline	52, 107, 231, 237
decomposable	38
decorate	249, 331
decoration	253, 287
decoy	254
decrease	84, 216
decree	50
decrepit	303
decry	281
dedicate	242, 303, 325
dedication	320
deduce	297
deduct	215
deep	167
deepness	170
defeat	196, 233
defeated	58
defect	253, 314
defendant	288
defense troops	83
defense	72, 194
defiance	154, 157, 244, 259
defiant	201
deficiency	182
deficit	110, 129
defile	154, 242
definite	19, 66, 222, 230, 245, 265
deflate	249
deflation	188
deforestation	325
deformation	237
deformed	275
deft	165
deftness	88
defunct	292
defy	328
degenerate	39, 281
dehydration	160
deity	132
delay	17, 277
delegate	90, 99
deliberate	79, 151, 199, 220
delicate	260, 281
delicious	252
delight	156, 194
delightful	189, 255
delineate	254
delinquent	286
deliver	173, 248
deliverance	123
deluge	51, 259
delusion	22
delve	28, 128
demand	113, 118, 259
demanding	19
demean	187
demeanor	88, 137
demise	116
democracy	320
democratic	296
demographics	247
demolish	89, 129, 138
demonstrate	139, 193, 216
demote	244
denial	218, 253, 259, 263, 296
denigration	315
denomination	275
denotation	198
denote	143
denounce	39, 112, 281
denunciation	121
deny	17, 109, 228, 274, 307, 315
depart	95
department head	308
departure	248
depend	28, 239
dependable	156, 264
dependence	153, 296
dependent	248
depict	88

Term	Pages	Term	Pages	Term	Pages
depiction	42	deterioration	111	digestion	51
deplete	204, 262	determine	94, 192, 198, 260, 280	dignity	102
deportation	297	determined	68, 205, 319	digress	72, 142
depository	127	deterrent	33, 55, 107	dilemma	105, 305
depot	127	detest	29	diligence	24
depreciate	154, 226	detract	264	diligent	18
depress	232, 270, 294	detractor	223	dim	121, 195
depressing	30	detrimental	148	dimension	149
depression	52, 137, 206	devalue	226	diminish	192, 226
deprivation	101	devastate	20, 138	diminutive	23
deprive	33	develop	226, 231, 281	diplomatic	320
depth	170, 192	development	19	direct	31, 212, 264, 287
deride	188	developmental	149	director	298
derivative	32	deviate	72, 142	disadvantage	216, 252
derive	264	device	106, 277, 307	disadvantageous	178
descend	163	devoid of	187	disagreeable	203, 330
descendent	153	devote	303, 325	disagreement	65, 76, 189, 308
describe	88, 254	devoted	178	disappear	39, 41, 141, 231
description	176	devotee	285	disappearance	254
desecrate	242	devotion	233	disappointed	226
desert	142, 326	devour	99, 198	disappointment	265
desertification	326	dexterity	88	disapproval	259, 303
deserving of	260	dexterous	21	disapprove	27, 122, 252
designate	77, 96, 175	diagnose	94	disassemble	304
desire	98, 152, 306	diagonal	165	disassociation	29
desist	44	dialect	61, 155	disaster	275
desolate	292, 313	dialogue	250	disastrous	214
despicable	193	dichotomy	187	disavow	109, 307
despondent	209	dictate	198	disbelief	149
destination	308	dictatorship	320	discard	270
destitute	204	dictionary	177	discharge	90, 132, 231, 309
destroy	20, 63, 66, 167, 217, 320	didactic	308	disciplinary	23
detach	159	diet	79	discipline	160
detached	76	differ	78	disciplined	285
detachment	192	difference	50, 187, 193, 207, 248	disclaim	274
detail	83	different	205, 248	disconcert	291
detailed	105	differentiate	57	discord	153
detect	39	difficult	21, 55	discordance	248
deter	315	diffusion	143	discordant with	111
deteriorate	39, 124, 281, 326	dig out	313	discount	165

discourage	27, 129, 228, 232, 315		311, 325	diversify	33
discouraged	24, 226	disreputable	34	divert	264, 318
discouragement	206	disrespect	242, 245, 313	divestment	121
discourse	331	disruptive	264	dividend	105
discover	39	dissect	94	divine	28, 171
discredit	303	disseminate	67, 237	division	162, 181
discreet	264	dissemination	110, 143	DNA	226
discrepancy	50, 220	dissension	85	do away with	52
discretion	154	dissent	124, 259	doctoral degree	292
discrimination	154	dissenter	90, 282	doctorate	292
discussion	331	dissention	308	doctrine	149
disdain	254	dissertation	215	document	82
disease	101, 265, ,272	dissident	44	documentation	152
disentanglement	176	dissimilar	44, 274	dodge	240
disguise	39, 209	dissimilarity	67, 73	dodging	116
disgust	127	dissimilarly	227	domain	176
disgusting	299	dissociate	274	domestic	154
dishonest	248	dissuade	228, 315	domesticated	204
dishonor	102	distance	96	domicile	160
disillusioned	226	distant	72	dominant	228
disinclination	21, 206	distasteful	82	dominate	160
disinclined	280	distinct	176, 205	domination	57
disliked	24	distinction	50	dominion	74, 243
disloyalty	233	distinctly	227	donate	259
disobedience	154	distinguish	286	donor	76, 220
disobey	32, 163	distinguished	112, 193	doorstep	196
disorder	113, 215, 315	distorted	275	dormant	110
disorganize	60	distortion	237	double	230
disorganized	115, 329	distracting	264	doubt	49, 155, 240
disoriented	298	distraction	330	doubtful	66, 118
dispensable	17	distressed	82	down and out	204
dispersal	182	distribute	237	downfall	116
disperse	171, 198, 285, 298, 314, 329	distribution	110, 182	downgrade	249
		district attorney	288	downright	171
dispersion	87	distrust	240	downsize	187
display	193, 270, 320	disturb	291	doze	123
disposable	17	disturbance	231	draft	149
disposition	242	disturbing	264	drag	83
disputable	39	divergence	162, 193	dramatic	182
dispute	49, 181, 189, 303	divergently	124	dramatist	222
disregard	165, 210, 303, 304,				

drastic 128	economic 83, 138	embryo 308
draw 40, 149, 264, 283	economical 22, 83, 111	emerge 39, 231
draw attention to 238	ecstasy 43	emergence 43, 116
draw the line 243	eddy 171	emigrant 282
drawback 252	edify 110	emigrate 105, 106
dreadful 277	edifying 308	eminent 193
dreary 130, 208, 316	educational 107, 210	emission 132
drop 18, 266	effect 164	emit 90, 285
dry 82, 209	effective 19	emotional 167
dryness 40, 51, 145	effectiveness 132	emotionless 285
dual 230	effectual 330	emphasize 154, 228, 238
duality 187	efficacy 132	empirical 94
dubious 57, 66	efficient 160	employ 30, 127
duct 165	effortlessly 211	employees 84
due to 302	egalitarianism 153	employment 181
dull 75, 182, 186, 216, 225, 270, 291	egg-shaped 94	empower 27, 99
duplicate 68, 160, 167	egocentric 93	emptiness 248
duplication 101	egoistic 298	empty headed 77
durable 260	elaborate 17, 221	empty 57, 187, 205
duty 18, 25, 263	elastic 143	emulate 40
dwell 95	elect 220	en masse 99
dwelling 43, 160	elegant 221	enactment 28, 45
dwindle 231	element 182	encase 149
dying 181	elevation 170	enchant 127
dynamic 270	elicit 99	enchanting 258
	eligible 50	enclave 243
E	eliminate 50, 73, 116, 217	enclose 253
earn 260	elimination 98	encode 105, 276, 315
earnings 57	elliptical 94	encoded 303
earthbound 79	eloquent 144	encounter 88, 265
earthly 33, 79, 108, 171, 229, 310	elucidate 143	encourage 22, 187, 232, 238
easily 211	elude 282	encouraged 226
easing 318	emancipate 176	encouragement 55, 206
easy-going 46	emancipation 110	encrypt 276, 315
easy 21, 55	embargo 99	encumber 264
eavesdrop 22	embarrass 254	end 52, 116, 232, 294
eccentric 105	embellish 331	endanger 51, 209
eclipse 165, 172	embezzlement 275	endangerment 123, 310
eco-friendly 38	embody 184	endeavor 227
ecological 127, 326	embrace 43	endorse 148

endorsement	142, 308, 317	enumerate	204	evasion	116
enduring	47	envelop	23, 149	even though	87
enemy	175, 187	environmental	326	evenhandedness	129
energetic	51, 284	envoy	99	evenly	238
energize	232	epic	286	event	177
energizing	293	epidemic	128, 288	ever-changing	68
enervated	155	episode	177	every now and then	29
enforce	304	epitaph	67, 320	evidence	146, 209, 232
engage	198, 327	equal	168, 205	evolutionary	149
engagement	116	equip	187	exacerbate	280
engender	44	equipped	195	exact	195
engrossing	258	equitable	304	exaggerate	161
engulf	110	equivalent	69, 168	exaggeration	20
enhance	249, 331	era	276	examine	28, 156, 293
enigmatic	88	eradicate	28	example	322
enjoy	100	erase	167	excavate	313
enlarge	216, 272	erect	116	excellent	186
enlighten	21, 110, 143, 215	erode	309	exceptional	64, 161, 173
enlightening	210	err	54	excerpt	121
enlist	78	errand	138	excess	110, 129, 182, 233, 293
enough	197, 210	erratic	33, 185	excessive	72, 111
enroll	156	error	41	excite	97, 252
ensuing	35, 133	erudite	77, 276	excited	167
ensure	61	eruption	309	exciting	182, 283
entail	309	escape	282	exclude	18, 43
entanglement	176	escort	141	exclusion	29
enter	34, 156	essence	83, 271	exclusive	21, 182
enterprise	237	essential	96, 194, 221, 255	excursion	73
enthrall	216	establish	28, 66	excuse	66, 247
enthusiasm	75	establishment	98	execute	106, 165
enthusiast	134	esteemed	24, 34	executive	298
enthusiastic	214, 226	estimate	33, 49	exemplify	216
enthusiastically	171	estimated	38, 189, 260	exemption	18
enticement	307	ethical	177, 227	exhale	40, 132
entirety	116, 121, 194	ethics	319	exhaust	94, 204, 299
entitled to	260	ethnicity	138	exhausting	293
entity	44, 63, 162	eulogy	315	exhibition	320
entourage	206	evacuation	143	exile	241, 249, 297
entrepreneur	72	evade	264, 282	exit	34
entry	218	evaluate	192, 237	exonerate	133, 275

exorbitant	72	extinction	254	familiarized	153
expand	27, 33, 187, 192, 249, 272	extinguish	116, 196	famine	188
expanse	89	extra	293	famous	89, 219
expansion	52, 277	extract	99, 121, 331	fancy	17
expansionism	139	extracurricular	149	fascinate	84
expat	282	extraordinary	41, 173, 283	fashionable	159
expatriate	282	extraterrestrial	205	fasting	226
expect	36	extravagant	17, 111, 164	fat	250
expectancy	17	extricate	331	fatal	73, 214, 293
expectation	208	extrinsic	34, 45	fatherly	139
expected	31, 107, 185, 291	extroverted	63	fathom	55
expediently	194	eyewitness	287	fatness	233
expedite	17, 326			favorable	269, 280
expedition	270	**F**		fear	41
expel	249	fabricate	320	fearful	197
expendable	155	face	27, 318	feasibility	149
expenditure	22	facet	227	feast	274
expense	22, 271	facile	21, 55	federal	182
experience	56, 262, 265	facilitate	17	federation	170
experienced	195	facility	40	fee	31, 88
expert	18, 170, 287, 327	fact	40, 148, 184	feeble	123
expertise	238	factual	140	feeling	71, 289
expiration	232	faculty	77, 155	fellowship	282
expired	292	fad	83, 159	felon	286
explain	139	fade	41, 141	felony	271
explanation	159, 176, 177	fail	156, 196	feminine	238
explicitly	194	failure	100, 233, 239, 265	ferocious	188
explode	256	faint	46	fertile	313
exploit	33, 89, 137	fair-mindedness	154	fertilize	161
exploitation	55, 331	fair practice	153	fervent	99, 148
explorer	261	fair	304	fickle	75, 264
explosion	309	faithfulness	233	fictional	156
exponent	94, 187	faithlessness	298	fidelity	298
exposure	39, 66	fake	17, 197, 248, 316	field	160, 217
express	143	fall	129, 215, 310	fight	241
expulsion	297	fallacy	166	figment	56
exquisite	221	falling-out	170	figurative	50, 183
extend	24, 255	false	243	figure	105, 135, 183, 220, 260
extensive	21, 293	familiar	107	file	173
extent	78	familiarization	192	filial	171

fill	187, 204, 221, 313	follow	23, 28, 31, 32, 40, 142, 210, 225	foster	28, 187
film	67			foundation	162, 205, 271
filthy	326	following	35, 194	founder	261
final	200, 234	foolish	214	fragile	260
financial	83, 138	for sale	281	fragment	107, 116
financing	121	forage	66	fragmentary	140
find fault	76	forbid	66	frail	123
finding	16	force	82, 183	framework	162, 205
fine	198	forceful	178, 270	frantic	161
finish	232	forecast	33	fraternity	245, 282
fire up	129	forego	284	free-spirited	151
first	200, 234	foregone conclusion	155	free of charge	281
firsthand	94, 287	foreign	87, 117, 154	free will	152
fiscal	138, 166	foremost	84	free	108, 253, 275, 324
fission	298	forensic	199	freedom	18, 85, 110, 194, 271
fissure	66	foresee	49	freight	243
fitting	248, 298	foreseeable	99, 185	frequently	63
fix	256	foreshadow	132	freshman	216
fix a limit	243	foresight	61	friendly	203, 216, 271, 330
fixable	332	forfeit	61	frighten	238, 316
fixation	84	forge ahead	140	frightful	107
fixed	74, 222	forgery	93	frivolous	293
flagrant	276	forgetful	89	from abroad	117
flamboyant	210	forgive	112	front page	315
flat	95	forgiveness	310	frown on	122
flaw	253	forgiving	300	frugal	22
flawless	326	forgo	137	fruitful	28, 179
fleeting	47	forlorn	254	fruitless	19
flexibility	172	formal	193	fulfillment	265
flexible	19, 25, 126, 238, 250	formation	232	full	57, 140, 187
flimsy	122	former	194	function	131, 176, 272
flippant	293	formidable	120, 150	functional	161
flood	259	formula	156, 315	functioning	110, 292
flourish	124, 326	formulate	149	fundamental	155, 131, 221
flow	143	forte	77	funnel	100
fluctuate	95, 318	forthcoming	133	furnish	249
fluctuation	172	fortification	27, 72	fusion	298
fluke	247	fortify	309	futile	28
fluorescent	121	fortune	239, 241, 253, 275, 313	futility	132
focus	306	fortune teller	85		
		fossil	255, 304		

G

game		35, 128
garment		309
garner		298
garnish		287
garrison		83
gather		171, 233, 237, 255, 329
gathering		87, 176, 182
gaze		161
gene		226
genealogical		32
general		104, 266
generate		63, 89
generation		276
genetic		133
genetically		265
genocide		254
genome		243
genre		132
gentle		188
genuine		17, 87, 93, 197, 281
geographic		55
geological		55
germ-free		77, 199
germinate		143
gestation		138
gesture		210
get		39, 56, 217, 296, 297, 326
get a degree		156
get hands on		146
get hold of		55
get rid of		50, 332
get underway		293
ghost		112
gifted		319
gigantic		23
gist		83
give		25, 35, 49, 56, 61, 98, 113, 190, 203, 212, 248
give precedence to		316
give rise to		44, 89, 141
give the green light		95
give way		328
giver		30, 65, 220
glacier		188
gloomy		23, 30, 209, 316
glorify		177
glossary		177
gluttonous		285
go		34, 39, 95, 124, 159, 163, 170, 184, 186, 262, 281
goal		308, 324
god		132
godly		171
good deed		117
good sense		154
good spirits		146
goods		107, 243
gossip		232
grade		237, 152
gradual		31, 90, 326
graduate		156
graduation		330
grant		315
grasp		137
gratuitous		281
grave		231
gravitational		166
greatest		239
greedy		177, 285
green		326
grief		43
grievance		155
grieve		250
gross		260, 171
grotesque		221
groundbreaking		50, 64
groundwork		205
group		275, 276
grow		143, 187, 226, 231
grown-up		67
grueling		55
grumble		232
guarantee		18, 61, 86
guard		51, 294
guarded		56, 58
guess		35, 172
guide		43, 141
guillotine		286
guilty conscience		85
guilty		270
gulp		198
gun down		296

H

habit		248, 296
hail		177
hall		291
hallmark		210
hallucination		56
halt		72, 141, 143, 293
hamper		22
hand		134, 137, 190
handful		294
haphazardly		331
happen		127
happening		19
happiness		43, 146, 225
happy		209, 236, 254
harassment		150
hardly		157
hardship		241
hardworking		18
harm		23, 310
harmful		148, 239
harmless		73, 109, 126, 212, 317
harmonious		124, 307
harmonize		129
harmonized		284
harmony		16, 248
harness		33

harvest	160, 305	hibernate	61	horrendous	260
hassle	194	hidden	176, 225, 322	horrible	260
hate	245, 254	hide	148, 193, 204, 218, 227, 238, 270	horrid	189
hatred	230	hideous	221	hospitable	271
haul	83	hiding	66, 93	hostile	307, 325
haunt	309	hierarchy	67	huge	23
have nothing to do with	302	hieroglyphics	199	humanitarian	325
hazardous	56, 317	high-class	144	humble	17, 121, 144, 298
hazy	122	high-volume	128	humbleness	249
headline	315	highlight	238	humdrum	283
headway	57	hijack	166, 212	humid	82
heal	29	hinder	16, 54, 277, 326	humidity	40
health	329	hindrance	23	humiliate	254
healthy	172	hindsight	61	humility	237, 249
hearsay	232, 287	hinge on[upon]	28	hunch	111, 148
heartache	146	hire	166	hunger	188
heartening	120	hireling	150	hunter	35
heat transfer	319	hit or miss	105	hurt	244, 270
heavenly	33, 79, 171	hitherto	143	hurtful	330
heavy	281	hoax	129	hybrid	320
hectic	161	hoist	266	hygienic	77
heed	210	hold back	38, 95, 99, 150, 155, 278	hyperbole	20
heedful	117	hold off	30, 61, 231, 270, 300	hypocritical	110
heel	77	hole	137	hypothesis	40, 184
hefty	332	holocaust	254	hypothesize	35, 134
hegemony	72, 138	holy ground	46	hypothetical	94, 140
height	170	homely	332		
heir	116	homicide	183		
help	244, 264, 277	homogeneity	36	ice mountain	188
helpful	239, 330	homogeneous	44, 320	iceberg	188
herald	171	hone	310	icon	188
here and there	151	honest	104, 248, 275	idealistic	68, 261
hereditary	45, 133	honesty	129, 331	identical	205
heretic	282	honor	199, 242, 327	identifiable	195
heritage	66	honorable	193	identified	49
hesitancy	112	honorary	172	identify	94, 286
hesitant	205, 266	hopeful	178	ideology	61
hesitate	276	hopeless	28, 209, 254	idle	51, 227, 251
heterogeneous	44	horizontal	62, 304	ignition	242
hiatus	221	horoscope	241	ignorance	51, 183, 238, 282

ignorant 117, 186, 276, 307	imperative 106	in reserve 62
ignore 22, 32, 54, 128, 165, 188, 210, 211, 220, 227, 325	imperfect 326	in retrospect 243
	imperialism 139	in the black 260
ill-boding 133	imperil 308	inability 21, 88, 144, 217
ill-fitted 298	impersonal 216, 287	inaccurate 195, 243
illegal 67, 210	impersonate 78, 117	inaction 121, 183
illegitimacy 287	impetus 23	inactive 51, 110, 250, 282
illicitness 287	implant 67	inactivity 63
illiteracy 282	implausible 99	inadequacy 182
illiterate 276	implement 106	inadequate 24, 122, 129, 210, 303
illness 313	implicate 274	inadvertently 100
illogical 41	implication 198	inanimate 162, 282
illuminate 143	implicitly 194	inappropriate 194, 203, 298
illusion 22	implosion 309	inapt 280
illustrate 88, 139	import 249	inattentive 124
imagery 116	important 261	inaugurate 232
imaginative 162, 278	impose 304	inborn 34
imbalance 172	impotent 73, 178	incapable 195
imitate 40, 56, 78, 117	impoverished 40, 208	incarceration 271, 332
imitation 62, 68, 93, 142, 316	impractical 151	incentive 33, 55
immaculate 326	impression 172	inception 44
immense 277	imprisonment 110, 271, 332	incessantly 115
immigrant 144	improbability 149	incident 177, 287
immigrate 105, 106	improbable 29, 261	incinerate 281
imminent 72	impromptu 104	incineration 269
immobile 222	improper 203, 313	incite 129, 250
immobilize 134, 305	improve 39, 249, 281, 310	inclination 77, 206
immoral 227	improvise 150	include 18
immorality 331	impulsive 151	incoherent 164
immune 62	impurity 283	income 57
immunize 163	in-word 16	incompatible 248
impact 172	in accord 111, 303	incompetence 144
impair 23, 159, 310, 321	in afterthought 243	incompetent 22, 35, 302
impairment 111	in essence 157	incomplete 140, 319
impart 155	in hindsight 243	inconceivable 295
impartial 261	in lieu of 51, 104, 111	inconclusiveness 155
impeachment 121	in line with 111	incongruent 183
impede 22, 30	in opposition to 111	inconsiderable 237
impediment 23, 32, 55	in order 115	inconsiderate 157
impend 41	in pieces 161	inconsistency 220
impending 133		

inconsistent	80, 183, 201	inertia	121	innocent	270
inconspicuous	89, 176	inevitable	34	innovative	34, 50
incorporate	18	inexhaustible	155	innumerable	162
incorrect	243	inexistence	292	inoculate	163
increase	73, 204, 215, 226	inexpediently	194	inquiry	139, 205
increasing	94	inexperience	238	inquisition	67, 205, 320
incredible	253	infamous	34	insect repellent	305
inculpable	270	infection	265	insecticide	305
incurable	293	infectious	314	inseminate	161
indebted	227	infer	172	insensitive	115, 272, 309
indecisive	205	inferior	193, 316	insert	331
indefinite	97, 161	infinite	276	insight	51
independence	153, 194	inflame	280	insignificant	63, 78, 106, 112, 173
independent	57	inflate	249, 258	insincere	99
indestructible	89	inflation	188	insinuated	46
indicate	132, 143, 227, 270	inflexible	238, 250	insolvent	260
indication	47	inflict	150	inspect	41
indict	133	influence	28, 172, 181	inspiration	28, 206
indicter	288	influx	143	instability	172
indifference	38, 75, 148	informal	193	install	232
indifferent	148, 214, 319	information	176	installation	40
indigenous	87, 117, 154	informative	210	installment	194
indirect	212	infrastructure	162	instead of	51
indiscreet	31	infrequently	63, 123	instigate	72
indispensable	83, 155, 255	infringe	249	instill	67
indistinct	251, 316	infringement	194	instinct	111
individual	52, 178, 327	ingenuity	144	instinctive	265
indolent	284	ingestion	226	institute	232
induce	16, 33	ingredient	106	instruct	110
indulge	38, 100	inhabit	95	instructive	308
indulgent	164	inhabitant	144	instrumental	261
industrial	142, 329	inhale	40, 68, 132	insubordination	154
industrialist	72	inherent	34, 45, 265	insubstantial	120
industrious	18	inherited	133, 216	insufficiency	182
ineffectiveness	181	inheritor	65, 116	insufficient	24, 128, 145, 197, 210
inefficient	21	inhibit	22, 95	insulate	23
inelasticity	172	initial	200	insulting	299
ineligible	50	initiate	52, 293	insusceptible	62
inept	21, 22, 35, 170, 319	innate	216, 265	integral	255
ineptness	88	inner parts	134	integrate	18, 314

integration	29	intrigue	84	irritation	156
integrity	199	intrinsic	34	isolate	56
intellect	111	introspective	271	item	182
intelligent	186	intrude	249	itemized bill	77
intelligible	121	intuition	61, 84, 111	itinerary	309
intended	199, 287	intuitive	265		
intensify	117, 183	invade	221	**J**	
intensive	326	invalid	174	jail	239
intent	247	invalidate	42, 66, 195, 209	jam	248
intentional	199, 304	invaluable	316	jargon	155
intentionally	100, 220	invariably	276	jeopardize	51, 308
interact	221	invention	74	jeopardized	131
intercept	166	inventive	34, 162	jeopardy	123
interest	148	inventiveness	144	join	225, 314
interfere	188	inventory	229	jointly	227
interim	89	invertebrate	229	joke	93
interior	134	investigate	41, 128	journal	29
interlude	166	investigation	205	journalism	205
intermediate	282	investment	121	journey	267, 308
intermission	45	invigorating	252, 293	joy	225
intermittently	238	invincible	89	joyful	236
intermix	175	invoice	77	judge	237, 332
international company	139	involuntary	218, 304	judgment	154
interpersonal	243	involve	309	judicial	199
interpret	173	involvement	176	junction	106
interpretation	177	invulnerable	64	junta	249
interrogate	232	ironhanded	80	jurisdiction	72, 176
interrupted	297	irrational	41	just as	111
interruption	166, 234	irregular	22, 33	justification	52
intersection	106	irregularity	248	jut out	294
interval	45	irregularly	123, 197, 238, 276	juvenile	67
intervene	188	irrelevant	145, 167, 211	juxtapose	293
intervention	144	irreparable	332		
inthing	83	irreplaceable	17	**K**	
intimately	320	irresistible	220	keep abreast of	23
intimidate	27, 238	irresolute	319	keep away from	127
intimidating	120	irresponsibility	216	keep back	99
intolerance	118	irresponsible	283	keep on	226
intolerant	95	irreversible	265, 332	keep up with	23
intricate	111	irrigation	51	keep	50, 99, 148, 211, 231

kill	296	layman	18	life-and-death	78
killing	183	laziness	24	life-threatening	231
kind	30, 42, 269, 300	lazy	18, 68	lifeless	121, 162
kindness	117	lead	31, 145, 228, 242	lift	266
kinetic	51	leadership	96	light	205, 293
kinship	67	leading	228	lighten	175
knowingly	79	learned	133, 216, 276	likelihood	206
knowledge	238	leave alone	188, 221	limb	219
knowledgeable	77	leave behind	142	limit	253
		leave	231, 314	limitation	154, 194
L		leftover	96	limited	25, 173, 248, 276, 293
labor	251	legal	50, 116, 142, 199, 210	line	173
laboriously	211	legality	287	lingo	61
lack	101, 160, 229, 250	legalization	98	lingual	271
lack of interest	84, 148	legalize	258	linguistic	271
lacking	69, 120, 210	legible	121	link	274
lackluster	75	legislation	28, 45	list	299
laden	205	legitimacy	287	literacy	282
ladylike	238	legitimate	67	literal	50, 183, 190
laid-back	307	lengthen	27, 170	litigant	288
lament	250	lengthy	140, 293	little	295
larceny	150	less	310	liveliness	121
large	61, 89, 237, 253, 267	lessen	192	lively	68, 75, 250
last	234	lesser	74	loathe	29, 230
late	101, 153	let go	231	loathsome	314
latent	322	let loose	168	local	80, 100, 182
latest	19, 198, 211	let off	112	location	36
latitude	194, 320	let out	132	locomotion	238
latter	194	lethal	73, 212	logical	214, 329
laud	76	lethargic	18	lone	230
lauded	263	lethargy	24	long-winded	140
laureate	117	level	304	long for	98
lavish	22, 83, 111	liability	216	longing	89
lawful	210	liable	181	longitude	321
lawfulness	287	liberal	95	look after	308
lawlessness	60	liberate	56, 108, 176, 247, 324	look the other way	66
lawsuit	177	liberation	85, 110, 332	looking into	139
lawyer	219	liberty	271	loom	41
lax	46, 183	license	308	loosely	183
lay	66, 113, 138	life	299	looseness	306

lose the way	217	make strides	138	matriarchy	151
lose	56, 100, 137, 196, 211, 217, 239, 258	make sure	61	matricentric	287
loudly	262	make up for	33, 151, 214	matriculate	156
low-status	144	make up	150	matter of course	104, 155
lower	187, 226, 266	make use of	30, 127	matter-of-fact	151
lowest	239	malady	315, 329	maturation	138
loyal	327	malfunction	272	mature	67
loyalist	282	malfunctioning	161	maxim	208, 266
loyalty	233, 263, 298	malicious	300	maximize	84, 216
lucid	108, 122	malignant	73, 109, 126	maximum	239
lucrative	18	malleable	126	meadow	217
lukewarm	133	malnourished	250	meager	122, 293
luminous	23, 121	manageable	150	mean	271
lure	254, 307	management	84	meaningful	174
		manager	298	means	29
		mandate	50	measurable	162

M

machinelike	261	mandatory	34, 61, 218	measure	45, 165, 183, 270, 273
machinery	283	maneuver	95	measurement	149
magic	321	manifest	106	meat-eater	269
magistrate	332	manipulate	89	mechanical	261
magnificent	255, 277, 287	manly	238	mechanism	29, 277, 307
magnitude	78, 183	manner	113	median	282
main character	145	manual	261	mediation	144
main point	83	manufacture	304	medicine	101
main	79, 167, 186	manuscript	195	mediocre	41
mainstream	294	many-sided	256	medium	29
maintain	100, 318, 332	map out	60	medley	203
maintenance	85, 96, 135, 261	mar	29, 331	meet together	198
majority	96	marginal	90, 265	meet	282
make	173, 260	marine	206	meeting	242, 318
make a pitch	148	marvel	188	meeting of leaders	267
make an effort	227	masculine	238	meltdown	100
make known	68, 162	mask	204, 238	membrane	67
make light of	36	mastery	217	memento	299
make off with	166	material	63, 74	menacing	133
make out	39, 215	materialistic	177	mend	256
make perfectly clear	156	materialize	141	mendable	332
make regular	57	maternal	139	menial	144
make sense of	276	mathematics	65	mental	62, 116, 120
makeshift	89, 326	matriarchal	287	mentor	164

mercenary	150	misdemeanor	117	monsoon	51
merchandise	107	misery	43	monumental	150, 286
merchant	251, 310	misfortune	241, 253	moon	79
merciless	269	misinterpret	215	moral	177, 227
merging	193	misinterpretation	45, 166	morale	272
merit-based system	133	misrepresent	71	morality	237
merit	60	miss	39, 260, 314	mortal	132
meritocracy	133	misshapen	221	most	167, 239
mesmerize	127, 216	mission	270	motherly	139
mess	215	mistake	166	motion	210
mess around with	91	mistaken belief	41	motionless	74, 282
mess up	54	misunderstand	55, 215	motivation	206
message	67	misunderstanding	45	motto	21, 266
metabolism	51	mitigate	117	mourn	250
metaphor	73	mixture	127	movable	222
metaphorical	50	mobile	74, 222	move	95, 105, 131, 140
meteorology	199	mobility	172	movement	238
method	186, 315	mocking	30	muddy	122
meticulous	105	model	118, 184	mull	46, 303
metropolitan	272	moderate	72, 167, 210	multinational	61, 139
microscopic	144	modern	19, 44, 65, 272	multitude	294
middle	282	modernize	129	mundane	283, 310
migrate	95, 105	modest	121, 298	municipal	139
mild	167	modesty	249	murder	183
milieu	49	modified	166	muscle in	212
millennium	233	modify	34, 314	muster	255
mimic	78, 117	moist	82	mutate	34
mind	210	moisten	209	mutilation	237
mindful	309	moisture	160	mutiny	244
minimize	84, 154, 161, 216	molecular	23	mutual	57, 227
minimum	239	mollify	305	myriad	162
minor offense	117	momentum	23	mysterious	88
minor	63, 228	money-making	178	mysticism	321
minority	96	money-oriented	177		
minuscule	144	money	142	**N**	
minute	23	moneyless	204	nadir	333
mirage	56	monitor	211	naive	67
misappropriation	275	monologue	250	naked eye	18
misconception	41	monopoly	133	name	19
misconstrue	55	monotonous	68, 130	named	49

nameless	49	nonexistent	156	obscured	56
nap	233	nonphysical	177	observant	71
narcissistic	298	nonpoisonous	212	observe	156, 163, 303, 327
narrative	318	nonstop	175	obsession	84
narrow-minded	33, 102, 118	nonthreatening	109	obsolete	65, 198, 211, 283, 292
national	144, 182	normal	186	obstacle	55
native	117, 144, 154	nostalgia	74	obstruct	244
natural	142, 211, 216, 281	nostalgic	89	obtain	56, 104
navigate	95, 217	not-for-profit	83, 142	obtuse	225
nearly	19	notable	219	obvious	176, 225, 276, 316, 322
neatness	215	noticeable	206, 251, 316	occasional	115, 276, 332
necessary	83	notorious	34, 101	occupational	311
necessitate	206	nourish	161	ocular	239
need	239, 259	nourishment	179, 277	of no account	150
negative	178, 269	novelty	74	of this world	101
neglect	76, 211, 227, 251, 303, 304	novice	164, 287	off-guard	124
negligence	261, 330	now and then	63	off and on	115
negligent	183	noxious animals	86, 172	off the record	71
net	111	nuance	198	offender	228, 331
neutral	261	nuisance	156, 194	offender	331
never-ending	144, 276	nullify	195	offense	189, 271, 299, 328
newest	198	numb	305	offer	71, 259
news	205	nursery	327	official language	61, 155
next to	76	nurture	227	officials	269
nimble	165, 225	nutrient	277	offset	151, 286
nitty-gritty	83	nutriment	277	offspring	45
no connection with	302			oil	255
no right to	260	**O**		old	19, 44, 211
nobility	148, 324	oath	111	old-fashioned	159
noblesse oblige	117	obedience	244	olfactory	305
noisy	168, 203	obedient	201, 327	ominous	133, 280
nominal	172	obesity	233	omnipotent	73
nominate	77, 96	objection	155	omnipresent	73
non-native	87	objective	52	omniscient	73
non-religious	101	obligated	227	omnivore	277
noncommercial	83, 142	obligation	18, 253, 327	on behalf of	45
noncompliance	111	obliterate	217	on guard	31
nonconformist	44, 282	oblivious	73, 89, 117	on level	62
nondiscriminatory	304	obnoxious	189	on schedule	167
nonessential	83, 155	obscene	68, 89, 328	on the contrary	124

on the dot	167	ornament	236, 253	overstate	161
on the loose	60	ostensible	127, 144	oversupply	129
on the side	62	otherworldly	205	overturn	193
on the verge	72	oust	141	overused phrase	115
on time	101	out-of-date	283	overweight	250
one-sided	60, 256	out-of-style	159	overwhelm	110, 150
one after another	123	out of action	110	owners	84
one at a time	99	out of date	65		
onset	41, 44	out of hand	62	**P**	
opaque	108, 122	out of proportion	145	pacify	309
open	72, 200, 248, 253	out of the question	151	pagan	285
open-minded	95, 102	outbreak	128, 302	paid	227
open to attack	58	outdated	198, 211	painstakingly	211
operable	293	outfit	187	pale	53
operation	161, 237	outgoing	63	pandemic	128
opinionated	102	outline	50, 123, 134, 254	paper trail	152
opponent	76, 87, 134, 175, 223, 321	outlying	90	paradigm	118
opportunity	32	outpouring	295	paradoxically	266
oppose	71, 117	outrageous	255	parallel	274
opposite number	77	outright	266	paralyze	134
oppositely	266	outside	243	paramount	74, 90
opposition	157, 187, 200, 230, 317	outskirts	243	paranoid	244
oppression	107	outstanding	41, 193, 332	paranormal	310
oppressive	80	outwardly	144	parch	82, 209
optical	239	outweigh	310	pardon	112, 281, 310
optimistic	24, 178	oval	94	parent	45, 171
option	34, 61, 128, 218, 220	overboard	72	parochial	255
oral	234	overcome	178	parody	62, 119
orbit	316	overflowing	140	parole	332
ordain	139	overhaul	199	part with	106, 155, 182, 194, 227
order	50, 60, 86, 101, 113, 215	overhear	22	partake	327
ordinary	20, 64, 105, 182, 263	overkill	110	partial	140, 267, 304
organic fuel	214	overlook	39, 156, 260	participate	198, 327
organism	162	overly	171	particle	107
organization	60, 245, 283	overpower	108, 196	partitioning	182
organize	66, 164, 284	overrate	36	partner	291
oriented	263	overseas	154	party	176
origin	164	oversee	211	pass on	22, 137, 146
original	68, 69, 78, 87, 117, 316	overshadow	172	passage	132, 165
originate	143, 264, 294	oversimplification	20	passerby	288

passion	75	perilous	195, 317	petroleum	255
passionate	214	perimeter	134	phantom	112
passive	250	period of immaturity	115	pharmaceutical	222
pasture	217	periodical	29	phase out	73
pat	331	peripheral	90	PhD	292
patent	68	permanent	47, 89, 326	phenomenal	161
paternal	139	permeate	162	phenomenon	19
path	64, 241	permission	99, 154, 219, 240, 313	philanthropic	93, 325
pathogen	199	permit	240, 315, 332	philanthropy	288
pathological	283	perpendicular	62	phobia	41
patriarchal	151, 287	perpetrate	100	phonetically	151
patricentric	287	perpetrator	331	photocopy	311
patron	122, 220	perpetual	75, 144	photosynthesis	56
patronage	317	perpetuate	100	physical	120, 239, 261
patronize	189	perplex	21, 156	physiological	62
pause	221, 234, 276	persecute	200	pick	200, 220, 298
pay attention to	165	perseverance	24	picturesque	316
pay for	184	persevere	276	piece	116
pay tribute to	85	persist	34, 318	piecemeal	90, 99
payment	22, 31, 57, 271, 299	persistence	24	pigmentation	134
peace	167, 168, 181, 231, 303	persistent	68	pilfering	150
peak	217, 267	personage	183	pilgrimage	73
peculiar	105, 206	personal	52, 216	piling up	94
pedestrian	288	personality	242	pillage	62
peer	161	personify	184	pilot	217
pen name	19	personnel	84	pinnacle	217, 333
penal	23, 33	perspective	186	pioneer	261
penetrable	89	perspiration	266	pious	178
penetrate	34	persuade	228, 315	pipe	165
penitentiary	239	pertain to	78, 211	pipeline	132
penny-pinching	83, 111	pertinent	167, 313	placate	305
per capita	35	pervade	162	place trust in	99
per person	35	pervasive	173	place	93
per se	96	pessimistic	24, 178	placid	167, 272
perceivable	195	pesticide	305	plagiarize	56
perception	41, 45	pestilence	288	plague	288
perceptive	115, 186, 265	pests	86	plain	111, 164
perennial	144	petition	274	plaintiff	288
perform	165	petrifaction	304	plan	150, 189, 247, 287, 309
performance	132, 233	petrify	316	plan of attack	201

plant and meat eater 277	portfolio 299	predominant 22, 167
plaster 211	portion 194	preeminent 73, 112
platitude 115	portrayal 42	preemptive 107, 299
plausible 29	pose 255, 294	pregnancy 138
play down 91, 161	position 197	prejudice 118, 154, 261
playwright 222	positive 178	preliminary 200
plea 118, 256	possibility 173	premeditate 150, 151, 189
pleasant 189, 203, 208, 299	possible 222	premise 184
pleasing 266	postpone 186, 321	premises 184
pleasure 156, 194	postulate 134	premonition 84
pledge 46	posture 294	preoccupation 84
plentiful 40, 129, 145	potent 178	preoccupy 309
plenty 197, 250	potential 173, 222	preparation 156
plethora 250	poverty-stricken 40	prepare 211, 291
pliant 143	powerful 150, 178	prerequisite 128
plot 259	powerless 73, 115	preschool 327
plummet 107	practicability 149	prescription 156, 221
plunder 62	practical 19, 68, 94, 157, 261	present 221, 327
plunge 107	practice 184, 297, 306	presentation 320
pneumonia 272	pragmatic 68, 261	presenter 30
point of view 197	praise 76, 155, 177, 217, 232, 252, 254	preservation 310
point out 175, 225, 227, 308	praiseworthy 314	preservative 78
pointless 179	prearranged 184	preserve 211, 273
poison 126	precarious 56, 118	preset 184
poisonous 172, 212	precedent 122	president 308
polarization 162	preceding 35	pressing 78
policy 45	precious 316	prestigious 112
polished 198	precipitate 233	presume 137
political 320	precipitation 145, 160	pretentious 121
politics 277	precise 195, 260	prevail 178, 310
poll 217	precisely 19, 183	prevalence 101
pollination 122	precondition 128, 299	prevent 16, 72, 95, 228, 244, 250
pollutant 283	predator 35, 128, 269	preventable 34
pollute 154	predecessor 153	prevention 33, 65
pompous 121	predetermined 184	preventive 107, 299
poor 40, 121, 208, 228, 287	predicament 105, 228, 305	previous 194
popularity 101	predict 33, 49, 189	prey 35, 128
populate 95, 292	predictable 99	priceless 316
population count 247	predisposition 206	pride 102, 249
portable 222	predominance 101, 138	primary 79, 186

primitive	19	promise	18, 46, 86, 111, 253	publicize	162
principal	131, 184	promising	133, 181, 280	pulling	166
principle	16, 149, 199, 321	promote	17, 22, 162, 244	pullout	167
prioritize	316	prompt	101	punctual	101, 153
prison	239	prone	280	punish	281
private	243	pronounced	56, 316	punitive	23
privilege	260, 327	pronouncement	176	purchasable	281
proactive	299	proof	40, 148, 209, 232	purchase	184
probability	17	propaganda	228	pure	172, 320
probation	332	propagate	89	purify	154
probe	41, 128	propel	30, 203, 283, 298	purposefully	100
problem	101	property	184	purposely	220
procedure	45, 140	prophet	85	pursuer	35
process	140, 211	proponent	134	push forward	233
proclaim	68, 171, 218	proportional	52, 151	put at risk	51
procrastinate	321	proportionate	303	put away	262
procure	56	proscribe	332	put down for	96
produce	16, 63, 160, 305	prosecutor	288	put down	46, 145, 188
productive	19, 28, 128, 313	prospect	149	put forward	109, 134
professedly	214	prospective	222	put in danger	209
professional	287, 327	prosper	124, 326	put in	331
professors	155	prosperity	239, 241	put into effect	106
proficiency	21, 238	protagonist	145	put off	321
proficient	35, 302	protect	23, 51, 58, 131, 209, 308	put on sale	184
profitable	18, 178	protection	68, 185, 194, 294, 310	put out	196
profiteering	55	protest	232	put to use	130
profound	167	prototype	68, 184	put together	320
profuse	24, 83	protrude	294	put up with	145
progeny	153	proverb	93, 208, 266	put up	116
progress	32, 57	provide	259, 278	putting an end to	98
progression	35, 45	provincial	272		
progressive	95	provisional	104, 326	**Q**	
prohibition	99	provoke	72, 85, 126, 250	quagmire	228
projected	189	prowess	217	qualification	98
proletariat	148, 324	proximity	96	qualified	195
proliferation	277	prudent	90, 157	quality	60, 289
prolific	128	pseudonym	19	quantifiable	162
prologue	200	psychological	62, 239	quarantine	56
prolong	170, 283	public	71	quarrel	76
prominent	56	publication	29	quarrelsome	204

quash	170	readable	121	reduce	117, 172, 187, 249
quell	145	real	17, 93, 156, 172, 197	reference	200
quench	310	realistic	68, 151, 261	referred to	211
question	44, 46, 232	reality	17, 22, 56, 101, 184	refine	310
questioning	139	realize	35	refined	211, 281, 328
queue	173	realm	176	refrain	38, 297
quick	225	reappearing	332	refreshing	252, 293
quicken	38	reason	52, 111, 297	refuge	112
quiet	42, 203, 231, 250, 262	reasonable	29, 60, 72, 244	refund	222
quit	118	reasoned	265	refusal	218, 253
quota	30	rebellious	327	refuse	30, 240, 315
quotation	200	rebuttal	255	refutation	255
quote	175	recant	228	regime	96, 109
		recede	104, 140	regiment	327
		receive	146	regional	182

R

race	138	receiver	30, 117	register	78
radiant	23, 195	receptacle	288	registrar	129
radiation	122	reception hall	291	regular	29, 63, 149, 238
radical	128	reception	274, 318	regulation	101, 253
radioactive rays	122	receptive	102	regulatory	207
rage	159	recession	52	regurgitate	244
raid	221	recipient	30, 65	rehabilitation	78
rainfall	145	reciprocal	57, 60, 227	rehearse	184
rainstorm	51	reckless	31, 283	reign	74, 96
raise	227, 266, 286	recognizable	195	reimbursement	222, 275
rampant	62	recognize	109	reinforcement	219
random	60, 222	recoil	328	reiterate	118
range	173, 236	recollective	89	reject	27, 42, 120, 175, 220, 240
ranking	67	recommend	122	rejection	263, 296
rapport	261	reconcile	129	rejuvenation	78
rare	73	reconstruct	199	rekindle	196
rarely	29	record-keeper	129	related	167, 211
rate	223	record	60, 82, 270	relationship	261
rational	41, 60, 71, 214, 244, 329	recorder	129	relative	19, 145
rationale	52	recover	134	relaxation	306
raw	142	recovery	78	release	56, 132, 168, 211, 231, 253, 278
raze	116	recruit	233	relentlessly	200
reactant	65	rectify	321	relevant	78, 167, 313
reactive	272	recurring	332	reliable	156
reactor	134	redo	199	reliance	153

relic	74	represent	189, 216	respiratory	68, 272
relief	318	representation	42, 116, 188	resplendent	121
relieve	126, 280, 310	representative	90, 99, 218, 296	respondent	305
relight	196	repress	99, 228	responder	305
religious	178	repression	107	responsibility	18, 216
relinquish	113, 134	reprimand	76, 121	responsible	270, 283
relish	29	reproach	217	responsive	272, 285
relocate	273	reproduce	160, 167	restore	294
reluctantly	266	republic	320	restrain	46, 168
remain	34, 278, 318	repudiate	49	restrained	60, 62, 203
remaining	111	repulsive	166	restraint	185
remains	39, 96, 292, 329	reputable	101	restrict	187
remarkable	173, 206	request	118, 198, 256, 259	restricted	155, 173
remedy	54, 101, 126	requested	74	restriction	99, 154, 185, 194
remembrance	74	require	206, 239	result	164, 324
reminiscence	74	required	34, 61	resuscitate	294
remnant	116, 304, 317	requirement	128	retail	266, 267
remorse	85	rescue	123	retain	142, 155, 211, 270, 314
remotely	320	reservation	112	retaliation	310
remoteness	96	reserve	244	retard	277
remove	28, 50, 255, 262	reserved	63	retention	85
remuneration	299	reservoir	244	retinue	206
render	173	residue	96	retreat	167
renegade	90	resign	118	retribution	310
renew	129, 196	resilient	250	retrieve	19, 134
renounce	30, 35, 109	resist	100, 241, 300	return	203
renovate	129	resistance	157	reusable	17
renowned	34	resistant	64, 201	reveal	85, 204, 209, 303
repair	261, 321	resolute	151	revenue	57
repayment	222	resolution	105	revere	245
repeat	118, 160	resolve	46, 129	revered	24
repeating	332	resolved	319	reverence	38, 313
repelling	166	resort to	30	revitalize	299
repentance	85	resource	252	revive	294, 299
replica	68, 316	resourceful	162	revoke	258
replicate	311	respect	145, 254	revolt	244
reply	232, 256	respectable	101, 193	revolutionary	128
report	159	respected	24	revolutionize	112
reporting	205	respectful	30, 297	revolve	316
repository	93	respectively	178	rewarding	18

rhythmically	321	
rich	208, 225	
ridicule	119, 254	
ridiculous	214	
rife	140	
right	62, 63, 167, 327	
righteous	177, 227	
rigid	250	
rigidity	172	
rigorous	21, 46	
rise	63, 215	
risk	86, 209	
risky	195	
rite	24	
ritual	24	
rival	145	
rivalry	200	
robust	123	
roll	69	
rookie	216, 287	
room	54	
root	28, 32	
rough	198, 281	
rouse	233	
routine	118, 149	
rowdy	168, 203	
ruckus	231	
ruin	63	
ruined	225	
rule over	108	
rule	45, 74, 101, 160, 321	
ruling	53	
rummage	66	
rumor	232	
run-down	303	
run-of-the-mill	41, 105	
run across	88, 126, 223, 272	
rural	272, 329	
rush	57, 272, 295	

S

sacrificial	244	
safe	56, 131, 195	
safeguard	185	
salient	206	
salvage	19	
salvation	123	
same	96	
sample	184, 322	
sanctify	285	
sanction	170	
sanctuary	46, 112	
sanguine	118	
sarcastic	30, 297	
satellite	79	
satire	62, 119	
satisfied	82	
satisfy	54, 247	
saturated	57	
save	19, 209, 273	
savings	22	
say clearly	71, 174	
saying	93	
scale	173	
scant	128, 129	
scapegoat	200	
scarce	73, 140, 145	
scarcity	129, 250	
scatter	171, 198, 329	
scattering	87	
scenic	316	
schedule	123, 309	
scholastic	107	
scoff at	85	
scold	76	
scooped	296	
scope	91	
scorn	254	
scourge	128	
scramble	105, 272, 276	

scribbled	121	
scrutiny	135	
scurry	272	
sea	206	
seal	137	
seaside	302	
second-to-none	84	
second thoughts	112	
secondary	74, 84	
secret	71, 276	
secrete	90	
secretion	266	
sect	275	
secular	101	
secure	195, 317	
security	185, 294	
sedated	168	
sedative	247	
see-through	108	
seek	66	
seer	85	
seize	71, 203	
seldom	29	
select	77	
self-centered	93	
self-denying	164	
self-esteem	272	
self-examining	271	
self-rule	153	
selfish	298, 325	
sell	184	
seller	251	
semantic	271	
semester	140	
semiconductor	90	
sensation	289	
sensational	182	
senseless	319	
sensible	41, 90, 151, 293	
sensitive	333	

sensual	266	shoreline	302	skeptical	66, 297
sentence	275, 281	short	293	skill	217
sentinels	83	shortage	110	skilled	22, 35
separate	44, 76, 96, 231, 255, 274, 314	shorten	27, 283	skillful	170
separation	170, 181, 193	show	193, 204, 270	slam into	314
separatist	44	showy	210	slaughter	254
septic	239	shrine	46	sleek	104
sequence	113	shrink	216, 226, 272	sleep	61, 123, 233
sequential	297	shrivel	272	slight	133, 265
series	69, 113	shroud	85	slogan	21
serious	63, 326	shun	27, 145, 127	slow	38, 233, 284
serve	54	shut down	134	sluggish	284
servitude	138	sibling	30	sluggishness	63
set a limit	243	sickness	329	slumber	123
set aside	230	side	227	small	226, 253, 277, 286, 332
set free	176, 281	side effect	32	smear	211
set in motion	134	sign	47	smoothness	237
set in stone	80, 126	sign up	78	smuggle	123
set side by side	293	signal	227	snare	324
set up	66	significant	20, 265	snoop	22
settle	33, 106	silently	262	snuff out	116
settled	227, 231	silhouette	50	so to speak	113
settlement	179, 189, 237	similar	44	soak up	285
settling	264	similarity	50, 65, 207	social class	153
setup	40	simple	97, 111	soft-spoken	63, 121
severe	19, 46	simplicity	176	soft spot	77
shading	165	simplified	178	soldier of fortune	150
shallow	271	simplify	17	solely	182
shame	102	simulation	101	solution	101
shameful	314	simultaneous	96, 231	solve	46
shapely	221	sinful	178	solvent	260
share	105	single	231, 294, 327	somber	30
sharp	115, 225	singular	230	soot	52
shatter	256	sink	294	soothe	102, 291
sheer	174	siphon	100	sophisticated	97
shield	27	sisterhood	245	sophomore	123
shift back and forth	46	site	36	sorority	245
shining	195	situation	126	sort	236
shocking	255	sizable	332	soul	271
shoot up	107	size	149	sour	252

Term	Page(s)	Term	Page(s)	Term	Page(s)
source	32, 308	spread throughout	162	stellar	228, 229
souvenir	299	spread	73, 143, 171, 211, 237, 277, 298	step	32, 183
sovereignty	57	springboard	119	step by step	90
span	24	spur	129	step down	109, 118
sparse	69	squad	327	sterile	236
spate	295	squadron	292	stiff	143, 225, 238
spatial	24	squash	145	stigma	102
spawn	63	stability	172	stimulate	28, 30, 97, 130, 232
speak	113	stable	80, 231	stimulus	33, 65
speak against	120	staff	84	stipulation	299
speak highly of	76, 122	stagnation	63	stir	233
spearhead	31	stalemate	57	stock	229, 262
specialist	18	stampede	57	stomp	223
specialize	33, 306, 327	standard language	155	stooge	200
specialty	160	standard speech	61	stop	226
species	42	standard	69, 165, 193	storage	93
specific	21, 206, 222	standardize	57	store	262
specify	17	standstill	57	straight	275
specimen	322	staple	79	straightforward	50, 88, 212
speck	107	stare	161	strain	281, 306
spectacular	316	start	294	strange	195, 197
spectrum	173	starting point	119	stranger	230
speculate	35	startling	107	strategy	79, 201
speculation	148	starvation	188, 226	streak	69
speculative	140	starving	250	streamlined	104, 178
speech	250	state-of-mind	91	strengthen	309
speed up	38, 326	state-of-the-art	65	strenuous	55
speed	223	state	174	stress	118, 154
spending plan	38	statement	263, 302	stretch over	24
sphere	91	stationary	74	stretchy	143
spin	316	stationery	74	strife	85
spiritual	101, 120, 177	statistics	135	striking	251, 332
splendid	287	status quo	85	stringent	19
splitting	298	status	153	strong	77, 250, 319
spoil	29, 331	staunch	99	structure	43, 322
spoken	234	stay	278	struggle	85
sponsor	189	steady	33, 183, 264, 328	student	84, 155, 164
sponsorship	317	steal	62	study	16, 217
spontaneous	151, 304	steel oneself against	291	stumped	263
sporadically	63	steer	30, 95, 217	stun	305

stupidity	51	summit	267	swap	285
sturdy	260	summon	286	sway	278
subconsciously	79	superficially	157	sweat	266
subject	28, 79	superintendent	333	sweet	252
subjective	52, 261	supernatural	310	swirl	171
subjects	120	superstitious	46	sworn statement	111
subjugate	108	supervisor	333	syllabus	123
subjugator	319	supervisory	207	symbol	73, 188, 210, 220
submerge	163	supplement	76, 263	symbolic	50, 218
submission	57, 154	supplemental	149	symbolize	184, 189
submissive	201	supplementary	84, 186	symmetrical	52
submit	190, 241	supply	229, 259	sympathetic	80, 269, 333
subordinate	74, 79	support	17, 28, 52, 54, 170, 189, 219, 261, 286	sympathizer	223
subordination	74, 138			symptom	47
subscribe	119	supporter	87, 90, 122, 187, 223, 321	syndicate	109
subsequent	55, 133	supposed	260	synopsis	295
subservience	74	supposedly	58, 214	synthetic	142
subsidiary	79, 145	suppress	28, 46, 162, 237	system	283
subsidy	52	suppression	277, 313	systematic	115, 331
substance	63, 98	supreme	73		
substantial	24, 63, 122, 237,	surface	163	**T**	
substitute	69, 252	surly	330	tabloid	295
subterfuge	129	surmise	172	tacitly	262
subterranean	108	surpass	310	taciturn	63
subtle	46, 276	surplus	129, 182, 250, 293	tack on	159
subtract	215	surprised	49	tackle	240
subtraction	192	surprising	107	tactful	157
subversive	327	surrender	25, 160, 178, 212, 221, 241, 244, 300	tactically	79
success	228, 239			tactics	201
successful	58, 178, 179	surveillance	135	take	64, 259, 327
successively	123	survey	217	take away	71, 76, 215
succinct	140	survive	25	take back	190, 228
succumb	25, 178	susceptible	58, 62, 64, 272	take down	143
sudden	32	suspend	186	take in	90, 285
suffering	146, 225, 313	suspension	234	take into custody	137
sufficient	120, 122, 129, 210	suspicion	240	take on	137, 240, 284
suffrage	63	suspicious	244	take out	331
suggest	132	sustain	314	takeover	192
suitable	194, 203	sustainability	135	take part in	198
summary	295	sustenance	135, 179	take place	127
		swallow	110, 198		

taking advantage	55	territory	89, 243	torment	225
taking off	143	testimonial	296	torrential	69
tale	318	testimony	207	totalitarian	320
talk	27, 315	theft	150, 275	touch	289
tame	188, 204	theoretical	94, 140	tout	218
tamper	91	theory	40	toxic	172, 212, 239
tangible	97	think	276	trace	317
tantamount	168	thinkable	295	tract	300
tap	33, 331	thought	130, 189	trade	285, 308
taper off	104	thoughtful	293	trademark	190, 210
tardy	101	thoughtlessness	61	tradeoff	179
target	128	thousand	233	trader	310
tariff	25	threaten	238	trading	47
tarnish	29, 310	threshold	196	tradition	66, 83, 248
task	82, 138	thrifty	22, 83	traditional	50, 128
taunt	85	thrive	124	tragedy	275
tax	25	through	289	trained	204
teacher	84, 155, 164	throw	141, 244, 270	trait	289, 302, 314
tear	89, 116, 129, 159	thrust	23	trajectory	64
tease	93	ticket	329	trample	223
technical	311	tidy	303, 326	tranquil	42
tedious	130	tie up with	314	transaction	47
teeming	140	tight spot	305	transcript	152
teenage	115	time	96, 153	transfer	273
temper	91	tiny	23, 144	transform	314
temporary	47, 89, 245, 265, 326, 332	tip over	193	transformation	326
tendency	77	tireless	155, 200	transformational	149
tender	142	tiring	293	transgress	163
tending	280	titanic	144	transgression	117
tension	306	to and fro	151	transient	47
tentative	245	to the point	140	transition	35
tepid	133	together	99	transitory	265
term	109	toil	251	translate	173
terminal	293	token	299	transmission	330
terminate	52, 294	tolerance	118, 154	transmit	146
termination	232	tolerant	19, 102	transmittable	314
terminology	155	tone	134	transnational	139
terrestrial	33, 79, 229	tool	106	transparent	108, 122
terrible	260	top	217	transplant	273
terrify	316	topsy-turvy	115	transport	83

trap	254	**U**		undergraduate	130, 155
travel	238, 267, 309	ubiquitous	73	underground	108
treacherous	317	ugly	221	underhanded	104
treachery	199, 298	ultimate	234	underlying	322
tread	53	unaccountability	216	undermine	54
treason	263	unaccountable	181	underrate	36
treasonous	327	unaccredited	241	underscore	154
treasure	126, 252	unaffected	62	understand	35, 55, 215
treasury	275	unafraid	197	understandable	16, 164
treatment	311	unaided vision	18	understanding	41, 45, 51, 118, 153, 230
tremble	328	unaltered	166		
tremendous	150, 277	unanimously	124	understatement	20
trend	83	unanticipated	31	undertake	284
trespass	249	unappreciated	24	undeserving	50
trial run	101	unauthorized	241	undetermined	184
tribulation	253	unavoidable	34	undomesticated	204
tribute	303, 315	unaware	117	unearthly	310
trigger	141	unbalanced	303	uneducated	77, 276
trimming	287	unbelievable	29, 253, 255	unenthusiastic	148
trite	278	unbiased	52, 261	unethical	227
triumph	178	uncaring	309, 333	unevenness	36
triumphant	58	uncertain	86, 225, 325	unexpected	99
trivial	20, 78, 106, 150	unchangeable	265	unfaithful	99
trouble	228, 294, 309	unchanging	68, 75, 201	unfaithfulness	233, 263
true-heartedness	298	unclear	164	unfamiliar	153, 195, 219, 307
trunk	219	uncloak	85	unfavorable	269
trust	240	uncommon	161	unflashy	210
trustworthy	66, 156, 253	unconcerned	82, 118	unfriendly	203, 216, 307, 320
truthful	248	unconditional	248	ungodly	178
tube	300	unconscionable	319	unhappy	254
tuition	31	uncontrolled	62	unhealthy	283
tumorous	109	unconventional	294	unheard-of	89
tumultuous	284	unconvincing	220	unhelpful	19, 261
turbulent	284	uncover	149	unification	29
turn	43, 54, 127, 233, 304, 318,	uncovering	39, 66	uniformity	16, 36
two-faced	110	undaunted	325	unify	57
two-sided	60	undefeatable	89	unilateral	57, 60, 256
type	42, 132, 275	underestimate	20, 36	unimaginable	295
typical	206, 294	underfed	250	unimaginative	34
tyrannical	80, 296	undergo	262, 264	unimportant	20, 56, 155, 193, 206
				unimpressive	287, 332

uninformative	210	unreal	156	urban	329
uninstall	232	unreasonable	41, 68, 244	urgent	78, 106
unintelligent	186	unrefined	198	use	94, 166, 226
unintentional	100, 189, 199, 220, 287, 304	unreflective	271	used to	307
		unrelated	78, 211, 274, 313	used	292
uninterested	285	unrelenting	68	useless	18, 174, 179, 210, 261, 330
uninteresting	258	unreliable	156	uselessness	132, 181
uninterrupted	69	unremarkable	64	usher	141
uninvited	74	unrestricted	79, 248	usurp	212
union	162, 181, 226, 298	unsacrificing	325	utilization	131
unique	206, 278	unsanitary	77, 236	utilize	127
unit	275	unseemly	298	utter	174, 266
universal	73, 80	unselfish	93		
unknowable	295	unsettled	298	**V**	
unknowing	73	unskilled	170, 302	vacant	187, 292
unknown	219, 230, 263	unskillful	165, 327	vacate	95
unleash	168	unsolicited	74	vaccinate	163
unlikelihood	149	unsophisticated	221	vacillate	95, 278
unlikely	34, 57	unstoppable	265	vague	16, 106, 195, 251, 316
unlikeness	65	unsubstantial	97	vain	28, 179
unlimited	79, 155	unsuitable	167	valid	67, 174
unlucky	280	untouched	166	validate	42, 195, 209
unmanageable	292	untrustworthy	101	valuable	20
unmask	209	unusual	22, 294	vanish	141
unnamed	49	unwarranted	67	vanquish	196
unnecessary	255	unwavering	151, 201	variable	75
unneeded	255	unwelcome	74	variation	16, 36, 207
unnoticeable	206	unwholesome	283	variety	203, 207
unoriginal	34, 278	unwillingness	206	velocity	223
unplanned	184	unwrap	149	vendor	251, 310
unpleasant	325	unyielding	126	venerate	245
unprecedented	64	up-and-down	80	vengeance	310
unpredictable	33, 185, 238, 264	up-to-date	211, 283	vengeful	300
unpretentious	17	up front	104	venom	126
unprincipled	319	up until that point	143	venture	121
unproductive	18, 58	upgrade	249	venue	36
unprofessional	18	uphold	35	verbal	234
unprofitable	178	upper class	148, 324	verbalize	71
unqualified	195	upright	304	verbatim	190
unquestionable	39	upset	247, 305	verdict	53
unravel	105				

verification	146	vote	63, 220, 329	well-provided	145
verified	140	voyage	95, 267	well-thought-of	101
verify	307	vulgar	328	well-to-do	204
vermin	86	vulnerable	58, 62, 89	wet	209
versatile	25			wetness	40
vertebrate	229	**W**		whimsical	60
vertical	62, 304	waive	113	whiten	175
vessel	288	wake up	233	whole	116, 121, 182, 194, 211
vestige	74, 317	walk	53, 288	wholesale	266, 267
veto	240	walkway	241	wicked	177
vex	288	wane	326	widespread	80, 173
via	289	ware	286	wield	130
vibrant	53	warehouse	127	wild	204, 283
vicinity	184	wares	107	wildness	185
vicious	188	warm	325	willing	218
victim	200, 331	warrant	86	winner	117
victimize	200	wary	31	wipe out	215
victorious	58	waste	39, 231	wise	90
view	292	wasted	303	wish for	306
vigilance	330	wasteful	22, 83	wishy-washy	205
vigilant	124, 319	watch	135, 211, 327	witchcraft	321
vigorous	123	watchful	124	withdraw	34, 140, 190, 259
vile	193	water buildup	160	withdrawal	121, 167
vindicate	274	waver	46, 57, 278	withering	181
vindictive	300	wavering	201, 319	withhold	100, 150, 255, 278, 297, 327
violate	163, 242	way out	105	withstand	300
violation	194	weak	178	witness	207
violent	188	weakness	77, 217	woe	146
virtually	157	wealthy	40, 204, 208, 225	womanly	238
visual	239	wear down	299, 309	wonder	188
vital	106, 261	weather science	199	word for word	177, 190
vivid	75, 186	weed	73	work	54, 110, 148, 161, 251, 324
vocational	311	weight	233	workout	297
void	57, 174	weighted	205	worldly	171
volatile	80, 185	welcome	241, 249	worldwide	128
volition	152	well-being	329	worried	82
volume	273	well-educated	77	worsen	39
voluntary	34, 61, 218	well-founded	67	worthless	316
vomit	244	well-grounded	97	worthy	50
vortex	171	well-known	71	wrap up	149

wreak havoc	20
write	74, 82, 170, 221
wrongdoer	228
wrongful	210

xerox	311

yearn	306
year	115, 123, 233
yield	68, 160, 300, 328

zeal	75
zenith	333
zoologist	273